Michael Noel

Microsoft® ISA Server 2006

Server 2006

UNLEASHED

 | 800 East 96th Street, Indianapolis, Indiana 46240 USA

Microsoft® ISA Server 2006 Unleashed

Copyright © 2008 by Sams Publishing

ISBN-13:   978-0-672-32919-7
ISBN-10:   0-672-32919-0

Library of Congress Cataloging-in-Publication Data on File

Printed in the United States on America

First Printing: November 2007

Trademarks

Warning and Disclaimer

Bulk Sales

Sams Publishing offers excellent discounts on this book when ordered in quantity for bulk purchases or special sales. For more information, please contact

U.S. Corporate and Government Sales
1-800-382-3419
corpsales@pearsontechgroup.com

For sales outside of the U.S., please contact

International Sales
international@pearsoned.com

Editor-in-Chief
Karen Gettman

Acquisitions Editor
Neil Rowe

Development Editor
Mark Renfrow

Managing Editor
Gina Kanouse

Project Editor
Jake McFarland

Copy Editor
Water Crest
Publishing

Indexer
Cheryl Lenser

Proofreader
Water Crest
Publishing

Technical Editor
Guy Yardeni

**Publishing
Coordinator**
Cindy Teeters

Series Designer
Gary Adair

Compositor
Jake McFarland

Contents at a Glance

Table of Contents

About the Author

Michael Noel, MS MVP, MCSE+I   Michael Noel has been involved in the computer industry for nearly two decades, and has significant real-world experience helping organizations realize business value from Information Technology infrastructure. Michael has authored several major best-selling industry books translated into seven languages with a total worldwide circulation of over 150,000 copies. Significant titles include *SharePoint 2007 Unleashed, Exchange Server 2007 Unleashed,* the upcoming *Windows Server 2008 Unleashed, ISA Server 2004 Unleashed, SharePoint 2003 Unleashed,* and many more. Currently a partner at Convergent Computing in the San Francisco Bay area, Michael's writings and worldwide public speaking experience leverage his real-world expertise designing, deploying, and administering IT infrastructure for his clients.

Dedication

I dedicate this book to my wife, Marina,
my eternal love and my best friend.

Acknowledgments

No book is an easy thing to write, particularly when dealing with a topic of considerable complexity and capabilities such as ISA Server. I really have to give credit to the ISA team at Microsoft, who has put together a fantastic product that has had a terrific track record with my clients. I wouldn't be able to write this book with a straight face if it wasn't for the hard-working folks who created and continue to update this product—thanks! A tip of the hat to the folks at Microsoft's Sydney office as well, including Ian Palangio and Gayan Peiris.

Thanks as well to all of my contributing writers who worked on this book and on the previous *ISA Server 2004 Unleashed* book. This includes Alec Minty, Tyson Kopczynski, Gennady Pinsky, Marina Noel, and Guy Yardeni, who gets an extra gold star for tech editing this latest edition. In addition, thanks to all of the technical team at Convergent Computing, most importantly Rand Morimoto, who are always there to bounce ideas off when I'm stuck in a rut.

As always, my family deserves so much of the credit as well, since they put up with their husband/son/father being lost in the computer lab once again, up all night writing. You guys make my life complete—I love you very much!

And thanks as well to you, the reader, whose advice and suggestions from previous books have all gone into this edition. I'd be happy to hear any advice you can give on this and my other books as well. I hope to see you at a conference or book event sometime in the future.... Happy reading!

We Want to Hear from You!

As the reader of this book, *you* are our most important critic and commentator. We value your opinion and want to know what we're doing right, what we could do better, what areas you'd like to see us publish in, and any other words of wisdom you're willing to pass our way.

As an associate publisher for Sams Publishing, I welcome your comments. You can email or write me directly to let me know what you did or didn't like about this book—as well as what we can do to make our books better.

Please note that I cannot help you with technical problems related to the topic of this book. We do have a User Services group, however, where I will forward specific technical questions related to the book.

When you write, please be sure to include this book's title and author as well as your name, email address, and phone number. I will carefully review your comments and share them with the author and editors who worked on the book.

Email: feedback@samspublishing.com

Mail: Neil Rowe
Senior Acquisitions Editor
Sams Publishing
800 East 96th Street
Indianapolis, IN 46240 USA

For more information about this book or another Sams Publishing title, visit our website at www.informit.com/title/9780672329197.

Reader Services

Visit our website and register this book at www.informit.com/title/9780672329197 for convenient access to any updates, downloads, or errata that might be available for this book.

Introduction

It is rare to run into that one product that impresses technical audiences in the way that ISA Server has managed to. As I prepared to write this book, what surprised me was not ISA's ability to wow and charm Microsoft-centric environments, but its ability to impress the Microsoft-skeptic crowds as well. These are the ones who have been skeptical of anything coming out of Redmond with "Security" in its title—for good reason in many cases. So, from its release, ISA faced a seemingly insurmountable uphill battle for acceptance, which makes its success even more impressive.

I have had the luxury of working closely with several of the best technologies Microsoft has produced: Active Directory, SharePoint, Exchange, and SQL Server. It therefore takes a powerful product for me to be impressed, and ISA Server 2006, and its closely related predecessor, ISA Server 2004, really has done that. ISA functionality is broad, with VPN, reverse-proxy, firewall, content-caching, and protocol-filtering capabilities. Marketing slogans are one thing, but this product really does live up to its billing. I have deployed, administered, and tested ISA Server at organizations of many sizes and functions, from city governments to banks to law firms to technology firms, and have had great success with the product. The breadth and depth of functionality that ISA provides makes my job designing security for these types of environments that much easier.

This book is the result of my experience and the experiences of my colleagues at Convergent Computing in working with ISA Server Standard and Enterprise versions, in the beta stages and in deployment. I wrote this book to be topical, so that you can easily browse to a particular section and follow easy-to-understand step-by-step scenarios. In addition, if you are looking for a good overview on ISA, the book can be read in sequence to give you a good solid understanding of the higher levels of security and functionality ISA can provide.

The Target Audience of This Book

This book is geared toward information technology professionals who have moderate to high levels of exposure to firewall, security, and network technologies. It is ideal for those administrators who need a good in-depth knowledge of how ISA works and how it can be used to perform common tasks. In addition, this book is ideal for security administrators who are looking to deploy ISA as an additional layer of security in an existing environment, particularly for securing Outlook Web Access, websites, and other internal services.

The Organization of This Book

This book is divided into four parts, as follows:

> ▶ **Part I: Designing, Exploring, and Understanding ISA Server 2006**—This section covers the basics of ISA Server 2006, including an overview of the technology, a walkthrough of the tools and features, and specific installation steps. In addition, design scenarios for ISA deployment are presented and analyzed, and migration steps from ISA 2000 are given.

> ▶ **Part II: Deploying ISA Server 2006**—This section covers the deployment of ISA technologies, discussing multiple common scenarios for which ISA is often used. Discussion surrounding ISA firewall, content caching, reverse proxy, and Enterprise version deployment is discussed, and step-by-step deployment guides are illustrated. In addition, detailed analysis of Virtual Private Network support, including both client and site-to-site VPN, is covered.

> ▶ **Part III: Securing Servers and Services with ISA Server 2006**—Part III focuses on the specifics of securing protocols and services using the built-in HTTP, FTP, RPC, and other filters in ISA Server 2006. Specific instructions on how to use ISA to secure Microsoft Exchange Outlook Web Access (OWA), including the common scenario of deploying ISA within the DMZ of an existing firewall, are outlined in depth. In addition, securing techniques for SharePoint sites, web servers, Outlook MAPI traffic, and other common scenarios are explained.

> ▶ **Part IV: Supporting an ISA Server 2006 Infrastructure**—The nuts and bolts of administering, maintaining, and monitoring an ISA Server 2006 environment are explained in this section, with particular emphasis on the day-to-day tasks that are needed for the "care and feeding" of ISA. Critical tasks that are often overlooked, such as automating ISA Server Configuration backups and documenting ISA Server rules, are presented and analyzed. Throughout this section, tips and tricks to keep ISA well maintained and working properly are outlined.

Conventions Used in This Book

The following conventions are used in this book:

CAUTION

Cautions alert you to common pitfalls that you should avoid.

TIP

Tips are used to highlight shortcuts, convenient techniques, or tools that can make a task easier. Tips also provide recommendations on best practices you should follow.

NOTE

Notes provide additional background information about a topic being described, beyond what is given in the chapter text. Often, notes are used to provide references to places where you can find more information about a particular topic.

SIDEBAR

A sidebar provides a deeper discussion or additional background to help illuminate a topic.

If you are like many out there recently tasked with an ISA project or simply looking for ways to bring security to the next level, this book is for you. I hope you enjoy reading it as much as I enjoyed creating it and working with the product.

PART I

Designing, Exploring, and Understanding ISA Server 2006

Introducing ISA Server 2006

The rise in the prevalence of computer viruses, threats, and exploits on the Internet has made it necessary for organizations of all shapes and sizes to reevaluate their protection strategies. No longer is it possible to ignore or minimize these threats because the damage they can cause can cripple a company's business functions. A solution to the increased sophistication and pervasiveness of these viruses and exploits is becoming increasingly necessary.

Corresponding with the growth of these threats has been the development and maturation of the Internet Security and Acceleration (ISA) Server product from Microsoft. The latest release of the product, ISA Server 2006, is fast becoming a business-critical component for many organizations who are finding that many of the traditional packet-filtering firewalls and technologies don't necessarily stand up to modern threats. The ISA Server 2006 product provides for that higher level of application security required, particularly for common tools such as Outlook Web Access (OWA), SharePoint Products and Technologies, and web applications.

In addition to a new array of firewall functionality, ISA Server 2006 provides robust Virtual Private Networking (VPN) support and enhanced web-caching capabilities, all within a simplified management interface. It also provides for a high degree of integration into an environment with existing security infrastructure in place, providing for an additional layer of security that could not have been achieved otherwise.

This book gives an in-depth analysis of the ISA Server product, with an emphasis on exploring "best practice" approaches that can be used when implementing an ISA

Server environment. These examples are gathered from real-world implementations and lessons learned from the field with the product. Because a majority of ISA Server implementations are established to complement—rather than replace—existing security infrastructure, particular emphasis is placed on the information and tools necessary to supplement these environments with ISA Server 2006. Third-party security tools, intrusion detection techniques, and firewall and VPN products working in coexistence with ISA Server 2006 are detailed throughout the chapters.

> **NOTE**
>
> The specific focus of this book is on the 2006 version of the product; all the examples and step-by-step guides assume the use of this latest version. For in-depth knowledge into the ISA Server 2004 product, we recommend reviewing the *ISA Server 2004 Unleashed* book by the same author and publisher.

Understanding the Need for ISA Server 2006

A great deal of confusion exists about the role that ISA Server can play in a network environment. Much of that confusion stems from the misconception that ISA Server is only a proxy server. ISA Server 2006 is, on the contrary, a fully functional firewall, VPN, web-caching proxy, and application reverse-proxy solution. In addition, ISA Server 2006 addresses specific business needs to provide a secured infrastructure and improve productivity through the proper application of its built-in functionality. Determining how these features can help to improve the security and productivity of an organization is subsequently of key importance.

In addition to the built-in functionality available within ISA Server 2006, a whole host of third-party integration solutions provides additional levels of security and functionality. Enhanced intrusion detection support, content filtering, web surfing restriction tools, and customized application filters all extend the capabilities of ISA Server and position it as a solution to a wide variety of security needs within organizations of many sizes.

Outlining the High Cost of Security Breaches

It is rare that a week goes by without a high-profile security breach, denial-of-service (DoS) attack, exploit, virus, or worm appearing in the news. The risks inherent in modern computing have been increasing exponentially, and effective counter-measures are required in any organization that expects to do business across the Internet.

It has become impossible to turn a blind eye toward these security threats. On the contrary, even organizations that would normally not be obvious candidates for attack from the Internet must secure their services because the vast majority of modern attacks do not focus on any one particular target, but sweep the Internet for any destination host, looking for vulnerabilities to exploit. Infection or exploitation of critical business infrastructure can be extremely costly for an organization. Many of the recent productivity gains in business have been attributed to advances in Information Technology functionality, and the loss of this functionality can severely impact the bottom line.

In addition to productivity losses, the legal environment for businesses has changed significantly in recent years. Regulations such as Sarbanes-Oxley (SOX), HIPAA, and Gramm-Leach-Blilely have changed the playing field by requiring a certain level of security and validation of private customer data. Organizations can now be sued or fined for substantial sums if proper security precautions are not taken to protect client data. The atmosphere surrounding these concerns provides the backdrop for the evolution and acceptance of the ISA Server 2006 product.

Outlining the Critical Role of Firewall Technology in a Modern Connected Infrastructure

It is widely understood today that valuable corporate assets cannot be exposed to direct access to the world's users on the Internet. In the beginning, however, the Internet was built on the concept that all connected networks could be trusted. It was not originally designed to provide robust security between networks, so security concepts needed to be developed to secure access between entities on the Internet. Special devices known as *firewalls* were created to block access to internal network resources for specific companies.

Originally, many organizations were not directly connected to the Internet. Often, even when a connection was created, there was no type of firewall put into place because the perception was that only government or high-security organizations required protection.

With the explosion of viruses, hacking attempts, and worms that began to proliferate, organizations soon began to understand that some type of firewall solution was required to block access to specific "dangerous" TCP or UDP ports that were used by the Internet's TCP/IP protocol. This type of firewall technology would inspect each arriving packet and accept or reject it based on the TCP or UDP port specified in the packet of information received.

Some of these firewalls were ASIC-based firewalls, which employed the use of solid-state microchips, with built-in packet-filtering technology. These firewalls, many of which are still used and deployed today, provided organizations with a quick and dirty way to filter Internet traffic, but did not allow for a high degree of customization because of their static nature.

The development of software-based firewalls coincided with the need for simpler management interfaces and the capability to make software changes to firewalls quickly and easily. Firewall products such as CheckPoint, Cisco, PIX, Sonicwall, and other popular firewalls are all software-based. ISA Server itself was built and developed as a software-based firewall, and has the ability to perform the traditional packet filtering that has become a virtual necessity on the Internet today.

More recently, however, holes in the capabilities of simple packet-based filtering technology have made a more sophisticated approach to filtering traffic for malicious or spurious content a necessity. ISA Server responds to these needs with the capabilities to perform Application-layer filtering on Internet traffic.

Understanding the Growing Need for Application-Layer Filtering

Nearly all organizations with a presence on the Internet have put some type of packet-filtering firewall technology into place to protect the internal network resources from attack. These types of packet-filter firewall technologies were useful in blocking specific types of network traffic, such as vulnerabilities that utilize the RPC protocol, by simply blocking negotiation ports or other high ports that the RPC protocol uses. Other ports, on the other hand, were often left wide open to support certain functionality, such as the TCP 80 port, utilized for HTTP web browsing. As previously mentioned, a packet-filter firewall is able to inspect only the header of a packet, understanding which port the data is meant to utilize, but unable to actually read the content. A good analogy to this would be if a border guard was instructed to allow only citizens with specific passports to enter the country, but had no way of inspecting their luggage for contraband or illegal substances.

The problem that is becoming more evident, however, is that the viruses, exploits, and attacks have adjusted to conform to this new landscape, and have started to realize that they can conceal the true malicious nature of their payload within the identity of an allowed port. For example, they can piggy-back their destructive payload over a "known good" port that is open on a packet-filter firewall. Many modern exploits, viruses, and "scumware," such as illegal file-sharing applications, piggy-back off the TCP 80 HTTP port, for example. Using the border guard analogy to illustrate, the smugglers realized that if they put their contraband in the luggage of a citizen from a country on the border guard's allowed list, they could smuggle it into the country without worrying that the guard would inspect the package. These types of exploits and attacks are not uncommon, and the list of known Application-level attacks continues to grow.

In the past, when an organization realized that it had been compromised through its traditional packet-filter firewall, the common knee-jerk reaction was to lock down access from the Internet in response to threats. For example, an exploit that would arrive over HTTP port 80 might prompt an organization to completely close access to that port for a temporary or semipermanent basis. This approach can greatly impact productivity, especially in a modern connected infrastructure that relies heavily on communications and collaboration with outside vendors and customers. Traditional security techniques involved a trade-off between security and productivity. The tighter a firewall was locked down, for example, the less functional and productive an end user could be.

In direct response to the need to maintain and increase levels of productivity without compromising security, Application-layer "stateful inspection" capabilities were built into ISA Server that could intelligently determine whether particular web traffic was legitimate. To illustrate, ISA Server inspects a TCP packet traveling across port 80 to determine whether it is a properly formatted HTTP request. Looking back to the smuggling analogy, ISA Server is like a border guard who not only checks the passports, but is also given an X-ray machine to check the luggage of each person crossing the border.

The more sophisticated Application-layer attacks become, the greater the need becomes for a security solution that can allow for a greater degree of productivity while reducing the types of risks that can exist in an environment that relies on simple packet-based filtering techniques.

For more information on the specifics of working with and setting up application-based filtering technology to secure inbound traffic and control access to internal resources, refer to Part III of this book, "Securing Servers and Services with ISA Server 2006."

Detailing the Additional Advantages of ISA Server

In addition to being a fully functional firewall solution, ISA Server contains a host of other security and productivity features. ISA Server is often deployed for other nonfirewall tasks such as Virtual Private Network (VPN) access, web caching, and intrusion detection. Taking it one step further, a slew of dedicated ISA hardware devices have become available from various manufacturers. An understanding of what these types of capabilities are and how they can best be utilized is key.

Allowing for More Intelligent Remote Access with Virtual Private Networks (VPNs)

In addition to having robust firewall capabilities, ISA Server is also a fully capable Virtual Private Network (VPN) solution. Built into the functionality of the product, VPN capabilities allow trusted users that exist outside a network to authenticate with ISA Server and gain elevated access to internal network resources. In addition to authenticating against Active Directory domains, ISA Server 2006 can utilize RADIUS (Remote Authentication Dial-In User Service) to authenticate users. This capability opens up a range of new architectural capabilities with ISA because the ISA server no longer is required to be a domain member to provide authentication between users. In addition, Internet Authentication Service (IAS) can be used to enable authentication between multiple domains that do not have trust relationships in place, as illustrated in Figure 1.1.

An added advantage to the Virtual Private Network support in ISA Server 2006 is the capability to treat VPN users as a separate network. This allows for a more granular policy control. For example, ISA can be configured to allow only authenticated VPN users to access an Exchange Server. Another function of ISA VPNs is to quarantine VPN clients that do not conform to an organization's security requirements into a restricted network in ISA that has access to only a small range of predetermined services.

> **NOTE**
>
> ISA Server 2006 supports both Point-to-Point Tunneling Protocol (PPTP) and Layer 2 Tunneling Protocol (L2TP) for VPN Connections.

For more information on how to set up, configure, and manage Virtual Private Networks with ISA Server 2006, refer to Chapters 9, "Enabling Client Remote Access with ISA Server 2006 Virtual Private Networks (VPNs)," and 10, "Extending ISA 2006 to Branch Offices with Site-to-Site VPNs."

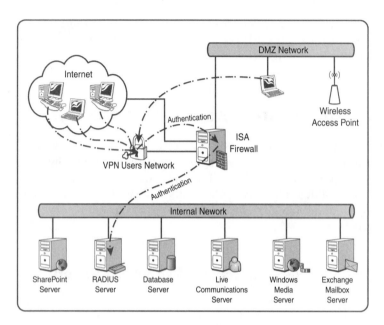

FIGURE 1.1   Utilizing Virtual Private Networks with ISA Server 2006.

Using Web Caching to Improve and Control Web Browsing

The "acceleration" portion of the Internet Security and Acceleration product refers to ISA Server's capability to act as a proxy for network clients, caching commonly used web sites and their associated graphics, text, and media, and serving them up to end users more quickly than if they had to access the content across the Internet. An additional benefit to this approach is the fact that all outbound web and FTP traffic is then scanned by ISA for threats, exploits, and restricted content. ISA has long been a product of choice for those seeking web-caching capabilities. In fact, the previous iteration of the product, Microsoft Proxy Server, was primarily used for that capability by itself in many organizations. ISA Server 2006 caching builds upon this success by further improving the system's caching capabilities.

Utilizing the caching capabilities of ISA Server 2006 is a straightforward and easy-to-deploy method of getting more bandwidth out of an Internet connection. In addition to the capability to cache requests made to web and FTP sites, ISA Server also provides for the capacity to provide commonly used content from web sites for caching by downloading it on a regular basis. Content download rules can be set up easily to update the cache on a regular basis for sites that administrators designate. This concept can further improve the speed and reliability of web and FTP browsing.

For more information on setting up and configuring ISA Server 2006 to act as a web-caching solution, refer to Chapter 8, "Deploying ISA Server 2006 as a Content Caching Server."

Reducing Setup and Configuration Time with an ISA Server 2006 Hardware Solution

One of the complaints with previous versions of the ISA Server product was the fact that it acted in many ways like a traditional server application. It was installed on a base Windows operating system that would subsequently need to be manually secured by a local administrator. This manual securing of the infrastructure on a device touted as a security solution caused many organizations to shy away from deploying it into their environment. In some cases, specific functionality that was offered by ISA Server but not offered by other firewall solutions was passed over in favor of more "traditional" firewalls, which did not require an operating system setup and security process.

To address this concern, Microsoft worked closely with several hardware vendors to offer prebuilt and prehardened ISA Server 2006 Hardware Appliances. These servers look and feel like traditional firewalls and come pre-built with multiple NICs, quick-restore CDs, and a presecured Windows Server 2003 Operating System installed. Many of the ISA servers deployed utilize these hardware devices, and their popularity is subsequently increasing.

There are many advantages to deploying an ISA Server solution using a dedicated hardware device. Installation time is greatly reduced, recovery is simplified, and many of these devices offer specialized functionality, such as specialized VPN appliances, caching servers, and enhanced intrusion detection capabilities.

Reducing Administrative Overhead and Potential for Errors with Simplified Management Tools

A major source of security breaches on all firewalls and security solutions comes down to simple misconfiguration of those devices by administrators. A robust, secure firewall solution becomes nothing more than a router if an administrator accidentally opens it up to all traffic. This concept is often glossed over during a security design process, but it is stunning how often simple typos or misconfigurations result in security breaches.

ISA Server 2006 sports a greatly simplified and easy-to-understand set of management tools that reduce the chance of security breaches through misconfiguration. Functionality is not sacrificed for the sake of simplicity, however, and ISA's simplified Management Console, shown in Figure 1.2, allows for a high degree of customization and functionality while simplifying the method in which this functionality is displayed.

NOTE

One of the most common methods hackers use to breach security is to take advantage of a misconfigured firewall. This was one of the main reasons that the ISA tools were simplified and the wizards streamlined, to reduce the chance that an overly complex interface would result in a security breach.

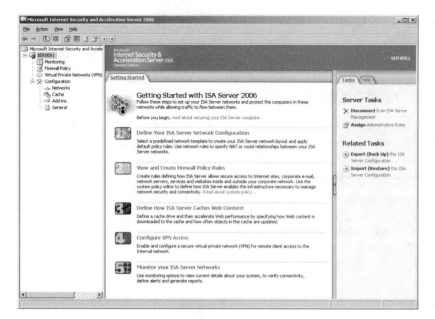

FIGURE 1.2   Using the ISA Server 2006 Management Console.

For more information about the ISA tools and how to effectively use them, refer to Chapter 3, "Exploring ISA Server 2006 Tools and Concepts."

Preserving Investment in Existing Security Solutions

One of the common misperceptions about ISA Server 2006 is that it is an "all or nothing" security solution. For example, it was thought that the goal of ISA was to replace other firewall or security devices with Microsoft-only devices. Subsequently, many Security Administrators were hesitant to consider deploying ISA, seeing it as a potential threat to existing firewalls and technologies. The reality of modern ISA deployments, however, is that they are most commonly deployed as an additional layer of security for an organization, not as a replacement for other security layers. For example, many ISA servers are being deployed as reverse-proxy devices that sit in the DMZ network of an existing firewall solution. As organizations have begun to realize that they do not need to put all their proverbial eggs in Microsoft's basket to be able to utilize some of ISA's enhanced functionality, many of the arguments against deploying ISA have become moot.

The real key to ISA's success lies within its flexibility and its capability to adapt to different security roles within an organization. For smaller organizations that require a complete firewall solution, it delivers. For other larger organizations that are simply looking to secure their Outlook Web Access (OWA) traffic from the Internet, it delivers as well. The different hats that ISA wears are numerous: VPN server, web proxy, Application-layer filter, RPC filter for WAN segment traffic, intrusion detection server, and many more. The capability of ISA to integrate and work with existing security solutions enables organizations to preserve their existing investment in security solutions.

NOTE

For more information on deploying ISA as an additional security layer to an existing third-party security environment, see Chapter 7, "Deploying ISA Server as a Reverse Proxy in an Existing Firewall DMZ."

Understanding the History of ISA Server 2006

Although ISA Server has only recently begun to gain wide industry acceptance, it actually has a long history relative to other computer products. The original version of this product, Proxy Server 1.x/2.x, was geared more toward web caching and proxy capabilities, but newer versions, namely ISA Server 2000, ISA Server 2004, and the newest version, ISA Server 2006, have stressed and focused on the security aspects of the product, improving them and adding functionality. To better understand where ISA Server is today, it is important to get a better understanding of how it got where it is.

Outlining Initial Microsoft Security Solutions

In the early days of networking, before the wide acceptance of the Internet, the focus of security was more directed toward making sure that files and folders on a network were kept safe from prying eyes. Communications between computers were deliberately built to be open and extensible, to facilitate the transfer of information between the devices on the network. As networking evolved, these networks became more and more interconnected, often to other networks that could not be trusted, such as the Internet in general. To protect computers from access via these outside networks, devices known as firewalls were placed between the untrusted and trusted networks to block access from the former to the latter.

While this was occurring, Microsoft products were changing and evolving to match the computing needs of the time, and focus was placed on making Microsoft products embrace the Internet. Focus was put on the need to provide enhanced access for clients to the Internet. As a direct result of this, the development of a product to provide web proxy capabilities to Microsoft clients took shape.

Exploring a New Product—Proxy Server

In 1996, the Internet browser wars between the Netscape Navigator product and Microsoft's Internet Explorer were in full swing, and Microsoft was constantly looking for ways to improve the capabilities of Internet Explorer. Netscape had begun to sell a web proxy product, which optimized Internet web browsing by caching the images and text from web pages to local servers, enabling clients to access them quickly. At this time, connections to the Internet were much more expensive, relatively speaking, and the need to take full advantage of the bandwidth provided to an organization created the need for products to optimize these connections.

In direct response to these needs, Microsoft released the first version (1.0) of Proxy Server, a new product to provide web proxy capabilities for clients. The capabilities of version 1.0

of the product were significantly less than those of Netscape or other proxy products available at this time, however, and industry support for the product was lacking.

Following closely on the release of version 1.0 was version 2.0 , which equalized many of the disparities between Microsoft's Proxy Server product and the competitors. Proxy Server 2.0 introduced the capability to create arrays of servers for redundancy and provided support for HTTP 1.1 and FTP. In addition, the capability to "reverse proxy" was added, protecting internal web servers by acting as a bastion host, or first layer of defense for untrusted traffic. The release of this version of the product was much more successful, and the Proxy Server product celebrated much wider industry acceptance as a web-caching and reverse-proxy product.

Unleashing a New Model: The Internet Security and Acceleration Server 2000

Although Proxy Server 2.0 provided for a wide array of security features, it did not enjoy broad industry acceptance as a security device for one reason or another. Microsoft wanted to focus more attention on the product's security capabilities, so it added more to the 3.0 version, and rebranded it as the Internet Security and Acceleration (ISA) Server 2000. This rebranding directed attention to its security capabilities, while still giving a nod to the web acceleration component, the caching capabilities.

ISA Server 2000 introduced an impressive new array of features, nearly all of which focused on turning it into a full-functioned security device. This version of the product was the first that marketed it as a firewall by and of itself. It was this claim that was greeted with skepticism by the security community, given the somewhat shaky track record that Microsoft products had at that time.

The politics of the security community being what they were, ISA Server 2000 faced an uphill battle for acceptance. In addition, deficiencies such as the lack of multi-network support, confusing firewall rules, and a haphazard interface limited the large-scale deployment of ISA 2000.

Unveiling the Next Generation: ISA Server 2004

While ISA Server 2000 was slowly gaining ground, the ISA Server team started work on the next version, code-named Stingray. The result of this project was the product released as the Internet Security and Acceleration Server 2004. This version of ISA was vastly improved over the previous versions of the product, and it quickly became noticed in the wider security community. In addition to fine-tuning and honing the capabilities it inherited from ISA Server 2000, ISA Server 2004 introduced a wide variety of new and improved security features that further extended its capabilities.

ISA Server 2004 was originally released with only a standard edition of the product. The Enterprise edition debuted the following year, expanding upon ISA's capabilities even further. Finally, predating the release of ISA Server 2006, Service Pack 2 for ISA Server 2004 added many of the same pieces of functionality recently included in ISA Server 2006, such as HTTP compression support, DiffServ, and other enhancements.

Expanding on ISA Server 2004's Success with ISA Server 2006

Microsoft released the next interim build of ISA Server 2004 as a new generation and relabeled it as ISA Server 2006. This version is similar in many ways to ISA Server 2004, with specific enhancements made to several key areas. In a way, it really can be thought of as ISA Server 2004 Service Pack 3, but instead it has been relabeled. The learning curve between ISA 2004 and ISA 2006 is not steep, however, and administrators familiar with ISA 2004 will immediately be familiar with the 2006 model. That said, the evolution of the ISA Server 2006 product to the spot that it inhabits today is impressive.

What's extremely important to note about ISA Server 2006 is that it is one of the first security products released by Microsoft that has really been taken seriously by the broader Internet Security community. ISA Server 2006 is a full-fledged Internet firewall, with Virtual Private Network (VPN) and web-caching capabilities to boot. The debate between pro-Microsoft and anti-Microsoft forces is far from over, but politics aside, the product that has been released is an impressive one.

Exploring ISA Server 2006's New Features

In addition to the enhanced features in ISA Server 2000, ISA Server 2004 and 2006 introduced the following new features:

▶ **Multiple network support and per-network policies**—ISA Server 2006 introduced the capability to set up and secure ISA between multiple networks. For example, you can set up ISA to act as a firewall between the Internet, an internal network, a perimeter (DMZ) network, a wireless access network, a VPN clients network, and many more. In addition, you can configure unique policies between each network, such as restricting traffic to a DMZ network or securing RPC traffic across WAN segments. For more information on this feature set, see Chapter 5, "Deploying ISA Server 2006 as a Firewall."

▶ **Support for complex and customizable protocols**—In addition to including a wide array of known protocol support for rules, ISA Server 2006 includes support for custom protocols. These protocols can be defined and specific filters can be created to scan for defined attack patterns in the custom traffic.

▶ **New server and OWA publishing rules**—ISA Server 2006 includes a vast assortment of server publishing rules, including sophisticated OWA publishing rules that utilize advanced functionality such as forms-based authentication and reverse-proxy capabilities. For additional reading on these features, see Chapter 12, "Securing Outlook Web Access (OWA) Traffic."

▶ **Remote Procedure Call (RPC) filtering support**—Of particular note in ISA Server 2006 was the addition of RPC filtering support, which enables an administrator to specify what type of RPC traffic will be allowed from one network to another. For example, a rule could be set up to allow only MAPI Exchange access or Active Directory replication traffic across segments, while blocking other RPC access, such as the kind that spawns attacks and exploits. For more information on RPC filtering, see Chapter 14, "Securing Web (HTTP) Traffic."

▶ **End-to-end secure web publishing capabilities**—The web publishing rules improved in ISA Server 2006 allow for end-to-end securing of Secure Sockets Layer (SSL) encrypted web traffic from client to ISA Server, and then back to web server. When the traffic is decrypted at the ISA Server, it can be inspected for viruses and HTTP exploits. The traffic is then re-encrypted before being sent to the web server.

▶ **RADIUS and SecurID authentication support**—In addition to supporting Active Directory authentication, ISA Server 2006 now supports authentication natively against a RADIUS or RSA SecurID authentication infrastructure. This enables an ISA Server to be a member of a workgroup, as opposed to a domain member.

▶ **Stateful inspection for VPN connections**—In this version of ISA Server, all traffic that passes through ISA is inspected for Application-layer attacks (stateful inspection). This includes VPN connections as well.

▶ **VPN quarantine control features**—ISA Server 2006 introduces the capability to provide granular control to VPN clients by enabling administrators to restrict new VPN connections to a separate quarantine network. This network can have strict access restrictions placed on it. In this model, VPN users are not moved into the regular VPN users network until it can be established that they satisfy certain criteria, such as the installation of virus-scanning software.

▶ **Enhanced monitoring, logging, and reporting**—ISA Server 2006 includes superb reporting, monitoring, and logging capabilities, including capabilities to write logs to a SQL-desktop version (MSDE) database. ISA can be configured to automatically generate rich reports for client web access, security events, protocol utilization, and much more. Monitoring of ISA is further enhanced with the use of the ISA Management Pack for Microsoft Operations Manager (MOM) 2000/2005. For more information on monitoring ISA Server, refer to Chapter 19, "Monitoring and Troubleshooting an ISA Server 2006 Environment."

▶ **Forms-based authentication for all web sites**—This includes cookie-based auth forms for SharePoint Products and Technologies, OWA, and other web sites. This is a new feature in the 2006 release of the product.

▶ **Enhanced branch office support tools**—Another feature new in ISA 2006, the support for branch office VPN using ISA Server has been greatly enhanced and streamlined with a new Branch Office VPN wizard.

The wide variety of features included in ISA Server 2006 makes it very versatile, and it can be deployed to take advantage of one, two, or multiple functions. For example, ISA could be deployed as a full-function firewall, allowing VPN access and web caching. Or it could be deployed simply to filter RPC connections between network segments. An added advantage to this flexibility is the fact that only those functions that are required are turned on. This reduces the surface area that is exposed to attack, reducing the overall threat.

Choosing the Operating System for ISA Server 2006

It is necessary to install and deploy ISA Server 2006 servers on the Windows Server 2003 platform. Improvements in reliability, functionality, and, most importantly, security dictate this. With ISA Server 2004, it was previously possible, though not recommended, to install ISA Server 2004 on the Windows 2000 Operating System. This is no longer an option with the 2006 version. In fact, 2006 requires both 2003 and Service Pack 1 at a minimum to be installed.

It is important to note that because the ISA server holds a very important security role, it is essential that you patch the operating system with the critical updates Microsoft releases. This includes the necessary Service Pack 1 or Windows Server 2003 R2 Edition and any new Service Packs for ISA Server 2006, when they become available, which both introduce advanced security and functionality. For more information on updating ISA Server and Windows with the latest in security and updates, see Chapter 2, "Installing ISA Server 2006."

Choosing Between ISA Server 2006 Enterprise or Standard Editions

ISA Server 2006 comes in two versions: an Enterprise version and a Standard version. Each version offers different functionality, with the Standard version of the product geared toward small and mid-sized organizations, and the Enterprise version designed for medium to large organizations. The Enterprise version of the software includes all the functionality of the Standard edition, but with the addition of the following:

▶ **Array Capabilities**—ISA Server 2006 Enterprise edition includes the capability to create *arrays*, which allow multiple servers connected to the same networks to act in tandem to process firewall, VPN, and cache requests. These arrays use the Cache Array Routing Protocol (CARP) to communicate changes and topology information.

▶ **Integrated Network Load Balancing (NLB)**—In addition to the general NLB support provided by the Standard version, the Enterprise version of ISA Server includes advanced integrated support for NLB, allowing an administrator to make changes and manage NLB directly from the ISA Management Console.

▶ **ADAM Centralized Storage**—A huge improvement over ISA Server 2000 Enterprise edition is the added capability for Enterprise Configuration information to be stored in a separate instance of Active Directory in Application Mode (ADAM), rather than in the internal Active Directory forest schema. This enables the external-facing ISA Enterprise servers to maintain their configuration in an isolated environment, without unnecessarily exposing internal Active Directory services to attack.

▶ **Centralized Management and Monitoring**—ISA Server Enterprise edition allows for management of a highly scalable ISA solution, with multiple ISA arrays in multiple locations. This allows for centralized management of a complex network infrastructure.

For more information on the advanced capabilities of the Enterprise edition of ISA Server 2006, refer to Chapter 6, "Deploying ISA Server Arrays with ISA Server 2006 Enterprise Edition."

Detailing Deployment Strategies with ISA Server 2006

What makes ISA Server stand out as a product is its versatility and capability to play the part of multiple roles in an environment. In addition to the capability to be deployed as a fully functional Application-layer firewall, ISA can also provide web caching, Virtual Private Network support, reverse proxy, and combinations of any of them. It is subsequently important to understand all the potential deployment scenarios for ISA when considering the product for deployment.

Deploying ISA Server 2006 as an Advanced Application-Layer Inspection Firewall

ISA Server 2006 was designed as a full-function firewall that provides for the type of functionality expected out of any other firewall device. At a base level, ISA enables you to block Internet traffic from using a specific port, such as the RPC or FTP ports, to access internal resources. This type of filtering, done by traditional firewalls as well, provides for filtering of Internet Protocol (IP) traffic at the Network layer (Layer 3). The difference between ISA and most other firewalls, however, comes with its capabilities to filter IP traffic at the more complex Application layer (Layer 7). This functionality enables an ISA firewall to intelligently determine whether or not IP traffic contains dangerous payloads, for example.

Because of the advanced IP filtering capabilities of ISA, it is becoming more common to see small to mid-sized organizations deploying ISA Server 2006 as a full-fledged edge firewall, similar to what is shown in Figure 1.3. ISA Server 2006 has passed many of the security tests that have been thrown at it, and it has proven to have firewall functionality beyond many of the more common firewall products on the market today.

For more information on the capabilities of ISA Server 2006 as a firewall device, refer to Chapter 5.

Securing Applications with ISA Server 2006's Reverse-Proxy Capabilities

Although ISA Server 2006 is marketed as an edge firewall, it is more common in organizations, particularly in mid-sized and larger ones, to see it deployed strictly for reverse-proxy capabilities. This functionality enables ISA to protect internal web and other application resources from external threats by acting as a bastion host.

To hosts on the Internet, the ISA Server looks and acts like a regular web or application server. Requests made by the client are then relayed back to the actual machine that performs the services, but not before being inspected for exploits or threats. In addition, it

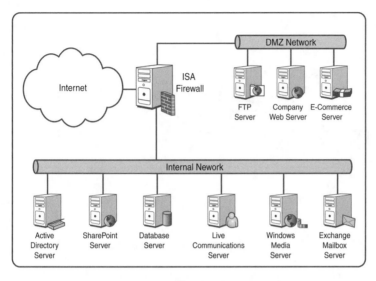

FIGURE 1.3   Deploying ISA Server 2006 as a firewall.

can also be configured to authenticate the user in advance before allowing requests to be relayed back, further securing the infrastructure.

For more information on utilizing the reverse-proxy capabilities of ISA Server, see the chapters in Part III.

Accelerating Internet Access with ISA Server 2006's Web-Caching Component

The original function of ISA Server when it was still known as Proxy Server was to act as a simple web proxy for client web traffic. This functionality is still available in ISA Server, even as the focus has been directed more to the system's firewall and VPN capabilities. By enabling the caching service on an ISA server, many organizations have realized improved access times for web and FTP services, while effectively increasing the available bandwidth of the Internet connection at the same time.

The concept of web and FTP caching in ISA Server 2006 is fairly straightforward. All clients configured to use ISA for caching send their requests for web pages through the ISA Server, similar to what is shown in Figure 1.4. If it is the first time that particular page has been opened, the ISA Server then goes out to the Internet, downloads the content requested, and then serves it back to the client, while at the same time keeping a local copy of the text, images, and other HTTP or FTP content. If another client on the network requests the same page, the caching mechanism delivers the local copy of the page to the user instead of going back to the Internet. This greatly speeds up access to web pages and improves the responsiveness of an Internet connection.

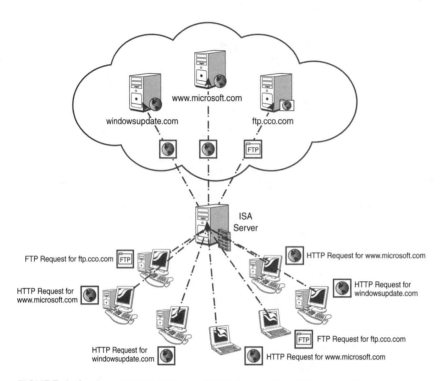

FIGURE 1.4   Deploying ISA Server 2006 as a web-caching server.

> **NOTE**
>
> An added advantage to using ISA Server 2006 as a content-caching server is that all of the HTTP traffic that clients request is scanned for exploits and viruses as well, decreasing the threat of clients being infected with spyware, viruses, and other scumware.

For more information on configuring ISA for web and FTP caching, refer to Chapter 8.

Controlling and Managing Client Access to Company Resources with Virtual Private Networks

Some of the more major improvements to ISA Server 2006 have been in the area of Virtual Private Networks (VPNs). VPN functionality has been greatly improved, and the flexibility of the VPNs for access rules is robust. Deployment of an ISA Server 2006 VPN solution is an increasingly common scenario for many organizations. The capabilities for clients to securely access internal resources from anywhere in the world is ideal for many organizations.

VPN deployment with ISA Server 2006 typically involves a secure, encrypted tunnel being set up between clients on the Internet and an Internet-facing ISA firewall. After the clients have authenticated, they are granted access to specific internal resources that are defined by the ISA administrator. The resources that can be accessed can be designated via access rules, so the control can be very granular.

In addition to this control, ISA Server also makes it possible to quarantine VPN users that do not comply with specific rules that can be set up. For example, ISA can be configured to quarantine clients that do not have antivirus programs installed. Different access rules can be configured for the Quarantine VPN Users network as well, restricting their access even further, for example.

Finally, ISA Server also includes the ability to set up site-to-site VPN connections to remote sites across the Internet. This enables networks to be joined across VPN links. An added advantage is that the Internet Key Exchange (IKE) protocol used to set up this connection can also be used to set up a site-to-site VPN between an ISA Server and another third-party VPN product. This functionality has been greatly enhanced over the 2004 version of the product as well.

For more information on working with VPNs in ISA Server 2006, refer to Chapters 9 and 10.

Using the Firewall Client to Control Individual User Access

In addition to the default capability to support traffic from any Internet client (SecureNAT clients), ISA includes the capability to restrict, control, and log individual user firewall access through the installation and configuration of ISA firewall clients. Although it is a less common deployment scenario by virtue of the need to install and support a client component, using the ISA Firewall Client can create scenarios that are more secure, and also enable an administrator to control firewall policy based on individual users or groups of users.

For more information on deployment scenarios involving the ISA Firewall Client, see Chapter 11, "Understanding Client Deployment Scenarios with ISA Server 2006."

Augmenting an Existing Security Environment with ISA Server 2006

One of the major steps forward for ISA Server was the change in focus from an assumption of ISA in a Microsoft-only environment to a focus where ISA is an additional layer of security to existing security technologies. ISA Server is being deployed more often recently to supplement security in many organizations, and this capability to "play well" with other firewalls and security applications is a welcome improvement.

Utilizing ISA Server 2006 in Conjunction with Other Firewalls

A common deployment scenario for ISA Server 2006 systems has been as a reverse proxy or dedicated VPN server that sits as a unihomed (single network card) server in the Perimeter (DMZ) network of an existing firewall. This is where the integration of ISA with other security devices really shines. The advantage to deploying ISA in this method is that it serves as an additional layer of security in an existing environment, improving the environment's overall security. Security works best in layers because it is more difficult to compromise a system that has multiple mechanisms that must be defeated before an unauthorized user is able to gain access.

To this end, ISA is proving to be a commonly used security tool that satisfies specific needs, rather than a whole host of needs at once. For example, a large number of ISA deployments serve a single purpose: to secure traffic to Outlook Web Access servers or other web-related servers while sitting in the DMZ of an existing packet-layer firewall, similar to what is shown in Figure 1.5. Of course, ISA can do more, but it is this capacity to do specific jobs very well that bodes well for ISA's acceptance among the overall security industry.

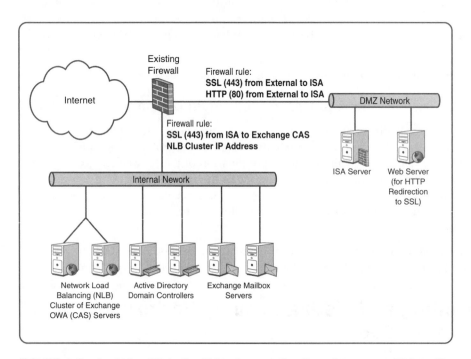

FIGURE 1.5   Deploying ISA in the DMZ of an existing firewall to secure OWA traffic.

For additional reading on this concept, see Chapter 7.

Deploying ISA Server 2006 in a RADIUS Authentication Environment

ISA Server 2006 supports authentication and logging against a Remote Authentication Dial-In User Service (RADIUS) environment, allowing for security integration in environments with an existing investment in RADIUS technologies. By providing this support, ISA also allows for scenarios where the ISA server is not a Windows NT/AD Domain Member. This decreases the overall threat associated with deploying an ISA server in certain circumstances, such as when it is deployed in the DMZ network of an existing firewall.

> **NOTE**
>
> The addition of RADIUS authentication support enables ISA to integrate with a vast array of third-party authentication mechanisms that can use RADIUS protocols to validate users. This substantially increases the breadth of ISA Server 2006 deployment options.

Administering and Maintaining an ISA Server 2006 Environment

After ISA is deployed, the important job of administering and maintaining the environment begins. Fortunately, ISA Server 2006 provides powerful yet easy-to-use tools to assist administrators in these tasks. The ease of use of these tools overshadows the impressive functionality that they provide. Thankfully, the straightforward approach that Microsoft took when designing the tools helps administrators to more easily administer and maintain an ISA Server environment.

Taking Advantage of Improvements in ISA Management Tools

The ISA Server Management Console, shown in Figure 1.6, provides straightforward wizards to assist with complex tasks, and puts all ISA's functionality at the fingertips of an administrator. Configuration, reporting, logging, monitoring, and securing can all be done from the centralized console, simplifying the management experience and making it less likely that configuration mistakes will result in security breaches.

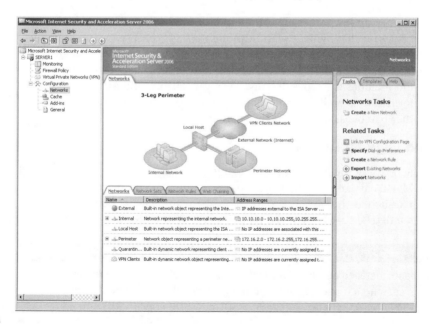

FIGURE 1.6   Using the ISA Server Management Console.

The ISA console also includes several built-in wizards and templates that enable an administrator to perform common functions and procedures, such as publishing a mail server, creating access rules, defining networks, and the like. For example, the New Network Wizard allows the creation of additional networks and their associated network rules quickly, easily, and securely. After the networks are created, the network rules and policies can then be modified to suit the needs of the organization. This offers administrators the best of both worlds, with the simplicity of a wizard combined with the power of a customizable toolbox.

For more information on administering ISA Server 2006, see Chapter 16, "Administering an ISA Server 2006 Environment."

Backing Up and Restoring ISA Server Environments

Backing up and restoring Windows environments has often been a complex and cumbersome process. Fortunately, ISA Server 2006 has learned a lesson from many of its firewall peers, and included an incredibly simple method of backing up the firewall configuration to an XML (essentially text) file that can be then re-imported on other ISA servers or saved for restoration purposes. In addition to the capability to back up the entire configuration to this file, individual ISA elements such as firewall rules can be backed up to individual files, allowing one-by-one restores of ISA elements. This flexibility allows for reduced restoration times and ease of recoverability of whole servers or individual elements.

For more information on backing up and restoring ISA Server 2006 environments, see Chapter 18, "Backing Up, Restoring, and Recovering an ISA Server 2006 Environment."

Maintaining an ISA Server Environment

The "care and feeding" of an ISA Server environment that has been put into place is a key component to an ISA Server deployment plan. Although ISA is typically low maintenance, there are still several important procedures and proactive steps that should be followed to keep ISA running smoothly. Chapter 17, "Maintaining ISA Server 2006," covers many of these procedures, and includes the types of daily, weekly, monthly, and quarterly tasks that should be performed to keep ISA in top shape. In addition, the concept of updating ISA with OS and other patches is covered in this chapter.

Monitoring and Logging Access

Deployed out of the box, ISA includes a robust logging mechanism that can be configured to use a SQL-style MSDE database for logging purposes. These logs can be easily queried, and powerful reports, such as the one shown in Figure 1.7, can be generated to provide administrators with a detailed analysis of the type of traffic sent across ISA servers.

NOTE

The MSDE Database, installed as an option with ISA Server 2006, is configured to allow only local access from a user logged in to the console. This prevents attacks such as SQL Slammer, which take advantage of a SQL or MSDE server with open ports to the network.

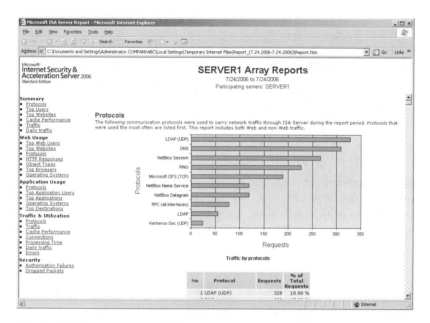

FIGURE 1.7   Viewing an ISA Server 2006 report.

It is critical to proactively respond to ISA alerts, intrusion attempts, and performance data generated by ISA servers; therefore, it may be prudent in certain cases to deploy a means of gathering ISA logging and performance data in a centralized location and automatically alerting on this information. Chapter 19 covers the use of the ISA Server 2006 Management Pack for Microsoft Operations Manager (MOM), which allows for proactive management, monitoring, and troubleshooting of an ISA environment.

Using ISA Server 2006 to Secure Applications

One of the distinct advantages to an ISA Server 2006 solution is the software's capability to scan all traffic that hits it for exploits and threats, before that traffic hits its intended target. As previously mentioned, ISA performs these functions through a process of scanning that traffic at the Application layer through a series of customizable filters, such as an HTTP filter for web traffic that knows to look for common exploit strategies like those employed by the Code Red, Nimbda, and Ject viruses. These capabilities are the central selling point for one of ISA's most popular features: the capability to secure and protect Internet-facing applications from attack.

Securing Exchange Outlook Web Access with ISA Server 2006

The current single most common deployment scenario for ISA Server 2006 involves an ISA Server being set up to provide reverse proxy to Exchange Outlook Web Access (OWA) servers. The ISA development team worked very closely with the Exchange development team when developing specific OWA filters for this, and the integration between the two technologies is very tight. In addition to the standard benefits that reverse-proxy capabilities provide, deploying ISA to secure OWA also has the following key selling points:

▶ **SSL to SSL end-to-end encryption**—ISA Server 2006 is one of the few reverse-proxy products to currently support end-to-end Secure Sockets Layer (SSL) support from the client to the ISA server and back to the Exchange OWA server. This functionality is provided via certificates installed on both Exchange and the ISA server, allowing the OWA traffic to be unencrypted at the ISA box, scanned for exploits, then reencrypted to the Exchange servers. This allows for a highly advanced ISA design, particularly in configurations where ISA is deployed in the DMZ zone of an existing firewall.

▶ **Forms-based authentication on ISA**—Introduced with Exchange Server 2003, forms-based authentication (FBA) enables users to authenticate against an OWA server by filling out information on a form, such as the one shown in Figure 1.8. This also has the added advantage of preventing any unauthenticated traffic from accessing the Exchange server.

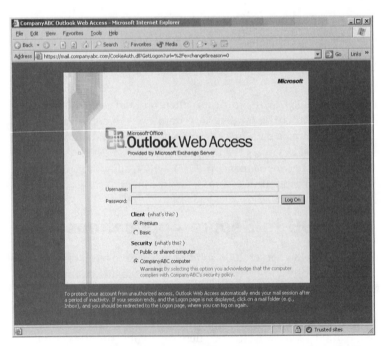

FIGURE 1.8   Using forms-based authentication to authenticate against OWA servers.

▶ **Unihomed ISA Server support**—ISA OWA Publishing also can be deployed on a unihomed (single network) card in the existing DMZ of a firewall such as a Cisco PIX or other packet-filter firewall. In fact, this is one of the more common deployment scenarios for ISA Server. This flexibility enables ISA to function as an appliance server that serves as a bastion host to Exchange services.

> **NOTE**
>
> Many Exchange deployment designs are replacing Exchange front-end servers in the DMZ with ISA servers in the DMZ that communicate with front-end servers in the internal network. This has the added advantage of securing the services in a DMZ configuration, but without opening the multitude of ports required by a front-end server to be able to communicate with Exchange database servers and Global Catalog servers.

In addition to filtering and protecting OWA traffic, ISA also includes custom filters to scan and protect other mail-related traffic such as Simple Mail Transport Protocol (SMTP) and Exchange MAPI (Outlook-style) access. For more information on securing mail-related services, including step-by-step deployment scenarios, see Chapter 12.

Locking Down Web Application Access

As previously mentioned, the HTTP filter included with ISA Server 2006 includes pre-installed knowledge to identify and eradicate HTTP threats before they access any web services, including traditional web servers and web applications. It is under this pretext that ISA can be deployed to secure external-facing web servers and web traffic. In addition, the HTTP filter is customizable, and can be modified or extended manually or can use third-party software products to do things such as limit specific HTTP calls, block executable downloads, or limit access to specific web sites. For more information on setting up ISA to secure web services, refer to Chapter 14, "Securing Web (HTTP) Traffic."

Securing Remote Procedure Call (RPC) Traffic

One of the more potent threats to Windows infrastructure in recent years has been the rise of viruses and exploits that take advantage of Remote Procedure Call (RPC) functions to take over computers and wreak havoc on client operating systems. Many of these threats have been extremely damaging to the infrastructure of organizations, and the method of containing the spread of them in the past has involved a complete shutdown of the RPC communications infrastructure between network segments.

ISA Server 2006 provides an invaluable tool against these types of RPC exploits through its capability to screen RPC traffic and intelligently open only those ports that are necessary for specific RPC services to function. For example, an ISA server could be positioned as a router between multiple network segments, a server segment, and client segments, and filter all RPC traffic between those segments, as the diagram in Figure 1.9 illustrates. It could then be configured to allow only Exchange MAPI Access (a form of RPC traffic) to that segment, blocking potentially infected clients from infecting servers or other clients on other segments.

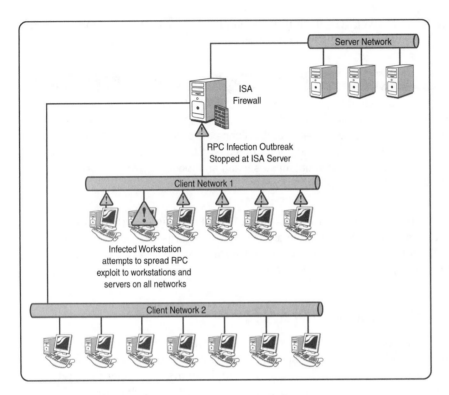

FIGURE 1.9   Securing RPC traffic between network segments.

For more information on the RPC filtering capabilities of ISA Server 2006, see Chapter 14.

Summary

The growth of Microsoft's Internet Security and Acceleration Server has corresponded with the increase in the types and quantities of threats faced by organizations on the Internet today. Fortunately for these organizations, the capabilities of ISA Server 2006 are many, and it has found a place in their security topology as a firewall, caching server, VPN device, reverse-proxy machine, RPC filter, and more.

ISA Server 2006's simple and eloquent design sits on top of a complex and capable security platform, capable of advanced Application-layer packet inspection, complex firewall rules, and multiple network support. Before deploying ISA, it is important to understand the specifics of what it can do and how to configure it. Consequently, the subsequent chapters of this book present detailed descriptions of ISA's capabilities, as well as step-by-step deployment scenarios, best practices, and tips to help organizations make the most out of an ISA Server investment.

Best Practices

▶ Become familiar with the wizards, toolbox, and tasks in the ISA Server Management Console.

▶ Consider deploying ISA Server 2006 as an additional security layer to an existing firewall environment, particularly where a strong investment currently exists.

▶ Consider the use of an ISA Server Hardware solution that provides prebuilt and presecured ISA solutions.

▶ Where possible, take advantage of the enhanced caching capabilities of ISA Server 2006, which are turned off by default.

▶ Secure Outlook Web Access (OWA) by using ISA reverse-proxy and forms-based authentication whenever possible.

▶ Consider deploying the Enterprise version of ISA Server 2006 if more than two ISA servers will be deployed or if there are advanced design considerations.

▶ Deploy ISA Server 2006 on the latest Windows and ISA security patches.

▶ Consider the use of third-party add-ins for ISA Server that can enable advanced intrusion detection, web-content filtering, improved VPN support, and much more.

▶ Document and back up the ISA Server 2006 configuration often to ensure quick recovery in disaster recovery scenarios.

Installing ISA Server 2006

This first step toward realizing ISA's real potential is, understandably enough, installing it on a server and testing it out. Although it seems simple, several critical security steps should be followed whenever ISA servers are set up. Many deployment scenarios call for the ISA server to be an edge service, facing the Internet or other secured networks in one fashion or another. Therefore, special care should be taken to ensure that the ISA server is secure and robust from the start.

This chapter covers all points related to ISA Server installation, including hardware and software prerequisites, operating system selection and installation, and patching and securing techniques.

It is recommended that you install and test ISA Server 2006 in a lab environment before deploying it into a production environment. This chapter provides a step-by-step installation process for ISA Server that will enable the administrator to work with ISA and can be used as a guideline for future deployment. After it is installed, key ISA functionality can be examined in Chapter 3, "Exploring ISA Server 2006 Tools and Concepts."

Reviewing ISA Server 2006 Prerequisites

Before you install ISA Server, it is essential to take several key prerequisites into account. Many of these prerequisites are required, and some are good general best practices. Reviewing them before deploying an ISA Server 2006 infrastructure is therefore recommended.

Reviewing Hardware Prerequisites

One of the advantages of ISA Server is its capability to be installed on standard, Intel/AMD-based server hardware. This helps to reduce the overall cost associated with deploying this type of security technology because replacement parts for server hardware are relatively inexpensive and easy to obtain. Many other solutions on the market today rely on proprietary hardware, which can be expensive to replace and/or difficult to obtain.

An ideal ISA Server implementation has redundant components and enough memory and processor speed to allow for the type of ISA functionality it will be responsible for. For example, an ISA server that solely acts as a firewall does not need as much processor overhead as one that also performs web caching and VPN connectivity.

ISA Server 2006 implementation should ideally be run on server-class hardware, such as rack-mountable or tower models from major hardware vendors. The 1U server models (or their tower equivalents) are the most commonly deployed server models used for ISA servers, although many other types of servers can also function in this capacity.

> **NOTE**
>
> When sizing and scoping hardware for ISA, keep in mind that for the current ISA Server 2006 licensing scheme, licenses are purchased on a per-processor basis. What this effectively means is that a dual-CPU server costs twice as much in licensing costs for ISA than a single-CPU server. For this reason, many organizations limit ISA servers to single-CPU servers, unless the load anticipated is great enough to warrant either multiple servers or multiple CPU machines.

Microsoft maintains a list of the minimal hardware requirements for ISA Server 2006 to run, as shown in Table 2.1. Bear in mind that these hardware levels are bare-minimum requirements and are not best-practice configurations. They support ISA deployments of 100 rules or less, require no special configurations, and require an Internet connection of less than 7Mb. Even in these cases, it may be wise to deploy more capable hardware for realistic deployments of ISA.

TABLE 2.1   Hardware Requirements

Component	Requirement
OS	Windows Server 2003 with SP1 or higher
Processor	Single 733MHz Pentium III equivalent
Memory	512MB of memory
Disk Space	150MB available (for installation of ISA software)
Network Cards / ISDN Adapter / Modem	One OS-compatible card per connected network

If an ISA server performs more functions, the configuration may require additional hardware and/or additional ISA servers. Details on exact server hardware deployment recommendations can be found in Chapter 4, "Designing an ISA Server 2006 Environment."

Understanding ISA Operating System Requirements

The ISA Server software itself requires only a few software prerequisites before it can be installed. The first and foremost is a Windows operating system (OS) on which to run. ISA Server 2006 installation can be performed on the following operating system versions:

▶ Windows Server 2003 Standard Edition (32 bit) with SP1

▶ Windows Server 2003 Enterprise Edition (32 bit) with SP1

▶ Windows Server 2003 R2 Standard Edition (32 bit)

▶ Windows Server 2003 R2 Enterprise Edition (32 bit)

> **NOTE**
>
> The previous version of ISA Server 2004 supported installation on Windows 2000. This is not supported anymore with ISA Server 2006. In addition, the new 64-bit version of Windows Server 2003 is not supported for ISA Server 2006, as there is no 64-bit version of ISA available currently.

Examining Windows and ISA Service Packs

In addition to the base operating system, ISA should be deployed on the latest Service Pack version for the OS itself. In fact, ISA Server 2006 requires at least SP1 for Windows Server 2003. The newer Windows Server 2003 R2 Edition is also supported. Windows Server 2003 SP1 included the following enhancements, which help to further secure ISA:

▶ **Cumulative security updates**—The entire list of updates and patches to Windows Server 2003 are included in the Service Pack 1 offering. This reduces the amount of time it takes to patch a Windows Server 2003 system.

▶ **Higher default security and privilege reduction on services**—Windows Server 2003 SP1 includes technology to reduce the running privilege of many services that run on the system. This way, if the service were to be compromised, the damage that could be done would be minimal because the exploit or virus would not have full administrative privilege.

▶ **Support for DEP (Data Execute Protection) hardware**—Microsoft has been working with hardware vendors on a technology called Data Execute Protection (DEP), which is essentially a way for the hardware, such as memory and processors, to physically not allow modification of code running within itself. This prevents a modification of base Windows functionality even if an exploit takes complete control of the system. Service Pack 1 is the first update to take advantage of DEP technology when it is installed on hardware that supports it.

▶ **Security Configuration Wizard**—One of the best additions to Service Pack 1 is the Security Configuration Wizard (SCW). SCW enables a server to be locked down easily via a wizard that scans for running services and provides advice and guidance throughout the process. SCW can also create security templates that can be used on multiple deployed servers, thus improving their overall security. Because SCW essentially shuts off all those subprocesses and applications that are not necessary for ISA to function, it effectively secures the ISA server by reducing the attack surface that is exposed on the server. A detailed description of using SCW to secure an ISA server is provided in the section of this chapter entitled "Securing the Operating System with the Security Configuration Wizard."

Outlining ISA Network Prerequisites

Unlike the older ISA Server 2000 edition, the newer version of ISA, including ISA Server 2004 and now ISA Server 2006 can be installed on and configured with rules for multiple networks. The only limitation to this concept is the number of network interface cards, ISDN adapters, or modems that can be physically installed in the server to provide for access to those networks. For example, the diagram in Figure 2.1 illustrates an ISA design where the ISA server is attached to a total of five different internal networks and the Internet, scanning and filtering the data sent across each network with a total of six network cards.

This type of flexibility within a network environment allows for a high degree of design freedom, allowing an ISA server to assume multiple roles within the network.

Procuring and Assembling ISA Hardware

After the prerequisites for ISA deployment have been taken into account, the specific hardware for ISA deployment can be procured and assembled. Exact number, placement, and design of ISA servers may require more advanced design, however. It is therefore important to review ISA design scenarios such as the ones demonstrated in Chapter 4.

Determining When to Deploy Dedicated ISA Hardware Appliances

An option for ISA deployment that did not exist in the past but is increasingly common in today's marketplace is the option to deploy ISA on dedicated, appliance hardware. These ISA *appliances* are similar in several ways to the many third-party firewall devices currently on the market. For example, several of the ISA appliances have network interfaces on the front of the appliance, and some even allow configuration of the server via an LCD panel on the front. It is highly recommended that you explore the ISA appliance options available on each manufacturer's websites. In addition, Microsoft provides a list of these hardware vendors at the following website:

http://www.microsoft.com/isaserver/partners

The concept of the ISA server as a dedicated security concept is a novel one for Microsoft, and several attractive options can be considered. It is advisable to examine each of the available hardware options before making design decisions on ISA Server deployment.

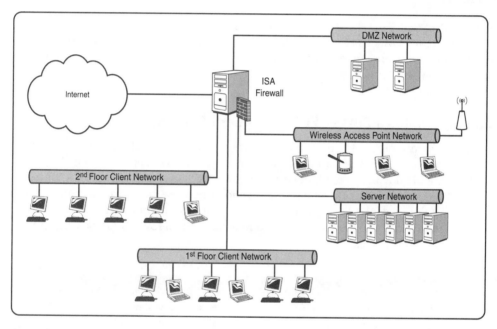

FIGURE 2.1   An ISA server deployed across multiple networks.

Optimizing ISA Server Hardware

ISA Server 2006 is not particularly processor or memory intensive, and its disk utilization is fairly low. The best investment when it comes to ISA server often comes with the addition of redundant components such as RAID1 hardware mirrors for the disks or multiple power supplies and fans. This helps to increase ISA's redundancy and robustness.

From a disk management perspective, ISA is commonly installed on a single physical disk that is partitioned into various logical partitions, depending on the server's role. At a minimum, all components can be installed on a single partition. To reduce the chance of logs filling up the operating system drive, a separate partition can be made for the ISA SQL Logs. Finally, if web caching is enabled on the server, the cache itself is often placed on a third partition. Although the size of each partition depends on the size of the drive being deployed, a common deployment scenario would be 8GB OS, 8GB logs, 16GB cache.

That said, the configuration of an ISA server's partitions is of small consequence to the overall functionality of the server, so there is no need to get involved in complex partitioning schemes or large amounts of disk space.

Building Windows Server 2003 as ISA's Operating System

The mechanism that lies at the base of ISA Server's functionality is the operating system. ISA draws from Windows its base network and kernel functionality, and it cannot be installed without it. Consequently, the operating system installation is the first step in the creation of a new ISA server.

Installing Windows Server 2003 Standard Edition

As previously mentioned, ISA Server 2006 software requires an operating system to supply needed core functionality. The operating system of choice for ISA Server 2006 is Windows Server 2003 Standard edition or Windows Server 2003 R2 Standard edition. The Windows Server 2003 operating system encompasses a myriad of new technologies and functionality, more than can be covered in this book. If additional reading on the capabilities of the operating system is desired, the recommended reference is *Windows Server 2003 R2 Edition Unleashed*, from Sams Publishing.

> **NOTE**
>
> It is highly recommended to install ISA Server 2006 on a clean, freshly-built operating system on a reformatted hard drive. If the server that will be used for ISA Server was previously running in a different capacity, the most secure and robust solution would be to completely reinstall the operating system using the procedure outlined in this section.

Installation of Windows Server 2003 is straightforward, and takes approximately 30 minutes to an hour to complete. The following step-by-step installation procedure illustrates the procedure for installation of standard Windows Server 2003 media. Many hardware manufacturers include special installation instructions and procedures that may vary from the procedure outlined here, but the concepts are roughly the same. To install Windows Server 2003 Standard edition, perform the following steps:

1. Insert the Windows Server 2003 Standard CD into the CD drive.
2. Power up the server and let it boot to the CD-ROM drive. If there is currently no operating system on the hard drive, it automatically boots into CD-ROM–based setup, as shown in Figure 2.2.

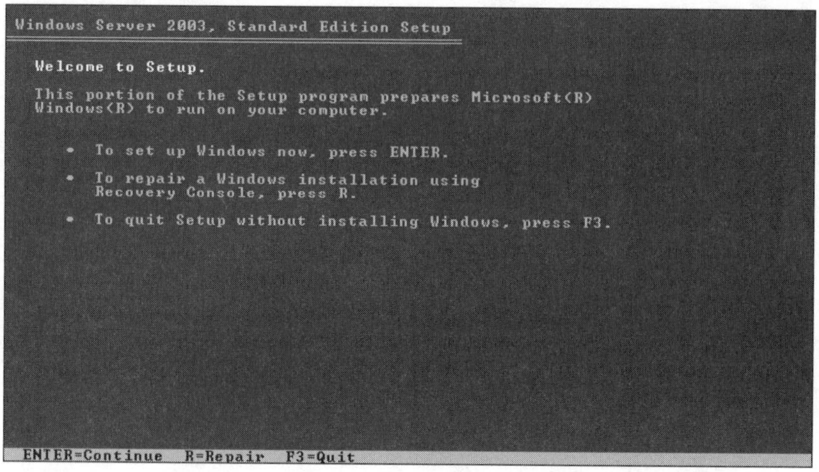

```
Windows Server 2003, Standard Edition Setup

    Welcome to Setup.

    This portion of the Setup program prepares Microsoft(R)
    Windows(R) to run on your computer.

        •  To set up Windows now, press ENTER.

        •  To repair a Windows installation using
           Recovery Console, press R.

        •  To quit Setup without installing Windows, press F3.




    ENTER=Continue   R=Repair   F3=Quit
```

FIGURE 2.2   Running the CD-ROM–based Windows Server 2003 setup.

3. When prompted, press Enter to start setting up Windows.

4. At the licensing agreement screen, read the license and then press F8 if you agree to the license agreement.

5. Select the physical disk on which Windows will be installed. Choose between the available disks shown by using the up and down arrows. When selected, press Enter to install.

6. At the next screen, choose Format the Partition Using the NTFS File System by selecting it and clicking Enter to continue.

Following this step, Windows Server 2003 Setup begins formatting the hard drive and copying files to it. After a reboot and more automatic installation routines, the setup process continues with the Regional and Language Options screen as follows:

1. Review the regional and language options and click Next to continue.

2. Enter a name and organization into the Personalization screen and click Next to continue.

3. Enter the product key for Windows. This is typically on the CD case or part of the license agreement purchased from Microsoft. Click Next after the key is entered.

4. Select which licensing mode will be used on the server, either Per Server or Per Device, and click Next to continue.

5. At the Computer Name and Administrator Password screen, enter a unique name for the server and type a cryptic password into the password fields, as shown in Figure 2.3. Click Next to continue.

FIGURE 2.3   Configuring the server name and administrator password.

6. Check the Date and Time Zone settings and click Next to continue.

The next screen to be displayed is where networking settings can be configured. Setup allows for automatic configuration (Typical Settings) or manual configuration (Custom Settings) options. Selecting Custom Settings allows for each installed Network Interface Card (NIC) to be configured with various options, such as Static IP addresses and custom protocols. Selecting Typical Settings bypasses these steps, although they can easily be set later.

1. To simplify the setup, select Typical Settings and click Next. Network settings should then be configured after the OS is installed.

2. Select whether the server is to be a member of a domain or a workgroup member. For this demonstration, choose Workgroup.

3. Click Next to Continue.

NOTE

The question of domain membership versus workgroup membership is a complex one. To ease installation, the server can simply be made a workgroup member, and domain membership can be added at a later time as necessary. For more information on whether or not to make an ISA server a domain member, see the section titled "Determining Domain Membership Versus Workgroup Isolation."

After more installation routines and reboots, setup is complete and the operating system can be logged into as the local Administrator and configured for ISA Server 2006. If Windows Server 2003 R2 Edition is being installed, you will be prompted to insert the second CD for R2 to complete the install.

Configuring Network Properties

Each deployed ISA Server 2006 server has its network settings configured uniquely, to match the network or networks to which the server is connected. It is important to understand the implications of how the network configuration affects ISA Setup. For example, the sample ISA server in Figure 2.4 illustrates how one ISA server that is connected to the Internet, an internal network, and a Perimeter (DMZ) network is configured.

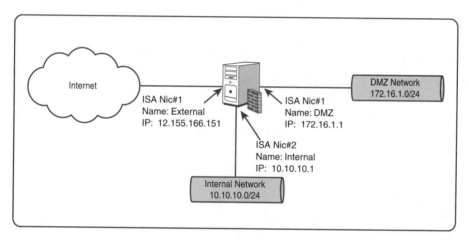

FIGURE 2.4   Looking at a sample ISA network layout.

NOTE

It is often highly useful to rename the network cards' display names on a server to help identify them during troubleshooting. For example, naming a NIC Internal, External, or DMZ helps to identify to which network it is attached. In addition, it may also be useful to identify to which physical port on the server the NIC corresponds, with names such as External (top), Internal (bottom), and DMZ (PCI).

ISA firewall rules rely heavily on the unique network settings of the server itself, and the assumption is made throughout this book that these settings are properly configured. It is therefore extremely important to have each of the Network Interface Cards (NICs) set up with the proper IP addresses, gateways, and other settings in advance of installing ISA Server.

Applying Windows Server 2003 Service Pack 1

The release of Service Pack 1 for Windows Server 2003 introduced a myriad of design and security improvements to the underlying architecture of Windows Server 2003. In addition, ISA Server 2006 now requires Service Pack 1 before installation of the ISA software can proceed.

> **NOTE**
>
> Many Windows Server 2003 CD packages come with SP1 already "baked in" to the media. This is also true for Windows Server 2003 R2 edition media. If this is the case, these steps can be skipped.

To update Windows Server 2003 with the Service Pack, obtain the SP1 media or download the Service Pack binaries from the following URL:

http://www.microsoft.com/windowsserver2003/downloads/servicepacks/sp1/default.mspx

After it is obtained, install the Service Pack by performing the following steps:

1. Start the installation by either double-clicking on the downloaded file or finding the update.exe file located with the Windows Server 2003 Service Pack 1 media (usually in the Update subdirectory).

2. At the welcome screen, as shown in Figure 2.5, click Next to continue.

FIGURE 2.5   Updating Windows Server 2003 with Service Pack 1.

3. Read the licensing agreement and select I Agree if in agreement. Click Next to continue.

4. Accept the defaults for the Uninstall directory and click Next to continue.

5. The Service Pack then begins the installation process, which will take 10–20 minutes to complete. Click Finish to end the Service Pack installation and reboot the server.

Updating and Patching the Operating System

In addition to the patches that were installed as part of the Service Pack, security updates and patches are constantly being released by Microsoft. It is highly advantageous to install the critical updates made available by Microsoft to the ISA server, particularly when it is first being built. These patches can be manually downloaded and installed, or they can be automatically applied by using Microsoft Update, as detailed in the following procedure:

1. While logged in as an account with local Administrator privilege, click on Start, All Programs, Microsoft Update.

NOTE

If Microsoft Update has never been used, the Windows Update link will be available. After clicking on it, it is recommended to click the link to install Microsoft Update instead. It is recommended to use Microsoft Update to secure an ISA server as it will identify not only Windows patches but ISA patches as well. This step by step assumes that Microsoft Update is used.

2. Depending on the Internet Explorer security settings, Internet Explorer may display an information notice that indicates that Enhanced Security is turned on. Check the box labeled In the Future, Do Not Show This Message and click OK to continue.

3. At this point, Microsoft Update may attempt to download and install the Windows Update control. Click Install to allow the control to install.

4. Depending on the version of Microsoft Update currently available, the Microsoft Update site may prompt for installation of the latest version of Windows Update software. If this is the case, click Install Now when prompted. If not, proceed with the installation.

The subsequent screen, shown in Figure 2.6, offers the option of performing an Express Install, which automatically chooses the critical security patches necessary and installs them, or a Custom Install, where the option to choose which particular patches—critical and non-critical—is offered. If more control over the patching process is required, then the Custom Install option is preferred. For a quick and easy update process, Express Install is the way to go. To continue with the installation, perform the following steps:

1. Click on Express Install to begin the patching process.

2. Depending on Internet Explorer settings, a prompt may appear that warns about sending information to trusted sites. Check the box labeled In the Future, Do Not Show This Message and click Yes. If the prompt does not appear, go to the next step.

3. If updates are available, they are listed under High Priority Updates. Click the Install button to install the patches.

4. Microsoft Update then downloads and installs the updates automatically. Upon completion, click Close.

5. Close the Internet Explorer Window.

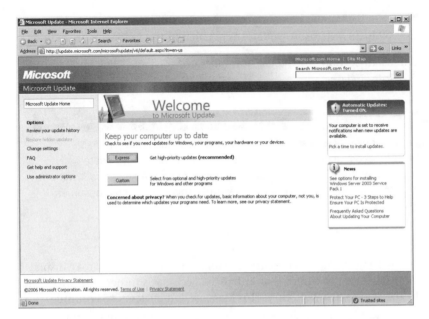

FIGURE 2.6   Running Microsoft Update.

TIP

Running Microsoft Update on an ongoing basis as part of a maintenance plan is a wise idea for keeping the server up to date with the most recent patches and fixes. For production servers, however, it is advisable to initially test those patches in a lab environment when possible. In addition, although enabling Automatic Updates to perform this function may seem ideal, it is not recommended to automatically install any updates on a running server, particularly a security-based server.

Determining Domain Membership Versus Workgroup Isolation

Before ISA Server 2006 is installed, a particularly important decision must be made: whether or not to make that server a member of an Active Directory domain. The answer to this question is not simple, but there is a general consensus that it is best to limit the scope of what is accessible by any server that is exposed to unsecured networks such as the Internet.

Although there are few concrete, easily identifiable security threats to back this up, it is general best practice to reduce the exposure that the ISA server has, and limit it to only the functionality that it needs. Consequently, one of the big improvements in ISA Server 2006 is its ability to run as a workgroup member, as opposed to a domain member. There are certain pieces of functionality that differ between each of these scenarios, and it is subsequently important to outline the deployment scenarios and functional limitations of both scenarios.

Understanding Deployment Scenarios with ISA Domain Members and ISA Workgroup Members

Installing ISA as a domain member is more common in smaller organizations that require greater simplicity and administrative flexibility. One of the main reasons for this is that these smaller organizations often deploy ISA as the main, edge-facing firewall for their networks. When ISA is deployed in this fashion, the reasons against domain membership become lessened because the server itself is directly exposed to network resources, and even if it were to be compromised, making it a domain member versus a nondomain member would not help things greatly.

One of the more common ISA deployment scenarios, on the other hand, involves ISA being set up as a unihomed (single NIC) server in the DMZ of an existing firewall. In nearly all these cases, the ISA server is not made a domain member because domain membership would require the server to open additional ports on the edge-facing firewall. In this situation, if the ISA server were to be compromised, there would be functional advantages to keeping the server out of the domain.

A third deployment scenario in use in certain organizations is the creation of a separate Active Directory forest, of which the ISA server is a member. This forest would be configured with a one-way trust from the main organizational forest, allowing ISA to perform domain-related activities without posing a threat to the internal domain accounts.

Working Around the Functional Limitations of Workgroup Membership

As previously mentioned, it may be advantageous to deploy ISA Server in a workgroup, in situations where the ISA server is deployed in the DMZ of an existing firewall, or for other reasons mentioned earlier. A few functional limitations must be taken into account, however, when determining deployment strategy for ISA. These limitations and their workarounds are as follows:

▶ **Local accounts used for administration**—Because ISA is not installed in the domain, local server accounts must be used for administration. On multiple servers, this requires setting up multiple accounts and maintaining multiple passwords. In addition, when remotely administering multiple servers, each server requires re-authenticating through the console each time it is accessed.

▶ **RADIUS or SecurID used for authentication**—Because domain authentication is not available, the ISA server must rely on RADIUS or SecurID authentication to be used to properly authenticate users. Because an Active Directory deployment can install the Internet Authentication Service (IAS) to provide RADIUS support, it is possible to leverage this to allow authentication of domain accounts through RADIUS on an ISA server that is not a domain member. More information on configuring IAS can be found in Chapter 9, "Enabling Client Remote Access with ISA Server 2006 Virtual Private Networks (VPNs)," and Chapter 14, "Securing Web (HTTP) Traffic."

▶ **Firewall client use disabled**—The one functional limitation that cannot be over-come in a workgroup membership scenario is the fact that the full-blown ISA client cannot be used. In reality, use of the full Firewall client, which provides advanced firewall connection rules and user-granular access control, is not widespread, so this may not factor into the equation. Because the SecureNAT client is supported, this minimizes the effects of this limitation. SecureNAT clients are essentially any client on the network (including those on the Internet) that can connect to the server and does not require any special client software to be installed. For more information on what the Firewall client can do, refer to Chapter 11, "Understanding Client Deployment Scenarios with ISA Server 2006."

Changing Domain Membership

If the decision has been made to make the ISA server a domain member, the following procedure can be used to add the server to a domain:

1. While logged in as an account with local administrative privilege, click Start, Control Panel, System.

2. Choose the Computer Name tab, as shown in Figure 2.7.

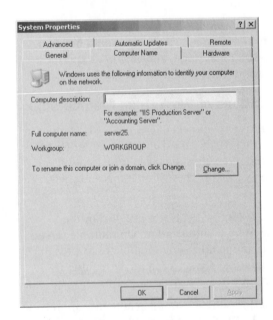

FIGURE 2.7   Changing domain membership.

3. Click the Change button.

4. Under the Member Of section, choose Domain and type in the name of the Active Directory domain of which the ISA server will be a member. Click OK when complete.

5. Enter the username and password of an account in the Active Directory domain that has the capability to add computers to the domain. Click OK when complete.

6. Click OK three times at the Welcome message, reboot warning, and close the dialog box.

7. Click Yes to restart the server.

Installing the ISA Server 2006 Software

After the base operating system has been deployed and configured, the task of installing the ISA Server 2006 software itself can take place. Although the initial installation procedure is relatively straightforward, several factors must be taken into account before you begin.

Reviewing ISA Software Component Prerequisites

Several components of ISA Server can be selected for installation during the setup process. These components are optional, depending on the role that the ISA server is to perform. Because it is always best to configure security with an eye toward reducing the overall security exposure, these components should be installed only if they are necessary for the functionality of the ISA server. With less services installed, the ISA server exposes less of a "signature" to the Internet. Just as design engineers for war planes limit what is installed on aircraft to reduce the overall radar signature, so too should ISA be configured with only those features enabled that are absolutely required.

The following components make up the core of ISA Server features and can be installed as options during the setup process:

▶ **Firewall Services**—This component contains all the key firewall functionality that controls and validates traffic sent across networks. It is almost always installed, unless only the management tools are being installed on a different machine.

▶ **Advanced Logging**—Choosing Advanced Logging installs the Microsoft Desktop/Data Engine (MSDE) to provide a database for the ISA logs. This makes it much easier to generate reports and to view log information and is a recommended option.

▶ **ISA Server Management**—The ISA Server Management tools simply install the ISA Management Console, which is normally installed on an ISA server. This component can also be separate from the ISA server to allow for remote management.

> **NOTE**
>
> The Message Screener and Client Installation Share components that were available in ISA Server 2004 have been removed from ISA Server 2006, largely because of the greater security risk they presented.

As soon as the various components have been reviewed, installation of ISA Server can begin.

Installing ISA Server 2006 Standard Edition

The installation process for ISA Server 2006 is not complex, but it requires some general knowledge of the various steps along the way to ensure that the services and functionality are properly configured.

NOTE

The procedure outlined in this chapter covers installation of the Standard version of ISA Server 2006. For the procedure to install the Enterprise version, refer to Chapter 6, "Deploying ISA Server Arrays with ISA Server 2006 Enterprise Edition."

To begin the ISA Server 2006 installation, perform the following steps:

1. Insert the ISA Server 2006 Standard media into the CD-ROM drive (or install from a network location).

2. From the dialog box, click on Install ISA Server 2006.

3. At the Welcome screen, click Next to continue.

4. Read the license agreement and select I Accept the Terms in the License Agreement if they are acceptable. Click Next.

5. Enter a username and an organization name into the fields on the Customer Information screen. In addition, enter the product serial number and then click Next to continue.
   The following screen allows for several installation options: Typical, and Custom. A Typical installation includes all ISA options. A Custom installation allows for the exclusion or inclusion of multiple ISA components.

6. Under type of installation, choose Custom and click Next to continue.

7. Under the Custom Setup options, as shown in Figure 2.8, review the installation features and choose which ones correspond to the functionality that the server will utilize. To add or remove components, click on the down-arrow key and choose This Feature, and All Subfeatures, Will Be Installed on Local Hard Drive.

8. After the features have been chosen, click Next to continue.

The next installation dialog box enables administrators to specify which network belongs to the internal network range, so that the appropriate network rules can be created. If this is an ISA server with a single NIC, then all IP addresses can be set up here. If it is a multi-NIC server, then it is appropriate to enter the proper IP range in this dialog box via the following procedure:

1. Click the Add button.

2. Enter the range or ranges of IP addresses that constitute the internal network range within the organization, similar to what is shown in Figure 2.9.

3. Click Add to move the entered range into the field.

NOTE

The Add Adapter button can be useful for automating this process. It detects the range in which a network adapter is installed and automatically adds it to the list.

4. Repeat for any additional internal IP ranges and click OK to continue.

5. Review the internal ranges in the next dialog box and click Next to continue.

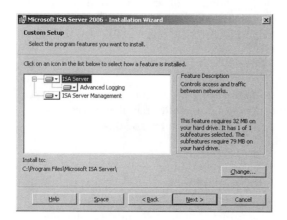

FIGURE 2.8   Performing a custom installation.

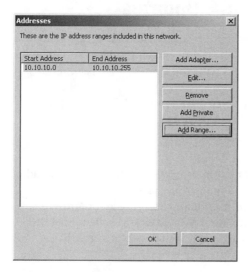

FIGURE 2.9   Specifying the internal network range.

The subsequent dialog box offers a setting that enables older (pre 4.x) Firewall clients to connect to and use the ISA Server 2006 environment. This setting is relevant to only those organizations with a previously deployed ISA 2000 environment that made use of the Firewall client and have not upgraded that client in advance of server setup. It is not recommended to enable this setting; it reduces the overall security of the ISA environment. For more information on the Firewall client, refer to Chapter 11. To continue, do the following:

1. Do not check the check box and click Next to Continue.

2. Review the list of services that will be stopped during the migration and click Next to continue. If installing over an RDP connection, an additional dialog box may appear alerting the administrator that a policy will be created to allow RDP to the box from the client that is currently connected.

3. Click Install to begin the installation process.

4. Click Finish when the wizard completes the setup process.

5. Close the Internet Explorer window that pops up automatically. This window prompts for the installation of ISA updates, which will be performed in later steps. Close all other dialog boxes as necessary.

Performing Post-Installation ISA Updates

ISA Server 2006 is an organic, constantly evolving set of technologies that occasionally needs patching and updating to stay ahead of the constantly evolving threats and exploits on the Internet. Subsequently, it is key to update ISA with the latest service packs and security patches available for the system, and to check for new updates as part of a regular maintenance plan. Using Microsoft Update (as opposed to only using Windows Update) will automatically detect the ISA patches that will be required for a server.

Installing Third-Party ISA Tools

The final step to ISA installation is the setup and configuration of any third-party ISA add-ons that may be required by the system. There are a whole host of security add-ons for ISA, which leverage ISA's Application-layer filtering technology to provide for anti-virus, spam filtering, enhanced VPN, intrusion detection, and other services. To view a list of ISA Server 2006's partners that produce these types of software, visit the following URL:

http://www.microsoft.com/isaserver/partners

Securing the Operating System with the Security Configuration Wizard

The most impressive and useful addition to Windows Server 2003 Service Pack 1 has to be the Security Configuration Wizard (SCW). SCW allows for a server to be completely locked down, except for the very specific services that it requires to perform specific duties. This way, a WINS server responds to only WINS requests, and a DNS server has only DNS enabled. This type of functionality was long sought after and is now available.

SCW enables administrators to build custom templates that can be exported to additional servers, thus streamlining the securing process when multiple systems are set up. In addition, current security templates can be imported into SCW to allow for existing intelligence to be maintained.

The advantages to using the SCW service on an ISA server are immediately identifiable. The ISA server, in that it is often directly exposed to the Internet, is vulnerable to attack, and should have all unnecessary services and ports shut down. The Firewall Service of ISA normally drops this type of activity, but it is always a good idea to put in an additional layer of security for good measure.

Installing the Security Configuration Wizard

Installing Service Pack 1 for Windows Server 2003 enables only the SCW service to be installed. It is not, however, installed by default, and must be set up from the Add or Remove Programs applet in Windows via the following procedure:

1. Logged in as a local administrator, click Start, Control Panel, Add or Remove Programs.

2. Click Add/Remove Windows Components.

3. Scroll down and check Security Configuration Wizard from the alphabetical list of components, as shown in Figure 2.10. Click Next to Continue.

4. Click Finish when the installation is complete.

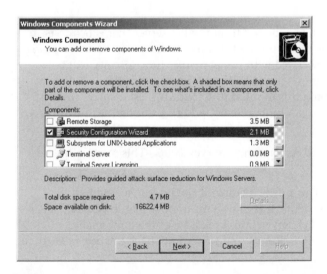

FIGURE 2.10   Installing the Security Configuration Wizard.

Creating a Custom ISA Security Template with the Security Configuration Wizard

The Security Configuration Wizard contains a wide variety of sometimes confusing securing options, and it is important to understand what each one does before securing ISA's Operating System. Too much securing, and ISA functionality could be crippled. Too little, and ISA is left insecure. It is therefore important to understand the SCW process.

Starting the SCW Template Creation   The following procedure outlines and explains the process for creating a custom security template with SCW that can be used to secure an ISA server:

1. Logged in as a local administrator, click Start, All Programs, Administrative Tools, Security Configuration Wizard.

2. At the welcome screen, click Next to continue.

3. From the list of actions to perform, select Create a New Security Policy and click Next to continue.

4. Enter the name of the server that is to be used as a baseline. For this example, the local server will be used, so click Next to continue.

5. After the processing is complete, click Next to continue.

6. On the Role-Based Service Configuration dialog box, click Next to continue.

The new dialog box, labeled Select Servers, enables administrators to define in what roles the server is allowed to function. Roles that are not specifically chosen are disabled through a process of disabling the corresponding service and locking down other functionality. Examine the list carefully, and click the arrow buttons to view additional information about each service.

Depending on what functionality will be required from the ISA server that is being set up, various roles must be assigned to the server during this process. If the roles are not configured during this step, the services associated with the particular functionality will be locked down. For example, if the Remote Access/VPN Server role is not checked, VPN access through ISA is disabled. Keeping this in mind, the following list displays some of the default roles that directly relate to ISA functionality. Additional roles may be displayed or may be necessary, and it is important to choose the ones that are required.

▶ **Microsoft Internet Security and Acceleration Server 2006**—This role is required for any ISA Server deployments.

▶ **Remote Access/VPN Server**—This role is required if the ISA server will handle Virtual Private Network (VPN) clients. It is important to note that, by default, VPN functionality is disabled on an ISA server, and it must be enabled manually. Consequently, the Security Configuration Wizard does not check the box next to this role by default because it doesn't see it as a running service. This box must be checked if future VPN functionality will be needed, however.

The other roles listed on this dialog box—such as DFS Server, Telnet Server, Print Server, and Internet Connection Sharing Server—should typically not be checked to maintain a smaller attack surface area on the ISA server. With the roles unchecked, their services are disabled.

NOTE

Unchecking the Print Server role disables the Spooler service, which effectively disables printing to and from the ISA server. It is generally best practice not to print from a server, particularly from a security server such as ISA.

Configuring SCW Roles and Options   To continue with the SCW, perform the following steps:

1. Check the roles that the server is to perform, and then click Next to continue.

2. Review the options on the Select Client Features dialog box, illustrated in Figure 2.11, which lists client features of the server. Check the appropriate boxes to enable functionality that the server requires.

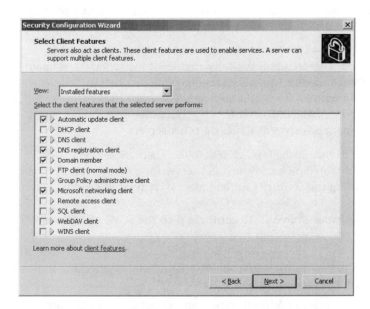

FIGURE 2.11   Selecting client roles for the Security Configuration Wizard.

The list of client roles that should be enabled on the server is no less complex than the server roles that were already configured. Properly securing an ISA server is contingent on configuring only those services that are necessary. Browse through the roles listed in the Client Features dialog box, clicking the arrows to view more information about each feature. The following are several features that may need to be enabled for an ISA server to function correctly, depending on its function:

- ▶ **Automatic Update Client**—This feature can be enabled if capability to automatically detect and download new patches for the operating system is required. In general, it is best practice to disable this functionality for an ISA server and instead set up a manual schedule of updating the operating system through a web browser or through manual patch execution on a regular basis.

- ▶ **DNS Client**—This feature is often enabled if the ISA server needs to contact DNS servers for the purposes of using the web (for patching) or contacting internal network services. In highly secure situations, however, this feature can be disabled and a static hosts file can be used for any name resolution required.

- ▶ **DNS Registration Client**—This service, although enabled by default, is best left disabled. The ISA server should not normally be writing its own records onto DNS servers. In most cases, if specific DNS records are required for internal resolution to an ISA server, for caching or another purpose, these records can be statically assigned.

- ▶ **Domain Member**—If the decision was previously made to configure ISA as a domain member, this feature needs to be enabled. If, however, it is being set up as a workgroup member, it should be disabled.

- ▶ **Microsoft Networking Client**—This service enables the ISA server to connect to other servers on a network. This feature is typically enabled if the server is a domain member. In other cases, such as with workgroup membership or when the ISA server is set up for a very specific purpose, such as a reverse-proxy server in the DMZ of an existing firewall, it would be disabled. Disabling this service disallows the ISA server from connecting to any mapped drives or shares on other servers.

The other client features listed in this dialog box, such as WINS client, SQL client, DHCP client, and so on, are rarely configured on a dedicated ISA server for security reasons. It is best to leave them disabled during the Security Configuration Wizard setup process.

Continuing with the SCW Configuration Process   To continue with the SCW, perform the following steps:

1. After checking the boxes for the features that will be enabled and unchecking those that will be disabled, click Next to continue.

2. On the next dialog box, titled Select Administration and Other Options, narrow down the list of options by clicking on the arrow in the View drop-down box and choosing Selected Options, as shown in Figure 2.12. The figure displays the options that remain after several options have been removed from the display.

   Sorting by Selected Options enables all the default options that the wizard automatically chooses to be displayed. Many of these options are unnecessary and a review and audit of each option should be undertaken. The rule of thumb with configuring

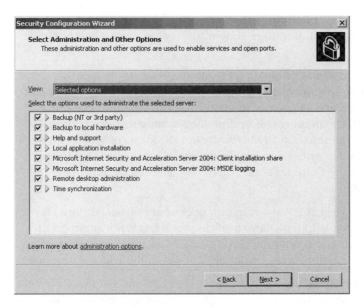

FIGURE 2.12   Selecting administration roles.

these and all the other SCW options is to enable (put a check mark) next to only those options that are absolutely necessary for the server to function.

The following list describes several of the options that can be enabled or disabled. It is important to thoroughly review each item to ensure that the server is properly secured.

▶ **Application Experience Lookup Service**—This service, installed with Windows Server 2003 Service Pack 1, is a new feature that automatically checks applications for compatibility issues when they are launched. This is an unnecessary service for an ISA server, and it should normally be disabled.

▶ **Application Installation from Group Policy**—This option should almost always be disabled on an ISA server because it is not good practice to have applications automatically installed, whether from Active Directory or any other location.

▶ **Backup (NT or 3rd Party)**—Enabling this option turns on the appropriate services and ports to allow the ISA server to be backed up with NTBackup or another third-party backup solution. Although backup functionality is a common feature, ISA can potentially disable this service if the configuration is manually exported to XML files on a regular basis. For more information on setting up this type of functionality, refer to Chapter 18, "Backing Up, Restoring, and Recovering an ISA Server 2006 Environment."

▶ **Back Up to Local Hardware**—This option goes hand in hand with the previous option. In fact, if it is enabled, the Backup (NT or third party) option must be enabled as well. This option enables the ISA server to perform backups to locally attached tapes or other media. Both these backup options can be enabled, depending on the backup method and procedure chosen. If they are not needed, they should be disabled.

▶ **Error Reporting**—Enabling this option allows faults and errors to be sent to Microsoft for troubleshooting and analysis. Although the information is never automatically sent, it is common best practice to disable this, unless troubleshooting a problem with Microsoft. Unchecking this option disables only the part of error reporting that sends the information to Microsoft, and the local console is still notified when a fault occurs. The entire error reporting service can be disabled in the System Properties under the Control Panel, if necessary, although this is not a common securing technique.

▶ **Help and Support**—The Help and Support option does what one would think: It enables display of Windows help topics and troubleshooting. It is not common to disable this because the service is not published to outside access, and it may be useful for troubleshooting in the future. It can be disabled, however, if it will not be utilized.

▶ **Link Tracking for Users' Shortcuts**—This service is typically not required for an ISA server. It proactively tracks the files to which a logged-in user has shortcuts and looks to see whether they have been renamed or moved. Because it requires the server to probe the network occasionally, it is recommended to disable this service.

▶ **Local Application Installation**—This option enables applications to be installed or modified on the ISA server. Because this also applies to patches and updates, it is not normally disabled. For the most paranoid environments, however, it can be disabled and then re-enabled when updates or new applications are necessary.

▶ **Microsoft Internet Security and Acceleration Server 2006: Client Installation Share**—This option allows the Firewall client share to exist on the ISA server for clients to use. While installed as part of a full installation, it should only be enabled if there is no other location on the network available to place the Firewall client installation files. If this functionality is required, however, it can be enabled.

▶ **Microsoft Internet Security and Acceleration Server 2006: MSDE Logging**—This option enables the Microsoft Desktop Engine (MSDE) SQL database to operate, which gives ISA the capability to perform advanced logging to a SQL-style database. For security reasons, the MSDE database is accessible only to local system access, which reduces the threat of SQL-borne viruses and exploits such as SQL Slammer. Although ISA is capable of logging to text or other formats, the advanced ISA logging capabilities are desirable in many cases, so it may be wise to install and maintain this. If it is not used, however, this should not be enabled.

▶ **Remote Desktop Administration**—Enabling this option allows for remote administration of the entire ISA server via the Remote Desktop Protocol (RDP). RDP administration of an ISA server is common for managing the ISA services, and it can simplify ISA configuration in the future. It is important to note that enabling this option simply keeps the Remote Desktop Administration service enabled, but the Firewall service of ISA blocks access from all systems unless specified in the System

Policy. If RDP will not be utilized, disable this option. For more information on remote administration of an ISA server, refer to Chapter 3.

► **Remote SCW Configuration and Analysis**—This option, when enabled, enables the Security Configuration Wizard to remotely configure the server. It should always be disabled on an ISA server because remote configuration requires the Windows Firewall to be installed, which cannot run on an ISA firewall.

► **Remote Windows Administration**—This option allows for remote administration of the MMC-related administrative tools on the server, such as the Event Viewer, Registry Editor, Performance Logs and Alerts, Local Users and Groups, and any of the administrative functions that can be remotely attached. In most cases, it is best to disable this option because remote administration of these services, even though explicitly blocked by the Firewall service, can be dangerous.

► **Shadow Copying**—The Shadow Copy Service takes snapshot backups of files on volumes that have been enabled for this service. This service is typically used on file servers, where data is dynamically changed on a regular basis and normally does not need to be installed and configured on an ISA server.

► **SQL Server Active Directory Helper**—This service should be disabled on an ISA server because its function is to allow a SQL Server to publish itself in Active Directory when certain permissions are used.

► **Time Synchronization**—The Time Synchronization option enables Network Time Protocol (NTP) to be used to keep the server's clock in synch. Keeping the clock synchronized to a known time source, such as pool.ntp.org or an internal NTP server, is an effective way to keep audit events and avoid replay attacks, so it is often good practice to keep this service enabled and subsequently configure ISA to use a time source. More information on using NTP with ISA can be found in Chapter 3. If this service is disabled, the clock should be manually synchronized with a known good time source on a regular basis.

► **Web Proxy Auto-Discovery**—The Web Proxy Auto-Discovery (WPAD) service permits certain HTTP traffic to be executed with fewer privileges than it would be normally. This would serve to strengthen security, but the service function becomes moot if web browsing is not performed. Because a server should not be used for web browsing, save for such activities as Windows Update, it is better to disable this option because it requires services such as the DHCP client, which can introduce other vulnerabilities.

► **Windows User Mode Driver Framework**—Part of the .NET Framework, this option turns on a service that is intended to provide a framework for drivers to behave properly and reduce system crashes. In general, this functionality is simply additional overhead and a potential security hole, so it is recommended to disable it on an ISA server. As always, all server drivers should be properly stress-tested and validated to avoid the types of problems that this service attempts to fix.

No additional Administrative options are necessary for ISA functionality, so it is therefore not recommended to enable any other options unless there is a very specific need to do so. Go on with the following steps:

1. After the list of selected options has been chosen, click Next to continue with the SCW process.

2. The next dialog box, labeled Select Additional Services, lists any custom services that may be required for the server to function. This list normally includes items such as hardware monitoring services that were installed with the operating system. Carefully look through the options and select only those that are absolutely necessary. Click Next to continue.

The Handling Unspecified Services dialog box to be displayed gives the option of configuring how to handle unspecified services. The two options provided are to not do anything with the unidentified service (Do Not Change the Startup Mode of the Service) or to shut down any services that were not identified in the SCW process (Disable the Service). For security purposes, it is best to configure the server to disable any unidentified services.

Locking Down Services with SCW   To continue with the SCW process, do the following:

1. Choose Disable the Service and then click Next to continue.

2. At the confirmation dialog box, similar to the one shown in Figure 2.13, look over each of the changes that SCW will make to ensure that they are accurate. After they are verified, click Next to continue.

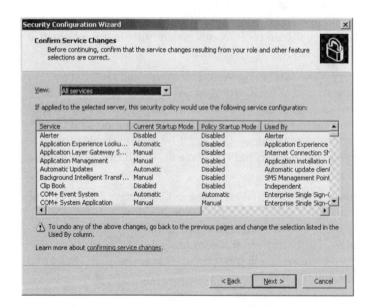

FIGURE 2.13   Confirming service changes with SCW.

3. The dialog box that follows contains a section that enables the Windows Firewall component to be configured. Because the Windows Firewall should not be used on an ISA Server 2006 system (ISA is a much more capable firewall), the check box for Skip This Section should be checked. Click Next to continue.

4. The next dialog box displayed offers the opportunity to modify Registry settings to block communication with particular types of clients. It is generally advisable not to skip this section, so the check box should not be checked. Click Next to continue.

The subsequent dialog box, shown in Figure 2.14, allows for the server to be locked down to accept only Server Message Block (SMB) traffic, which is Microsoft's file and print traffic, that has been digitally signed. Because most ISA server implementations do not allow SMB traffic to reach the server, this setting becomes moot. However, if the Firewall client share is configured, SMB traffic is allowed, and it is much more secure to force the SMB traffic to be digitally signed, so as to avoid "man in the middle" types of exploits against the ISA server.

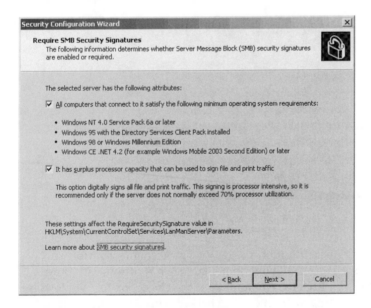

FIGURE 2.14   Configuring SMB signing options.

Although it is true that enabling this option prevents downlevel clients (Windows 3.1, Windows 95/98 without the Directory Services Client, Windows NT pre–Service Pack 6a) from connecting to the Firewall client share, they are not supported by the Firewall client, so it is not desirable to grant them access.

Even without the Firewall client share in place, it may be advisable to configure these options to add an additional layer of security to ISA, in the event that a problem with the

Firewall service allows SMB traffic to be sent to the machine. To continue with the Template creation, do the following:

1. Ensure that both check boxes on the SMB Security Signatures dialog box are checked, and click Next to continue.

2. The subsequent dialog box, shown in Figure 2.15, controls outbound authentication levels, which, in addition to the default, Domain Accounts, should also include the Local Accounts on the remote computer setting, if the server will be used for site-to-site VPN access. Site-to-site VPN with ISA 2006 requires local accounts, and if this box is not checked, the VPN tunnel will fail. Click Next to continue.

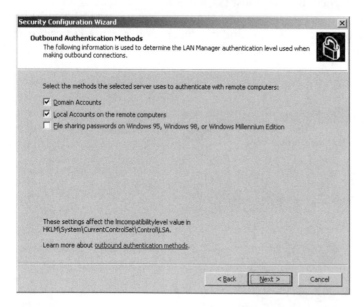

FIGURE 2.15   Configuring outbound authentication methods.

The next dialog box, Outbound Authentication Using Domain Accounts, controls LAN Manager authentication levels. In nearly all environments, except for those with down-level (pre–Windows NT 4.0 Service Pack 6a) environments, the check box for Windows NT 4.0 Service Pack 6a or Later Operating Systems can be checked. This strengthens the authentication level used for outbound connections, making it less likely that passwords will be decrypted through the use of brute-force techniques.

In addition, the setting for Clocks That Are Synchronized with the Selected Server's Clock can be checked if there is a clock synchronization scheme in place, such as NTP, or if the domain controllers in the domain are Windows Server 2003 or greater. Once again, this affects only outbound attempts to communicate with file servers from the ISA server, which is often disabled, so many of these options may seem redundant and unnecessary. As previously mentioned, however, it is ideal to configure as many layers of security as possible without breaking functionality, and there are very few downsides to configuring these options, so it is always a good idea to set them.

Continue with the following steps:

1. Check both boxes on the Outbound Authentication by using the Domain Account dialog box (if the criteria mentioned earlier has been satisfied) and click Next to continue.

2. Uncheck (disable support for the lower security forms of authentication) the two boxes on the subsequent dialog box that configure inbound authentication methods.

3. Review the Registry changes that will be made on the subsequent dialog box, similar to the ones shown in Figure 2.16. Click Next to continue.

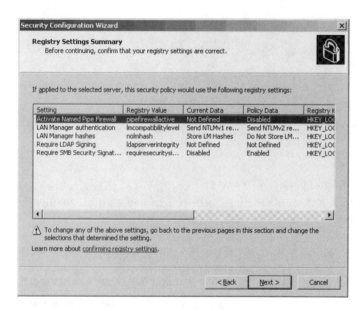

FIGURE 2.16   Confirming Registry Settings changes in SCW.

4. The Audit Policy dialog box is for configuring audit settings. Because it is highly recommended to audit who logs in to an ISA server, it is advisable not to skip this section. Click Next to continue.

5. On the next dialog box, labeled System Audit Policy, change the setting to Audit Successful and Unsuccessful Activities. Although more processor intensive, it helps increase the security of the ISA server. Click Next to continue.

6. Review the Audit Policy summary on the next dialog box. Leave the box checked to include the SCWAudit.inf security template, which properly sets System Access Control Lists (SACLS) for file-level audit access. Click Next to continue.

7. Under Save Security Policy, click Next to continue.

The next set of options are for specifying where the XML-based file that contains the security policy that SCW creates will be saved. Enter a path for saving the policy and a name for the policy, similar to what is shown in Figure 2.17. It may also be helpful to include a description of the security policy.

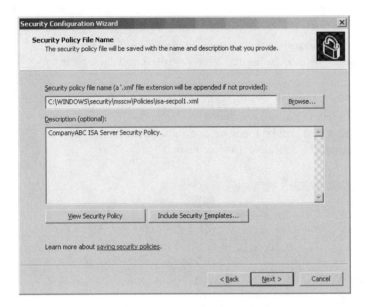

FIGURE 2.17   Saving the Security Policy file.

If the View Security Policy button is clicked, the SCW Viewer is invoked to enable the policy options to be viewed. In addition, the Include Security Templates button enables you to add preconfigured security template (.inf) files to the security policy.

Applying the SCW Template   To apply the SCW Template that was created, do the following:

1. After entering a path, name, and description for the policy, click Next to continue.
2. The choice to apply the security policy now or at a later time is given in the next dialog box. For this example, choose Apply Now and click Next to continue.
3. When complete, click Next to continue.
4. Click Finish at the summary page.

Summary

Installation of ISA Server is not limited to the task of inserting the ISA CD and running through a simple wizard. Proper ISA installation also involves patching the system and securing and locking down the OS with tools such as the Security Configuration Wizard. Proper configuration of an ISA server when it is first set up is the best way to minimize the risk of instability and problems down the road.

Best Practices

▶ Use the Security Configuration Wizard to lock down the Windows Server 2003 operating system.

▶ Install only those ISA Server 2006 and Windows Server 2003 features that are needed.

- ▶ Build an ISA server on a clean installation of the operating system.

- ▶ Consider the use of ISA Hardware Solutions and/or third-party add-ons that increase the capabilities of ISA.

- ▶ In general, deploy ISA Server 2006 as a workgroup member if it will be deployed in the DMZ of an existing firewall, and deploy it as a domain member if it will be deployed as a full-function firewall.

CHAPTER 3

Exploring ISA Server 2006 Tools and Concepts

After ISA Server has been installed, the intimidating task of configuring it and customizing it to fit organizational needs begins. An ISA server is a very customizable and powerful security solution, but the proper rules, parameters, and settings must be configured before it can perform any of its promised functions.

Fortunately, ISA Server 2006 makes management and configuration relatively straightforward to perform, particularly when it is compared with some of the other security solutions on the market. With this in mind, it is subsequently important to understand how to use the tools that ISA provides and to become familiar with its interface before becoming proficient in leveraging its functionality.

This chapter focuses on presenting and explaining the various ISA components and terminology that are central to its operation and functionality. Each of the components in the ISA Server Management Console is explained, and instructions on how to use them are presented. Because of the quantity of topics, they are covered at a high level in this chapter, but references to other chapters that go into more specifics are given when applicable.

Exploring the ISA Server 2006 Management Console

The centerpiece to ISA Server 2006 is the Management Console. The ISA Management Console contains the majority of the features and tools that are necessary for configuring ISA's various functions. Firewall rules, network rules, caching configuration, VPN functionality, and many more functions are contained within the console itself, and an understanding of ISA is incomplete without a solid familiarity with the Console.

Defining ISA Server Console Terminology and Architecture

The ISA Server 2006 Console, shown in Figure 3.1 is very similar to the ISA Server 2004 Console. The new model for the console is a vast improvement over the older ISA 2000 Console, which was not very logically structured and made information and tools difficult to locate. The 2004/2006 Console, on the other hand, logically groups common tasks together and structures the tools and information in a way that is intuitive and convenient.

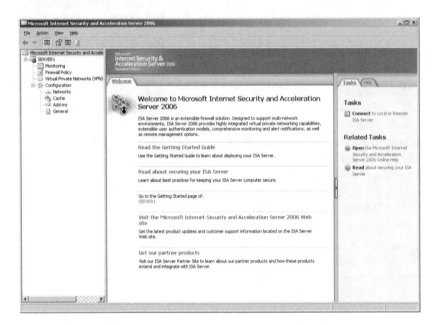

FIGURE 3.1   Viewing the ISA Server 2006 Management Console.

The ISA Console can be launched by clicking Start, All Programs, Microsoft ISA Server, ISA Server Management. Because of the way the console is structured, it is best viewed at a screen resolution of 1024×768 or greater.

Exploring ISA Console Panes

Each area within the ISA Server Console has a specific name by which it is referenced. The names of these areas—or panes, as they are called—make it easier to identify where specific information is, and provide a common language that can be used when troubleshooting ISA issues. This book refers to the particular panes by name throughout the chapters, so it is important to understand the terminology in advance. The following is a list of the panes included in the ISA Console and their respective functions:

▶ **Scope Pane**—The pane on the left side of the console is known as the Scope pane. The Scope pane displays the Console Tree, also known as the Node Tree, which is a navigation component that helps to quickly change between the various nodes.

▶ **Details Pane**—The Details pane is the large pane in the bottom center of the ISA Console. This pane displays information specific to the node itself, such as server log activity, firewall rules, network sets, and other server status items.

▶ **Task Pane**—The Task pane is the section on the right side of the Console that displays common tasks and wizards that can be invoked. This pane also typically contains multiple tabs for the different options available in the particular node chosen. One tab that is present for each node is the Help tab, which displays useful help information about topics particular to the node selected.

TIP

When not in use, the Task Pane can be hidden from view by clicking on the Open/Close Task Pane arrow, which appears as long oval with a > arrow in the middle of it. To open the Task pane back up, simply click on the Open/Close Task Pane arrow again. If you close the Task pane when it is not needed, more space is available for viewing rules or monitoring ISA configuration.

Examining ISA Console Nodes

The Scope pane contains a list of nodes, or logical configuration units that group together tasks and views related to a specific portion of ISA functionality. Clicking on each node in the console tree displays the information that is particular to that node. For example, cache-related information is stored in the Cache node, VPN information in the Virtual Private Networks node, and so on.

Switching between nodes involves just clicking on each individual node in the Scope pane. Each time a new node is selected, the information displayed in the Details pane and the Task Pane changes to display information specific to that particular node.

The nodes available in ISA Server 2006 Standard Edition are the following:

▶ Monitoring
▶ Firewall Policy
▶ Virtual Private Networks (VPN)
▶ Configuration
▶ Networks
▶ Cache
▶ Add-ins
▶ General

Additional information about the contents of each of these nodes is provided in the next sections of this chapter.

NOTE

ISA Server 2006 Enterprise Edition contains several additional nodes, not listed in this list. For more information on the Enterprise-specific nodes, refer to Chapter 6, "Deploying ISA Server Arrays with ISA Server 2006 Enterprise Edition."

Configuring Networks with ISA Console Network Wizards and Tools

One of the first tasks that is normally performed on a new ISA server is the configuration of the networks and the associated network rules. This instructs ISA how to handle traffic and provides a base on which firewall rules can be built. For example, an ISA server with three network adapters that are physically connected to three different networks should configure the networks in the console so that ISA understands what IP addresses should exist on each network and how to handle the traffic that comes from those networks.

Exploring the Networks Node

The Networks node, illustrated in Figure 3.2, contains configuration settings for Networks Sets and Network Rules and provides wizards that assist in the creation and designation of these elements. The Task Pane for the Networks node contains three tabs: Tasks, Templates, and Help. Each of these tabs contains specific functionality and wizards related to ISA's network configuration.

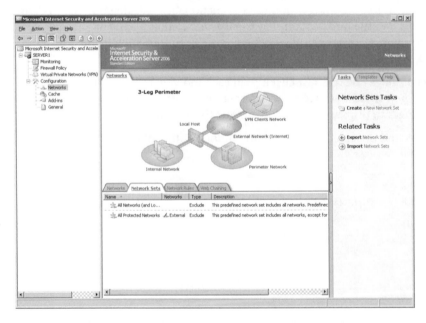

FIGURE 3.2   Viewing the Networks node of the ISA Management Console.

In the Details pane of the Networks node, there are four unique tabs: Networks, Network Sets, Network Rules, and Web Chaining. Each tab lists its own content, such as a list of the current network rules.

Understanding the Definition of ISA Networks

The term *network* in ISA should not be confused with the concept of subnets; the two terms are distinct in the ISA world. An ISA network is defined as the grouping of physical subnets that form a network topology that is attached to a single ISA Server network adapter. So, a single ISA "network" could be composed of multiple physical networks. Take, for example, the diagram illustrated in Figure 3.3. Even though there are eight physical subnets, all connected to each other with switches, routers, and gateways, ISA sees these individual subnets as only two networks—an internal network and a perimeter network—because it has network adapters attached to only a single subnet on each of the networks. To further illustrate, a unihomed (single NIC) server would see the range of all IP addresses on the Internet as a single ISA network. This concept is important to understand.

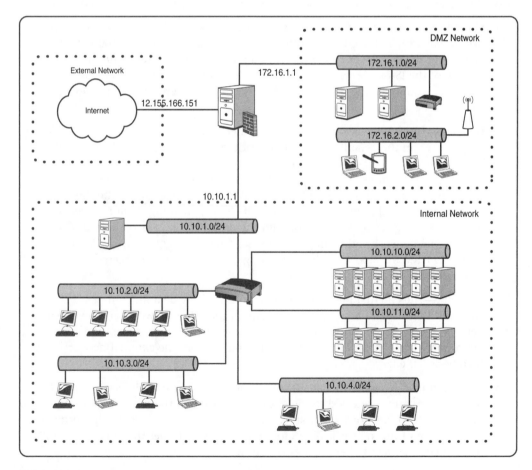

FIGURE 3.3   Examining ISA network concepts.

In Figure 3.3, for example, ISA is physically connected to only the 10.10.1.x/24 network, but accepts the traffic that is routed from the subnets "behind" this subnet as belonging to the aggregate network topology. This assumes that all the subnets are properly listed in ISA's definition of the network itself.

CAUTION

If an ISA server is configured improperly with multiple networks that are not physically attached to the ISA server, it assumes that those networks are disconnected and reports a 14147 error. Any responses that are received from that disconnected network are assumed to be IP spoofing attempts and are ignored. It is subsequently important to configure all the physical network subnets properly within the definition of the network to avoid this issue.

New networks that are created in ISA share these common characteristics. A few networks created by default on an ISA server operate in slightly different ways, as defined here:

▶ **Local Host**—This network represents the local ISA server itself and cannot be modified. It exists to facilitate the creation of rules that have to do with traffic that originates from the ISA server. For example, if a ping request was sent from the command prompt of the ISA server, that request would originate from the Local Host network, and there would need to be a specific firewall rule and network rule to allow the request to be sent.

▶ **Internal**—The internal network is a default network that represents the full range of IP addresses on the default protected network in an organization. The internal network possesses certain special functionality that is not contained in the other networks. For example, default System Policy rules are created to allow the ISA server itself to access services on the internal network. In addition, the internal network has special implications for firewall clients, enabling them to access local resources directly, as opposed to through the firewall itself. For more information on the internal network and its implications, see Chapters 5, "Deploying ISA Server 2006 as a Firewall," and 11, "Understanding Client Deployment Scenarios with ISA Server 2006."

▶ **External**—The external network is unique in that it, by default, contains all IP addresses that haven't been specified in any of the other networks. The external network is considered untrusted by default, and all connections from the external network are blocked. Specific rules allowing traffic from the external network must then be specified.

▶ **VPN Clients**—This network consists of all the individual IP addresses of VPN clients who are currently connected to the ISA server. Although the network cannot be deleted, VPN connections are disabled by default, and must be explicitly turned on. The creation of this network allows for granular firewall rules that affect only VPN users, such as allowing them to access only specific servers.

▶ **Quarantined VPN Clients**—The Quarantined VPN Clients network is similar to the VPN Clients network, except that it contains those VPN clients that haven't passed specific security restrictions set by the administrator. For more information on configuring this network, refer to Chapter 9, "Enabling Client Remote Access with ISA Server 2006 Virtual Private Networks (VPNs)."

Keeping these concepts in mind, the process of defining networks in ISA subsequently involves mapping out the entire subnet topology of a network and then defining it within the ISA Console Network node.

Outlining Network Sets

A *network set* is a logical grouping of networks that makes it easier to apply rules and policies to multiple networks at the same time. For example, a rule could be generated to allow web browsing from the All Protected Networks network set. This makes it easier to apply the rule by avoiding creating multiple rules or having to select each individual network for the rule.

The following lists the two default network sets and which networks are included in each:

▶ **All Networks (and Local Host)**—This network, as the name implies, contains all networks that are designated on the ISA server, including the local host. Any new networks that are created are automatically added to the network set.

▶ **All Protected Networks**—The All Protected Networks network set contains all networks except for the external network. As with the previous network set, any new networks are automatically added to this group unless specifically excluded.

Network sets can be created from scratch and customized as necessary. For example, it may be useful to create a network set to logically organize all the client networks, to make it easier to set up rules to restrict their access to a server network. To create a custom network set, perform the following steps:

1. Open the ISA Server Management Console (Start, All Programs, Microsoft ISA Server, ISA Server Management).

2. In the console tree, expand the Configuration node by clicking on the plus sign to its left and select the Networks node by clicking on it once.

3. In the Details pane, select the Network Sets tab, if not already selected.

4. In the Task Pane on the right, select the Tasks tab, if not already selected.

5. Under the Tasks tab, click the link for Create a New Network Set.

6. At the welcome screen for the wizard, enter a name for the network set. Click Next to continue

7. Under the Network Selection screen, check which networks to include in the network set, such as what is shown in Figure 3.4, and click Next to continue.

8. Click Finish to create the new network set.

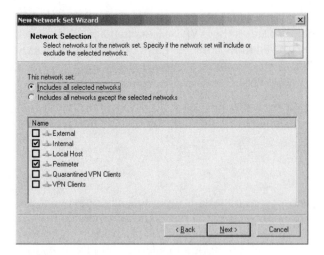

FIGURE 3.4   Creating a new network set.

Defining Network Templates

To assist with the task of setting up ISA network settings, Microsoft has included a powerful and helpful wizard, the New Network Wizard. The New Network Wizard allows ISA administrators to apply network templates to the ISA server, which automatically configure the appropriate network sets and rules based on standard settings that are most commonly deployed for the type of network design chosen. For example, a simple ISA server with two network adapters, one connected to the Internet and the other connected to the internal network, could apply the Edge Firewall template. That template would then configure common settings for this design, such as allowing web access for clients in the internal network and blocking all inbound traffic from the external network.

The following default network templates are included in ISA Server 2006 Standard Edition:

▶ **Edge Firewall**—This template configures the ISA server as a dual-NIC system that provides traditional firewall functionality, with one NIC connected to the Internet and the other to the internal network.

▶ **3-Leg Perimeter**—This template expands the Edge Firewall template design to include a third NIC connected to a Perimeter (DMZ) network.

▶ **Front Firewall**—A front firewall is an ISA server that is deployed as a dual-NIC server, but one that works in combination with a back firewall to provide two routes out of a network that is sandwiched between both ISA firewalls.

▶ **Back Firewall**—The Back Firewall template applies rules that provide for the second ISA server in the Front/Back Firewall design just described.

▶ **Single Network Adapter**—A Single Network Adapter template, commonly deployed for caching-only servers or for reverse-proxy capabilities in an existing packet-filter firewall DMZ, provides a template for a server with a single NIC. Although not a traditional firewall, this configuration is actually quite common.

For more information about using the New Network Wizard to apply network templates, see the chapters in Part II, "Deploying ISA Server 2006," especially Chapter 5.

Exploring Network Rules

A network rule in ISA Server is a mechanism that defines the relationship between networks. For example, the network rules defined in Figure 3.5 define how traffic is transmitted between the source and destination networks. The network rules defined allow VPN clients to be routed to the internal network, for the Perimeter (DMZ) network to be accessible, and for Internet access from protected client networks to be defined.

Of particular note is the network rule relationships that are set up, which are either *Route* or *NAT*. A Route relationship basically defines that the clients on one network can access the clients on the other network by their real IP addresses, with ISA acting as a router for the traffic.

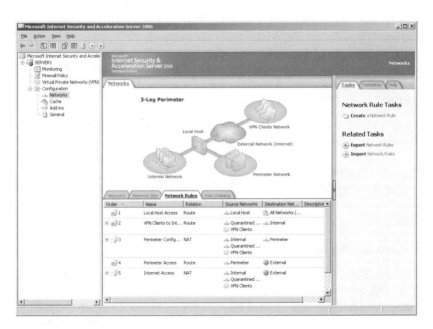

FIGURE 3.5   Examining network rules.

The NAT route relationship refers to Network Address Translation, which effectively hides the original IP address of the requesting client, and translates that IP address into an IP address on the destination network, as illustrated in Figure 3.6. NAT translations are common between private internal networks (10.x.x.x, 172.16.x.x, 192.168.x.x, and so forth) and external IP addresses on the Internet. This enables an organization to utilize a small number of external addresses while still providing network connectivity to internal clients.

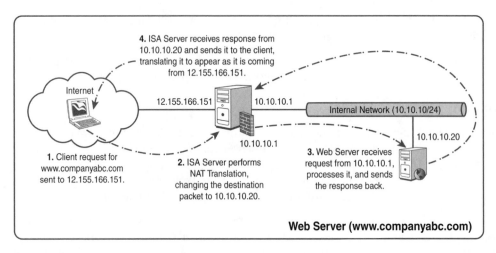

4. ISA Server receives response from 10.10.10.20 and sends it to the client, translating it to appear as it is coming from 12.155.166.151.

Internet

12.155.166.151   10.10.10.1

Internal Network (10.10.10/24)

10.10.10.1

10.10.10.20

1. Client request for www.companyabc.com sent to 12.155.166.151.

2. ISA Server performs NAT Translation, changing the destination packet to 10.10.10.20.

3. Web Server receives request from 10.10.10.1, processes it, and sends the response back.

Web Server (www.companyabc.com)

FIGURE 3.6   Understanding Network Address Translation (NAT).

Incidentally, simply because a network rule is created, it does not automatically mean that clients between the networks will be able to communicate between each other. The network rule simply establishes how allowed communication will be transmitted. It is still up to the administrator to establish the particular firewall rules that must be in place to allow specific types of communication to occur between the network, such as allowing web traffic or server publishing between the networks.

The same concept applies to thinking in the reverse direction as well. A common mistake ISA administrators make, particularly when first configuring an ISA server, is to create firewall rules without corresponding network rules to provide a relationship between the networks specified in the firewall rule. This makes it difficult to troubleshoot why the firewall rule is not working, as ISA does not automatically explain that both rules must be in place. It is subsequently important to define the network rules in advance, in order to establish the relationship between two networks before the firewall rules are created.

Running the Network Template Wizard

ISA Server 2006 streamlines the ISA configuration process with the addition of the Network Template Wizard, which automates the creation of networks, network rules, and firewall rules per common deployment scenarios for ISA. The Network Template Wizard, run by clicking on one of the templates in the Templates tab of the Task Pane, makes it easier to deploy and configure an ISA server, or at least gives administrators a head start toward configuration of the server.

The Network Template Wizard is straightforward to use for the application of a network template. After the template is in place, additional networks can be added, changes to network rules can be made, and any additional customization required can be performed.

In the following step-by-step procedure, the New Network Wizard is used to apply a 3-Leg Perimeter network template. The same general approach can be used when applying any of the other templates as well.

1. Open the ISA Server Console by clicking on Start, All Programs, Microsoft ISA Server, ISA Server Management.

2. Select the Networks node by clicking on it in the console tree.

3. Select the Templates tab in the Task Pane on the right.

4. Click on 3-Leg Perimeter from the list of templates.

5. At the Welcome dialog box, as shown in Figure 3.7, click Next to continue.

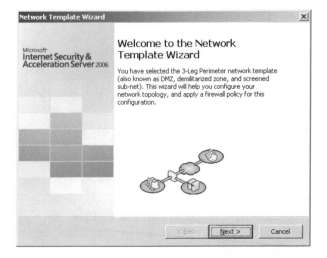

FIGURE 3.7   Running the Network Template Wizard.

The subsequent dialog box allows for the opportunity to export the current configuration to an XML-based text file, effectively backing up the configuration in the event that there is a problem created by the wizard. For a production ISA server, it would be wise to export the configuration at this point, but for a new server with no prior configuration done, this step is unnecessary. To continue with the template installation, do the following:

1. Ignore the Export dialog box and click Next to continue.

2. At the subsequent dialog box, which allows for the internal network to be configured, click Add Adapter.

3. Check the box for the NIC that is attached to the internal network, as shown in Figure 3.8.

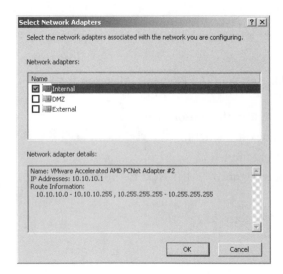

FIGURE 3.8   Defining the internal network.

The Add Adapter button in the Network Template Wizard automatically adds the IP addresses associated with the network adapter chosen, including any routes that the adapter may have configured. This can be a convenient way to establish the IP range of which the internal network will be composed.

In addition, the Internal Network IP Addresses dialog box also allows for entire ranges of private IP addresses to be added to the internal network. Because private addresses such as 10.0.0.0–10.255.255.255, 172.16.0.0–172.31.255.255, and 192.168.0.0–192.168.255.255 are not routable on the Internet (Internet routers are configured to drop all packets for clients in internal ranges), it may be easier and just as secure to configure the internal ranges by adding an entire Private IP range. Continue with the steps as follows:

1. When finished adding all IP ranges of which the internal network will be composed, click Next to continue.

2. At the next dialog box, shown in Figure 3.9, add the IP addresses associated with the Perimeter (DMZ) network, using the same process outlined previously. If a different template that did not have a Perimeter network were chosen, this step would be skipped.

3. Click Next when finished adding IP addresses to the Perimeter network.

In the following dialog box, shown in Figure 3.10 and titled Select a Firewall Policy, several options for default firewall policies are given. These default options create standard firewall policies based on common configurations as follows:

▶ **Block All**—This option does not create any firewall rules automatically. It is up to the administrator to create the appropriate policies after the wizard has been run.

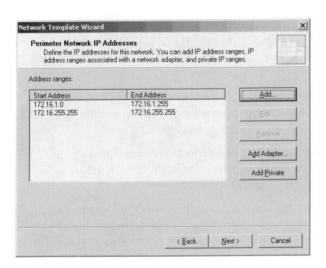

FIGURE 3.9   Defining Perimeter network IP address ranges.

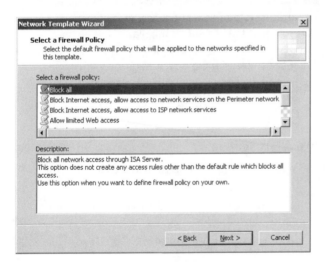

FIGURE 3.10   Selecting a firewall policy.

▶ **Block Internet Access, Allow Access to Network Services on the Perimeter Network**—This policy creates default rules that allow only limited DNS traffic from the Internet network to the DMZ network.

▶ **Block Internet Access, Allow Access to ISP Network Services**—This option creates rules that allow DNS access only from internal clients to the external network. It is used in situations when clients get their DNS services from an Internet Service Provider (ISP).

▶ **Allow Limited Web Access**—This option, more common in many organizations, creates firewall rules that allow web browsing via the HTTP, HTTPS, and FTP ports to the external network. It also creates rules that grant VPN clients full access to the internal network.

▶ **Allow Limited Web Access, Allow Access to Network Services on Perimeter Network**—This option configures the same rules as the preceding option, but with the addition of DNS access to the DMZ network as well.

▶ **Allow Limited Web Access and Access to ISP Network Services**—This option configures the same rules as the Allow Limited Web Access option, with an additional rule to allow DNS to the external network (for ISP services).

▶ **Allow Unrestricted Access**—This option, while definitely not the most secure, opens all ports from the internal protected networks to the Internet and to the DMZ network. It does not, however, allow the external network to have any type of access to internal networks.

TIP

After the wizard has configured these auto-generated rules, it is highly recommended to audit and customize them to match the role that the ISA server will play in the organization. Although the wizard creates rules based on common scenarios, in many cases they will require additional customization to comply with the organization's security policies. More information on customizing firewall rules is presented in later sections of this chapter.

To continue the template application, do the following:

1. Choose a firewall policy from the options, using the criteria listed as a guideline. Click Next to continue.

2. Review the options on the completion dialog box and click Finish to create and apply the template, network rules, and firewall rules.

3. Click the Apply button that appears in the upper portion of the Details pane, as shown in Figure 3.11.

4. Click OK at the configuration confirmation dialog box.

NOTE

Similar to other security products, ISA Server does not automatically apply changes made to the configuration. Instead, these changes must be either applied or discarded. Whenever changes are made, the Apply and Discard buttons are displayed in the Details pane. Before Apply has been clicked, the changes made will not go into effect.

For more information on performing these activities, including more step-by-step descriptions of the process, refer to Chapter 5.

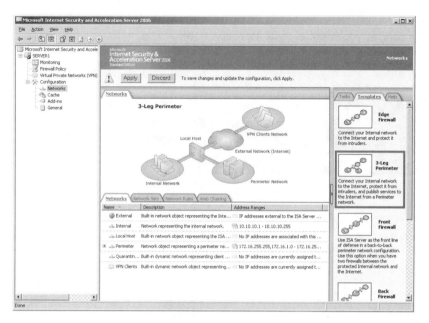

FIGURE 3.11   Applying firewall changes.

Understanding Web Chaining

The Web Chaining tab, located in the Details pane of the console, allows for additional network functionality. Web chaining allows relationships between multiple ISA servers to be established for the purposes of directing and optimizing web browsing traffic. For example, a web chaining rule could be created to force clients in a remote site to use the ISA server of the central location for specific types of content. This allows administrators to more intelligently route web content requests.

For detailed information on configuring web chaining, refer to Chapter 8, "Deploying ISA Server 2006 as a Content Caching Server."

Exploring Firewall Policy Settings

The heart and soul of ISA functionality lies in the Firewall Policy settings. These settings control the behavior of ISA and how it responds to traffic sent to it, and are therefore very important. It is critical to understand the functionality and terminology of the Firewall Policy settings, or run the risk of a misconfiguration that could jeopardize the server's security.

Examining the Firewall Policy Node

The Firewall Policy node, shown in Figure 3.12, contains several critical and commonly used tools in the ISA Console. The Details pane details the rules deployed on the server. The rules are, by default, sorted by the order in which they are applied, with the first rules applied at the top of the list. This concept, familiar to many who are used to working with other firewalls, is a relatively new concept for ISA Server, introduced with version 2004; ISA 2000 did not apply rules in a logical order.

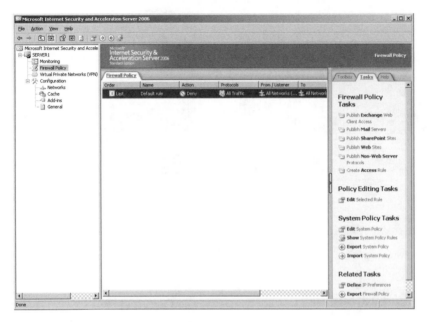

FIGURE 3.12   Viewing the Firewall Policy node.

In the Task Pane on the right, three tabs are presented. The requisite Help tab displays common questions and help topics related to firewall policy. The Tasks tab contains a list of common tasks related to the node. Lastly, the Toolbox tab contains a very useful list of the elements in the ISA server, such as network entities, content types, protocol descriptions, and the like.

Understanding Firewall Access Rules

A Firewall Access rule is simply a mechanism by which access is granted or denied for specific types of traffic through the ISA server. Rules are the means by which specific ports, applications, and other types of network traffic are either blocked or opened. If, for example, web access to the Internet is necessary for clients on the Internet network of an ISA configuration, a specific Firewall Access rule needs to be configured to specifically allow this type of access.

In Figure 3.13, for example, several default rules that were created from the Network Template Wizard are illustrated.

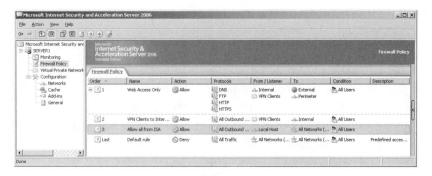

FIGURE 3.13   Exploring sample firewall rules.

In this example, four rules control the flow of traffic and specify what is allowed and what is denied through the firewall. Each rule in the Details pane can be sorted by multiple variables, listed as follows:

▶ **Order**—The order of the rule determines when it is processed. Whenever any type of traffic arrives at the ISA server, the firewall rules are applied in order, from lowest number to highest. If a match is made for the type of traffic, that firewall rule is processed and no further rules are parsed.

▶ **Name**—Names of rules are displayed in the console to aid in the identification of what each rule does. Names chosen for rules should ideally indicate the rule's function.

▶ **Action**—The action of a rule is one of two choices: Allow or Deny. For obvious reasons, it is critical to ensure that the rules have this field set properly.

▶ **Protocols**—The Protocols column displays to what common or custom-defined protocols the particular rule applies, such as HTTP, FTP, DNS, and others.

▶ **From/Listener**—The From/Listener column displays the network or listener from which rule traffic will arrive. ISA examines only the traffic from this network when applying the rule.

▶ **To**—The To column represents the destination of traffic. Only traffic sent to this network or set of networks will have the particular rule applied.

▶ **Condition**—The Condition column allows for individual rules to only apply to particular users or groups of users. User granularity can be allowed only when the Firewall Client is deployed, so this is often simply set to All Users when the full client is not deployed.

Advanced information on configuring access rules can be found in Chapter 5.

Examining Publishing Rules and the Concept of Reverse Proxy

A server publishing rule is more complicated than a simple network access rule, in that it allows the ISA server to mimic a destination server such as a web server and act as a reverse proxy server to the client requests. A reverse proxy server is a system that acts as a bastion host for requesting clients, protecting the server from direct attack by proxying all requests that are sent to it, making them go through the reverse proxy server itself.

ISA Server 2006 is commonly deployed for its reverse-proxy capabilities, particularly in its ability to secure web servers and Exchange Outlook Web Access (OWA). Through reverse proxy, clients on the Internet are directed to the external IP address of the ISA server, which they think is the actual server for the services that they require. In reality, ISA performs Network Address Translation (NAT), scans the traffic for exploits and threats at the Application layer, and forwards the traffic back to the server. This greatly reduces the threat posed by having servers and services exposed to the Internet.

Server publishing rules in ISA Server allow for advanced services securing SQL servers, Exchange servers, Web servers, SharePoint sites, RPC services, and many other prede-fined options. For more information on configuring and using server publishing rules, see Chapter 5.

Understanding System Policy Rules and the System Policy Editor

System policies are often misunderstood or not taken into consideration, but are a funda-mental component to every ISA installation. System policies are essentially a default set of firewall policies that allow the ISA server to perform various system functions. Without system policies in place, ISA would be unable to perform any network functions at all, such as Windows Update, without them being specifically designated in manually created firewall policies.

Basically speaking, system policies are really just firewall policies that have been preconfig-ured, but are hidden from view. Because the task of configuring an ISA server would be time-consuming and ominous, these policies were configured as part of the firewall instal-lation. It is wise, however, to examine each of these policies to ensure that they are truly necessary for the role that the ISA server will play in the organization. To view the system policies, click on the Show System Policy Rules link in the Tasks tab of the Firewall Policy node. Some of the default system policies are illustrated in Figure 3.14.

To edit the system policy rules, right-click any one of the rules and click Edit System Policy. This displays the System Policy Editor dialog box, as shown in Figure 3.15.

The System Policy Editor allows for advanced configuration of the system policy rules in place on the server. It is in this location that particular types of system access can be denied or enabled, based on the organization's particular security needs. For more infor-mation on editing the system policy, see Chapter 15, "Securing RPC Traffic."

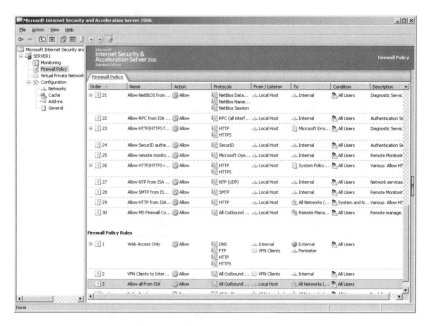

FIGURE 3.14   Viewing system policies.

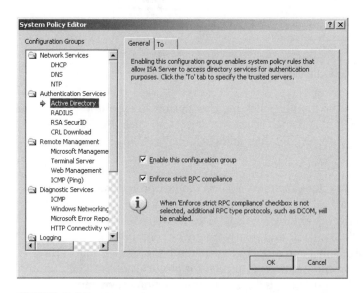

FIGURE 3.15   Editing the system policy.

Defining the Contents of the Firewall Policy Toolbox

The Firewall Policy toolbox, shown in Figure 3.16, is an extremely useful function that organizes all the individual components of the firewall policies into one logical area. The toolbox is easily accessed by clicking on the toolbox tab in the Task Pane.

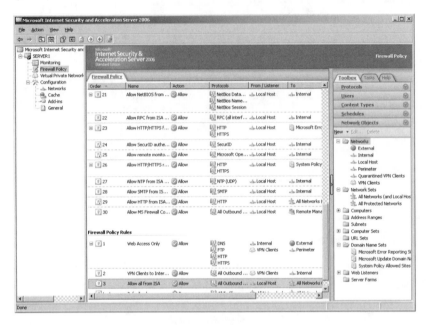

FIGURE 3.16   Examining the Firewall Policy toolbox.

To examine individual items in the toolbox, click the down arrow to expand the particular section, such as Schedules or Users, and then select the object and click the Edit button. To create new objects, select the object container and click the New button.

The toolbox comprises the following elements:

▶ **Protocols**—The Protocols toolbox contains a list of defined protocols that are used to communicate across networks. Common protocols such as DNS, HTTP, SMTP, POP, Telnet, MSN Messenger, and Ping are listed here, as well as more obscure protocols such as RIP, H.323, MMS, RTSP, and many others. By containing definitions for these protocols, you can easily configure ISA to create rules to block or allow them as necessary. In addition, you can create custom rules for protocols not in ISA's default list by clicking the New button in the toolbox. For information on creating custom and advanced protocol support, see Chapter 15.

▶ **Users**—The Users toolbox contains groupings of users that are useful for bulk application of firewall rules and other settings. The default groups created by ISA are All Authenticated Users, All Users, and System and Network Service. New groups can be created to logically organize different types of users to facilitate the creation of policies and rules. For more information on users and groups within ISA Server, refer to Chapter 11.

▶ **Content Types**—The Content Types toolbox allows for different applications and files to be organized according to the type of content they are. For example, a file that is downloaded via the web may be an audio file, an image, text, video, or any of several other options. Files that are grouped by content type can be controlled more easily, giving the ISA administrator an easy way to perform such actions as not allowing specific types of dangerous executables or other file types to be accessed. For more information on configuring and creating content types, see Chapter 15.

▶ **Schedules**—The Schedules toolbox allows for custom time schedules to be created. This can be extremely useful if there are organization-specific schedules that need to be consistently applied to multiple rules or parameters within projects. For example, a custom schedule could be created for scheduled maintenance, such as the dialog box shown in Figure 3.17 illustrates. This schedule can then be applied to default rules that deny connections during those periods of time.

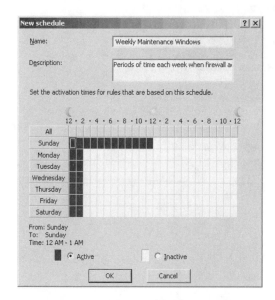

FIGURE 3.17   Creating a custom schedule.

▶ **Network Objects**—The Network Objects toolbox is perhaps the most important and commonly used of the toolboxes. All the configured network-related objects are listed in the toolbox, such as the Network Sets, Computer Sets, URL Sets, Address Ranges, and more. Even though the logical location for this toolbox would normally be under the network node, it has been placed with the rest of the toolboxes in the Firewall Policy node, so it is important to understand that distinction when looking for network settings, such as the location and configuration of web listeners and subnets. More information on using the Network Objects toolbox, including step-by-step descriptions, can be found in Chapter 5.

The toolbox serves as a "one-stop-shop" for many configuration settings in ISA, and can make the life of an administrator much easier through the creation of custom schedules, content types, users, protocols, and network objects. For these reasons, it is highly advisable to become familiar with these options.

Navigating the Monitoring Node Options

One of the biggest improvements to ISA Server has been the addition of multiple robust and capable logging and monitoring options. The key to troubleshooting an ISA server is understanding what type of activity is currently occurring, whether packets are being denied or granted, or whether the firewall is being attacked. The Monitoring node, illustrated in Figure 3.18, is the portal toward accessing the logging and monitoring capabilities of ISA Server, and is one of the most valuable tools in the ISA Server Console.

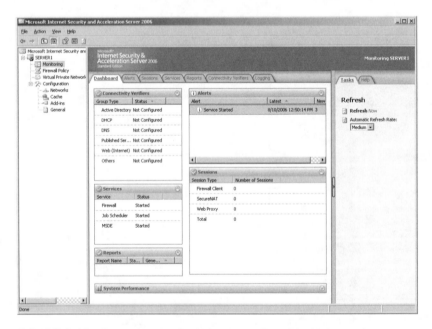

FIGURE 3.18   Examining the Dashboard tab of the Monitoring node.

Within the Monitoring node of the ISA Server Console, there are seven tabs in the Details pane that link to different monitoring and reporting functions that the ISA server provides. These tabs are ordered as follows:

▶ Dashboard

▶ Alerts

▶ Sessions

▶ Services

▶ Reports

▶ Connectivity Verifiers

▶ Logging

When selecting an individual tab, the Tasks and Help tabs in the Task Pane change their content to reflect the type of functions and common help questions specific to the tab chosen.

This section on the monitoring node covers the high-level detail present in the node. For additional reading on the topic, including best practices, step-by-step descriptions, and examples, see Chapter 19, "Monitoring and Troubleshooting an ISA Server 2006 Environment."

Configuring the Dashboard

The Dashboard is a monitoring function of ISA that allows for multiple monitoring indicators and other real-time information to be displayed in a centralized console, such as the Dashboard shown in Figure 3.18. The Dashboard contains individual monitoring components that track activity on the ISA server, such as alerts, sessions, reports, and overall system performance. The information presented in the Dashboard is generated from the settings configured in the various other tabs of the Monitoring node.

The Dashboard is a good place to "park" the ISA Server Console when it is not actively being used, as it can be used to quickly determine the status of the ISA server at a glance.

Viewing Alerts

Alerts are a useful mechanism for ISA Server to communicate information, warning, and error messages to administrators through the Monitoring console. The Alerts tab, shown in Figure 3.19, links to information about individual alerts. Clicking on each alert displays information specific to that alert on the bottom of the Details pane.

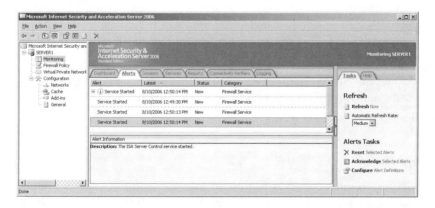

FIGURE 3.19   Viewing alerts.

The Alert mechanism in ISA Server 2006 is a simple yet powerful tool to give advance warning to administrators of attacks on the firewall, misconfigurations, or other errors.

Alerts can be customized by clicking on the Configure Alert Definitions link in the Task Pane. This link summons the Alert Definitions dialog box, as shown in Figure 3.20. This dialog box allows for specific alerts to be configured and customized when existing alerts are double-clicked. This allows for specific actions to be taken in the event of problems, such as email warnings to be sent to administrators, services to be stopped, or programs to be run.

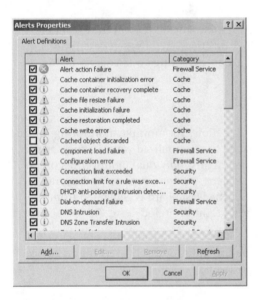

FIGURE 3.20   Setting alert definitions.

Monitoring Sessions and Services

Every time a device such as a computer or server communicates with the ISA server, that particular session is logged and displayed in the Sessions tab of the Monitoring node. This tab enables individual client sessions to be listed and monitored. Individual sessions can also be disconnected from this tab, via the Disconnect Session link in the Tasks pane.

In addition to the Sessions tab, the server can be monitored via the Services tab, shown in Figure 3.21, which shows the current status of each of the critical ISA Services. Each service can be stopped from this console, and the length of time that the service has been running is also displayed.

Generating Reports

ISA's reporting mechanism is one of the best features of the application. It enables administrators to quickly create useful, accurate reports pulled from data in the ISA logs, such as the one shown in Figure 3.22.

FIGURE 3.21   Viewing the Services node.

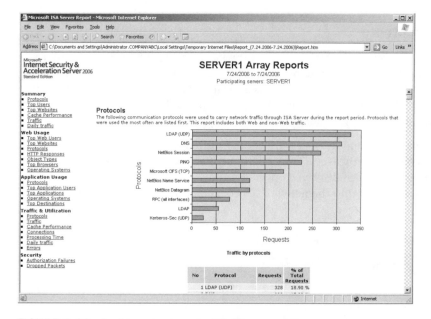

FIGURE 3.22   Looking at a sample ISA Server report.

ISA Reports analyze activity that occurs on the ISA server over a period of time, and can include the following fields of information:

▶ **Summary**—The report summary includes the most commonly utilized report findings, such as the most utilized protocols, the top users and websites, cache performance, and traffic patterns.

▶ **Web Usage**—The Web Usage field generated by ISA includes specifics on how the web is being used by ISA clients, such as the types of objects requested, the most commonly accessed web sites, and other facts.

▶ **Application Usage**—Application usage analyzes the types of applications that are accessed through ISA, including the protocols and operating systems used to access them.

▶ **Traffic and Utilization**—Traffic and utilization refer to the types of network data traffic that flow through ISA, any errors encountered, and the performance of the content cache.

▶ **Security**—The Security field focuses on identifying authorization failures, which can indicate hacking attempts, and a dropped packet analysis, which together enable ISA administrators to perform intrusion detection.

Each of the report fields specified can be customized further to include additional information. In addition, ISA reports can be automatically generated on a defined basis and saved to a remote network location for viewing by other administrators and for archive purposes.

Verifying Connectivity

Connectivity verifiers in the Monitoring node of the ISA Console are mechanisms that allow administrators to perform simple monitoring on network services and functionality. They make it possible to monitor certain servers and sites via an up/down services analysis. For example, a DNS Verifier might send DNS queries to the local DNS server to ensure that it is operational. If the verifier fails to contact the service, an alert is generated.

ISA Server 2006 organizes various connectivity verifiers into different group types, which can be chosen when running the New Connectivity Verifier Wizard, as shown in Figure 3.23. These group types are then displayed on the Dashboard, which allows for quick up/down status on services within the network. The default group types are listed as follows:

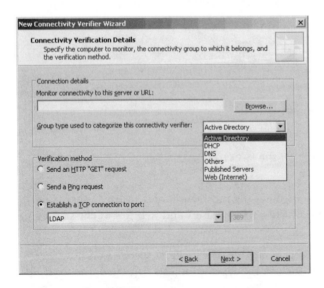

FIGURE 3.23   Choosing connectivity verifier group types.

▶ **Active Directory**—This type of connectivity verifier attempts to establish a Light Directory Access Protocol (LDAP) connection to an Active Directory Domain Controller.

▶ **DHCP**—A DHCP verifier simply sends Ping requests to a local DHCP server to verify that the DHCP server is responding.

▶ **DNS**—A DNS connectivity verifier is configured by default to also Ping DNS servers to validate functionality. It can be customized to send requests to the DNS service as well, however.

▶ **Others**—By default, this group type is used to organize any custom connectivity verifiers created by the administrator. It uses Ping by default, but can also be modified to attempt to connect to any number of ports.

▶ **Published Servers**—The Published Servers Group type is used to organize verifiers to servers for which ISA has publishing rules set up.

▶ **Web (Internet)**—The Web (Internet) group is used for verifying outbound Internet connectivity by performing occasional HTTP "GET" requests to web servers on the Internet.

Logging ISA Access

The Logging tab in the Monitoring node gives administrators an extremely useful tool for troubleshooting connection failures and monitoring content flow. The Logging tab allows the ISA activity to be displayed in real time, with each and every network packet sent and processed by the ISA server displayed in the Details pane, such as the logs shown in Figure 3.24.

The logging tab is a great troubleshooting tool for ISA Server. For example, if a new server publishing rule has been established, but it doesn't allow traffic the way the administrator intended, the ISA logging tab can be referenced to view the real-time communications to the server and determine whether the packets are being dropped, and which rule is dropping them. This function alone makes the logging component of ISA Server one of the most commonly accessed modules in the console.

Working with the Virtual Private Networks Node

A Virtual Private Network is an encrypted "tunnel" from an untrusted network such as the Internet into a trusted network, such as an organization's internal network. ISA Server 2006 possesses a wide array of VPN capabilities, all of which can be accessed through the Virtual Private Networks node in the ISA Server Console, as shown in Figure 3.25.

This section of the chapter covers the ISA Server Console settings in the VPN node at a high level, describing the general options available and giving an idea of what VPN tools are available in the console. For advanced VPN design, configuration, and step-by-step descriptions, see Chapters 9 and 10, "Extending ISA Server 2006 to Branch Offices with Site-to-Site VPNs."

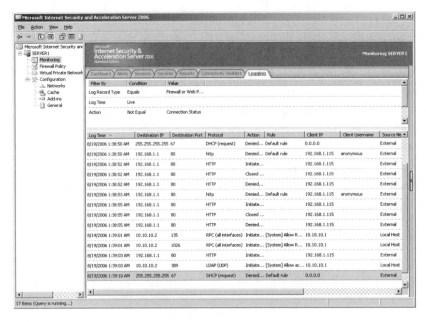

FIGURE 3.24   Viewing ISA Server logs.

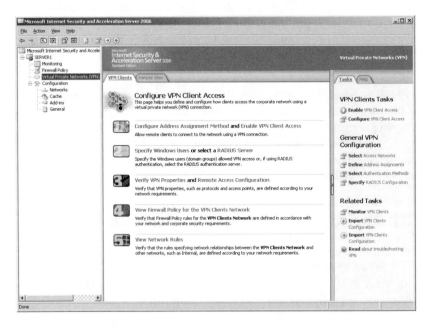

FIGURE 3.25   Examining the Virtual Private Network (VPN) node in the ISA Console.

Enabling and Configuring VPN Client Access

By default, VPN access through ISA Server is not enabled, and it must be turned on before VPN capabilities can be reviewed. Before it can be turned on, the address assignment method must be established. Typically, this involves using a Dynamic Host Configuration Protocol (DHCP) server in the network, but a static assignment method can also be used. For in-depth information on this topic, see Chapter 9. If DHCP will be used, turning on VPN functionality can be performed as follows:

1. Open the ISA Server Management Console (Start, All Programs, Microsoft ISA Server, ISA Server Management).

2. In the console tree, select Define Address Assignments.
   Prior to this step, the VPN node must be selected. In addition, the name of the detail pane link that should be selected next is Configure Address Assignments.

3. Select Dynamic Host Configuration Protocol (DHCP), as shown in Figure 3.26, and click OK.

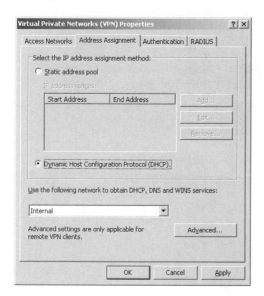

FIGURE 3.26   Enabling VPN client access.

4. In the Tasks tab of the Task Pane, click the Enable VPN Client Access button.

5. Click the Apply button on the top of the Details pane.

6. Click OK when the success dialog box is displayed.

NOTE

The VPN functionality of ISA Server relies on the Routing and Remote Access Service of Windows Server 2003, and requires it to be started for VPN clients to be able to connect. If a Security Policy is in place to disable this service, it will create problems with VPNs, so it is subsequently important to validate that RRAS functionality is enabled if the ISA server will need to process VPN requests.

After VPN client access has been granted, the VPN client settings can be configured by clicking on the Configure VPN Client Access link in the Tasks pane. This link invokes the VPN Clients Properties dialog box, shown in Figure 3.27, where the following settings can be configured:

▶ **Maximum number of VPN clients allowed**—The default is 100, but it can be throttled based on the server's capacity.

▶ **The specific Active Directory groups that can be granted remote access**—This option is relevant only if the server is a member of an AD domain. For non-AD domain member ISA servers, Remote Dial-In Authentication Service (RADIUS) authentication can be used to specify which users have access.

▶ **What type of VPN protocols will be allowed**—The two options are the Point-to-Point Tunneling Protocol (PPTP) and the Layer 2 Tunneling Protocol (L2TP).

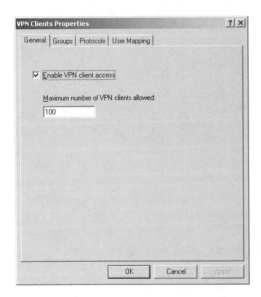

FIGURE 3.27   Setting VPN client properties.

▶ **Whether or not user mapping will be enabled**—User mapping allows for non–Windows authenticated users to be mapped to AD users so that user-based policies can be applied.

Configuring Remote Access Configuration

Many of the options associated with VPNs in ISA Server can be found in the Remote Access configuration dialog box, accessible via the Select Access Networks link in the Task Pane. The dialog box invoked via this link, shown in Figure 3.28, allows for the configuration of Remote Access properties specific to VPN access, but not necessarily specific to clients. These include the following settings:

▶ Networks from which VPN clients can connect.

▶ Address assignment properties, such as automatic VPN client IP address assignment via the Dynamic Host Configuration Protocol (DHCP).

▶ Authentication methods allowed. This includes such protocols as Microsoft encrypted authentication version 2 (MS-CHAPv2), Extensible Authentication Protocol (EAP, for smartcards), and other downlevel encryption methods.

▶ Remote Dial-In User Service (RADIUS) settings.

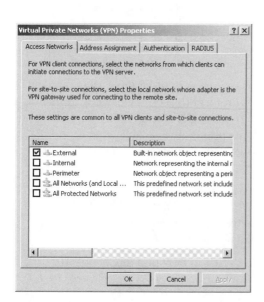

FIGURE 3.28   Configuring Remote Access settings.

Creating Remote Site Networks for Site-to-Site VPNs

ISA Server 2006 also includes the capability to create encrypted tunnels between two disparate networks in an organization that are connected through the Internet. This allows for communication across the Internet to be scrambled so that it cannot be read by a third party. ISA provides this capability through its Remote Site VPN capabilities.

The Remote Site VPN options, available on the Remote Sites tab in the Details pane of the VPN node, allow for the creation and configuration of Remote Site networks for site-to-site VPNs. These site-to-site VPN networks enable an organization to connect remote networks together, creating one complete, routable, and logical network, such as the one shown in Figure 3.29.

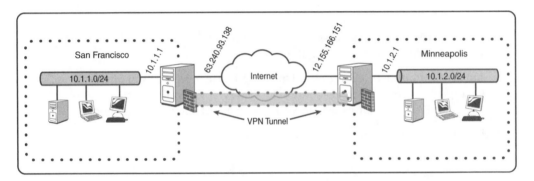

FIGURE 3.29   Understanding a site-to-site VPN.

When configuring a site-to-site VPN between two ISA Server 2006 systems, the option exists to secure the traffic by using the IP Security Protocol (IPSec), the Layer 2 Tunneling Protocol (L2TP) over IPSec, or the Point-to-Point Tunneling Protocol (PPTP), depending on the individual organizational security needs. These options are available when running the Create Site-to-Site Connection Wizard that is launched from the Create VPN Site-to-Site Connection link in the Task Pane.

In addition to supporting a destination ISA Server 2006 system for site-to-site VPN, ISA Server also supports connecting to a third-party VPN gateway that supports the IPSec protocol. This greatly extends ISA's reach because third-party firewall solutions that may already be in place are potential candidates for ISA site-to-site VPNs.

Specific configuration information for site-to-site VPNs can be found in Chapter 10.

Understanding VPN Quarantine

The concept of the VPN quarantine network is fairly straightforward, although its implementation is not necessarily so. Essentially, VPN quarantine refers to the capability to have ISA place a client that does not conform to specific criteria into a special quarantined VPN clients network. This network can then be limited to only a specific set of low-risk activities. For example, it may be useful to validate that all clients have approved anti-virus software installed before full access to the network is granted.

VPN quarantine is not on by default, and must be specifically set up and configured. Chapter 9 contains step-by-step procedures, but the configuration of VPN quarantine consists of two processes. The first process involves configuring VPN client computers with a special listener that reports to the ISA server if the client passes specified criteria that are necessary for full access. The second component, illustrated in Figure 3.30, involves checking the box in the Quarantined VPN Clients Properties dialog box.

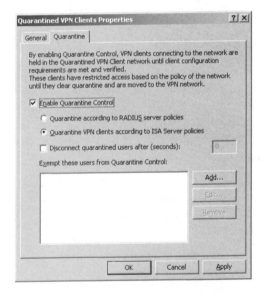

FIGURE 3.30   Enabling VPN quarantine.

Unlike the other VPN settings, you can invoke this dialog box in the Networks node by double-clicking on the quarantined VPN clients network listed under the Networks tab of the Details pane.

Examining the Cache Node Settings

The Cache node in the ISA Server Console, shown in Figure 3.31, is where content caching can be enabled and configured on an ISA server. Although not enabled by default in the ISA Console, enabling caching can improve network performance and response time by saving copies of images, text, and other data that clients download from web and FTP sites on the Internet and making them available to the next client that requests information from that particular site.

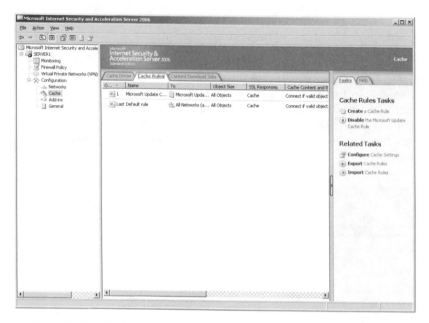

FIGURE 3.31   Viewing the ISA Console Cache node.

This section contains a high-level description of the settings available in the ISA Server Console under the Cache node. Further information on deploying ISA Server for its content-caching capabilities can be found in Chapter 8.

Enabling Caching

It is not immediately evident how to enable caching, in that it is disabled by default when ISA is deployed. Caching is enabled when physical drive space is made available to the caching service. To perform this action, follow these steps:

1. Open the ISA Server 2006 Management Console (Start, All Programs, Microsoft ISA Server, ISA Server Management).

2. From the console tree, select the Cache node by clicking on it.

3. In the Task Pane, click the link entitled Define Cache Drives (Enable Caching).

4. In the Define Cache Drives dialog box, select the drive where the cache will be stored.

5. Enter the Maximum cache size in megabytes in the field provided, and click the Set button.

6. Click the OK button.

7. Click the Apply button that is displayed at the top of the Details pane.

8. When presented with the option to restart the services or not, as shown in Figure 3.32, select Save the Changes and Restart the Services and click OK.

9. Click OK when finished.

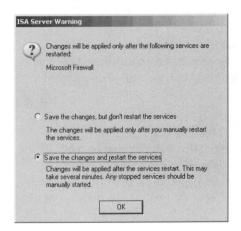

FIGURE 3.32   Enabling caching.

> **NOTE**
>
> Unlike most other changes made in the ISA Console, configuring cache drives is one of the changes that requires a restart of the firewall service, as noted in the preceding procedure.

Understanding Cache Rules

Caching behavior by ISA is made granular and more configurable through the addition of specific caching rules. Each caching rule allows for specific types of content to be processed in different ways, depending on the needs of the administrator.

By default, when caching is enabled, a default cache rule is put into place that caches objects based on default settings. Additional caching rules can be configured by clicking on the Create a Cache Rule link in the Tasks tab. Each rule created can contain the following customizations:

- ▶ Source and destination networks
- ▶ What types of items are retrieved and stored in the cache
- ▶ HTTP caching settings, such as the Time to Live (TTL) of objects retrieved
- ▶ File Transfer Protocol (FTP) caching settings
- ▶ Secure Sockets Layer (SSL)–specific settings
- ▶ Object size limitations

Just as with firewall rules, caching rules are applied in order, from top to bottom, until a match is made. Through the creation of multiple caching rules, fine-grained control over the caching settings of the clients can be achieved.

Examining Content Download Jobs

The final set of options available under the Cache node revolves around the capability of the ISA caching engine to automatically download content based on a defined schedule. This can be useful if specific websites need to be always up to date and quickly available to internal clients.

Content download jobs can be enabled and configured via the Content Download Jobs tab in the Details pane of the Cache node. When configuring this setting up via the Schedule a Content Download Job link in the Tasks tab, two changes must be made to the configuration. These changes, shown in the dialog box in Figure 3.33, are to allow the Local Host to listen for web proxy requests via a rule, and enabling a special system policy rule. After these settings are automatically configured, specific content download jobs can be created.

FIGURE 3.33   Enabling content download jobs.

Content download jobs can be scheduled weekly, daily, hourly, or only once, as needed. They also can be configured to browse and download the content of only a single URL page on the Internet, or to follow a certain number of links "deep" from the page that is being accessed.

CAUTION

Care should be taken to not configure content download jobs to be too aggressive because they can consume exponential amounts of bandwidth, depending on the depth of the links that will be followed. For example, a simple page with five links on it, and five links on its subpages, would access only six total pages if the content download job were to be configured to scour pages one link deep. If the job were changed to two links deep, however, a total of 31 pages would need to be accessed. This could pose a serious drain on the Internet bandwidth available if not configured properly.

Configuring Add-Ins

One of the biggest advantages to ISA Server 2006 is its ability to have its base application-filtering engine easily extended with third-party add-in functionality. This makes ISA a strong candidate for software to provide advanced web filtering, anti-virus applications, intrusion detection filters, and additional VPN capabilities.

All the add-ins to ISA Server, including the default add-ins that are installed with ISA itself, can be viewed from within the Add-ins node of the console tree, as shown in Figure 3.34. This section takes a high-level look at the add-in options available in the Add-ins node of the ISA Console. Additional information on specific add-ins can be found in Part III of this book, "Securing Servers and Services with ISA Server 2006."

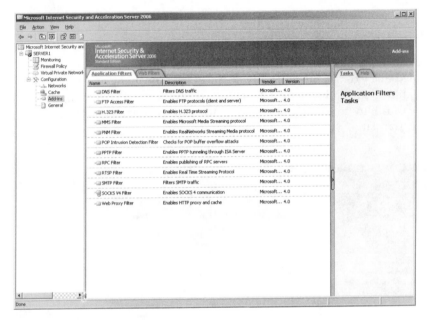

FIGURE 3.34   Examining the Add-ins node of the ISA Console.

Exploring Application Filters

Application filters in ISA were specifically created to examine the traffic being passed through the server and make sure that it is not simply a piggy-backed exploit or attack. Each application filter contains language specific to the protocol it is filtering, so it can identify and block traffic that does not comply with the proper use of the protocol. The following application filters are configured by default in ISA Server 2006:

- ▶ DNS filter
- ▶ FTP Access filter
- ▶ H.323 filter
- ▶ MMS filter
- ▶ PNM filter
- ▶ POP Intrusion Detection filter
- ▶ PPTP filter

▶ RPC filter

▶ RTSP filter

▶ SMTP filter

▶ SOCKS V4 filter

▶ Web Proxy filter

Examining Web Filters

In addition to the default application filters available with ISA Server 2006, a series of web filters is also installed that extends the capability of ISA to scan incoming web (HTTP) packets. These web filters, shown in Figure 3.35, allow for advanced HTTP filtering capabilities, such as the capability to secure Outlook Web Access (OWA) traffic, or the capability to perform Link Translation.

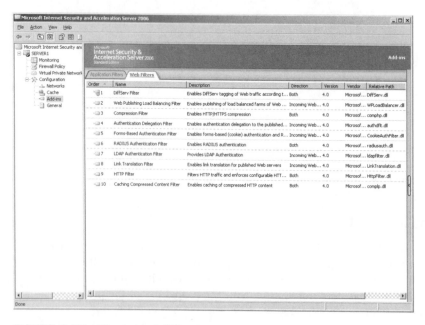

FIGURE 3.35   Viewing web filters in the Add-ins node.

The web filters in ISA are accessible via the Web Filters tab in the Details pane of the Add-ins node. For more specific information on using web filters, refer to Chapter 14, "Securing Web (HTTP) and SharePoint Site Traffic."

Exploring the ISA General Node

Any of the settings that were not explicitly defined in the other nodes of the ISA console were placed together in the General node. The General node, shown in Figure 3.36, contains several links to key functionality that are not found anywhere else, and is therefore important to explore.

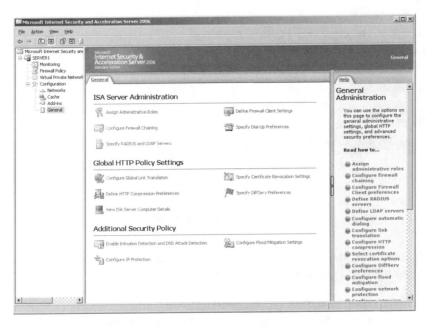

FIGURE 3.36   Exploring the General node in the ISA Console.

Delegating ISA Administration

The first link listed under the ISA General node is the Administration Delegation link. This link makes it possible to enable other administrators within an organization to monitor and/or administer the ISA Server Console. The delegation process is streamlined through the use of a wizard, which leads administrators through the entire process.

To allow an individual or a group of users to administer the ISA Server system, perform the following steps:

1. Open the ISA Server Management Console (Start, All Programs, Microsoft ISA Server, ISA Server Management).
2. From the console tree, select the General tab by clicking on it.

3. In the Details pane, click the Assign Administrative Roles link.

4. In the Delegate Control dialog box, click the Add button to add a group or user.

5. In the Administration Delegation dialog box, enter the name of the group or user that will be added, similar to the example shown in Figure 3.37.

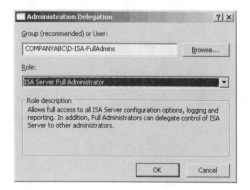

FIGURE 3.37   Delegating ISA administration.

Users or groups can be local accounts, or they can be domain accounts if the ISA server is joined to an Active Directory domain.

Under the Role field in this dialog box, three types of administrators are available to choose from, each with its own varying level of permissions and abilities. The three types are as follows:

▶ **ISA Server Monitoring Auditor**—Members of this role can view the ISA monitoring console and items such as the Dashboard but cannot configure any of the settings.

▶ **ISA Server Auditor**—Members of this role can monitor ISA and are also capable of customizing monitoring components. All other ISA configuration components are listed as read-only for members of this role.

▶ **ISA Server Full Administrator**—A Full Administrator can configure and change any ISA Server components.

To complete the Admin role assignment, do the following:

1. Choose the role of the administrator to be added using the criteria already outlined. Click OK when finished.

2. Click the Add button and repeat the procedure for any additional groups or users that will be added.

3. After returning to the dialog box, as shown in Figure 3.38, review the addition(s) and click OK to finish.

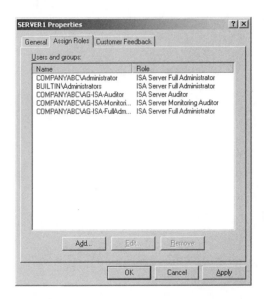

FIGURE 3.38   Specifying groups to be added as ISA administrators.

4. Click the Apply button at the top of the Details pane.

5. Click OK at the confirmation dialog box.

Configuring Firewall Chaining

Firewall chaining is an additional option that can be configured via the General node. With firewall chaining, multiple ISA servers can be configured to forward client requests to upstream ISA servers. This enables them to be routed to "parent" ISA servers, for the purposes of directing the flow of traffic from one network to another.

Firewall chaining settings can be set up by clicking the Configure Firewall Chaining link in the Details pane.

Defining Firewall Client Parameters

The full-featured Firewall client, available as an option for ISA implementations, allows for customized user-based policies and application-specific filtering using Winsock-compatible applications. Specific Firewall client settings are available in the General node of the ISA Server Console by clicking on the Define Firewall Client Settings link. These settings allow for options such as whether or not downlevel (ISA 2000) client connections will be allowed and what type of Winsock applications to support through the Firewall client, as shown in Figure 3.39.

For additional information on using the Firewall client, see Chapter 11.

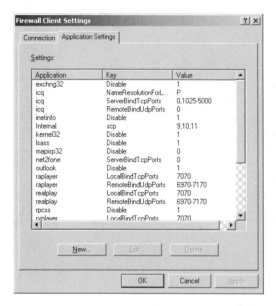

FIGURE 3.39   Defining Firewall client settings.

Exploring Link Translation

Link translation, an option fully explained in Chapter 14, is a process by which a web server published through ISA Server automatically translates embedded links in the page into a different format. This can be useful when a web server, such as an intranet server, provides links to internal server names that are not resolvable on the Internet. Through the process of link translation, these internal names, such as http://server20, can be translated into a publicly accessible link names, such as https://sharepoint.companyabc.com, for example.

The General node makes it possible to configure what type of content is parsed for link translation via the Configure Global Link Translation link. This link invokes the dialog box shown in Figure 3.40, which enables administrators to choose additional content types to be parsed for link translations, as well as the ability to enter global mappings and other settings.

When these options are selected, individual web publishing rules that are configured with link translation can then apply those link translation options to the additional content types chosen from this list.

Configuring Dial-Up Preferences

The Specify Dial-Up Preferences link in the Details pane allows ISA Server to be configured to utilize dial-up networking to establish links to specific networks. The options available in this link allow for specific dial-up account information, dial-up preferences, and dial-up connection information to be entered and configured for ISA servers that require this type of capability.

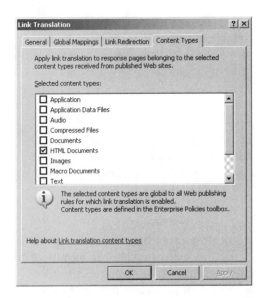

FIGURE 3.40   Configuring link translation options.

Examining Certificate Revocation Options

The Specify Certificate Revocation Settings link makes it possible to have the ISA server check incoming client certificates to make sure that they are not in the Certificate Revocation List (CRL). The dialog box shown in Figure 3.41 illustrates the default options for certificate revocation in an ISA server.

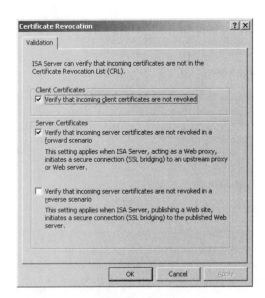

FIGURE 3.41   Configuring certificate revocation options.

Although ISA can easily check incoming client certificates, the ISA server can check only to see whether a server certificate has been revoked if it initiates the Secure Sockets Layer (SSL) connection itself, normally performed when the server is configured as a web proxy for the clients. This option can further secure web browsing for clients by making sure that server certificates on the Internet are valid.

Viewing ISA Server Details

ISA Server details, such as the specific version used, the product ID, the installation directory, and the creation date of the server, are accessible via the View ISA Server Computer Details link in the Details pane. These details are mainly useful for determining the current version of ISA Server that is running on the server.

Controlling Flood Mitigation Settings

ISA Server 2006 introduces a new console setting that attempts to limit the ability of rogue systems to flood an ISA server with spurious requests. This limits Denial of Service (DoS) attacks and also helps to identify unnecessarily chatty clients. These settings, shown in Figure 3.42, are controlled through the Configure Flood Mitigation Settings link in the General node.

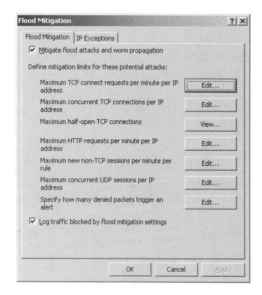

FIGURE 3.42   Examining Flood Mitigation settings.

By default, individual clients that access an ISA server are limited to a specific number of connections per second, per rule. In certain cases, exceptions may need to be made if individual servers need to establish a large number of connections, such as in the case of an

SMTP or DNS server. These settings can be configured under the IP Exceptions tab of this dialog box.

Determining whether exceptions need to be made can be accomplished by checking the alerts in the Monitoring node and looking for specific alerts that indicate that a session was terminated because of connection limit settings.

Setting Intrusion Detection Thresholds

Intrusion detection settings, covered in detail in Chapter 19, can be configured by clicking the Enable Intrusion Detection and DNS Attack Detection link in the Details pane. These options, shown in Figure 3.43, allow for the customization of what types of attacks will be reported as alerts in the ISA Console.

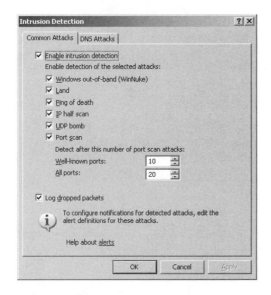

FIGURE 3.43   Enabling intrusion detection filters.

It is recommended to enable all the intrusion detection filters and to closely watch for these type of attacks. An increase in intrusion detection attempts can signal a full-blown attack against the ISA server.

Defining RADIUS and LDAP Servers

Remote Dial-In User Service (RADIUS) and Light Directory Access Protocol (LDAP) Servers can be configured by clicking the Specify RADIUS and LDAP Servers link in the General node of the Console. These types of servers are typically utilized for authentication when the ISA server is not a member of an Active Directory domain and/or when the server is configured as an appliance reverse proxy server in the DMZ of an existing firewall.

For more information on this concept, reference Chapter 7, "Deploying ISA Server as a Reverse Proxy in an Existing Firewall DMZ."

Configuring IP Protection

The IP Preference settings, invoked via the Configure IP Protection link, allow for advanced IP options filtering to be configured, as shown in Figure 3.44. This allows for IP characteristics such as time stamp, router alert, strict source route, and others to be blocked or allowed.

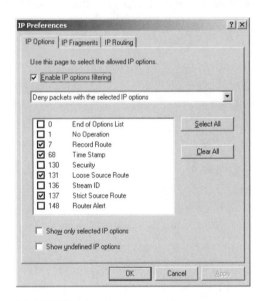

FIGURE 3.44   Setting IP preferences.

In addition to filtering based on IP options, this dialog box also allows for IP routing to be enabled, which allows for original packets received by the ISA server to be forwarded to their destinations. If this option is not enabled, ISA repackages the data in its own packet and forwards it to the destination server—a more secure option, but one that requires additional overhead on the server. For more information on these options, see Chapter 15.

Specifying DiffServ Preferences

ISA Server 2004 Service Pack 2 introduced the ability for ISA Server to provide for Quality of Service (QoS) for IP traffic through the implementation of IP DiffServ. This feature was ported over to ISA Server 2006 as well. DiffServ allows administrators to give priority to traffic sent to specific domains, URLs, or originating from particular networks. Using this concept, an ISA admin can prioritize the traffic that passes through the server.

DiffServ settings are controlled through the HTTP DiffServ applet, shown in Figure 3.45, which can be invoked by clicking the Specific DiffServ Preferences link.

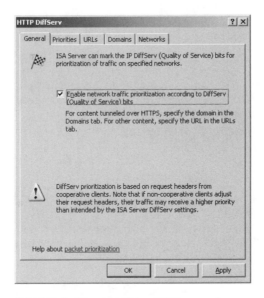

FIGURE 3.45   Specifying DiffServ preferences.

Defining HTTP Compression Preferences

Another new feature introduced was the ability to compress HTTP packets that pass through the ISA server. This helps to reduce the overall bandwidth required for web surfing. The HTTP Compression settings can be configured by clicking on the Define HTTP Compression Preferences link, which launches the dialog box shown in Figure 3.46.

Network clients specified under the Return Compressed Data tab will have their HTTP responses compressed. In addition, the ISA server will request that web servers listed under the Request Compressed Data tab compress their HTTP traffic. If there are no systems listed under these tabs, compression does not occur.

Summary

The ISA Server Management Console is an extremely valuable, flexible tool that provides for nearly all ISA functionality and configuration. Navigating the console tree and exploring the various nodes available is an important part of understanding how ISA works, and what tools are available for configuration of the server.

This chapter covered the high-level details of each portion of the ISA Management Console, with emphasis placed on introducing ISA administrators to the tools available to make their lives easier. Additional information on each of the sections covered can be found in the subsequent chapters on deploying, configuring, and supporting ISA infrastructure.

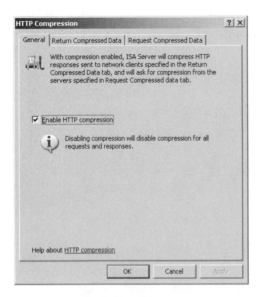

FIGURE 3.46   Defining HTTP Compression preferences.

Best Practices

▶ When possible, become familiar with the ISA Server Console before becoming involved in production ISA Server configuration.

▶ Use the Help tab in the Tasks pane for more information about the specific console node selected.

▶ When not in use, park the ISA Server Console on the Dashboard of the Monitoring node so that you can quickly glance at and see updated real-time ISA status.

▶ Enable only those options on the ISA server that are absolutely necessary.

▶ Use the logging mechanism in ISA Server to troubleshoot firewall rule creation.

▶ Delegate administration based on group membership whenever possible, rather than on individual users.

CHAPTER 4

Designing an ISA Server 2006 Environment

The success of an ISA Server implementation depends largely on its design. ISA Server 2006 is a complex, capable system that can assume multiple roles in the organization. It is therefore important to first understand what the security needs are, and then match those needs to the various pieces of ISA Server functionality.

Because ISA can assume multiple roles, a proper ISA design does not always fit cookie-cutter style roles. In fact, many ISA server designs involve multiple ISA servers distributed across multiple network locations. The need to provide for network security has evolved to encompass both external and internal traffic within an organization, and ISA Server 2006 provides the tools to perform these tasks.

This chapter focuses on the design factors that are involved in an ISA Server 2006 deployment. Particular focus is placed on establishing a proper security methodology to avoid mistakes in deployment. So as to ensure a secure and updated design, specific steps to upgrade existing ISA 2000 Servers to ISA Server 2006 are presented as well. Finally, sample designs of small-, medium-, and large-sized organizations are presented.

Preparing for an ISA Server 2006 Design

When designing ISA Server implementations of any size, it is important to establish and utilize a design methodology that is proven to have successful results. There are many different ways of approaching this, and different methodologies have varying levels of success, depending on the specific needs of the organization. In general, it is best practice to follow whatever design methodology has proven to work best in the past. That said, a common design methodology for ISA Server that works well is one that focuses on outlining current security needs and goals and matches them to specific ISA functionality.

Identifying Security Goals and Objectives

Although seemingly straightforward, it is often difficult to define what goals or objectives ISA Server 2006 is meant to achieve. Many organizations are looking for "better security," but have a tough time identifying specifically what they mean by "better." Without knowing the question, it is impossible to properly define the answer, so it is important to properly outline these goals and objectives in advance.

Every organization has different needs in this category, and it is impossible to list them all. However, some of the more common goals and objectives of an ISA server design project are the following:

- ▶ Secure access to Internet-facing services

- ▶ Provide for the capability to monitor traffic between network segments

- ▶ Provide for the capability to report on Internet traffic patterns

- ▶ Reduce the amount of Internet bandwidth consumed

- ▶ Enable employees to securely access network resources from remote locations

- ▶ Design an infrastructure that is compliant with government regulations such as HIPAA or Sarbanes-Oxley

- ▶ Reduce the overhead and complexity associated with managing security infrastructure

The first stage in a design process is to map out these goals and objectives in advance to provide for a common roadmap. This information is then used for later portions of the design project.

Documenting and Discovering Existing Environment Settings

It's often surprising how many organizations do not maintain an updated set of diagrams or documentation about their existing network and security infrastructure. When it comes down to it, there is often not enough time available for IT organizations that are already stretched thin to maintain these types of materials. Unfortunately, however, it is very important to keep this type of information handy, particularly in light of new governmental regulations such as Sarbanes-Oxley, which stipulate the need for identifiable documented processes.

Before designing an ISA implementation, it is therefore important to gather any and all updated documentation to determine the nature of the environment in which ISA will be installed. During deployment of an ISA server is not the time to discover that there are multiple previously unidentified networks attached via ad-hoc routers in dusty closets.

If a network diagram is not available, it is highly recommended to create one, using Microsoft Visio or another similar network diagramming tool. This will make it easier to visualize the project and logically design the location of ISA servers.

In addition to mapping out the locations of routers, switches, and the logical network as a whole, it is a good idea to match up the network design with the overall location of computers and computer services. Understanding where critical servers are logically located on a network, and where client workstations are located, can be useful in determining where to place ISA servers. For example, if a client network is composed of workstations from a department that is prone to virus infestations or exploits, it might prove helpful to place an ISA server between that network and a separate network of mission-critical servers.

When all is said and done, an ISA server design process is only as complete as the knowledge that was used to create it. It is therefore important to understand how the current environment is structured before you try to decide where and how to utilize ISA.

Matching Goals and Objectives to ISA Features

It may seem trite, but many ISA design sessions start with a lack of understanding of what the organization needs to get out of ISA. Or, in other cases, ISA is required for a specific reason, such as to secure Outlook Web Access (OWA) from the Internet, but the fact that it can be used for more than this is never realized. It is therefore important to maintain a list of what types of functionality are necessary in an environment and what ISA features correspond with this functionality. For example, Table 4.1 depicts several common goals and objectives and what ISA features correspond to those particular needs.

Managing a Deployment Project

One of the most difficult parts of deploying a technical solution is managing the project itself. Often, security solutions, particularly Microsoft security solutions, become part of a political—or even an almost religious—topic for many of the organizations who seek to deploy them. In addition, care must be taken to manage and control other aspects of ISA design and deployment. The following are areas of particular note for ISA Server 2006 deployments:

▶ **Defining the project**—It is not enough to simply define what will be deployed, but rather it is necessary to explain the "why" of the project. What critical functionality does ISA bring into an environment? Why should management shell out the money necessary to deploy yet another set of servers? Defining and documenting the project at an early stage can help it get out of the gates early on.

▶ **Outlining the project scope**—Determining the size, complexity, and level of deployment are critical factors in the success of an ISA project. A well-defined set of boundaries to which the project will be limited helps to minimize the amount of testing that will need to be done and also helps to sell the project to a targeted audience.

▶ **Organizing technology champions**—If no one champions a new product, the technology dies, either before it is implemented or shortly afterward. Technologies such

TABLE 4.1   Matching ISA Functionality to Goals and Objectives

Goal or Objective	ISA Functionality
Secure Exchange Outlook Web Access from the Internet.	Deploy ISA Server 2006 for reverse-proxy functionality by using mail publishing rules.
Audit all network access to a specific server service, such as a web server.	Deploy ISA Server 2006 between network segments and implement web publishing rules. Audit the traffic by logging it to a SQL database.
Protect Exchange servers from RPC-based attacks from clients on the internal network.	Secure all Exchange servers behind ISA servers, using RPC filtering to filter out all non-MAPI RPC traffic.
Deploy redundant content-caching solution for clients to allow for HTTP and FTP proxy to the Internet.	Deploy ISA Server 2006 Enterprise Edition to allow for network load balancing. Use the proxy functionality of ISA server to provide for HTTP and FTP content caching.
Connect remote sites across the Internet to a single logical network.	Deploy site-to-site Virtual Private Networks with ISA Server 2006.
Enact strict limitations on client access to services and data, for governmental compliance reasons such as those dictated by Sarbanes-Oxley.	Deploy ISA Server Firewall client software to all systems and monitor, restrict, and audit access to services.
Secure web services from the Internet by using advanced Application-layer filtering techniques, traffic.	Deploy a unihomed ISA server in the DMZ of the existing firewall. Configure web publishing rules to filter the HTTP.

as ISA Server require those who use it to be at least somewhat interested in the type of functionality that it can provide. For example, creating champions may simply involve showing an Exchange administrator what is possible with ISA mail publishing rules for Outlook Web Access. Or, a manager evaluating the plethora of expensive VPN solutions may become an ISA technology champion after he or she finds the low-cost and highly functional ISA VPN solutions tempting. The more support ISA can get, the easier it is to manage the project to completion.

▶ **Convincing the skeptics**—The reality today is that there is a great deal of skepticism regarding Microsoft security technologies. This skepticism is partly based on the bad experiences many security admins have had in the past with exploits and security holes in Microsoft products. This makes a product such as ISA Server a tougher sell to this audience. In this scenario, ISA is often best sold as an additional layer to existing security technologies, rather than as a replacement for them. In addition, as with any technology, if the impression is that a fundamental redesign of existing network or security architecture is necessary to deploy ISA, it will have a more difficult time gaining approval.

▶ **Controlling the costs**—Although a full ISA Server 2006 deployment with multiple arrays of ISA Enterprise Edition servers running on robust multi-processor systems can end up being quite expensive, most ISA deployments are actually quite low cost, particularly when they are compared to similar solutions. A single-processor ISA Server 2006 Standard system running on server hardware, for example, can easily be contained to a small licensing charge (around $1300 per processor or so) and the price of the hardware. Because there are no client licenses to purchase, this makes ISA itself a fairly inexpensive solution to deploy.

▶ **Containing the impact**—It is critical that the level of impact that the deployed solution will have is mitigated as much as possible. The success of an IT project is often defined by the level of "pain" that the end users end up feeling after the migration project. Fortunately, ISA deployments are easy to set up in parallel to existing deployed environments, reducing the risk that they have and allowing for an extensive pilot of the technology before it is fully deployed.

▶ **Training the resources**—Because ISA is a new technology, the skills to administer and maintain the environment are not always present in an IT infrastructure. Formal training in ISA Server administration may be warranted, but are not necessarily required if using references such as this book. The key to a successful project post-implementation comes down to how smoothly the new environment dovetails with existing processes and environmental procedures. Training in advance the people who will work with the product is key toward reaching this goal.

Documenting the Design

Although often the most important step in a design process, the documentation of an ISA design is often overlooked. It cannot be stressed enough that good documentation is critical for IT projects, particularly ones involving security and remote access considerations.

With this in mind, it is of the utmost importance that the design decisions chosen for an ISA deployment are documented and diagrammed. This information becomes very useful down the line when questions about why a system was deployed the way that it was are asked. For more information on techniques for documenting ISA Server, see Chapter 20, "Documenting an ISA Server 2006 Environment."

CAUTION

Documentation for ISA configuration and deployment should be highly restricted, and not made available to anyone who does not absolutely need the information in it. Spreading information on how an ISA environment is configured is akin to giving the war plans to an enemy army in advance of a battle.

Migrating from ISA Server 2000/2004 to ISA Server 2006

Part of an ISA design process involves examining existing ISA deployments and migrating those servers to ISA Server 2006. Fortunately, Microsoft provides for a robust and straight-forward set of tools to migrate existing ISA 2000 servers to ISA Server 2006. From a design perspective, it is important to first understand the functional differences between ISA 2000, ISA 2004, and ISA Server 2006, so that the design can take them into account.

Exploring Differences Between ISA 2000 and ISA Server 2004/2006

ISA 2000 was a very capable product that provided for a great deal of firewall and proxy capabilities. Compared to the features of ISA Server 2004/2006, however, the older version of the software falls short in several key categories. This new functionality, along with a higher overall degree of security, drives organizations to upgrade to the newer version.

The following key features comprise the bulk of the new features and improvements introduced to ISA Server 2006:

▶ **Multi-network support**—One of the most visible changes between ISA 2000 and ISA 2006 is the capability of ISA 2006 to support multiple defined networks, each with its own defined relationships. This allows for unique policies that can be applied to each network, and the networks can be used as part of firewall rules.

▶ **Improved Application-layer filtering**—The Layer 7 (Application layer) filtering capabilities of ISA Server 2006 have been greatly enhanced to include per-rule–based HTTP stateful inspection, RPC filtering support, and link translator features.

▶ **Enhanced monitoring and reporting**—Another welcome improvement to ISA 2006 is the introduction of robust and real-time log viewing. This greatly aids in the troubleshooting of firewall rules and connections. The addition of monitoring and reporting features such as connection verifiers, report publishing, MSDE logging options, and real-time session monitoring greatly improves this area for ISA admins.

▶ **Greatly improved management interface**—The GUI Admin tool in ISA Server 2006 was streamlined and greatly improved over the ISA 2000 console. In addition to overall ease of use, ISA 2006 added multiple wizards to help with common tasks, network templates that can easily be applied, and centralized logging, reporting, and storage of firewall policy in the Enterprise version of the software.

▶ **Export and import functionality**—The capability of ISA Server 2006 to export out individual elements or entire ISA configurations to simple XML text files that can be imported into separate servers greatly enhances the backup and restore options available to ISA admins.

▶ **Virtual Private Network improvements**—ISA Server 2006 added new VPN enhancements such as support for VPN Quarantine, SecureNAT client support, stateful filtering for VPN clients, and support for third-party IPSec tunnel mode for site-to-site VPNs.

▶ **Content-caching updates**—The web and FTP proxy options for ISA have been expanded to include RADIUS support for authentication, improved cache rules, and the creation of CARP-enabled caching arrays in the Enterprise version.

▶ **Enhanced firewall rules**—Support for multiple default protocols has been added to ISA, including the capability to support complex protocols when using the ISA Firewall client. In addition, enhancements to server publishing for services such as OWA, websites, SharePoint, FTP sites, and other firewall rules have been included.

Migrating ISA 2000 to ISA Server 2006

There is no direct upgrade path for ISA 2000 systems to ISA 2006. The only supported method of upgrading an existing ISA 2000 server to ISA 2006 is by migrating the server's settings to ISA 2004, and then migrating from 2004 to 2006. This procedure is outlined in this section.

There are two basic options for migration of ISA 2000 settings to ISA Server 2004. The first procedure involves an in-place upgrade of an existing ISA 2000 server to ISA Server 2004. It is highly recommended that you avoid this technique at all costs because it does not always produce desirable results and can produce a system with existing security holes and the mess left over from migrating from one environment to another.

The preferred migration option for ISA Server 2004 is to run the ISA Server Migration tool to export out the settings of an ISA 2000 server to an XML file, which can then be imported on another newly installed ISA Server 2004 system running on Windows Server 2003. This option allows for the creation of a brand-new ISA server from scratch, without any of the configuration or operating system problems of the ISA 2000 server.

To perform this type of ISA 2000 migration to ISA Server 2004, perform the following steps:

> **NOTE**
>
> To upgrade the Standard version of ISA 2000, the Standard version CD for ISA Server 2006 must be used. Likewise, to upgrade from the Enterprise version of ISA 2000, the ISA Server 2006 Enterprise CD must be used. If the intent is to upgrade between different versions (that is, ISA 2000 Standard to ISA Server 2006 Enterprise), the only supported migration path is to run the migration wizard, copy the configuration to the same version, and then export the individual rules to XML files and transfer them over to the new version of the server.

1. From the ISA 2000 server, insert the ISA Server 2004 CD into the CD drive (or double-click the `autorun.exe` file).
2. Click on the Run Migration Wizard link.
3. At the Welcome dialog box, click Next to continue.
4. At the subsequent dialog box, type in a name of the folder to which the XML file will be saved, as well as a name for the file, similar to what is shown in Figure 4.1. The Browse button can also be used.

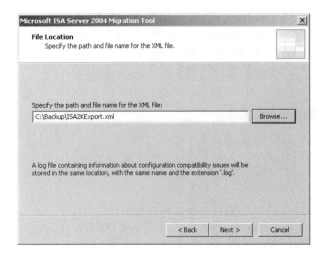

FIGURE 4.1   Using the ISA Server 2004 Migration wizard to export ISA 2000 settings.

5. After a name for the file has been entered, click Next to continue.

6. Click the Create button to start the export.

7. After the export has finished, click Next to continue.

8. Click the Finish button.

The exported XML file, if opened from Notepad, looks similar to the one shown in Figure 4.2. At this point, the file is ready to import to an ISA Server 2004 system.

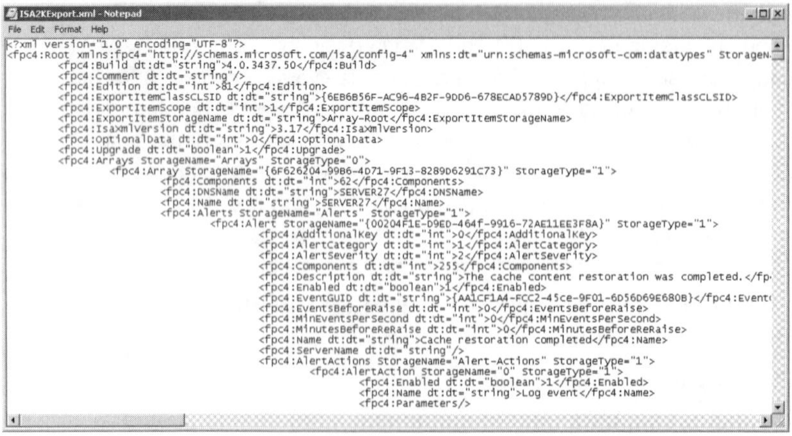

FIGURE 4.2   Viewing the export XML file for ISA Server 2004.

After the XML file has been physically made accessible from the new server, it can then be imported via the following process:

1. On the ISA Server 2004 system, open the ISA Console.

2. Right-click the server name in the Scope pane and click on Import.

3. When prompted with the warning dialog box in Figure 4.3, click Yes.

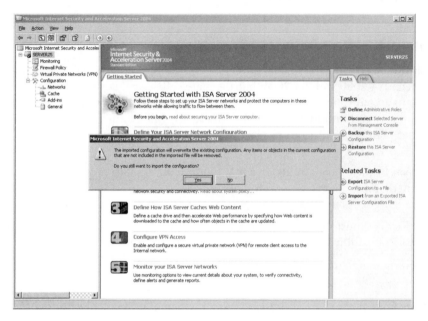

FIGURE 4.3   Importing the ISA 2000 settings onto an ISA Server 2004 system.

CAUTION

As the dialog box indicates, performing this restore operation results in any current settings being overwritten. Ensure that there are no customizations in place on the server before restoring from an ISA 2000 Export file.

---

4. Select the XML file from the ISA 2000 backup procedure and click Import.

5. Click OK when the import is finished.

6. Click Apply at the top of the Central Details pane.

After the migration process, and before the migrated settings are upgraded to ISA 2006, the mess of ISA 2000 rules that have been migrated should be scrutinized. One of the most noticeable characteristics of an ISA Server 2004 server that has just had ISA 2000 migration rules exported to it is the sheer number of confusing and redundant rules set up in the firewall policy. The ISA Server Migration wizard exports out all unique rules on the server itself, which are then imported onto the ISA 2004 server. In many cases, however, this creates many rules that are already covered by system policy rules or other default rules that may be configured on a server.

Taking this into account, this may be an ideal time to clean up some of the old ISA 2000 rules. To mitigate the risk associated with this action, it is ideal to simply disable the rules for a period of time before they are deleted completely. This way, if a rule turns out to have been necessary, it can be easily reenabled and nothing needs to be created from scratch.

Migrating from ISA 2004 to ISA 2006

The migration path between ISA Server 2004 and ISA Server 2006 is more straightforward than the one between ISA 2000 and ISA 2004, but there are still several key factors that need to be taken into account. Just as with the ISA 2000–2004 upgrade, it is highly recommended to build a new server and then export and import the rules configuration from the old server, rather than performing an in-place upgrade of the server itself.

Performing an In-Place Upgrade from ISA 2004 to ISA 2006   If an in-place upgrade is necessary, several key criteria must be reviewed, as follows:

▶ All ISA 2004 log files must be copied to an alternate location, as ISA 2006 starts with a brand-new, incompatible log format and will erase any existing logs.

▶ The SMTP Screener and Firewall client share components must be uninstalled before beginning the upgrade, as they are not supported in ISA 2006.

▶ It is highly recommended to back up the existing configuration before beginning the upgrade process.

▶ In-place upgrades cannot be used between version types. For example, an ISA 2004 Standard Edition server cannot be upgraded to ISA Server 2006 Enterprise Edition, and vice versa. The only supported method to accomplish this is to export out individual rules to XML files and import them into the new version.

▶ The Windows version must be upgraded to meet the minimum requirements for ISA 2006, which is either Windows Server 2003 SP1 or R2 Editions.

As previously mentioned, in-place upgrades are generally not the best method to transition between ISA versions. If an in-place upgrade is required, however, performing the upgrade is as simple as running ISA 2006 setup from the ISA 2006 media and accepting the defaults.

Migrating Between ISA 2004 and ISA 2006 Using the Export Wizard   The preferable way to upgrade an ISA 2004 server is to export out the rule configuration from the ISA 2004 server and then import them into the new ISA 2006 server. This allows for a fresh configuration to be maintained and also has the advantage of easy failback to the old server in the event of issues.

Existing rules and settings from an ISA 2004 server XML export are all that are needed to migrate rules and settings from 2004 to 2006. In addition, any SSL certificates that are installed on the old 2004 server must be transferred and installed on the 2006 server as well.

To export the configuration from an ISA 2004 server, perform the following steps:

1. From the ISA Server 2004 Management Console, click on the server name in the scope pane.

2. In the Tasks tab of the Tasks pane, click the link labeled Backup This ISA Server Configuration.

3. Enter a file name and file path that the XML backup file will be saved to and click Backup.

4. When prompted with the dialog box in Figure 4.4, enter a password that will be used to encrypt the XML file and click OK.

FIGURE 4.4   Exporting out the config from the ISA 2004 system.

5. Click OK when the backup is complete.

After the configuration has been exported, the XML file that was generated can be copied over to the 2006 system and imported via the process outlined as follows:

1. From the ISA Server 2006 Management Console, click on the server name in the scope pane.

2. In the Tasks tab of the Tasks pane, click the link labeled Import (Restore) This ISA Server Configuration.

3. At the wizard screen, click Next to start.

4. Click the Browse button to locate the XML file that came from the 2004 system.

5. Navigate to the XML file, click on it, and then click Open, Next to continue.

6. When prompted with the dialog box in Figure 4.5, click OK to indicate that you are prepared to upgrade the settings in the XML file to those compatible with ISA 2006.

FIGURE 4.5   Importing the 2004 XML into a 2006 server.

7. Enter the password used to encrypt the file into the subsequent dialog box and click Next.

8. Click Finish to start the import process.

9. Click OK when complete, then click Apply and OK within the console to save the changes.

At this point, the new 2006 system will be an exact mirror of the old 2004 system, and the actual migration between the two servers involves a simple IP address swap between the systems. If any problems exist with the new server, the old 2004 system can be easily replaced, as all of its original settings are still intact.

Determining the Number and Placement of ISA Servers

ISA Server sizing concepts are not particularly complex, but often depend on the role that ISA will fill in an environment. In general, most organizations rarely tax the processor and memory utilization on an ISA server on updated server hardware, assuming that the server is used primarily for Internet-related traffic, such as web publishing or mail publishing rules. When an ISA server starts to be used for content caching, on the other hand, knowing the number of clients that will access the system becomes very important.

Sizing an ISA Server Deployment

Although there are no hard and fast guidelines for ISA Server 2006 sizing, some general suggested hardware minimums, shown in Table 4.2, should be followed when deploying an ISA server.

> **NOTE**
>
> Table 4.2 lists only the minimal levels for a server with the indicated number of users. It is often wise to increase the capabilities of the server to avoid overtaxing its resources, particularly if it will act as a proxy server.

Choosing Between ISA Server Standard Edition and ISA Server Enterprise Edition

There is a fairly hefty difference in cost between the Standard version of ISA Server 2006 and the Enterprise version. It is therefore important to map out whether or not the Enterprise Edition is required. In general, Enterprise Edition deployments are required when any one of the following factors are true:

▶ Server failover and redundancy using network load balancing is required.

▶ Centralized logging to a SQL database for multiple ISA servers is required.

▶ Centralized firewall policy and/or array functionality is needed.

TABLE 4.2   Sizing ISA Server Hardware

	To 50 Users	50–500 Users	500+ Users
Processor	Single 767MHz Pentium III or equivalent	Single 2GHz Pentium III/IV or equivalent	Dual 2GHz Pentium III/IV or equivalent (or greater)
Memory	512MB of memory	1GB of memory	2GB of memory (or greater)
Disk Space	150MB available (for installation of ISA software), plus space for logs and caching	150MB available (for installation of ISA software), plus space for logs and caching	8GB OS partition 10GB+ logs partition Additional 18GB+ partition for caching (if necessary)

▶ Support for Cache Array Routing Protocol (CARP) web proxy traffic to optimize content caching for clients is required.

For more information on the Enterprise version of ISA Server, refer to Chapter 6, "Deploying ISA Server Arrays with ISA Server 2006 Enterprise Edition."

Deploying ISA to Branch Offices

The branch office deployment scenario is common for ISA configurations. In many cases, the ISA server in the branch office may be the first line of defense for that particular office. In addition, site-to-site VPNs can be created easily between ISA servers in remote and parent sites, joining them together into a single contiguous network.

During the ISA design process, it is important to take into account the individual needs of each branch office and to examine whether a local install of ISA is relevant to that particular office.

Prototyping a Test ISA Server Deployment

Before an ISA server design can go into effect, it is ideal to test the design in an isolated prototype lab environment. Setting up this type of environment helps to address any problems in advance of the deployment of the ISA servers to a production environment. This mitigates the inherent risks in the project, and can prove to be quite useful as a training tool and test bed for new rules and ISA settings.

Setting Up a Prototype Lab for ISA Server 2006

To set up an ISA Server 2006 prototype, it is important to simulate as closely as possible the way that the ISA server will be deployed and also set up any servers or components that will be tested. For example, if an ISA server is to be set up to secure MAPI access to Exchange mailbox servers, it would be necessary to restore those servers onto spare hardware in an isolated setting and then test the new ISA server against that environment.

The key to a successful prototype environment is closely linked to how it reflects the true production settings. In an ideal world, all servers and settings would be exactly matched in the prototype lab. In reality, however, the expense associated with such a comprehensive prototype environment would make the project cost prohibitive. What this means is that in most cases, the prototype environment ends up being a partial reflection of the most critical services, which are then tested for functionality.

Emulating and Testing ISA Settings

The design process should have already created a design document that illustrates exactly how an ISA environment will be configured. Ideally, it will include information on individual ISA elements, such as server publishing rules and networks that need to be created. This information can be used to generate the various rules and settings that will be required to test the components in the prototype lab.

After all components are in place and the rules have been configured, testing against the ISA environment can take place. Ideally, the testing would involve emulating the steps a user would take to access the particular services or systems that are being protected by the ISA server. For example, it might include testing inbound OWA access across an ISA Server publishing rule. After all types of access that can feasibly be tested are fully tested, the information gleaned from the prototype testing can be used to modify the design if necessary.

Exporting Prototype Lab Configs

One of the most advantageous features of ISA that greatly assists in prototype testing is the capability to export out individual ISA elements to XML files for import on other systems. This concept, useful for backups of the system, can also be used to export out "known good" configurations from a prototype lab and import them onto the actual production servers.

Ideally, a prototype lab would remain in place to test the functionality of new rules or configuration settings in the ISA environment. Anytime a change would need to be made, it could be easily created on the prototype ISA server, tested, exported to XML, and then imported onto a production server.

Piloting an ISA Server Deployment

The logical step that follows an ISA prototype would be a pilot phase, where the functionality tested in the lab is extended into a production environment, but only to a small subset of users. This can prove to be tricky to set up, in some cases, but easier in others.

Organizing a Pilot Group

The first step in setting up an ISA pilot is to find a subset of users who would be willing to test out the new ISA functionality. Ideally, the total sum of pilot users would be between 5% and 10% of the total number of users in an organization. These users should also be willing to fill out checklists and reports following their pilot testing. This information can be then used to modify the ISA configuration one last time before it is deployed to full production use.

Understanding ISA Pilot Scenarios

Depending on the purpose of an ISA deployment, it may or may not prove difficult to establish a pilot group. The following scenarios and their pilot considerations are listed next:

- ▶ **ISA deployed as a forward proxy server**—This scenario is the easiest to pilot. The list of pilot users' workstations can be forced to use the ISA proxy server for web caching through the deployment of an Active Directory group policy.

- ▶ **ISA deployed as a reverse proxy server**—Setting up ISA as a reverse proxy server, for such things as OWA publishing and web server publishing, can be piloted by creating a temporary web presence for the new ISA pilot configuration. To take an OWA example as an illustration, if the old OWA access was through mail.companyabc.com, and the ISA server was set up to protect this traffic, then a second host called mail2.companyabc.com could be temporarily created to allow the pilot users to test OWA access through the reverse-proxy server. After the pilot has validated the configuration, the mail2 record can be retired and mail.companyabc.com can be directed to the ISA implementation only.

- ▶ **ISA deployed as a full edge firewall**—When ISA is deployed as a full-blown edge (Internet-facing) firewall, then pilot deployments are more complex to administer, given the fact that traffic from the Internet, by default, wants to go through a single patch. If both the old configuration and the new ISA edge firewall are deployed at the same time, it is feasible to test out ISA access in this manner, by essentially having two sets of gateways into the environment until the pilot can be completed and the old environment retired.

- ▶ **ISA deployed between network segments**—This scenario is similar to the edge firewall scenario. The only difference is that the ISA server is meant to be placed between internal network segments to monitor the traffic going between those segments. Because the network traffic is going to try to go through the standard route, rather than through the new ISA servers, this presents a challenge. The best solutions to this problem involve creating an alternate patch for the pilot users and hard-coding routes on their workstations so that they can test access through the ISA server.

Running Penetration Tests and Attacks Against the Pilot Infrastructure

A pilot infrastructure should ideally be tested for vulnerabilities and overall performance. The best and most effective way to do this is by using third-party hacking and exploit tools to attempt penetration tests against the ISA environment. Because this is likely to occur for any Internet-facing (or often even trusted network-facing) systems, it is important to put ISA through the hoops and test out the design in this manner.

Implementing the ISA Server Design

After successful prototype and pilot phases, and any modifications that arise from these projects, the ISA server design can be fully implemented in production for all users. In many cases, this involves simply re-routing traffic to the ISA servers. To use the previous reverse-proxy example, after the pilot has finished, the regular mail.companyabc.com record can be directed to point at the ISA server. The same concept applies to the other ISA deployment scenarios as well.

Validating Functionality

Before the ISA design project can be considered a success, it must ideally be validated against all normal client and server traffic. Ideally, this would involve enlisting the support of members of each of the business units within an organization to test the type of standard business applications and processes that were previously performed. This should be done very shortly after the implementation of the ISA server has gone into place, such as on the Saturday after the Friday night implementation.

By getting different business units involved in the testing of the infrastructure and obtaining their sign-off that all their business needs have been met, the success of the project can be more easily ensured.

Supporting the ISA Environment Long Term

After the ISA Server 2006 solution has been put into place, the task of administering, maintaining, and general "care and feeding" of the environment needs to take place. There are many factors to bear in mind for long-term ISA support, and more information about this topic can be found in Chapters 16, "Administering an ISA Server 2006 Environment," and 17, "Maintaining ISA Server 2006."

Designing ISA Server 2006 for Organizations of Varying Sizes

Every organization has different needs, and the fact that ISA fits into so many roles means that there are vast numbers of ISA server deployment scenarios. That said, certain typical best-practice ISA server deployment options are commonly seen in many organizations. These deployment options tend to be seen in organizations of specific sizes. To better illustrate this concept, three sample organizations of varying sizes are illustrated in this section to give an example of how ISA is often used today.

Examining an ISA Server 2006 Deployment for a Small Organization

CompanyABC is a 30-person law firm with an office in Minneapolis, MN. All local workstations run in a single, switched network at the office. Several remote users require access to resources in the office from home and while traveling. Often, clients visiting the offices request wireless Internet access, and employees request similar functionality.

The ISA design that CompanyABC deployed, illustrated in Figure 4.6, incorporates a single ISA Server 2006 Standard server as the edge firewall for the organization.

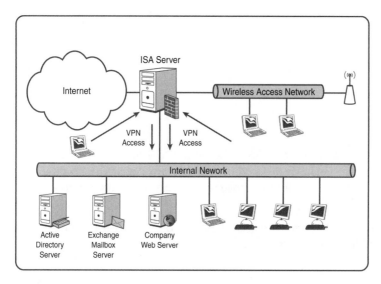

FIGURE 4.6   Examining an ISA deployment at a small organization.

Three network cards are present in the ISA server, allowing the server to be connected to three physical networks: the Internet, the internal network, and a secured wireless network. All employees on the Internet and on the wireless network must establish VPN connections with the ISA server before gaining access to internal company resources. A web server for the company is secured via ISA reverse-proxy functionality and web server publishing rules. In addition, the ISA server provides for content caching for all internal and wireless clients, to speed up and further secure web browsing.

Through this simple, yet robust design, CompanyABC is able to meet its security requirements through the deployment of a single ISA server that takes advantage of numerous ISA features.

Examining an ISA Server 2006 Deployment for a Mid-Sized Organization

OrganizationY is a city government in the state of Hawaii. With 2000 employees, the city IT department must manage not only external threats, but internal viruses and exploits that often crop up on city desktops and laptops. The city needed to secure its farm of servers, but still maintain functionality for clients on the network.

OrganizationY deployed a single ISA Server 2006 Standard Edition server with six network cards, as illustrated in Figure 4.7. Each network card is attached to a separate physical network within the organization, as follows:

▶ Internet

▶ DMZ network

▶ Wireless access network

▶ First-floor client network

▶ Second-floor client network

▶ Server network

The ISA server is configured to allow only specific types of traffic from the client, wireless, and DMZ networks to the server network. Specifically, the server is configured to filter RPC traffic to allow only MAPI access to an Exchange server, print functionality to a specific print server, and similar rules.

By deploying ISA in this manner, OrganizationY is able to mitigate the threat posed by viruses or exploits that may infect their deployed workstations.

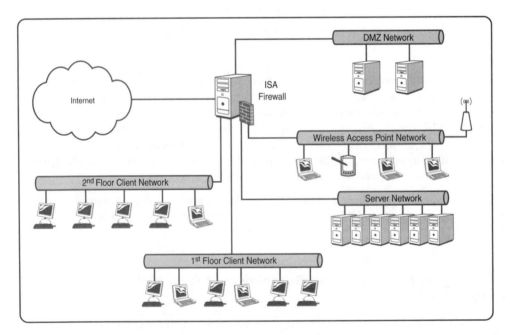

FIGURE 4.7   Examining an ISA deployment at a mid-sized organization.

Examining an ISA Server 2006 Deployment for a Large Organization

CompanyA is a large financial services organization with 20,000 employees distributed among three major sites in New York, Tokyo, and Paris. CompanyA has had trouble in the past securing and auditing access to their email services. When the decision was made to upgrade their existing Exchange 5.5 environment to Exchange Server 2003, a design process was followed to further secure the environment within the confines of the existing network and security infrastructure. The results of this design are reflected in Figure 4.8.

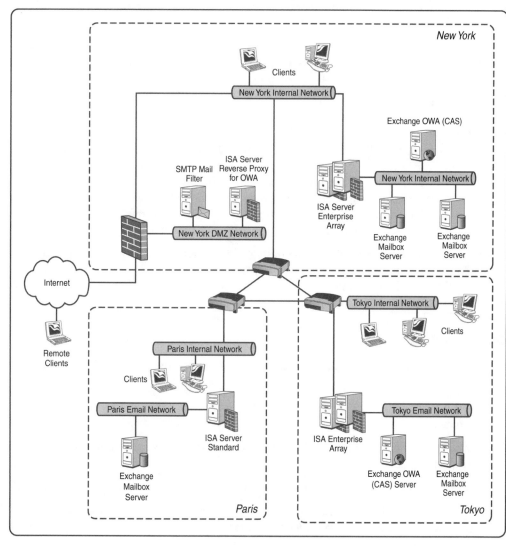

FIGURE 4.8   Examining an ISA deployment at a large organization.

CompanyA secured access to its email environment by placing all email-related components behind ISA servers. In New York, inbound email is sent to a SMTP Smarthost that scans for viruses and spam and then forwards the messages to the New York Exchange Servers behind an enterprise array of ISA servers. The ISA array is configured to allow the SMTP inbound traffic from the Smarthost. All other traffic is restricted to inbound MAPI from clients, which is then audited and tracked.

In the DMZ of the existing packet-filter firewall, an ISA server exists to provide reverse proxy to Exchange Outlook Web Access. Because of the need to fit into the existing security model, the ISA server is deployed as a single-NIC server that is homed to the DMZ network. The packet-filter firewall is then configured to allow only port 443 to the ISA server and out of the ISA server to the internal front-end server.

In remote locations, Exchange services are protected by ISA servers as well, operating in the same capacity. All traffic sent between these isolated networks is scanned at the Application layer by ISA servers.

Summary

Simply tearing open the ISA Server 2006 box and quickly installing the software onto a system is not the best strategy, in most cases, because the power and functionality of the environment call for a well thought-out design process that takes into account how the functionality of ISA can be applied to address specific organizational needs. Through the use of basic design and project management skills, ISA can be leveraged in a way that takes full advantage of the various types of functionality the environment can provide.

The design decisions reached during the design process can subsequently be tested and validated in a prototype lab and a pilot deployment, before they are implemented in production. Following this basic methodology, along with proper design, can help to ensure the success of an ISA project.

Best Practices

- ▶ Document the design of an ISA environment and store the documents in a secured location.

- ▶ Test ISA design in an isolated prototype lab environment before implementing it in production.

- ▶ Make a list of goals and objectives for ISA design that can subsequently be matched to specific pieces of ISA functionality.

- ▶ Look for ISA technology champions who will assist in pushing an ISA project forward.

- ▶ Consider increasing processor and memory capacity if ISA is used for content caching for an expanding number of clients.

- ▶ Run penetration tests against a pilot ISA deployment to validate the environment's security.

PART II

Deploying ISA Server 2006

Deploying ISA Server 2006 as a Firewall

ISA Server has become successful mainly because of its flexibility and capability to assume many roles within an organization. The fact that it can easily be configured as a network traffic filter, a web proxy server, a reverse-proxy device, or a VPN solution gives administrators and architects a great deal of freedom in designing ISA solutions for their organizations.

All these deployment scenarios take advantage of a particular portion of ISA functionality, each supplying an answer to a particular need. The deployment option that truly takes full advantage of all the features in ISA Server 2006, however, is the full-blown edge firewall scenario. This ultimately is the ideal role around which ISA was designed, and it fills the role quite well.

This chapter focuses on deployment scenarios involving ISA Server 2006 being used as an Application-Layer Firewall (ALF) for organizations. A discussion of the capabilities of ISA firewalls is presented, and step-by-step guides to deploying them are presented. Specifics on firewall-specific ISA components, such as network rules, firewall rules, the system policy, and network templates, are discussed and outlined.

ISA as a Full-Function Security Firewall

To better understand ISA Server 2006 as a product, it is important to understand its beginnings and the environment around which it was designed. First and foremost, general security concepts relating to ISA should be reviewed. This is of particular importance as there is a great deal of confusion about what ISA Server really is. This confusion has been increased in recent months as Microsoft has made ISA Server a part of the ForeFront line of Security products.

Defining the Concept of a Firewall

The idea of a computer firewall has evolved over time. In the beginning, the first networks were isolated and unconnected. With the rising need to collaborate between different organizations, the networks were joined together, eventually creating a worldwide network that became what we know as the Internet. Along with the advantages of being able to communicate with systems all over the world came the disadvantages of being exposed to those same systems.

Thus was born the network firewall, named to reflect the concept of an architectural barrier constructed to slow the spread of fires from one part of a building to another. Initially, firewalls simply blocked all access from the "untrusted" network to the "trusted" internal network, and allowed only traffic out of the network. As technology progressed, however, the need to share internal information with outside clients and vendors arose, driving the need for firewall administrators to "open ports" on the firewall to allow for specific types of traffic, such as HTTP web traffic, into the internal network.

Initially, filtering traffic at the packet layer proved to be successful in thwarting hacking attempts, which traditionally required for certain "dangerous" ports to be open to succeed. Eventually, however, virus and exploit writers realized that if their dangerous payloads were encased in commonly allowed protocols such as HTTP, they could freely pass through packet-filter firewalls and into the internal network unobstructed.

These types of exploits gave rise to extremely damaging viruses such as Code Red, Nimda, and Slammer. Many of these viruses and exploits sailed right through traditional firewalls and wreaked havoc upon internal servers. To make matters worse, internal "trusted" clients would get infected with a virus, exploit, or spyware application, which would then launch a set of attacks behind the firewall at unprotected servers and other workstations.

It quickly became obvious that some type of solution was needed to determine what type of traffic was legitimate and what was a potential exploit. This gave rise to firewall technologies such as ISA Server 2006, which provided for stateful inspection of the traffic at the Application layer of the TCP/IP stack.

Filtering Traffic at the Application Layer

Network traffic is logically divided into multiple layers of what is called the Open System Interconnection (OSI) Reference model. Each layer in the OSI model provides for different types of TCP/IP functionality, as follows:

- ▶ **Layer 1: Physical**—The Physical layer is the lowest layer in the OSI model, and it deals with the actual ones and zeros that are transmitted to and from network devices.

- ▶ **Layer 2: Data Link**—The Data Link layer deals with error detection and handling, basic addressing at the hardware (MAC address) level, and conflict avoidance. It is at this layer that the boundaries of the local network are defined.

▶ **Layer 3: Network**—The Network layer of the OSI model encapsulates information into multiple logical "packets" of information, and deals with routing them to specific IP addresses across multiple networks.

▶ **Layer 4: Transport**—The Transport layer of the TCP/IP stack is where the information about the specific "port" that the packets are to utilize is identified. Standard packet-filter firewalls can deny or accept traffic at this level.

▶ **Layer 5: Session**—The Session layer deals with establishing individual sessions between client and target systems. It is at this layer that services such as NetBIOS and RPC operate.

▶ **Layer 6: Presentation**—The Presentation layer (which, depending on the protocol, is not always used) deals with translating the way data is presented between disparate platforms. It is also where some compression and encryption (SSL, for example) can take place.

▶ **Layer 7: Application**—The Application layer is the top layer in the stack, and the one that deals with providing services and programs that use the network for specific functionality. It is at this level that protocols such as HTTP, FTP, and SMTP exist and are processed. Application-layer firewalls such as ISA Server can understand the specific protocols at the Application layer.

The deficiency in firewall devices that use packet-filtering technologies only is that the true nature of the traffic cannot be determined at this layer. A standard exploit, for example, can include a simple HTTP header, with the exploit itself hidden in the body of the packet. If that packet is scanned at the Application layer with ISA Server 2006, however, it can be determined whether a packet is truly legitimate. In addition, filters can be written to look for specific types of traffic in Application-layer protocols. For example, the HTTP filter in ISA Server can be modified to block directory traversal attacks that include HTTP strings that include multiple dots (..).

Deploying ISA Server 2006 as a firewall device gives an environment Application-layer inspection capabilities. Indeed, this is one of the most distinct advantages to deploying ISA in this fashion. All traffic that passes through the ISA box is scanned at the Application layer, providing for a great degree of flexibility in what type of traffic is allowed and what is denied.

Understanding Common Myths and Misperceptions About ISA

ISA Server has always faced an uphill battle for acceptance, based mainly on the fact that Microsoft has only recently put a strong emphasis on security in its products. Since the Trustworthy Computing initiative a few years back, however, the emphasis has shifted to "Security first, functionality second." How big of an effect the Trustworthy Computing initiative has had is debatable, but needless to say, the security provided by ISA Server 2006 is quite respectable.

Despite this fact, however, there is a great deal of confusion and misunderstanding of what ISA really is and what type of functionality it supports. It's easy to dismiss ISA as simply another "Microsoft BOB," but the reality is that a growing number of organizations are finding that ISA Server 2006 provides an excellent fit into their environments, and allows for a degree of security previously nonexistent. At a minimum, ISA should at least be evaluated for inclusion into an environment, particularly for functions in which it currently excels, such as securing Outlook Web Access or providing for secured web proxy functionality.

Keeping this in mind, several key misconceptions about ISA Server 2006 should be dispelled. These misconceptions are as follows:

▶ **ISA Server 2006 is only a proxy server**—This misconception often stems from the history of ISA Server, when it was named Proxy Server 1.x/2.x. One of the reasons for the name change to the Internet Security and Acceleration Server was to move away from this concept, and highlight the fact that ISA is a security device at heart.

▶ **ISA clients require special client software**—Some organizations avoid looking at ISA as a solution under the mistaken belief that if clients are to utilize ISA Server, they need special client software. Although there is an ISA Firewall client that provides for advanced securing and auditing functionality, it is not required to utilize this type of client to use ISA Server. ISA can easily scan and filter traffic from any type of client on any connected network.

▶ **ISA Server is not a real firewall**—This misconception is often manifested in the fact that ISA is often referred to as simply "the ISA server," and packet-filter solutions are referred to as "the firewall." In reality, ISA owns as much or more of a claim to the title of "firewall" as it filters network traffic across all layers of the network model, and not just the lower layers as traditional packet filter firewalls provide. If a distinction needs to be made between the technologies, a good term to use to describe ISA could be an Application-Layer Firewall (ALF).

▶ **ISA can't be deployed unless it completely replaces existing firewalls and security infrastructure**—Microsoft is partly to blame for this misconception. The marketing push for ISA and the examples that are used on their websites essentially position ISA as the end-all security solution, meant to replace all other firewalls, stateful inspection devices, and intrusion detection systems. In reality, however, a large number of ISA servers currently deployed exist in the DMZ of an existing firewall and provide an additional layer of security to existing security and firewall protections. In reality, it becomes much easier to sell ISA as a solution if security administrators understand that existing security is not replaced, but only added to.

▶ **ISA servers have to be domain members**—This misconception alone has kept many organizations away from deploying ISA in their environments. The truth is that ISA 2000 was severely limited if it wasn't a domain member, and Microsoft sought to fix this with ISA Server 2006. Fortunately, Microsoft has provided for much improved support of ISA servers that are not domain members. The capability to use RADIUS servers for authentication and Active Directory in Application Mode (ADAM) for storage of Enterprise arrays allows for workgroup member ISA servers to have the same capabilities as domain members.

Multi-Networking with ISA Server 2006

ISA Server 2006 introduced "multi-networking" support. What this means is that it is possible to deploy an ISA server across multiple physical network segments, as illustrated in Figure 5.1. The goal of this is to filter, control, and monitor the traffic that traverses between the networks. In essence, this allows ISA to then become a true firewall for the traffic between multiple network segments.

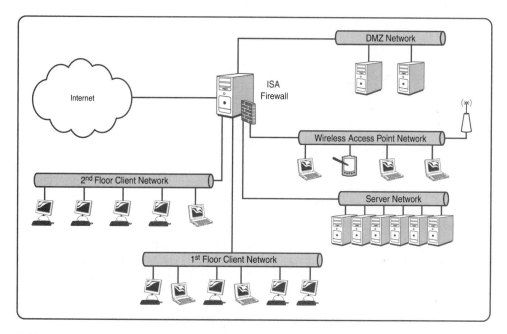

FIGURE 5.1   Examining ISA multi-networking support.

This functionality is a true departure from the tedious ISA 2000 concept of the Local Address Table (LAT), which effectively allowed for a concept of only an internal network and an external network. Now, with ISA Server 2006, multiple networks can be configured, and specific ISA rules can be established based on the network origin and destination.

Setting Up a Perimeter Network with ISA

Multi-networking capabilities in ISA Server 2006 allow for the creation of a traditional perimeter (DMZ) network. This network model, shown in Figure 5.2, isolates Internet-facing services into a dedicated network that has little access to resources in the internal network. The idea behind this model is that if one of the servers in the DMZ were to be compromised, the attacker would have access to only DMZ resources, and would not be able to directly hit any of the clients or servers on the internal network.

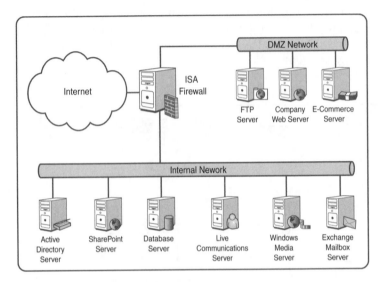

FIGURE 5.2   Viewing a perimeter network model.

Establishing a perimeter network is as simple as putting a third network card into an ISA firewall and setting up a dedicated network. The third NIC is then plugged into that network to establish ISA's presence in the network and force traffic through the ISA server. The final step is to define the IP address of the network in the ISA console and to set up the network and firewall rules between the new perimeter network and the internal network. More information on these topics, including step-by-step instructions, can be found later in this chapter.

Deploying Additional Networks

ISA is not limited to three defined networks. On the contrary, the software is limited only to setting up as many networks as there are network cards in the server itself. Theoretically, additional networks can be established for wireless access points, server-only networks, client networks, and any other type of network. Defining the network is as straightforward as configuring the proper network definitions and network rules in the ISA console.

Defining ISA Firewall Networks

As previously mentioned, ISA is fully capable of supporting numerous networks, and makes it possible to create firewall rules that specifically allow or deny traffic from certain networks to other networks. For example, HTTP traffic could be allowed by default from the internal network to the external network, but not from the internal network to the perimeter network. Many different scenarios exist for these types of deployments, and it is therefore ideal to gain a better understanding of how ISA defines networks and how an ISA firewall can be set up to protect them.

Understanding ISA's Concept of a Network

The standard definition of a network, loosely described, is quite simply a group of inter-connected computers and network devices, all able to communicate with each other on the same segment.

ISA Server 2006, on the other hand, actually defines a network in a somewhat different way. A network in ISA Server 2006 is all the connected physical networks that are routable from one of ISA's network cards. For example, in Figure 5.3, ISA defines the physical network subnets of 10.10.1.x, 10.10.2.x, 10.10.3.x, 10.10.10.x, and 10.10.11.x as one ISA network, because only a single network card is connected to the logical grouping of subnets (10.10.1.1).

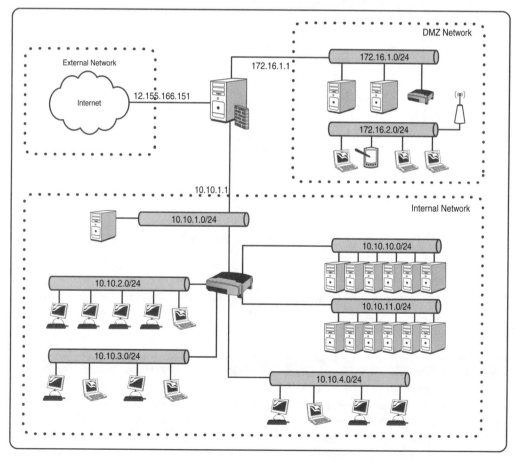

FIGURE 5.3   Understanding ISA networks.

Any time ISA sees source IP addresses within the range that it has defined for this network, it assumes that they originated from that network.

CAUTION

It is important to list all the physical subnets of which a network is composed in the ISA Console. If all subnets are not listed, ISA assumes that clients in unlisted subnets are simply spoofing their IP addresses, and denies them access through the server.

Each network is defined on the ISA server itself and can be viewed from the Networks tab of the Networks node, similar to what is shown in Figure 5.4.

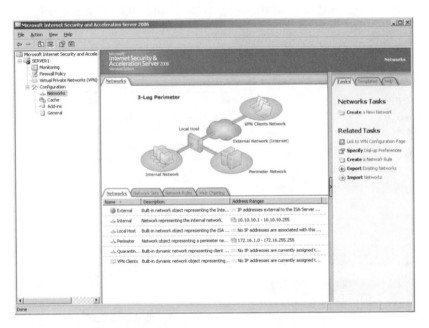

FIGURE 5.4   Viewing ISA networks.

Creation of new networks can be accomplished by using the Create a New Network task in the Tasks pane or through running the Network Template wizard, described in the following section of this chapter.

NOTE

One important factor to keep in mind when connecting ISA to a complex routed network such as the one displayed in Figure 5.4 is that manual "route add" statements need to be added to the route table within ISA to allow it to properly route the traffic that is destined for those subnets that are not directly attached to it. For example, one statement that would be added to the ISA server in the figure would be:

route -p add 172.16.2.0 mask 255.255.255.0 172.16.1.254

This statement would add a persistent route (the -p tells it to always re-create the route statement after a reboot) that tells ISA that any traffic in the 172.16.2.0/24 network should be routed through the 172.16.1.254 address, which in this example corresponds to the IP of the router illustrated in the DMZ network.

Understanding Network Rules with ISA Server 2006

Network rules in ISA Server 2006 define the relationships that exist between the various defined ISA networks. Two types of relationships can be defined as part of ISA network rules, and it is important to understand the differences between the two. The two forms of network relationships are the following:

▶ **Network Address Translation (NAT)**—A NAT relationship between networks is one where the source IP of a client is hidden, and instead replaced by the IP address of the ISA server on the destination network. This is most often the type of relationship that exists between a private IP range on an internal network, such as 10.x.x.x or 192.168.x.x, and a public IP range, such as the IP addresses on the Internet. In this scenario, when a client with an IP address of 10.10.10.200 tries to access a web server on the Internet, the web server sees the request coming from the Internet IP address (such as 63.240.93.138) of the ISA server. This concept allows for large IP ranges to be established on an internal network without any waste of the dwindling supply of public IP addresses on the Internet. NAT relationships in ISA Server 2006 are one-way.

▶ **Route**—A route relationship defined between ISA networks essentially allows the ISA server to act as a router between two distinct network segments. When resources from one network are requested in another, the requester and the target see the real IP addresses of each other. Simply creating a route relationship does not open communications between networks, however: ISA requires firewall rules to be set up for that functionality. The relationship simply defines how allowed traffic will be handled. Route relationships in ISA Server 2006 are two-way.

Working with the Default Network Templates

ISA Server 2006 streamlines the way that networks, network rules, and firewall rules are applied to new servers by including default templates that can be applied to servers. These templates define what role an ISA server holds and sets up the appropriate types of access to match that role.

Network templates support various ISA deployment options, including firewall deployments. The various network templates that are included in ISA Server 2006 Standard Edition are as follows:

▶ **Edge Firewall**—This template configures the ISA server as a dual-NIC system that provides traditional firewall functionality, with one NIC connected to the Internet and the other to the internal network. This template is the traditional deployment model for ISA Server.

▶ **3-Leg Perimeter**—This template expands the edge firewall template design to include a third-NIC connected to a Perimeter (DMZ) network.

▶ **Front Firewall**—A front firewall is an ISA server that is deployed as a dual-NIC server, but one that works in combination with a back firewall to provide two routes out of a network that is sandwiched between both ISA firewalls.

▶ **Back Firewall**—The back firewall template applies rules that provide for the second ISA server in the front/back firewall design already described.

▶ **Single Network Adapter**—A single network adapter template, commonly deployed for caching-only servers or for reverse-proxy capabilities in an existing packet-filter firewall DMZ, provides a template for a server with a single NIC. Although not a traditional firewall, this configuration is actually quite common for securing services such as OWA and web sites.

Deploying an ISA Firewall Using the Edge Firewall Template

When deploying ISA Server 2006 as a firewall, which is the focus of this particular chapter, several of the default network templates can be used to configure the initial server settings. Each template is used in different scenarios, depending on the specific firewall role that the ISA server is to fulfill. The most basic ISA firewall is the edge server role, and the process for configuring an edge server is described in the following section.

> **NOTE**
>
> If the firewall to be deployed has three NICs and will be deployed with a perimeter (DMZ) network, the 3-leg perimeter template would be the logical choice instead. A specific example of deploying the 3-leg perimeter network template is provided in Chapter 3, "Exploring ISA Server 2006 Tools and Concepts."

To use the Network Template wizard to configure a new ISA Server system as an edge firewall, perform the following steps:

1. Open the ISA Server Management Console and select the Networks node by clicking on it in the console tree.

2. Select the Templates tab in the Tasks pane.

3. Click on Edge Firewall from the list of templates, as shown in Figure 5.5.

4. At the Welcome dialog box, click Next to continue.

5. Ignore the Export dialog box and click Next to continue.

> **CAUTION**
>
> The Network Template wizard overwrites current configuration settings, including firewall policy rules and network rules. It was designed to be used when deploying new servers, and would normally not be used to modify existing settings. If a new network were added, for example, it would make more sense to simply manually create the network, rather than have the Template wizard overwrite existing customizations.

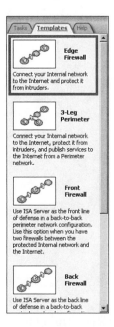

FIGURE 5.5   Viewing the network templates.

6. At the subsequent dialog box, which allows for the internal network to be configured, click Add Adapter.

7. Check the box for the network card that is attached to the internal network.

8. When finished adding all IP ranges that should compose the internal network, click
   Next to continue.
   The subsequent dialog box, shown in Figure 5.6, allows for the creation of a default
   policy, which will automatically create firewall rules based on the needs of the organization. Carefully review which policy will be needed by clicking on each option to
   see which rules will be created. The policies listed are described as follows:

   ▶ **Block All**—This option does not create any firewall rules automatically. It is up
     to the administrator to create the appropriate policies after the wizard has been
     run.

   ▶ **Block Internet Access, Allow Access to ISP Network Services**—This option
     creates rules that only allow DNS access from internal clients to the external
     network. It is used in situations when clients get their DNS services from an
     Internet Service Provider (ISP).

   ▶ **Allow Limited Web Access**—This option, more common in many organiza-
     tions, creates firewall rules that allow web browsing via the HTTP, HTTPS, and
     FTP ports to the external network. It also creates rules that grant VPN clients
     full access to the internal network.

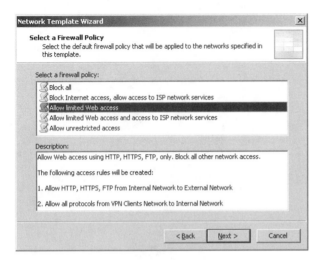

FIGURE 5.6   Creating a default policy for the ISA network template.

> ▶ **Allow Limited Web Access and Access to ISP Network Services**—This option
>   configures the same rules as the Allow Limited Web Access option, with an
>   additional rule to allow DNS to the external network (for ISP services).

> ▶ **Allow Unrestricted Access**—This option, although definitely not the most
>   secure, opens all ports from the internal protected networks to the Internet
>   and to the DMZ network. It does not, however, allow the external network to
>   have any type of access to internal networks.

9. Select the firewall policy from the options, using the preceding criteria as a guide-
    line. In this example, the Allow Limited Web Access and Access to ISP Network
    Services policy is chosen. Click Next to continue.

10. Review the options on the completion dialog box and click Finish to create the
    template, network rules, and firewall rules.

11. Click the Apply button that appears in the upper portion of the Details pane.

12. Click OK at the configuration confirmation dialog box.

Reviewing and Modifying Network Rules

After the wizard has completed, the networks, network rules, and firewall rules will have
been created and can be customized as necessary. In certain cases, it may be necessary to
modify some of the settings that the wizard created, particularly if changes have been
made or new networks need to be added to an environment after it has been placed into
production.

Modifying Network Rules

Network rules, after they are put into place, are not changed often because the relationship between networks is often quite static. In certain cases, however, modifications may be necessary. If those circumstances arise, the task of modifying the rules is relatively straightforward. To modify an existing network rule, perform the following steps:

1. From the ISA Console, click on the Networks node in the console tree.
2. Click on the Network Rules tab in the Details pane.
3. Double-click on the particular network rule to be modified.
4. From the dialog box shown in Figure 5.7, reconfigure the network rules as necessary, making changes to Source Networks, Destination Networks, or the Network Relationship.

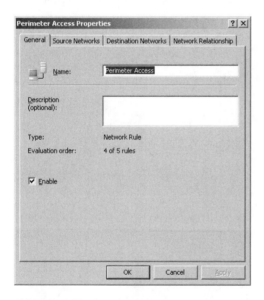

FIGURE 5.7   Modifying network rules.

5. Click OK when the changes are complete.
6. Click Apply to apply the changes and then click OK.

Creating New Network Rules

Creating a new network rule is primarily done only when a major change to the ISA firewall configuration has taken place, such as when a new network has been added to the server. In addition, this procedure can be used if the Network Template wizard is not run on a new server and manual methods of configuring the network rules are required. To create a new network rule, perform the following tasks:

1. From the ISA Console, click on the Networks node in the console tree.
2. Click on the Network Rules tab in the Details pane.
3. Click on the Tasks tab in the Tasks pane.
4. Click the link entitled Create a New Network Rule.
5. Enter a descriptive name for the network rule and click Next to continue.
6. On the Network Traffic Sources dialog box, click Add.
7. Select the network or network set that will be added as a source of the rule and then click Add, Close, and Next to continue.
8. For destination, click Add and perform the same process, this time selecting the network or network set that will be the destination set. Click Next when complete.
9. Select the type of relationship to configure, NAT or Route, as shown in Figure 5.8. Click Next to continue.

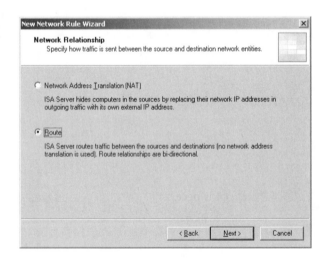

FIGURE 5.8   Creating new network rules.

10. Review the settings and click Finish.
11. Click Apply and then click OK to enable the new rule.

Understanding Firewall Policy Rules

Firewall policy rules are distinct from network rules in that they define what types of traffic and applications will be supported between the network segments. For example, an administrator may want to configure a firewall rule to allow web traffic from internal clients to the Internet. Firewall policy rules, shown in Figure 5.9, are the heart of ISA's firewall functionality. They define what is allowed and what is denied for specific networks, users, and protocols.

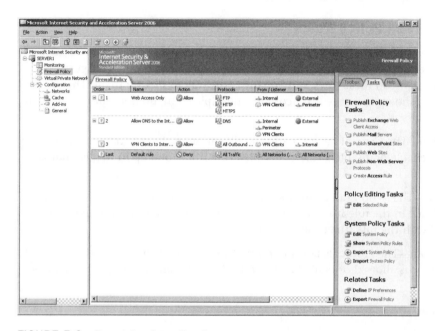

FIGURE 5.9   Examining firewall policy.

Firewall policy configuration should be well understood before ISA administration is attempted. Incorrectly configured rules can open up the wrong type of access to an environment and invite hackers in. It is therefore important to audit these settings on a regular basis as well to ensure that they are set in the way that is necessary for functional security.

The basic rule of thumb with ISA firewall policy rules is to deny all traffic unless a specific need has been established that the traffic will be allowed. The key to a successful ISA firewall deployment is to identify the entire range of functionality that will be necessary in advance, and then to create individual rules to reflect that functionality.

Firewall rules are applied to network traffic from top to bottom in the list. This is important to note because specific rules may need to be applied before other ones are. For example, if a rule at the top of the list is set to deny HTTP traffic to a particular network segment, and a later rule allows it, the traffic is denied because it hits the upper rule first. Rule placement is therefore an important component of an ISA firewall policy.

To move rules up or down in the policy list, select a rule by clicking on it and then click the link entitled Move Selected Rules Down or Move Selected Rules Up, depending on the specific need.

It should be noted that the last rule on an ISA server is the default rule to deny all traffic if not already specified. So if there isn't a specific rule above the default rule that allows for a certain protocol or activity, that protocol is blocked by the default rule. This rule exists to preserve security: The ISA server is configured to allow only predefined activities to occur, and anything not explicitly stated is disallowed.

Modifying Firewall Policy Rules

If the Network Template wizard was run, and a default policy other than Block All was enacted, then a set of predefined rules should already exist on the newly configured ISA server. Double-clicking on these rules individually is the way to modify them. The properties box for a rule, shown in Figure 5.10, contains multiple configuration options on each of the tabs as follows:

- ▶ **General tab**—The General tab allows for modification of the rule name and also can be used to enable or disable a rule. A disabled rule still shows up in the list, but is not applied.

- ▶ **Action tab**—The Action tab defines whether the rule allows or denies the type of traffic defined in the rule itself. In addition, it gives the option of logging traffic associated with the rule (the default) or not.

- ▶ **Protocols tab**—The Protocols tab is important in the rule definition. It defines what type of traffic is allowed or denied by the rule. The rule can be configured to apply

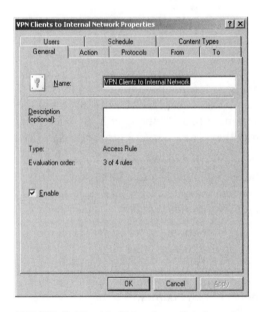

FIGURE 5.10   Modifying firewall policy rules.

to all outbound traffic, selected protocols, or all outbound traffic except for the types selected. Default protocol definitions that come with ISA Server can be used, as well as any custom protocol definitions that are created. In addition, this tab is where the port filtering and Application-layer filtering options are accessed, via the Filtering and Ports buttons.

▶ **From tab**—The From tab simply defines from which network or networks the originating traffic to which the rule applies will come.

▶ **To tab**—The To tab reverses this, and makes it possible to define for what destination network or networks the particular traffic is aimed.

▶ **Users tab**—The Users tab, normally set to All Users by default, is used only when the full ISA Firewall client is deployed on client desktops. The client software allows unique users to be identified, allowing for specific rules to apply to each one as a group or individual user. For example, a group could be created whose members have full web access, whereas others are restricted.

▶ **Schedule tab**—The Schedule tab allows for the rule to apply during only specific intervals, and to be inactive in others.

▶ **Content Types tab**—The Content Types tab enables an administrator to specify whether the rule is applied to only specific types of HTTP traffic, or whether it applies to all traffic.

After any changes are made, click the OK button, click Apply in the Details pane, and click OK again to save changes to the rule.

Creating Firewall Policy Rules

Firewall policy rules are powerful and highly customizable, and can be used to set up and secure access to a wide range of services and protocols. So it may seem surprising that creating an access rule to allow or deny specific types of traffic is relatively straightforward. To set up a new rule, perform the following steps:

1. From the ISA Management Console, click on the Firewall Policy node in the console tree.

2. Click on the Tasks tab in the Tasks pane.

3. Click the link entitled Create Access Rule.

4. Enter a descriptive name for the new rule and click Next.

5. Select whether the rule will allow or deny traffic and click Next.

6. On the next dialog box, choose whether the rule will apply to all traffic, all traffic except certain protocols, or selected protocols. In this example, Selected protocols is selected. Click the Add button to add them.

7. To add the protocols, select them from the Protocols list shown in Figure 5.11 and click Add and then Close. The list is sorted by category to provide for ease of selection.

FIGURE 5.11   Creating firewall access rules.

8. Click Next to continue to the Source Network dialog box.

9. Click Add to add a source for the rule and then select the source network by clicking Add and then clicking Close.

10. Click Next to continue to the Destination Network dialog box.

11. At the Destination Network dialog box, click Add to add a destination for the rule, select the destination network by clicking Add and then clicking Close, and click Next to continue.

12. Leave the User Sets dialog box at the defaults and click Next.

13. Review the settings and click Finish.

14. Click Apply in the Details pane and click OK after it has been confirmed.

Examining Advanced ISA Firewall Concepts

In general, creation of firewall policy rules and network policy rules comprise the bulk of the types of activities that an ISA firewall administrator will perform. Specific advanced tasks, however, should be understood when deploying ISA Server as a firewall.

Publishing Servers and Services

ISA Server 2006 can secure and "publish" a server to make it available to outside resources. The "publishing" of servers involves making web servers, OWA servers, SharePoint sites, Citrix servers, and the like available to the outside without directly exposing them to the traffic. The advantage to using ISA to publish servers is that it enables the ISA server to pre-authenticate connections to services and act as a bastion host to the network traffic, making sure that internal servers are never directly accessed from the Internet.

ISA Server 2006 supports publishing multiple types of servers, and it is important to understand how to set this up. Publishing scenarios, including step-by-step guides, are listed in Part III of this book, "Securing Servers and Services with ISA Server 2006."

Reviewing and Modifying the ISA System Policy

By default, ISA Server 2006 uses a set of firewall policy rules that grant the Localhost network specific types of functionality and access. Without system policies, for example, an ISA server itself would not be able to perform tasks such as pinging internal servers or updating software on the Windows Update website. Because the default rule is to deny all traffic unless otherwise specified, it is necessary to set up system policy rules to support specific types of access from the local ISA server.

System policy rules are enabled, but are not shown by default in ISA Server 2006. To view the system policy rules, click on the Show System Policy Rules link in the Tasks tab of the Firewall Policy node. The system policy rules, partially shown in Figure 5.12, are extensive, and it is important to understand what types of functionality are provided by each individual policy rule.

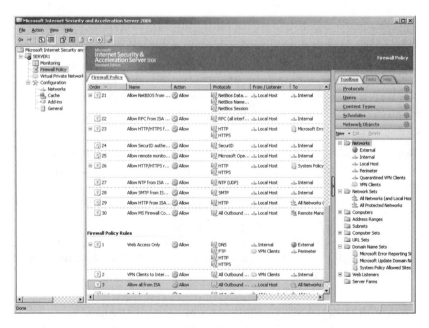

FIGURE 5.12   Viewing default system policy rules.

All the system policy rules are configurable through the System Policy Editor, shown in Figure 5.13. The System Policy Editor can be invoked simply by double-clicking on any of the system policy rules listed.

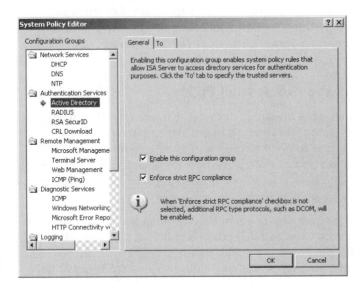

FIGURE 5.13   Editing system policies in the System Policy Editor.

The System Policy Editor divides the system policies into various configuration groups, which are subsequently organized into parent configuration groups as follows:

▶ **Network Services**—The Network Services configuration group contains the DHCP, DNS, and NTP configuration groups, which allow for the designation of how the ISA server interacts with these services. For example, configuring the DNS configuration group enables an ISA server to communicate using DNS protocols to the servers listed in the group.

▶ **Authentication Services**—The Authentication Services group contains the configuration groups for Active Directory, RADIUS, RSA SecurID, and CRL Download. Modifying these settings makes it possible to specify these types of authentication services, as well as enforce strict RPC compliance to Active Directory servers.

▶ **Remote Management**—The Remote Management group contains the Microsoft Management Console, Terminal Server, and ICMP (Ping) configuration groups. Modifying these settings allows for management of the ISA server, such as pinging ISA and using MMC consoles to access the server.

▶ **Diagnostic Services**—The Diagnostic Services group contains the ICMP, Windows Networking, Microsoft Error Reporting, and HTTP Connectivity Verifiers configuration groups, which enable the ISA server itself to report on health-related issues, as well as ping other systems on a network.

▶ **Logging**—The Logging group contains the Remote NetBIOS Logging and Remote SQL Logging configuration groups, which enable the ISA server to send its logs to other servers, such as an internal SQL database.

▶ **Remote Monitoring**—The Remote Monitoring group contains the Remote Performance Monitoring, Microsoft Operations Manager, and SMTP configuration groups, which enable monitoring services such as MOM to access the ISA server and SMTP emails to be sent from ISA.

▶ **Various**—The Various group contains the Scheduled Download Jobs and the Allowed Sites configuration groups. Of particular note is the Allowed Sites configuration group, which defines the System Policy Allowed Sites, as shown in Figure 5.14. Unless specific websites are added into this list, the ISA server cannot access them.

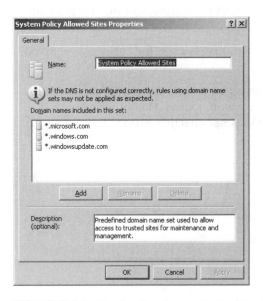

FIGURE 5.14   Viewing the System Policy Allowed Sites list.

Troubleshooting why an ISA server cannot perform certain functionality should always include a visit to the System Policy Editor. The built-in system policy rules allow for the configuration of multiple deployment scenarios with ISA Server 2006.

Summary

ISA Server 2006 fills many roles at many organizations. In certain environments, it provides dedicated web-proxy capabilities. In other locations, it serves as a dedicated OWA reverse-proxy server. All these deployment scenarios utilize specific pieces of ISA functionality, but the full range of ISA functionality can only be had when it is deployed as a dedicated Application-layer firewall.

The capability of ISA firewalls to provide for robust and secure stateful inspection of all traffic passing through them gives them an added edge over traditional packet-filtering firewalls. In addition, the capability to provide for advanced logging, server publishing, and VPN functionality positions ISA squarely in many environments for the long term.

Best Practices

- ▶ Deploy an ISA-secured perimeter network to isolate Internet-facing services from the rest of the internal network.

- ▶ Get acquainted with the System Policy Editor, and understand what default system policy rules are in place on the ISA server.

- ▶ Use the Network Template wizard for the initial configuration of a new ISA server, but manually create networks and network rules for any changes that are made after the server goes into production.

- ▶ Create access rules on the firewall only when there is a specific business need to do so. If there is not, leave the traffic denied.

- ▶ Create networks in ISA to correspond with each network card that is connected to a logical grouping of subnets connected by network routers. Do not create individual networks for multiple subnets to which ISA is not directly connected.

CHAPTER 6

Deploying ISA Server Arrays with ISA Server 2006 Enterprise Edition

ISA Server 2006 is a remarkably adaptable, scalable system that provides for a variety of deployment scenarios for organizations of many sizes. The Standard version of ISA Server 2006, for example, can be deployed as an edge firewall, reverse-proxy server, content-caching box, VPN server, or a combination of these roles. These capabilities satisfy the needs of many small to mid-sized organizations, but for those mid-sized to large organizations wanting to take advantage of those same features, Microsoft offers the Enterprise version of the software.

The Enterprise version of ISA Server 2006 enables organizations to scale their ISA implementations outward, providing for redundancy through Network Load Balancing (NLB) and making it possible to create standardized security configurations. With the Enterprise Edition, all the capabilities of the Standard Edition are extended and made more manageable, enabling ISA to scale to deployments of multiple sizes.

This chapter focuses on deployment scenarios involving the Enterprise version of ISA Server 2006. Differences between the Standard and Enterprise versions are discussed, and best-practice design considerations for the Enterprise version are outlined. In addition, a step-by-step process for configuring a load-balanced ISA Server 2006 Enterprise environment is outlined.

> **NOTE**
>
> The focus of this chapter is directly on those features of the Enterprise Edition that are different from the Standard, and that require different design and configuration. All other chapters in this book apply to the Standard Edition. The functionality in those chapters is the same as with the Enterprise Edition. Subsequently, if additional information on specific topics is desired, such as VPN support with the Enterprise Edition, the VPN chapters of this book should be referenced.

Understanding ISA Server 2006 Enterprise Edition

Unlike most Microsoft products, the Standard and Enterprise versions of the old version of ISA Server, ISA Server 2004 were released separately, approximately a half year apart from each other. This caused some confusion over what the Enterprise Edition was, and what distinguished it from the Standard version and the previous Standard and Enterprise versions of ISA 2000. With ISA Server 2006, however, they were released together, but there was still considerable confusion between the two different products. To more fully understand the Enterprise version, it is important first to note the differences between Standard and Enterprise.

Exploring the Differences Between the Standard and Enterprise Versions of ISA Server 2006

The Enterprise version of ISA Server 2006 contains all the features and functionality of the Standard version, in addition to the following features:

▶ **Network Load Balancing (NLB) Support**—Only the Enterprise version of ISA Server 2006 supports Network Load Balancing (NLB) clusters, allowing for automatic failover and load balancing of services across array members.

▶ **Cache Array Routing Protocol (CARP) Support**—The Enterprise version supports the Cache Array Routing Protocol (CARP) to properly balance web proxy requests across an array.

▶ **Configuration Storage Server (CSS)**—One of the biggest differences between Standard and Enterprise is that the Enterprise Edition uses a Configuration Storage Server (CSS) to store ISA rules and configuration. A CSS is an Active Directory in Application Mode (ADAM) implementation (essentially a "light" version of an Active Directory forest) and can be installed on non–ISA servers. This also allows for centralized management of ISA servers.

▶ **Enterprise and Array Policy Support**—As opposed to the Standard version, which allows only a single set of rules to be applied, ISA Enterprise allows a combination of global Enterprise policy rules, and individual array rules that are used in combination with one another.

Designing an ISA Server 2006 Enterprise Edition Environment

The Enterprise version of ISA Server 2006 is designed in a different way than the Standard version is. For instance, the CSS component itself changes the entire design equation. The concept of arrays also makes an ISA Enterprise version unique. It is subsequently important to understand what design factors must be taken into account when dealing with the EE.

The first design decision that must be made with the Enterprise Edition is where to store the CSS. The CSS is a critical server in an ISA topology, and can be installed on any Windows 2000/2003 server in an environment. In certain cases, it is installed on the actual ISA server itself, and in other cases, it is installed on a dedicated machine or on a domain controller.

In smaller environments, the CSS would be installed directly on the ISA server. In larger and more secure environments, however, the CSS would be installed on systems within the network, such as in the ISA environment displayed in Figure 6.1.

Because the Content Storage Server is essentially an LDAP-compliant, scaled-down version of an Active Directory forest, it can easily be replicated to multiple areas in an organization. It is ideal to configure at least one replica of the CSS server to maintain redundancy of ISA management.

NOTE

Although the ISA servers get their configuration information from a CSS server, they do not shut down or fail if the CSS is down. Instead, they continue to process rules based on the last configuration given to them from the CSS server.

The example illustrated in this chapter uses a single CSS server installed on an internal domain controller, as shown in Figure 6.2. In addition, step-by-step deployment guides to setting up two ISA Server 2006 Enterprise servers running as edge firewalls in a network load balanced array of ISA servers are outlined.

Although ISA Server Enterprise allows for a myriad of deployment models, this deployment scenario illustrates one of the more common ISA deployment scenarios, which is one that takes full advantage of ISA functionality. Other common deployment models, such as ISA deployment in a workgroup and unihomed ISA reverse-proxy systems, are similar in many ways, with slight variations to implementation.

Deploying the Configuration Storage Server (CSS)

The Configuration Storage Server (CSS) is the central repository for all of ISA's rules and configuration information, and is therefore an extremely important piece of the ISA Enterprise Environment. ISA Standard version does not have a CSS equivalent because the rules and configuration of the Standard version are all stored locally. It is important to understand how to deploy and work within the CSS model before deploying and administering ISA Server 2006 Enterprise Edition.

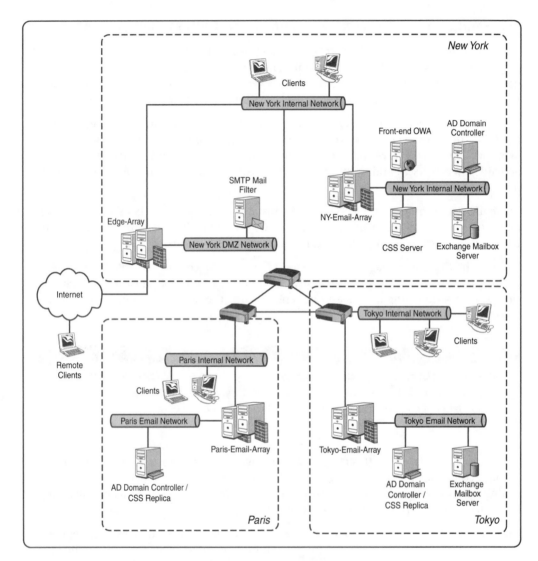

FIGURE 6.1   Examining a complex ISA Enterprise deployment.

Determining CSS Placement

As previously mentioned, there are several deployment scenarios for the CSS, starting with simpler, smaller deployments and moving up to larger deployments. These scenarios are as follows:

▶ CSS installed on the ISA server itself

▶ CSS installed on a separate server or servers running other services, such as a domain controller

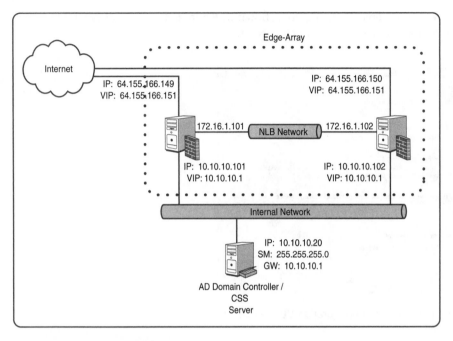

FIGURE 6.2   Conceptualizing the CSS deployment model illustrated in this chapter.

▶ CSS on a dedicated server

▶ Multiple CSS servers on multiple types of different servers

With CSS, the important thing to remember is that it should be secured and made highly redundant. In addition, there should be a local CSS replica relatively close to the ISA arrays themselves. The ISA servers need to constantly communicate to the CSS server to check for changes in policy.

Installing CSS

As soon as the decision has been made about where to install the CSS server, the install process can begin. The following procedure describes the installation of CSS onto a separate server—in this case, a domain controller:

1. Insert the ISA Server 2006 Media in the server's CD drive and wait for the setup dialog box to automatically appear. If it does not appear, double-click on the ISAAutorun.exe file in the root of the media directory.

2. Click on Install ISA Server 2006.

3. At the welcome screen, click Next to continue.

4. Select I Accept the Terms in the License Agreement and click Next.

5. Enter a User Name, Organization Name, and the Product Serial Number and click Next.

6. From the Setup Scenarios dialog box, shown in Figure 6.3, select to Install Configuration Storage Server and click Next.

FIGURE 6.3   Installing the Configuration Storage Server.

7. In the Component Selection dialog box, where ISA Server Management and Configuration Storage Server are selected for installation, leave the selections at the default and click Next.

8. From the Enterprise Installation Options, shown in Figure 6.4, select to Create a New ISA Server Enterprise and click Next.

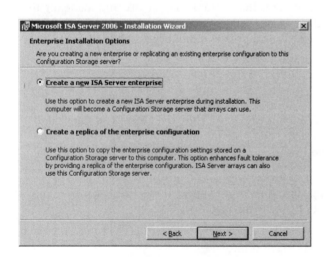

FIGURE 6.4   Creating a new ISA Server Enterprise.

9. At the warning dialog box about creating a new CSS, click Next.

10. If the CSS will be installed on a domain controller, the dialog box shown in Figure 6.5 will prompt for credentials that the CSS service will run under to be displayed. Enter the username and password of a domain admin account and click Next to continue.

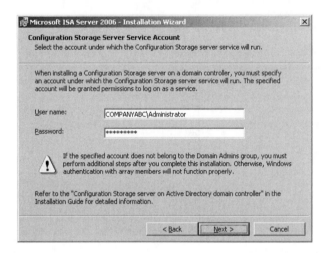

FIGURE 6.5   Configuring the login account for the CSS service.

11. Click the Install button to begin installing files.

12. After installation, click Finish.

13. Following installation, review the Protect the ISA Server Computer recommendations provided. This web file provides best-practice information on securing ISA components.

Setting Up Additional CSS Replicas

After the initial Enterprise has been created, it's possible to generate additional replicas of the Enterprise itself by re-running the setup and choosing to create a replica instead of a new Enterprise.

Setting Up Enterprise Networks and Policies

With a CSS Enterprise in place, the groundwork can be laid for the eventual introduction of the ISA servers. The key is to preconfigure information that will be global for all ISA servers and arrays within an organization. The ISA admin console, a default installation option on a CSS server, is used in this capacity, and can be run even before official ISA servers are installed. The console, shown in Figure 6.6, is slightly different than the Standard Edition console. Several Enterprise options have been added.

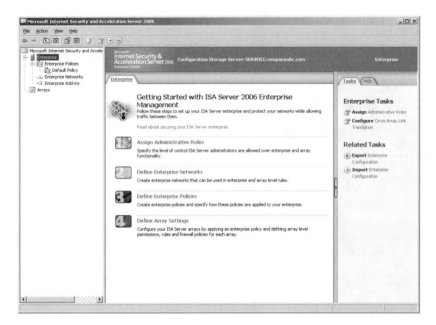

FIGURE 6.6   Exploring the ISA Enterprise admin console.

Although it is possible to wait to configure the options in the console until the servers are installed, it is often preferable to preconfigure them.

Delegating Administration of ISA

The first step that should be performed after the CSS Enterprise has been established is the delegation of administration to individual users or, preferably, groups of users. To delegate administration to a group, for example, perform the following steps:

1. On the server where CSS was installed, start the ISA Server 2006 Enterprise Admin Console (Start, All Programs, Microsoft ISA Server, ISA Server Management).

2. From the console tree, click on the Enterprise node.

3. In the Tasks tab of the Tasks pane, click on the link Assign Administrative Roles.

4. Click the Add button.

5. Enter the DOMAIN\Groupname into the Group or User field (or use the Browse button) and select a role that matches the group chosen, as is illustrated in Figure 6.7.

6. Click the Add button to add groups as necessary.

7. Click OK to close the dialog box.

8. Click Apply and then click OK to save the changes.

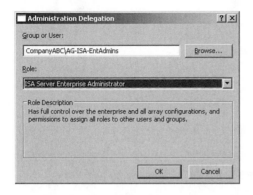

FIGURE 6.7   Delegating administration in ISA Enterprise Edition.

Defining Enterprise Networks

The Enterprise Console enables Enterprise networks to be defined and configured before ISA servers are installed. An Enterprise network is one that is defined for use by all ISA servers and arrays within an organization. For example, if a company's network were composed of three locations—Miami, Kiev, and Sapporo—and each location utilized a different network subnet, then each of these subnets could be defined within CSS as Enterprise networks. This makes it easier to create rules that apply to traffic to and from these networks and ensures that any changes made to the networks (such as new subnets added) are applied globally across all ISA servers.

In this example, a single internal network (10.10.10.0/24) is defined in the CSS Console as follows:

1. From the ISA Enterprise Console, navigate through the console tree to Enterprise, Enterprise Networks.

2. In the Tasks tab of the Tasks pane, click the link for Create a New Network.

3. When the wizard appears, enter a name for the network, such as CompanyABC-Internal, and click Next.

4. Under the Network Addresses dialog box, click Add Range.

5. Enter a Start address and an End address that define the internal network, as shown in Figure 6.8, and click OK.

6. Click Next.

7. Click Finish, Apply, and OK.

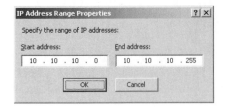

FIGURE 6.8   Defining the Enterprise internal network.

Establishing Enterprise Network Rules

Along with the Enterprise networks, Enterprise network rules can be defined to describe the relationship, either Route or NAT, between the various networks. In this example, a NAT relationship is configured between the newly created CompanyABC-Internal network and the external network as follows:

1. From the Enterprise Networks node in the console tree, click on the Create a Network Rule link in the Tasks tab of the Tasks pane.

2. Enter a name for the network rule, such as NAT—External and Internal, and click Next.

3. In the Network Traffic Sources, click the Add button.

4. Under Enterprise Networks, choose CompanyABC-Internal (or equivalent) and click Add.

5. Select External and click Add.

6. Click Close and click Next.

7. Under the Network Traffic Destinations dialog box, click Add.

8. Under Enterprise Networks, choose CompanyABC-Internal and click Add, then repeat for External. Click Close and Next when done.

9. Under Network Relationship, shown in Figure 6.9, choose Network Address Translation (NAT) and click Next to continue.

10. Click Finish, Apply, and OK to save the changes.

Creating Enterprise Policies

An Enterprise policy is one that, as the name suggests, is global to the entire ISA Enterprise. Enterprise policies are vessels for Enterprise access rules, and can be populated with various access rules that are global for all parts of an organization. It is convenient to create Enterprise policies to make it easier to implement global changes that may be dictated at an organization. For example, an Enterprise policy could be set up with several Enterprise access rules that allow web access and FTP access. A change in organizational policy to allow the Remote Desktop Protocol for all networks could be easily modified by adding an additional Enterprise access rule to an existing Enterprise policy.

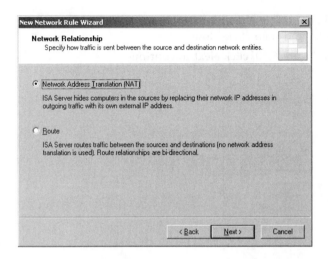

FIGURE 6.9   Defining the network relationship between ISA Enterprise networks.

By default, a single Enterprise policy already exists, with a default access rule to deny all connections. This is by design for security purposes. To create an additional Enterprise policy, do the following:

1. From the ISA Enterprise Console, click on the Enterprise Policies node.
2. In the Tasks tab of the Tasks pane, click the link for Create New Enterprise Policy.
3. Enter a name for the policy, such as CompanyABC Policy, and click Next.
4. Click Finish, Apply, and OK.

Creating Enterprise Access Rules for the Enterprise Policy

Each Enterprise policy can be populated with various Enterprise access rules. To create a single rule allowing web access, for example, perform the following steps:

1. From the ISA Console, navigate to Enterprise, Enterprise Policies, CompanyABC Policy (or equivalent).
2. From the Tasks tab in the Tasks pane, click the link for Create Enterprise Access Rule.
3. Enter a name for the Access rule, such as Web Access, and click Next.
4. Under Rule Action, select Allow and click Next.
5. Under the Protocols dialog box, choose Selected Protocols and click the Add button.

6. Under Common Protocols, choose HTTP and click Add, choose HTTPS and click Add, choose DNS and click Add, and then click Close.

7. At the dialog box displayed in Figure 6.10, click Next to continue.

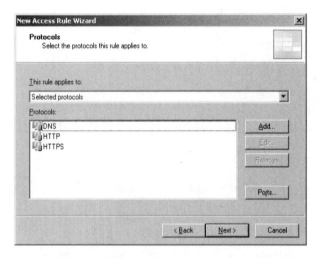

FIGURE 6.10   Adding a Web Access rule to the Enterprise policy.

8. From the Access Rule sources, click the Add button.

9. Under Enterprise Networks, choose CompanyABC-Internal (or equivalent), click Add, and then click Close.

10. Click Next to continue.

11. Under Access Rule Destinations, click the Add button.

12. Under Enterprise Networks, select the External network and click Add and Close.

13. Click Next to continue.

14. Under User Sets, accept the default of all users and click Next.

15. Verify the configuration in the final dialog box, shown in Figure 6.11, and click Finish.

16. Click Apply and OK to save the changes.

Changing the Order of Enterprise Policy Rules

With ISA Server 2006 Standard Edition, firewall policy rules are implemented in order from top to bottom. This is true as well with the Enterprise Edition, with one twist on the theme. Enterprise policies can be implemented either before array rules (described in later sections of this book) or after those array rules. They can be moved from one section to another, similar to what is displayed in Figure 6.12.

This concept can be useful if it's necessary to specify which rule is applied, and whether it is applied before or after different array rules are applied.

FIGURE 6.11   Finalizing a Web Access rule in the Enterprise policy.

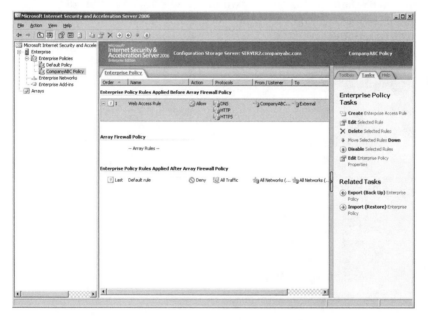

FIGURE 6.12   Changing the order of an Enterprise policy rule.

Creating and Configuring Arrays

ISA 2000 Enterprise Edition introduced the concept of an array, and ISA Server 2006 Enterprise improved upon it. Essentially, an array is a grouping of ISA servers that have the same NIC configuration and are connected to the same networks. They are meant to act as redundant load-balanced members of a network team, either with integrated Windows Load Balancing or through the use of a third-party load balancer.

For example, an organization may have an array of ISA servers acting as edge firewalls for an organization. If one of the array members were to go down, the other one would shoulder the load. There also may be other arrays within the organization that protect other critical network segments from internal intrusion. Essentially, arrays provide a critical measure of load balancing and redundancy to a security environment.

Creating Arrays

Arrays can be defined in CSS before the ISA servers have been installed. In this example, a single edge-firewall array is created via the following procedure:

1. From the ISA Enterprise Admin Console, click on the Arrays node in the console tree.

2. In the Tasks tab, click the Create New Array link.

3. Enter a name for the array, such as Edge-Array.

4. Under the Array DNS Name dialog box, shown in Figure 6.13, enter the Fully Qualified Domain Name (FQDN) of the array, such as edge-array.companyabc.com, and click Next to continue.

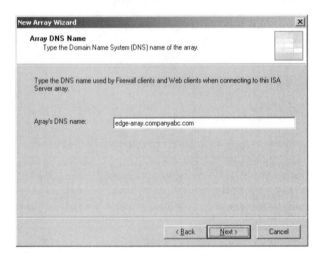

FIGURE 6.13   Creating an array.

5. In the Assign Enterprise Policy dialog box, select the customized policy previously created from the drop-down box, such as CompanyABC Policy, and click Next to continue.

6. Under the types of array firewall policy rules that can be created, leave all checked, as displayed in Figure 6.14, and click Next to continue.

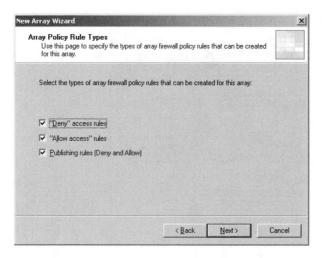

FIGURE 6.14   Defining array policy rule types.

NOTE

The Array Policy Rule Types dialog box allows the array to be restricted to specific types of rules, such as deny, allow, or publishing rules. This can be useful for securing an array.

7. Click Finish, OK, Apply, and OK to save the settings.

Configuring Array Settings

Creating an array opens up an entirely new set of nodes in the ISA Enterprise Admin Console, as shown in Figure 6.15. In fact, the array nodes may look familiar to an administrator familiar with the Standard version because they are nearly identical to that version.

To view and modify properties for the array, right-click on the array name and choose Properties. The following tabs, shown in Figure 6.16, are available for review of an array:

▶ **General**—Name and description of the array.

▶ **Policy Settings**—Which Enterprise policy to apply to the array and what types of policy rule can be applied.

▶ **Configuration Storage**—The FQDN of the main CSS server and an alternate server (if necessary), in addition to the definition of how often the CSS is checked for updates.

▶ **Intra-Array Credentials**—Defines what type of credentials (domain or workgroup) are used for intra-array communications.

▶ **Published Configuration Storage**—Used for environments where the CSS server is secured across a VPN connection.

▶ **Assign Roles**—Allows for delegation of administration at the array level.

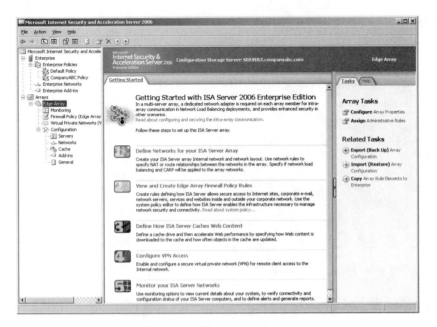

FIGURE 6.15   Examining the newly created array console settings.

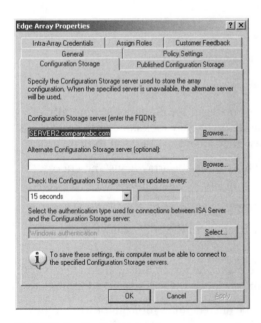

FIGURE 6.16   Examining the array properties tabs.

Creating the NLB Array Network

If Windows Network Load Balancing (NLB) will be used for the ISA servers, then an additional NIC needs to be added and an isolated network created between those two servers, as shown in Figure 6.2. This network is solely devoted to NLB traffic, which is required because the NLB operates only in unicast mode.

As well as being physically set up to provide for NLB, the network needs to be defined within the array. To define this network, do the following:

1. In the ISA Enterprise Admin Console, click on Arrays, Edge-Array (Array Name), Configuration, Networks node in the console tree.

2. In the Tasks tab of the Tasks pane, click the link for Create a New Network.

3. In the Network Name field, enter **Edge-Array-NLB** and click Next.

4. In the Network Type dialog box, shown in Figure 6.17, select Perimeter Network and click Next.

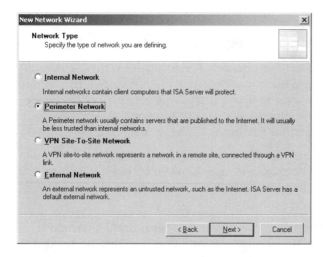

FIGURE 6.17   Creating the NLB Array network.

5. Under Network Addresses, click Add Range.

6. Enter a start address and end address, such as 172.16.1.0 and 172.16.1.255, and click OK.

7. After the address is entered, click Next to continue.

8. Click Finish, Apply, and OK.

Defining Array Policies

After the array has been configured, standard firewall policies can be defined for the array. These policies follow the same concepts as the Standard version follows, and specific chapters in this book can be used to configure these policies. For example, a mail publishing rule can be used to secure an OWA site through the array, or a SQL Server can be published. The options are nearly endless.

As previously mentioned, the specific array policies are applied after the initial enterprise policies are, and before the final enterprise policies.

Installing and Configuring ISA Enterprise Servers

After all the preconfiguration via the CSS has been performed, the actual installation of ISA Server 2006 Enterprise Edition can be accomplished. Many of the same design factors that applied to the Standard version also apply to the Enterprise version, but it is useful to review these prerequisites and best practices before installing ISA.

Satisfying ISA Server Installation Prerequisites

ISA Server 2006 Enterprise version has the same hardware prerequisites as the Standard version, with Microsoft recommending a minimum of 256MB of RAM, a 550MHz Pentium II, and 150MB of disk space to operate. That said, an Enterprise deployment of ISA Server should never be installed on hardware as limited as that, and additional RAM (1GB or more), faster processors, and more disk space will invariably be needed.

It is difficult to pin down the exact hardware that will be required, but ISA itself does not require much in terms of resources. Performance metrics allow for up to a T3 of network input into an ISA server before an additional server is needed, so it is not common to run into performance issues when a system is properly sized.

ISA Server 2006 Enterprise Edition can run on either Windows Server 2003 or Windows 2000 Server versions, but it is *highly* recommended to install it on Windows Server 2003 only. This version is the most secure and integrates better with ISA Server 2006.

ISA Server 2006 operates if it is installed onto servers that are domain members, and it also functions on servers that are not domain members (workgroup members). Workgroup member ISA servers require server certificates to be installed between CSS members, however, and also are limited to authenticating users using the RADIUS protocol.

Adding the ISA Server(s) to the Managed ISA Server Computer Set

Before any ISA servers can be added to an array, they must be defined on the CSS server, in a group known as the "Managed ISA Server Computers" computer set. This predefined computer set exists to further secure the ISA environment by ensuring that only the proper servers are installed into the ISA Enterprise.

To add a server or servers into this computer set, perform the following steps:

1. From the ISA Management console on the CSS server, navigate to Arrays - ArrayName (i.e., Edge-Array) - Firewall Policy.

2. In the Tasks pane, click on the Toolbox tab.

3. Navigate to Network Objects - Computer Sets.

4. Right-click on the Managed ISA Server Computers computer set and choose Properties.

5. Click the Add button and choose Computer from the drop-down box.

6. Enter the name of the ISA server that will be added and an IP address, as illustrated in Figure 6.18.

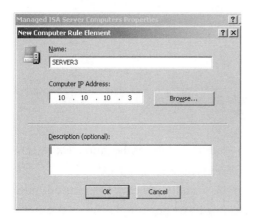

FIGURE 6.18   Adding an ISA server to the Managed ISA Server computer set.

7. Click OK to save the changes.

8. Repeat steps 5–7 for any additional ISA servers to be installed.

9. When servers have been added, as illustrated in Figure 6.19, click OK, Apply, and OK to save the changes.

Installing the Enterprise Edition on the Server

After a server for ISA has been identified, the operating system should be installed with default options. See Chapter 2, "Installing ISA Server 2006," for a step-by-step guide to this process. After the OS is installed, the server should be added to the domain (if it will be a domain member). Afterward, ISA can be installed via the following process:

1. Insert the ISA Server 2006 Enterprise Edition media into the server and wait for the autorun screen to be displayed (or double-click on the ISAAutorun.exe file).

2. Click the Install ISA Server 2006 link.

3. Click the Next button.

4. At the license agreement dialog box, click I Accept the Terms in the License Agreement and click Next.

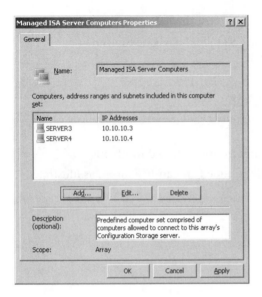

FIGURE 6.19   Finalizing the addition of the servers to the computer set.

5. Enter a User Name, Organization Name, and Product Serial Number and click Next.

6. Under Setup Scenarios, select Install ISA Server Services and click Next.

7. In the Component Selection dialog box, leave the defaults and click Next to continue.

8. On the Locate Configuration Storage Server dialog box, shown in Figure 6.20, enter the FQDN of the CSS server (for example, server2.companyabc.com) and click Next to continue.

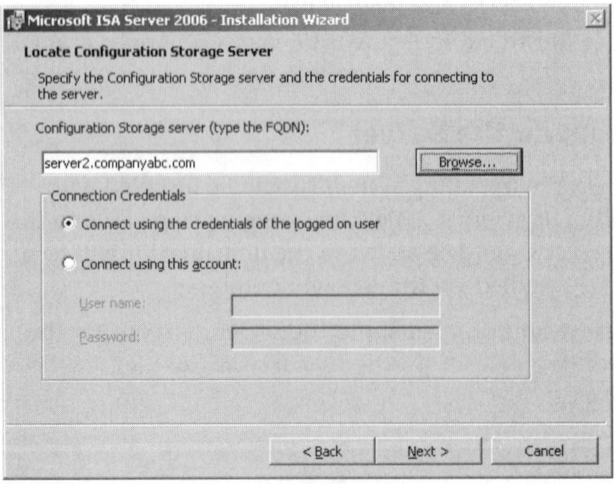

FIGURE 6.20   Installing the ISA Server services.

9. Under Array Membership, select Join an Existing Array and click Next.

10. Under the Join Existing Array dialog box, shown in Figure 6.21, enter the Array name (or browse to select) and click Next.

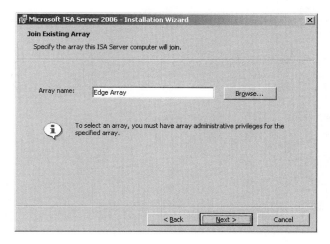

FIGURE 6.21   Joining the server to an array.

11. The subsequent dialog box allows for the type of authentication to be selected. This enables nondomain ISA servers to have a certificate installed. In this example, because the servers are domain members, choose Windows authentication and click Next.

12. In the Internal Network dialog box, click the Add button. In the subsequent Addresses dialog box, click the Add Network button.

13. Check the box for the previously defined internal network, such as what is displayed in Figure 6.22, and then click OK.

14. Click OK, Next, and Next to continue.

15. Click Install.

16. Click the Finish button when installation completes.

After ISA setup, the install process opens Internet Explorer and provides links to ISA resources at Microsoft. It is important to check the latest list of patches and downloads on these links and install them if they are required.

In this scenario, two ISA servers are installed and deployed. The second server should be installed through the same process as was defined previously. The one difference to this process is that the internal network is not prompted for definition; it is defined already.

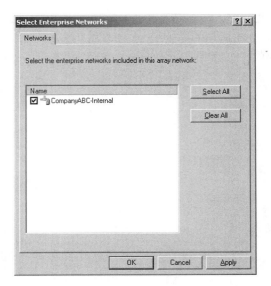

FIGURE 6.22   Picking an Enterprise network.

Configuring the Intra-Array Communication IP Address

Each array member needs to be configured to use the proper IP address on the NLB isolated network for communications between array members. To configure this setting, do the following:

1. From the ISA Console on the newly installed server, navigate to Arrays, Edge-Array, Configuration, Servers.

2. In the Details pane, right-click the server name and choose Properties.

3. Select the Communication tab.

4. Choose the IP address of the array network adapter from the drop-down box, as shown in Figure 6.23.

5. Click OK, Apply, and OK.

Perform the same process on the second server as well. The array members are now ready for additional rule and array configuration. The final step in this scenario is to enable load balancing of network traffic and cache traffic.

Configuring Network Load Balancing and Cache Array Routing Protocol (CARP) Support

Network Load Balancing (NLB) is a Windows service that enables network traffic to be shared between multiple servers, while appearing to the client to be captured and processed by a single server's IP address. It provides for load sharing between NLB cluster members, and also provides for redundancy if one of the NLB members becomes unavailable. Only the Enterprise version of ISA Server 2006 natively supports NLB.

The Cache Array Routing Protocol (CARP) is a protocol that helps to balance content-caching traffic sent to a network server. It is also supported only with the Enterprise version.

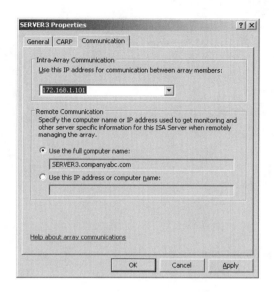

FIGURE 6.23   Selecting the intra-array communication IP address.

Understanding Bi-Directional Affinity with Network Load Balancing (NLB)

One of the main challenges faced by the ISA team in regards to Network Load Balancing was enabling and supporting bi-directional affinity with NLB. Bi-directional affinity is basically needed to ensure that traffic sent from one network to another, and sent back to the client from that remote network, is properly sent and received through the same ISA server the entire time. If bi-directional affinity is not enabled, then traffic sent through one ISA server might be routed through the NLB cluster to the wrong server, which causes sporadic serious issues.

Enabling NLB for ISA Networks

To enable NLB on an ISA member server, perform the following procedure on each server:

1. From the ISA Server Admin Console, navigate through the console tree to Arrays, Edge-Array, Configuration, Networks node.

2. In the Tasks tab of the Tasks pane, click the link for Enable Network Load Balancing Integration.

3. At the welcome screen, click Next to continue.

4. At the Select Load Balanced Networks dialog box, check the boxes next to the external and internal networks (do not check the box for the Edge-Array-NLB network).

5. With the external network selected, click Set Virtual IP.

6. Enter an IP and mask of the virtual IP that will be set up for the external network (for example, 12.155.166.151, Mask:255.255.255.0) and click OK.

7. Click on the internal network, and then click the Set Virtual IP button.

8. Enter an IP and mask of the virtual IP for the internal network, as shown in Figure 6.24, and click OK.

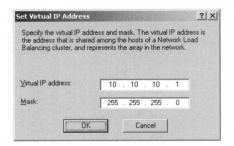

FIGURE 6.24   Entering the virtual IP for the internal network.

9. Click Next to continue.

10. Click Finish.

11. Click the Apply button at the top of the Details pane.

12. When prompted with the warning shown in Figure 6.25, click Save the Changes and Restart the Services and click OK.

13. Click OK.

With NLB in place, the ISA servers act as a single virtual IP address (VIP). Clients can be configured to use this IP address as their gateway, or it can be used as the destination for reverse proxy or server publishing rules.

Defining Cache Drives for CARP

Before the Cache Array Routing Protocol (CARP) can be enabled to provide for redundancy and enhancement of caching services, the actual cache drives first need to be configured on each ISA server. Perform the following process on each server:

1. From the ISA Console, navigate to Arrays, Edge-Array, Configuration, Cache.

2. Right-click on the server and choose Properties.

3. Under Maximum Cache Size, enter a number less than the total amount of space, as shown in Figure 6.26, and choose Set and OK.

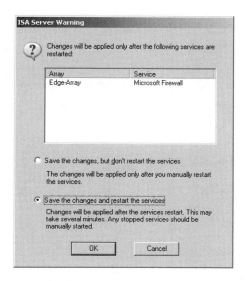

FIGURE 6.25   Restarting the services for NLB support.

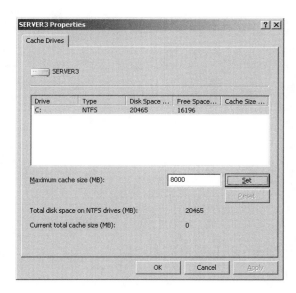

FIGURE 6.26   Enabling caching.

4. Click Apply.

5. When prompted, select to Save the Changes and Restart the Services and click OK.

Enabling CARP Support

After the cache drives have been defined, CARP can be easily enabled via the following process:

1. From the ISA Admin Console, navigate to Arrays, Edge-Array, Configuration, Networks.
2. In the Details pane, select the Networks tab.
3. Right-click on the internal network and choose Properties.
4. Click on the CARP tab.
5. Check the box for Enable CARP on This Network, as shown in Figure 6.27.

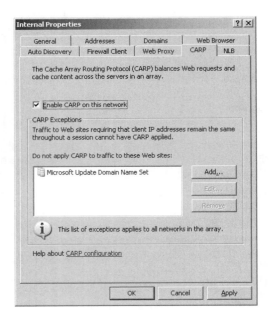

FIGURE 6.27   Enabling CARP.

6. Click on the Web Proxy tab.
7. Make sure that the Enable Web Proxy Clients is checked and click OK.
8. Click Apply and OK to save the changes.

Summary

ISA Server 2006 Enterprise Edition not only contains all the advanced firewall, VPN, and caching capabilities of the Standard version, it also allows for server redundancy and load balancing and the creation of common enterprise policies across an organization. Creating arrays, deploying Content Storage Servers, and establishing Enterprise networks are just some of the ways that the Enterprise Edition can be used to further secure and enhance the functionality of an environment.

Best Practices

► Install more than one CSS replica in an organization to provide for redundancy.

► Deploy CSS replicas on dedicated servers in large organizations, and on other multi-tasking servers such as domain controllers in mid-sized organizations.

► Enable Network Load Balancing for server redundancy.

► Synchronize all the ISA server clocks to an NTP time source to ensure that they are writing timestamps into logs accurately.

CHAPTER 7

Deploying ISA Server as a Reverse Proxy in an Existing Firewall DMZ

Although ISA Server can fit many roles within organizations, such as VPN server, edge firewall, content-caching device, and many more, it is not always used to fill these roles. In many deployment scenarios, ISA Server 2006 is used solely in its reverse-proxy functionality. In these configurations, ISA is typically deployed in the Perimeter (DMZ) network of an existing firewall, and protects web and related services such as Exchange Outlook Web Access (OWA) from external intrusion and attack. Although it does not take full advantage of ISA features, this is a perfectly valid deployment scenario, and a relatively common one at that.

Many organizations are finding that ISA Server 2006 provides for a relatively inexpensive solution to the problem of securing Internet-facing services. It doesn't require them to replace existing firewall or security infrastructure or make ISA a domain member. An ISA server, deployed with a single NIC, looks and acts like the target web or OWA server, while instead acting as a proxy for the traffic, intercepting it and scanning it at the Application layer of the TCP/IP stack. Indeed, this is often how ISA first makes it into an organization: as security dictates an answer to the problems faced when services are exposed to the Internet.

This chapter focuses on the deployment scenarios involved with deploying ISA as a Security Appliance in the DMZ network of an existing firewall. The differences in setup and configuration between this model and the other ISA deployment models are outlined, and best-practice configuration information on deploying ISA in this manner is provided, including such common tasks as securing OWA, SharePoint sites, and web servers.

ISA Server 2006 as a Security Appliance

An ISA server with a single connected NIC interface is still a very powerful tool. Although not a full firewall while deployed like this, the ISA server becomes a security appliance, similar to many of the other security products that are available. This deployment scenario is exceedingly common, so it is important to understand what ISA can do when deployed as a unihomed server, and what limitations it has as well.

Understanding How Reverse Proxies Work

To understand first what a reverse proxy is, it is important to fully define what a proxy server does in the first place. ISA Server 2006 was originally named Proxy Server 1.x/2.x. (The 2006 version is technically the 5.x version of the product.) The product was designed to assist clients in retrieving web and FTP content from the Internet, but had the clients route all their requests through the server.

The advantage to this approach is that Internet browsing is optimized because the server keeps copies of the pages that are accessed so that when another client requests the same page, the server simply gives that client the cached copy that it made. This eases Internet bandwidth constraints and accelerates the flow of content to the client. For more information on traditional forward proxy with ISA Server 2006, refer to Chapter 8, "Deploying ISA Server 2006 as a Content Caching Server."

Reverse proxy works in a similar way, except in this case the clients are on the Internet, and the server that is being accessed is in the organization's environment. This concept gave rise to the term "reverse" proxy, in that the client/server relationship is flipped when compared to a standard "forward" proxy. For example, Figure 7.1 illustrates how a reverse proxy protects internal servers by acting as a bastion host to the traffic.

The one additional difference between reverse proxy and forward proxy is that the reverse proxy does not cache the traffic, but instead only exists to secure the connection to the server by preventing any direct communications from untrusted networks to hit the servers.

There are many other reverse-proxy products in the market today. Some are considerably more expensive, and a small handful are less expensive than ISA Server 2006. For many organizations, however, the reverse-proxy capabilities of ISA Server have earned it a place as a dedicated security device deployed in the DMZs of their firewalls.

Deploying a Unihomed ISA Server as a Security Appliance

It is important to note that ISA Server 2006 does an extremely good job at providing reverse-proxy capabilities to organizations, in addition to the other types of functionality that it possesses. It was specifically designed to understand the types of communications that are supposed to occur over commonly used services such as Outlook Web Access and standard web page access. These factors have positioned ISA as one of the more attractive options for securing these particular services.

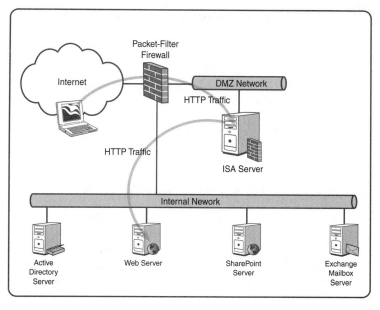

FIGURE 7.1   Understanding how reverse-proxy servers work.

That said, many organizations are not willing to simply throw away existing security infrastructure, such as packet-filter firewalls, VPN solutions, intrusion detection equipment, and the like. The real advantage in ISA's case is that it is not necessary to replace anything currently in place. Deploying ISA as a dedicated reverse-proxy security appliance simply adds a layer of security to an environment, and the only configuration required to existing firewalls in this deployment scenario is creating rules for the type of traffic (such as HTTP or HTTPS) needed to process the request.

One of the key points to this type of deployment scenario is that it removes the "religious" debates about Microsoft products from the conversation. It no longer becomes necessary to try to convince skeptical security personnel that the keys to the entire organization should be held by a Microsoft product. Instead, ISA is deployed and governed by the rules set forth by the existing security infrastructure. This also keeps Exchange front-end servers and other types of application servers and their need for "swiss-cheese" firewall rules out of the DMZ.

NOTE

It should be pointed out that this chapter does not imply that ISA Server 2006 is not capable of filling other roles within an organization such as edge firewall, VPN server, or caching solution. It simply points out that ISA can be, and is often, deployed in other types of scenarios, such as this one, and can be a welcome improvement to the security of organizations without any modifications to existing infrastructure.

Understanding the Capabilities of ISA Server 2006 Reverse Proxy

Unihomed ISA servers do not have the full range of capabilities that multi-homed ISA servers do, such as the edge firewall and network-filtering firewall that deployment scenarios offer. That said, however, the reverse-proxy capabilities that ISA does offer are quite powerful, and may be all that is necessary for ISA Server to be considered a success in an organization. For example, securing Exchange Outlook Web Access (OWA) with publishing rules, which can be easily accomplished on a unihomed server, is quite likely the single most common deployment scenario for ISA today. In addition, ISA possesses the capability to publish and secure other web servers, Microsoft SharePoint sites, and certain other applications as well.

Defining Web Server Publishing Rules for Reverse Proxy

ISA Server 2006 reverse proxy makes it possible to secure web and other services through a logical construct known as a web server publishing rule. A web server publishing rule is a firewall policy rule that uses specific filters to monitor web traffic and force that traffic to conform to specific conventions. For example, particular web server publishing rules can be set up to allow Internet access to a web server, but to restrict that access to particular subdirectories on the server, and to require that only specific HTTP commands are used.

There are many variations of web server publishing rules, and it is important to understand how different web publishing rules can be set up.

> **NOTE**
>
> Web server publishing rules are unique in that only they (along with web-based mail publishing rules such as OWA rules) can be used when an ISA server is deployed with a single NIC. Other types of server publishing rules, such as RPC publishing rules, DNS publishing rules, Telnet publishing rules, and any non-HTTP–based rules, cannot be set up on a single-NIC ISA server.

The process for setting up web server publishing rules is almost exactly the same for multi-homed and unihomed ISA servers. The only difference is that when the rule is created, the source network for the unihomed server doesn't apply, and can be set to All Networks. (ISA sees everything that is not local as a single network.) With this understanding in mind, more specific information on setting up web server publishing rules can be found in Chapter 14, "Securing Web (HTTP) Traffic."

Deploying Unihomed ISA Server 2006 Security Appliances

Setup and configuration of unihomed ISA Server 2006 servers is effectively the same as the setup of a standard ISA server, with one major difference: the number of network cards. ISA Server 2006, in this type of reverse-proxy scenario, simply processes web and other traffic and then forwards it on to its destination. Because the traffic does not need to flow from one network to another in this case, ISA does not require more than a single NIC. It relies on the network topology to route the server requests.

To perform the initial setup and configuration steps for a unihomed ISA Server 2006 system, follow the configuration steps outlined in Chapter 2, "Installing ISA Server 2006."

Applying the Single Network Adapter Network Template to a Unihomed ISA Server

After installation, it is ideal to configure the server with one of the preexisting network templates that are available on the ISA server. Fortunately, a unihomed ISA server template exists, which can be easily utilized to set up the initial configuration of the ISA server. To deploy this network template, perform the following steps:

1. In the console tree of the ISA Management Console, expand SERVERNAME, Configuration, Networks.

2. Click on the Templates tab in the task pane, as shown in Figure 7.2.

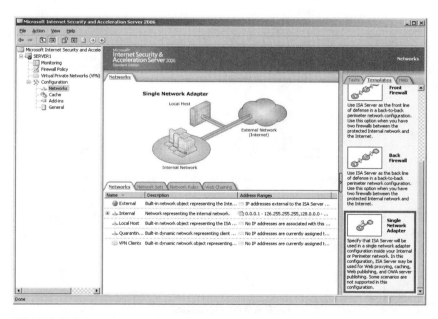

FIGURE 7.2   Deploying the single network adapter network template.

3. Scroll down and click on the single network adapter template. You may be warned about disabling additional adapters.

4. At the wizard welcome screen, click Next to continue.

5. The option to export the current configuration is given. Because this is a new server install, this is skipped, so click Next to continue.

CAUTION

The Network template wizard overwrites any settings currently on the server, so it is important to back them up if the server has any rules or configuration that need to be saved.

6. The subsequent dialog box, Internal Network IP Addresses, shown in Figure 7.3, automatically inputs the entire TCP/IP address range as part of the internal network. Because there is only one NIC, ISA logically groups all IP addresses into a single network, so click Next to accept the defaults.

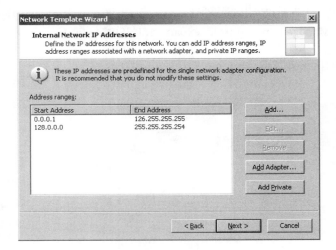

FIGURE 7.3   Defining internal IP addresses for a unihomed ISA server.

7. Click on Apply Default Web Proxying and Caching Configuration, as shown in Figure 7.4, and click Next.

8. Click Finish.

9. Click Apply, then click OK to save the changes.

Deploying a Preconfigured ISA Hardware Appliance

One of the perceived advantages to out-of-the-box security solutions is that they are simple to set up. Simply pull them out of the box, plug them in, and configure a few settings. These ready-built solutions often compete directly with ISA Server, offering

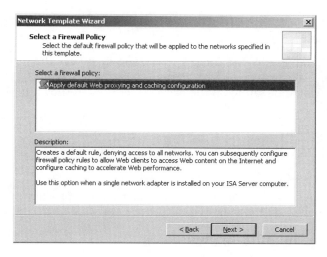

FIGURE 7.4   Applying a default firewall policy for the unihomed server network template.

instant setup and security. In response to this, Microsoft has worked with major security and hardware vendors to produce ISA hardware appliance solutions.

These solutions offer all the advantages of the ready-built security solutions, with the increased capabilities of ISA Server 2006. They come preinstalled, preconfigured, and presecured, and some even include LCD panels that allow for console-less configuration of the ISA server itself. These solutions can appeal to many organizations that are looking for a quick and easy way to take advantage of ISA Server 2006's reverse-proxy (or other) capabilities. For the latest list of devices built for ISA Server 2006, see the Microsoft ISA Partner website at the following URL:

http://www.microsoft.com/isaserver/partners/default.asp

Configuring Existing Firewalls to Utilize ISA Server 2006 Reverse Proxy

For various reasons, it may not be feasible or desired to replace an existing firewall with an ISA server firewall. In these circumstances, the ISA server can still be utilized for reverse-proxy capabilities, and it can be deployed in the DMZ of the existing firewall.

What this effectively means is that ISA server effectively can be treated as an isolated web server from the firewall's perspective. The configuration steps on the packet-filter firewall are therefore straightforward.

Understanding Packet-Filter Firewall Configuration for ISA Server Publishing

Simply opening the proper port (HTTP and/or SSL) to the ISA server, and then from the ISA server to the Internal web server, is all that is necessary. For example, the following rule illustrates the firewall rules that would be set up on the packet-filter firewall shown in Figure 7.5:

▶ NAT 12.155.166.151 to 172.16.1.21

▶ Allow 443 from External to 172.16.1.21

▶ Allow 443 from 172.16.1.21 to 10.10.10.20

Each firewall product will have a different way of configuring rules. Consult the product documentation for information on how to set these up.

Isolating and Securing an ISA Security Appliance

This concept drives home the real benefit of ISA in the DMZ: isolating and protecting the web services from direct physical access from the Internet. In this design, even if an attacker were able to compromise and overcome the ISA server, he or she would be isolated in the DMZ of the firewall, and able to communicate over only a single port to a single server in the internal network. This adds another security layer into an already secure environment, and enables ISA to scan the traffic at the Application layer, adding yet another layer of security.

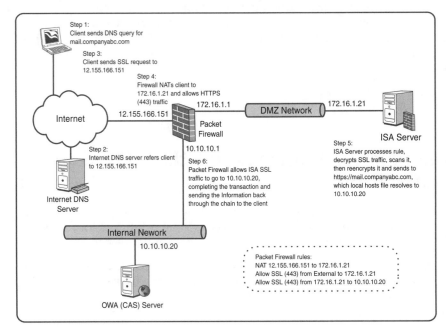

FIGURE 7.5   Viewing the steps involved in an ISA reverse-proxy scenario.

Publishing and Securing Services in an Existing DMZ

In general, there are few differences involved when securing various services in a unihomed server configuration. In most instances, the main difference in the rules that are set up relates to the networks from which the specific HTTP or HTTPS listeners will listen to requests, shown on the Networks tab of a specific listener.

For a standard (multihomed) ISA server, different listeners listen for connections from various networks, depending on the particular rule and functionality required. For example, an OWA publishing rule may listen to requests from the external network (the Internet) and publish the server on the internal network. Because the unihomed ISA server doesn't know the difference between all networks, it is important to make the change to the particular listener and adjust it to listen to All Networks for the rule to work properly.

> **NOTE**
>
> This is an important concept to understand. Throughout this book, the assumption is made that a multi-homed server is set up. When the step-by-step guides in those chapters get to the point where the listening network is set up, simply change it to All Networks and configure the rest of the rule the way that the rest of the procedure lists. This ensures that web rules will work for a unihomed ISA configuration.

Configuring a Unihomed ISA Server to Reverse Proxy Exchange Outlook Web Access

Of special note is securing Outlook Web Access (OWA) with a unihomed ISA configuration because this type of scenario is very popular and very common. Aside from the same listener network consideration previously mentioned, one more very important step must be taken on ISA servers to allow the OWA publishing rules outlined in Chapter 12, "Securing Outlook Web Access (OWA) Traffic," to work. The unihomed ISA server must resolve the Fully Qualified Domain Name (for example, mail.companyabc.com) to the internal web server when SSL encryption is in use, to ensure that the full host header is properly passed through the entire SSL chain.

To explain further, when the client on the Internet sends a web request to go to https://mail.companyabc.com, external DNS servers point the client to an IP address on the external firewall, shown in Figure 7.5. The firewall, configured with the rules mentioned in the preceding section, forwards the HTTPS request to the ISA server, which then decrypts it and repackages it as an SSL packet to send to the OWA server on the internal network.

The tricky part is when this packet gets repackaged and sent back to the OWA server. Many administrators have made the mistake of simply selecting to forward the traffic to the internal name of the OWA server, such as server20.companyabc.com. The problem with this is that the SSL traffic then arrives at the OWA server without the proper host header (mail.companyabc.com). This causes the communications to fail, and the client to receive an HTTP error that says the "Target principal name is incorrect."

The key to fixing this is to make sure that the OWA publishing rule is configured to publish the server name the same way that the SSL Certificate is configured, such as what is shown in Figure 7.6.

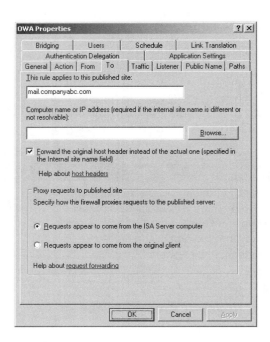

FIGURE 7.6   Checking the server publishing name of an OWA publishing rule.

Or course, the real catch to all of this is that the FQDN of the original host header will either be found unresolvable by the ISA server or end up forwarding the traffic back to the external interface, which is definitely not wanted. Instead, the traffic needs to be redirected to point to the internal OWA server through the use of a hosts file on the ISA server itself. This may be just the internal IP address, if a route relationship is set up between the DMZ and the internal network, or it may be the NAT IP address that the packet-filter firewall has configured for the OWA server.

In either case, the hosts file should be modified to enter the appropriate information. The hosts file is located in the following directory on the ISA server:

\windows\system32\drivers\etc

It can be modified in a text editor such as Notepad, as shown in Figure 7.7.

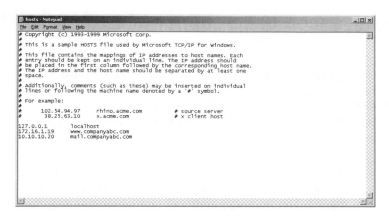

FIGURE 7.7   Editing a hosts file.

The lines beginning with # are comments, and can be removed if desired. A hosts file works when an IP address is entered on the first part of the line, a tab is inputted, and then the fully qualified domain name that will be associated with that IP address is entered. A hosts file will always override what is in DNS, so it is important to document the setting in case the IP address of the OWA server is ever changed.

After the hosts file is modified, traffic will point to the proper server immediately, and the entire SSL chain will use the proper host header information.

Configuring a Unihomed ISA Server to Reverse Proxy Web Services

Reverse proxy of a web server is almost exactly the same on a unihomed server as a multihomed one, just as it was with the OWA publishing rules. The same issues regarding host headers and end-to-end SSL encryption apply as well, and should be taken into account. For step-by-step guides to securing web traffic, see Chapter 14.

One common mistake made when using ISA as a reverse-proxy system in an existing DMZ is to configure a web publishing rule to make the traffic appear to come from the original client's IP instead of ISA's IP. This confuses most firewalls, who assume that the traffic is being spoofed, and it is subsequently dropped. In a unihomed DMZ deployment, ISA should typically be configured to make the traffic appear to come from itself. This setting can be found on the To tab of the publishing rule, such as what is shown in Figure 7.6.

7

Understanding Advanced ISA Security in Enterprise Environments

In general, the larger the environment, the more likely it is that ISA will be deployed in a unihomed ISA configuration. This has less to do with deficiencies in ISA itself and more to do with the investment that these organizations have with their existing security infrastructure. For many, it is simply too difficult, time-consuming, or politically challenging to replace firewalls, SSL-VPNs, and other security infrastructure with a new system such as ISA Server 2006.

What these organizations are finding, however, is that ISA as a reverse proxy is a valid option for them, and can be configured to secure and protect internal company resources. What happens in many cases is that ISA gets deployed in this scenario, and eventually finds its way into other layers of an organization's security infrastructure after ISA's features are gradually understood.

Large organizations have specific special needs that aren't fully met by a standard ISA deployment. Fortunately, the Enterprise version of the product provides for these needs, above and beyond the capabilities of the Standard version.

Deploying ISA Security Appliances for Redundancy and Load Balancing

To achieve redundancy of ISA components requires either the use of a third-party load-balancing solution or the inclusion of an internal load-balancing solution, such as Network Load Balancing (NLB).

Unfortunately, ISA Server 2006 Standard edition does not natively support Network Load Balancing (NLB). This has to do with the limitations of ISA Standard in properly matching load-balanced traffic sent between two separate networks (also known as *bi-directional affinity*).

> **NOTE**
>
> Because the limitations of ISA Server 2006 Standard with Network Load Balancing are related to issues of bi-directional affinity, it is theoretically possible to use NLB between different unihomed ISA Standard servers. Although this is possible, it is not a supported configuration and is not recommended.

Larger organizations, when deploying unihomed ISA servers, often turn to the Enterprise version to provide failover of services by using NLB. This enables the reverse-proxy functionality to remain up and running upon the failure of a single server. For these organizations, downtime of an OWA site or a company website is simply not acceptable, and the Enterprise version of the software supports improving the overall uptime of the solution.

For more information on ISA Server 2006 Enterprise Edition, see Chapter 6, "Deploying ISA Server Arrays with ISA Server 2006 Enterprise Edition."

Monitoring and Intrusion Detection on ISA Servers in the DMZ

Monitoring an ISA server in a firewall's DMZ can prove to be particularly challenging. The firewall itself is often configured to not allow remote access traffic over common ports, such as the MMC console (RPC-based) access or Remote Desktop Protocol (RDP). For this type of access to be allowed, the ISA server must first allow it, and then the firewall itself must allow it as well. This involves opening the proper ports on the firewall from management consoles to the ISA server itself. In worst-case scenarios, management of ISA itself can take place only via the attached keyboard, mouse, and video connection on the server itself.

For more information on monitoring an ISA server, see Chapter 19, "Monitoring and Troubleshooting ISA Server 2006."

Summary

Although it doesn't take full advantage of all ISA Server 2006 has to offer, the deployment scenario of an ISA server in the DMZ of an existing firewall is very common, and can be a useful component of a broad security strategy. ISA Server 2006 is a relatively cost-effective approach to maximizing the security of edge-facing web services. This includes common attack targets such as Outlook Web Access servers, SharePoint sites, and any other websites.

ISA Server 2006 contains preconfigured and intelligent rules that allow for the configuration of reverse-proxy capabilities that scan, filter, and reprocess the traffic sent to web servers, allowing for intelligent web filtering in addition to hard-to-find capabilities such as end-to-end SSL processing. For those organizations that are not in a position to restructure their existing security configuration, these capabilities provide them with an impressive additional layer of security without making any fundamental changes to their environment.

Best Practices

- ▶ If the existing security configuration cannot be changed, consider ISA Server 2006 for reverse-proxy configuration in the DMZ of existing firewalls.

- ▶ Use the Enterprise version of ISA Server 2006 if redundancy and failover of ISA functionality is needed.

- ▶ Never install any IIS components (except the SMTP service) directly on an ISA server.

- ▶ Use RADIUS or SecurID authentication when the ISA server is not a domain member.

- ▶ Use a hosts file on the ISA server to properly resolve the FQDN of SSL-encrypted web pages, and use the full name in the ISA rule.

- ▶ If needing a prebuilt, preconfigured security solution for reverse-proxy capabilities, consider the ISA Server 2006 appliances provided by third-party vendors.

▶ When deployed in a unihomed DMZ configuration, change ISA web publishing rules to make the traffic appear to come from the ISA server itself, not the original client IP. This will avoid the packet-filter firewall from thinking the traffic is spoofed and dropping it.

▶ Follow the securing procedures outlined in the other chapters of this book, only changing the listener network to point to All Networks when ISA is deployed as a unihomed server.

CHAPTER 8

Deploying ISA Server 2006 as a Content Caching Server

This chapter focuses on the information necessary to deploy ISA Server 2006 as a content-caching server. Design scenarios and optimization techniques for content caching are presented, and step-by-step guides to deployment are given. In addition, information on how to create custom download jobs and how to automatically configure proxy clients is outlined.

Understanding the Acceleration Component of the Internet Acceleration Server 2006

ISA Server has a long history of providing web proxy access to network clients. In fact, the original name of the product, before it was rechristened as the Internet Security and Acceleration Server, was Proxy Server. The Proxy Server component of ISA is still strong and robust, but it has been overshadowed by the strong emphasis on the firewall and security aspects of the application. This should not detract from the fact that ISA still provides for excellent web and FTP proxy capabilities through its content-caching technologies.

The "acceleration" in the title of ISA Server 2006 refers to these capabilities. Web caching enables web and FTP browsing to be optimized because local copies of commonly accessed files are stored on the server. They are downloaded only once and then made available to multiple clients. This increases the response time of web browsing and decreases an organization's overall bandwidth needs.

Improving Web Access by Caching Content

The concept of content caching is not overly complex, and the key to its success lies in its simplicity. Content caching works by saving local copies of web data on the hard drive of the caching server and making that information available to the next clients that request the same information from the same site.

The example shown in Figure 8.1 serves as an illustration: If Client1, configured to use ISAServer1 as a proxy server, were to browse to the home page of www.microsoft.com and www.cco.com, ISAServer1 would first check whether it had a recent local copy of the websites accessed. If it did not, it would then initiate an HTTP request directly to the www.cco.com and www.microsoft.com websites. When the websites return the text and images associated with the site to ISAServer1, the server keeps a local copy and then forwards the information back to the requesting Client1.

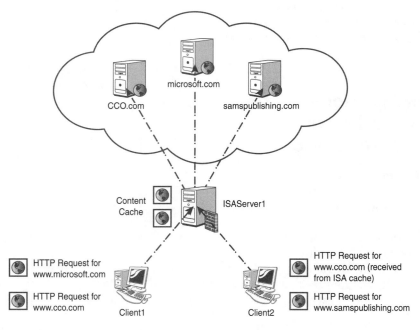

FIGURE 8.1   Understanding the ISA server content-caching process.

Later, Client2 requests information from the websites of www.cco.com and www.samspublishing.com. The ISA server checks the local cache and finds that it already has a recent copy of www.cco.com, so it forwards this information directly to Client2. Because the www.samspublishing.com information is not stored locally, however, the server goes through the requesting process again and subsequently stores this information locally so that it is available for the next client that requests it.

Protecting and Monitoring Client Web Access

In the early days of proxy servers, the goal of the server was to reduce the amount of total Internet bandwidth consumed by web browsing. The cost of bandwidth was more expensive, comparatively speaking, and many organizations looked to proxy server solutions to save on the expense of maintaining an Internet connection.

Although bandwidth savings are still a potential reason for deploying a proxy server, bandwidth costs have become less of a factor and client security and control has become more of a factor. What organizations have found is that having a dedicated proxy server enables all communications from clients to external websites to be monitored and controlled.

A welcome side effect to using ISA Server 2006 to provide for proxy server functionality is that clients avoid making direct connections from the internal network to the Internet. Best-practice security design stipulates that client workstations (which are more vulnerable to attack, spyware and virus infection, and other exploits) should not have direct, unsupervised access out to an untrusted network such as the Internet.

By funneling all client web traffic through the ISA server for proxy functionality, organizations have newfound control over monitoring, filtering, and protecting client web and FTP traffic. This also allows for highly functional third-party proxy add-ons that provide for intelligent filtering of client traffic to block access to particular types of websites and/or scanning of the traffic for viruses, exploits, and spyware.

Pre-Caching Commonly Used Content

ISA Server 2006 content-caching capability includes the capability to automatically download content on a predefined basis to make it fresh and available to clients on the network. For example, a law firm could set up a content download job that refreshes content from online legal websites that are commonly used in the firm. Data can be retrieved quickly from internal clients, but the information is still known to be fresh.

Designing ISA Server 2006 Caching Solutions

ISA Server 2006 content-caching solutions typically fit into one of two models. In the first model, the ISA server acts as an edge firewall to a network, such as what is shown in Figure 8.2. In this case, the ISA server provides for full firewall functionality to the clients on the network, monitoring and securing all traffic to the clients on the network. In addition, the server acts as a web and FTP proxy for the internal clients.

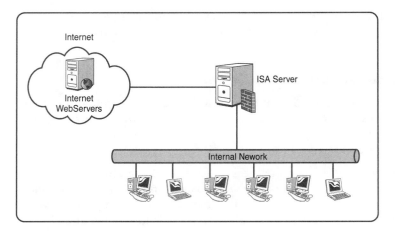

FIGURE 8.2   Understanding the edge firewall content-caching model.

The second content-caching deployment model for ISA Server 2006 is one where the ISA server provides for caching to only the clients on the network, similar to what is shown in Figure 8.3. In this model, the ISA server is used as a cache-only server, with a single network interface connected to either the internal or the DMZ network of an organization. This model, which was the common deployment model for ISA's predecessor, Proxy Server 1.x/2.x, allows for proxy capabilities, but doesn't take full advantage of the firewall functionality in the server.

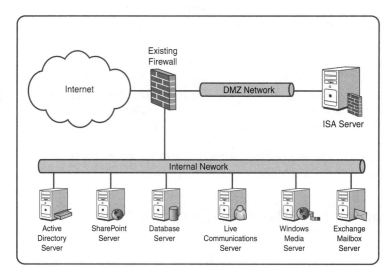

FIGURE 8.3   Understanding the caching-only server model.

From a content-caching perspective, both deployment models for ISA are essentially the same. For some organizations, deploying a full-blown edge firewall and content-caching proxy server is ideal. For other organizations with an existing investment in security and firewall technologies, it may make sense to deploy a unihomed (single NIC) ISA server in the DMZ of the existing firewall to take advantage of the content-caching capabilities, as well as to provide for reverse-proxy functionality. For more information on this type of deployment scenario, refer to Chapter 7, "Deploying ISA Server as a Reverse Proxy in an Existing Firewall DMZ."

Understanding the Types of Proxy Servers

Proxy servers handle traffic in different ways, depending on how they are configured. In general, all proxy servers fall into one of three categories: forward proxy, transparent proxy, or reverse proxy. A single server can hold more than one of these roles; the roles simply refer to the type of proxying that the server handles, as follows:

▶ **Forward proxy**—A forward proxy is a traditional proxy server that clients are aware of and to which they send their web requests directly (rather than to the Internet). This type of proxy requires some way for the client browser to be configured to point directly to the proxy server.

▶ **Transparent proxy**—A transparent proxy provides for proxy functionality, but is invisible to the client workstation. A transparent proxy can be set up in ISA if the web traffic from the workstations flows directly through the ISA server in some fashion, such as when the ISA server acts as an edge firewall.

▶ **Reverse proxy**—Reverse proxy refers to the proxy server's capability to handle requests made from the Internet to internal web servers. One common reverse proxy scenario would involve ISA handling all traffic sent to a publicly accessible Outlook Web Access (OWA) server. Reverse proxy provides for enhanced security by not exposing internal web servers directly to the Internet.

Sizing Hardware Components for an ISA Caching Server

For firewall purposes, it is difficult to overload an ISA server, simply because only so much data typically can be pushed at an ISA server through a standard Internet connection. For example, the rule of thumb with ISA Server is to assume that each T1 supplied to ISA adds an additional 2.5% of CPU utilization. This allows for theoretical ISA deployments of a single server on an Internet connection of up to T3 status.

Content caching, however, changes the performance equation somewhat because the amount of processor utilization required by the system increases. This is particularly so if ISA will be used as a transparent proxy, where clients are not aware that they are using a proxy. Transparent proxy servers, described in more detail later in this chapter, utilize approximately twice as much processor time as regular forward proxy servers. Even with this knowledge taken into account, however, adding ISA servers to an environment for performance reasons becomes an issue only when the number of proxy clients approaches 1000. That said, all these factors should be taken into account when designing an ISA server implementation.

NOTE

ISA Server licensing operates on a per-processor basis. Subsequently, a dual-CPU server costs twice as much to license as a single-CPU system. Because adding processors produces diminishing returns from a performance perspective (doubling the number of CPUs increases performance by only 50% in most cases), it is most cost effective to deploy single-CPU ISA servers where possible. In larger environments, it makes sense to add CPUs when performance dictates it, but it is important to keep in mind the licensing issue when scoping possible ISA configurations.

ISA Server 2006 by itself does not require much in the realm of disk space. Enabling content caching on an ISA server, on the other hand, requires a large amount of disk space to be made available to the server in the form of the ISA cache file. This file can be predefined as a certain size, and it is important to allow as much space as will be required by the server to store the cache images and text. Depending on the level of usage that the proxy server will see, this could end up being a cache drive of 10–50GB.

A good rule of thumb would be to configure an ISA server with an OS partition of 10GB or so, a dedicated log drive of 10–30GB, and a cache drive of 10–50GB, if space allows. These are not hard and fast rules, but it is important to allow for the most ideal configuration for ISA caching.

Deploying Caching Redundancy with the Cache Array Routing Protocol (CARP)

For large environments, it may become necessary to deploy more than one caching server to provide for redundancy and load balancing of web caching. The Enterprise version of ISA Server 2006 allows for the creation of arrays of ISA servers that utilize the Network Load Balancing (NLB) protocol to provide for failover and load-sharing capabilities. In addition, Enterprise ISA servers support the Cache Array Routing Protocol (CARP), which provides for intelligent redirection of clients to individual ISA array members, based on the presence of cached data on those servers. This helps to further extend the caching capabilities of ISA Server 2006.

For more information on configuring ISA Server 2006 Enterprise Edition, see Chapter 6, "Deploying ISA Server Arrays with ISA Server 2006 Enterprise Edition."

Enabling ISA Server 2006 as a Web-Caching Server

The first step to configuring and utilizing the content-caching functionality on an ISA server is to enable the caching functionality. After it has been enabled, advanced cache settings and content download jobs can be set up and enabled.

Configuring ISA Server to Provide Web-Caching Capabilities

By default, content caching is not enabled on an ISA server. Instead, it must be turned on to enable an ISA server to provide for web-caching capabilities. Turning on this functionality is as straightforward as defining the size of the cache drive. After the cache drive has been defined, caching is set up and ready to go on the server. To set this up, perform the following steps:

1. From the ISA Management Console, select the Cache node from the console tree.

2. In the Tasks pane, select the Tasks tab and click on the link entitled Define Cache Drives (Enable Caching).

3. From the subsequent dialog box, shown in Figure 8.4, define the size of the cache drive by selecting the drive on which it will be placed and entering a maximum size into the field. Click the Set button to save the changes and then click OK.

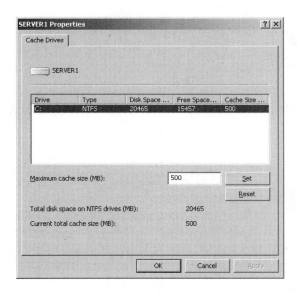

FIGURE 8.4   Enabling caching functionality in ISA.

4. Click Apply in the Central Details pane.

CAUTION

Most ISA changes do not require the firewall service to be restarted. Changing the cache drive size, however, is one of the few exceptions. If the ISA server has been placed into production, it should be noted that continuing with this procedure restarts the firewall service and kills the current connections to the server.

5. When prompted, select to Save the Changes and restart the services. Click OK.

6. Click OK when the changes are complete.

Changing Default Cache Settings

To process cache objects, ISA Server 2006 uses a series of default settings. To access and modify them, click on the Configure Cache Settings link in the Tasks tab of the Tasks pane. The Cache Settings dialog box, shown in Figure 8.5, contains a General tab that displays the size of the cache, as well as an Advanced tab.

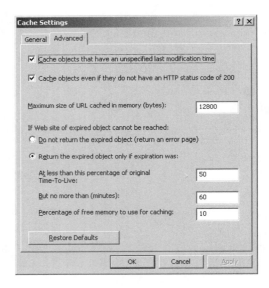

FIGURE 8.5   Modifying cache settings.

The Advanced tab allows for the customization of the maximum size of URLs that can be cached, and whether to cache objects with an unknown last time that they were modified. In addition, the default behavior, along with how expired content should be handled, is displayed if the original website cannot be reached. For example, if the www.cco.com website was previously accessed and was downloaded to the cache, but the entry has expired, the server could be configured to either error out (if the Do Not Return the Expired Object option is checked) or return the object to the requestor based on the amount of time since the Time-to-Live (TTL) of the object has expired (the default).

The Time-to-Live of a cache object is the amount of time that the object remains valid in a cache before it expires and needs to be refreshed. Without TTL settings on cached objects, stale data could potentially be returned to requesting clients.

Configuring Cache Rules

After caching has been enabled on an ISA server, specific rules must be set up to configure how ISA handles caching traffic. By default, a single Last Default Rule for caching exists on the server and can be viewed under the Cache Rules tab in the Central Details pane. The settings in this rule can be utilized, or different cache rules can be configured to be processed before the default rule. This can be useful in scenarios where different cache policies are created for different clients, such as forcing caching for clients in the internal network, but turning it off for servers in the DMZ. To create a cache rule, perform the following steps:

1. In the Tasks pane of the Cache node, click the link labeled Create a Cache Rule.
2. Enter a descriptive name for the cache rule and click Next to continue.
3. Click the Add button to define to which source network entities the cache rule will apply.
4. Select the source network, network sets, computers, or other network objects from the list and click Add for each one. Click Close when finished.
5. Click Next to continue.

From the subsequent dialog box, shown in Figure 8.6, the rule can be configured to modify the behavior of how cached objects are returned to the requestor. The three options are as follows:

- ▶ **Only if a Valid Version of the Object Exists in the Cache. If No Valid Version Exists, Route the Request to the Server**—In this scenario, which is the default option, a requesting client has a cached object returned only if the object exists in the cache and has not expired. If there is not a current version, the ISA server routes the request to the web server on the Internet.

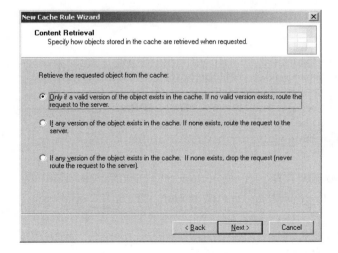

FIGURE 8.6   Setting up a cache rule in ISA.

▶ **If Any Version of the Object Exists in the Cache. If None Exists, Route the Request to the Server**—For this option, the ISA server returns an object in the cache, even if it has expired. If it does not exist in the cache, it routes the request to the web server on the Internet. This option can run the risk of supplying stale data to requesting clients.

▶ **If Any Version of the Object Exists in the Cache. If None Exists, Drop the Request (Never Route the Request to the Server)**—With this option, clients get web data only from objects that exist in the cache. If an object isn't in the cache, the request fails. This is a highly restrictive option, but is useful in scenarios where only specific content is meant to be made available to web-browsing clients, and that content is made available with Content download jobs.

Select the default content retrieval behavior and click Next; this invokes the subsequent dialog box, which allows for advanced options such as caching dynamic content or offline browsing responses and customization of what type of content will be cached, such as the following:

▶ **Never, No Content Will Ever Be Cached**—If this option is chosen, the cache rule stipulates that the content will never be cached, regardless of whether or not the source and request header indicate to do so. This basically tells the cache rule to never cache the content.

▶ **If Source and Request Headers Indicate to Cache**—This setting (the default) relies on the source and request headers of the object that is retrieved to determine whether it is cached.

To continue with the process, do the following:

1. Select what type of cache content settings to utilize and click Next to continue.
2. Check whether SSL responses will be cached or not, or if a size limit to cached objects will be configured.
3. Click Next to continue.

The subsequent dialog box, shown in Figure 8.7, allows for the core customization of HTTP caching settings, such as whether to enable HTTP caching, and what the content's default TTL is. If a longer TTL is set, objects remain in the cache for longer periods of time, although the risk that they will become stale becomes larger. If the TTL is shortened, objects returned are less likely to be stale, but the server has to update the records more often, increasing the amount of bandwidth required. To continue, perform the following steps:

1. Make any necessary changes to the HTTP caching options and click Next to continue.
2. Check to enable FTP caching, if required, and set the default TTL for FTP objects. Click Next to continue.
3. Click Finish to create the rule.
4. Click Apply and then click OK when finished.

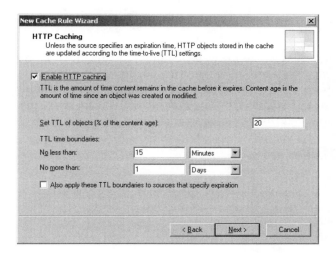

FIGURE 8.7   Customizing HTTP caching settings.

Any number of cache rules can be configured, each with different settings. This allows for the creation of granular cache options that can be set on a per-network or even per-computer basis.

Configuring Proxy Web Chaining

ISA Server 2006 proxy servers, or even a third-party proxy product, can be chained together inline so that proxy traffic is routed through both servers. This concept is known as *web chaining* with ISA Server 2006, and it allows for the optimization of multiple proxy servers by requiring users in different locations to use local ISA servers for proxy first, and then to use a centralized one, for example.

To create a web-chaining rule, perform the following steps:

1. Open the ISA Server Management Console (Start, All Programs, Microsoft ISA Server, ISA Server Management).
2. In the console tree, select the Networks node by clicking on it.
3. In the Details pane, select the Web Chaining tab.
4. In the Tasks pane, click on the Tasks tab, if it is not already selected.
5. Select the link titled Create New Web Chaining Rule in the Tasks pane.
6. At the Welcome dialog box, enter a name for the web-chaining rule. Click Next to continue.
7. At the Web Chaining Rule Destination dialog box, click the Add button.
8. When presented with the Add Network Entities dialog box, select the networks, network sets, individual computers, subnets, or other destinations to which the rule is to apply. Click Add when selected.

9. Select additional network entities as necessary. Click Close when finished and Next to continue.

The next dialog box, shown in Figure 8.8, is where the web-chaining functionality options are set, such as whether the requesting clients are sent to another upstream ISA proxy cache server, or whether the requests are retrieved directly from the specified destination (the default). To configure the ISA server as a downstream server in a web chain, select the option titled Redirect Request to a Specified Upstream Server and click Next to continue.

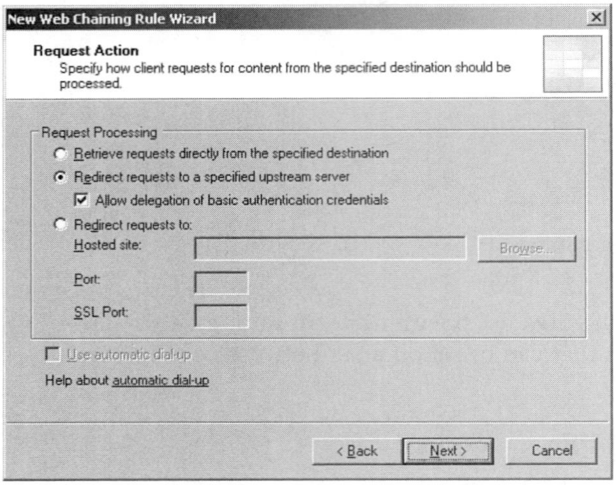

FIGURE 8.8   Creating a web-chaining rule.

1. Enter the name of the upstream proxy server, what ports are to be used (typically 8080), and what account to use for authentication. Click Next to continue.

2. Under the Backup Action dialog box, choose how to respond if the upstream server is not responding. This can be useful because it can avoid allowing the upstream server to be a single point of failure. Select the option desired and click Next to continue.

3. Click Finish to apply the web-chaining rule.

4. Click Apply and OK to save the changes to ISA.

Setting Up a Content Download Job

Content download jobs in ISA Server 2006 enable administrators to proactively download content from websites and make it quickly available to requesting clients. This functionality enables organizations to quickly gain access to fresh content from web pages that are relevant to their organizations. Of course, overuse of content download jobs can also end up spuriously wasting available bandwidth, so they should be configured only if necessary.

To create a content download job, do the following:

1. Select the Cache node from the Scope pane.

2. Select the Content Download Jobs tab from the Central Details pane.

3. From the Tasks tab in the Tasks pane, click the link for Schedule a Content Download Job. If prompted to enable the jobs, click Yes, Apply, and OK and then run through steps 1–3 again.

4. Enter a name for the content download job and click Next.

5. Define the download frequency for the job—one time only, one scheduled time, daily, or weekly—and click Next to continue.

6. Enter the URL of the site from which to download, such as what is shown in Figure 8.9. Also, indicate how many links deep the site is to be scanned and whether to follow outside links (not recommended). Click Next to continue.

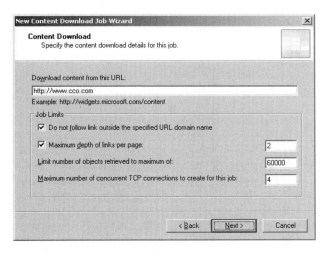

FIGURE 8.9   Setting up a content download job.

7. Enable the individual cache content settings and TTL settings for the job and click Next to continue.

8. Review the results of the wizard and click Finish.

Taking Advantage of HTTP Compression for Caching

A newer feature in ISA Server is the ability to compress HTTP traffic that flows through it in a caching scenario. Compressing the traffic has significant advantages in speed and overall bandwidth utilization. It is important to understand the capabilities and limitations of HTTP compression in ISA Server, however.

HTTP compression will only occur if the web server and web client both support the industry standard Deflate and GZIP algorithms. This applies to Windows 2000 and greater version of IIS and also to Internet Explorer 4.x and greater.

> **NOTE**
>
> Enabling HTTP compression for a network element is a global policy setting that
> applies to all rules pertaining to the network element that it applies to.

The HTTP compression settings for ISA can be found under the General node in the
Details pane. Clicking on the Define HTTP Compression Preferences link invokes the
HTTP Compression dialog box, shown in Figure 8.10. This dialog box is divided into three
tabs, the General tab simply allows for HTTP compression to be turned on and off. The
Return Compressed Data tab allows an administrator to define which clients will be
subject to HTTP compression. Finally, the Request Compressed Data tab allows an administrator to define when HTTP compression is requested based off of the destination of the
traffic. Each one of the settings also allows for exceptions to be made for individual
network entities.

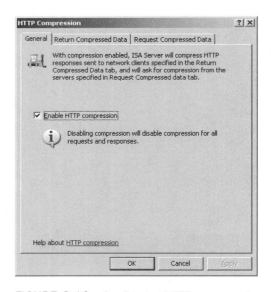

FIGURE 8.10   Configuring HTTP compression settings.

Configuring Proxy Clients

Configuring the ISA server for proxy functionality is only one half of the puzzle for
enabling web-proxy capabilities. If the ISA server is to be used for this purpose, the clients
must be configured in one way or another. Several different options exist for setting this
up, including some that are more labor intensive and other options that streamline the
process. Understanding how the clients can be configured is therefore important when
deploying a proxy infrastructure.

Enabling an ISA Transparent Proxy

The simplest way to configure clients to use ISA as a proxy server is to not configure anything on the clients at all. If an ISA server can be configured to be inline to the web-browsing traffic, such as when it is set up as an edge firewall, then the ISA server automatically caches the HTTP client requests, assuming that caching has been enabled on the server. This type of proxy is referred to as a *transparent* proxy, in that it does not require any client configuration and requires clients to have only a normal TCP/IP stack.

The downside to transparent proxy is that the traffic is not optimized, and the server has to work twice as hard to process the requests because the client cannot optimize the requests based on the presence of a proxy server. In addition, certain HTTP-based applications may not work properly through a transparent proxy, so it is important to test application compatibility in advance of deploying this type of scenario.

> **NOTE**
>
> Transparent proxy is effective when it's necessary to enable proxy capability on heterogeneous clients that utilize multiple operating systems and different types of browsers. It intercepts the HTTP commands as they pass through the system. This does not require any additional customization on the part of the client.

Manually Configuring Client Proxy Settings

If a forward proxy, rather than a transparent proxy, is to be set up for clients to use, they must be directed to use that client through a modification to their Internet Explorer settings. This modification can be done through different techniques. The most straightforward (albeit most user-intensive) technique is to simply manually enter the forward proxy information directly into Internet Explorer. To do this, perform the following tasks:

> **NOTE**
>
> Different versions of Internet Explorer and other browsers utilize slightly different methods for changing these settings. Although the options are different, the settings are typically similar. Check the Help file for the browser to identify how to change proxy server settings.

1. Open Internet Explorer and click Tools, Internet Options.
2. Go to the Connections tab.
3. Click on the LAN Settings button.
4. To configure manual proxy server settings, enter the necessary information into the LAN Settings dialog box, shown in Figure 8.11. The check box to Use a Proxy Server should be checked, and the IP address or host address and port of the ISA server should be entered.

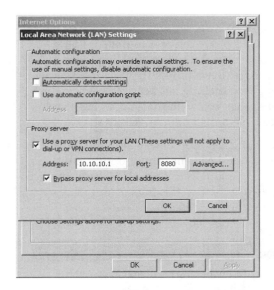

FIGURE 8.11   Manually configuring client proxy settings in Internet Explorer.

5. Review the proxy server settings and click OK and OK to save the settings.

Creating an Active Directory Group Policy Object (GPO) to Streamline the Deployment of Client Cache Settings

In an Active Directory domain that is inhabited by clients that use Internet Explorer, the setting for configuring a forward proxy server can be automatically applied to client workstations through the use of a Group Policy Object (GPO). GPOs allow for bulk enforcement of settings on systems in a domain, and can be very useful in the automation of proxy server settings. To create a GPO, perform the following tasks:

> **NOTE**
>
> The step-by-step process outlined here utilizes a tool known as the Group Policy Management Console (GPMC), which greatly simplifies the way that Active Directory GPOs are applied. It is highly recommended to install this tool for the application and modification of GPO settings. It can be downloaded from Microsoft at the following URL:
>
> http://www.microsoft.com/technet/prodtechnol/windowsserver2003/technologies/management/gp/default.mspx

1. Log in as a domain admin on an internal domain controller (not the ISA server).

2. Open the Group Policy Management Console (see the note about installing this earlier in this chapter) by clicking on Start, Run, and then typing **gpmc.msc** into the field and clicking OK.

3. Navigate to the Organization Unit where the user objects to which the proxy settings are applied and maintained. This may also be a top-level OU.

4. Right-click the OU and select Create and Link a GPO Here, as shown in Figure 8.12.

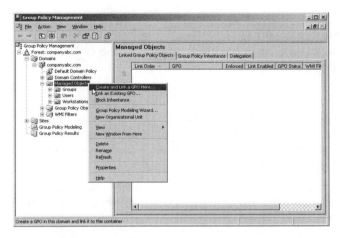

FIGURE 8.12   Creating an Active Directory GPO for client proxy server configuration.

5. Enter a descriptive name for the GPO and click OK.

6. Right-click the newly created GPO and click Edit.

7. Drill down under User Configuration, Windows Settings, Internet Explorer Maintenance, Connection.

8. Double-click on the Proxy Settings object in the right pane.

9. Check the box labeled Enable Proxy Settings.

10. Enter the IP address or DNS name of the proxy server, as well as which port should be used (8080 is the default). Enter any exceptions as well.

11. When finished making changes, click OK and close the Group Policy Object Editor and GPMC.

CAUTION

Group Policy settings can be very powerful, and they should be tested on a small sub-set of users initially. After the desired functionality has been verified, the GPO can then be linked to a more global OU and applied to all users.

Configuring Proxy Client Auto Discovery with DHCP

If all clients are not domain members, or if an alternate approach to automatically configuring clients with proxy server settings is needed, clients can be configured for auto discovery of proxy settings. Auto discovery can be set up to use one of two methods: discovery via the Dynamic Host Configuration Protocol (DHCP) or via the Domain Name System (DNS). Depending on how an environment is set up, one or both of the options can be set up to ensure that the client proxy settings are properly configured.

> **TIP**
>
> If both DHCP and DNS auto discovery are enabled, the client attempts to use DHCP first, and, that failing, then uses DNS.

For auto discovery to work, the Internet Explorer systems first need to be configured to automatically detect proxy settings. They do so when the Automatically Detect Settings check box is checked in the dialog box shown previously in Figure 8.11. Because this is the default setting, it should make this easier to configure.

Auto discovery uses a file that is automatically generated on the ISA server, known as the Web Proxy Auto Discovery (WPAD) file. Clients that are pointed to this file are automatically configured to use a proxy server.

Assuming that a DHCP server has already been set up in the internal network, use the following steps to set up client auto discovery through DHCP:

1. From the internal server that is running DHCP (not the ISA server), open the DHCP Console (Start, All Programs, Administrative Tools, DHCP).

2. Right-click on the name of the server in the left pane and select Set Predefined Options.

3. Click the Add button.

4. Enter in **Wpad** for the name of the option, enter data type of **String**, a code of **252**, and a description, as shown in Figure 8.13.

FIGURE 8.13   Configuring a WPAD entry in DHCP for client auto discovery of proxy server settings.

5. Click OK.

6. In the String field, enter in a value of **http://10.10.10.1:8080/wpad.dat** (where 10.10.10.1 is the IP address of the ISA server; a DNS hostname can be used as well if it is configured).

7. Click OK.

8. Close the DHCP Console.

With this setting enabled, every client that receives a DHCP lease and is configured for auto discovery is eligible to point to the ISA server as a proxy.

> **NOTE**
>
> The biggest downside to DHCP auto discovery is that clients must have local administrator rights on their machines to have the proxy server setting changed via this technique. If local users do not have those rights, then DNS auto discovery should be used instead of, or in combination with, DHCP auto discovery.

Configuring Proxy Client Auto Discovery with DNS

The Domain Name Service (DNS) is also a likely place for auto discovery information to be published. Using a WPAD entry in each forward lookup zone where clients need proxy server settings configured is an ideal way to automate the deployment of the settings.

Assuming DNS and a forward lookup zone is set up in an environment, auto discovery can be enabled through the following technique:

1. Log in with admin rights to the DNS server.

2. Open the DNS Console (Start, All Programs, Administrative Tools, DNS).

A host record that corresponds with ISA is required, so it is necessary to set one up in advance if it hasn't already been configured. To create one, right-click on the forward lookup zone and select New Host (A), enter a name for the host (such as proxy. companyabc.com) and the internal IP address of the ISA server, and click Add Host. This hostname is used in later steps.

To create the CNAME record for the ISA server, do the following:

1. While in the DNS Console, right-click the forward lookup zone where the setting is to be applied and click New Alias (CNAME).

2. For the alias name, enter **Wpad**, and enter the Fully Qualified Domain Name that corresponds to the Host record that was just created (for example, proxy. companyabc.com), similar to what is shown in Figure 8.14.

8

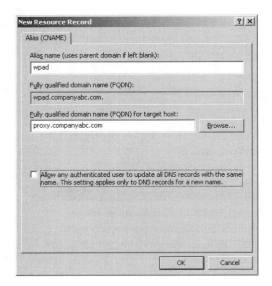

FIGURE 8.14   Configuring a WPAD entry in DNS for client auto discovery of proxy server settings.

3. Click OK to save the CNAME record.

This technique enables all Internet Explorer clients that are configured to use the forward lookup zone in DNS to automatically configure their proxy server information, which can be highly useful in automating the deployment of the proxy client.

Summary

ISA Server 2006 provides organizations with a wide variety of tools and functionality, including robust content caching and web proxy functionality. Taking advantage of these capabilities enables these organizations to improve web browsing and save on Internet bandwidth costs, while also making it possible to audit, monitor, and protect client access to the Internet. This functionality, coupled with its other capabilities, further extends the usefulness of the software and allows for flexible deployment strategies.

Best Practices

▶ Consider using ISA for web and FTP caching scenarios, particularly if it is already deployed as an edge firewall.

▶ Chain ISA proxy servers if it's necessary to provide faster local content caching that passes requests up to a centralized proxy server location.

▶ For redundancy of ISA caching environments, consider the use of the Enterprise version of the software and the Cache Array Routing Protocol (CARP).

▶ For clients in a domain environment, consider the use of Group Policy Objects (GPOs) to configure proxy server settings.

▶ Use a combination of DHCP auto discovery and DNS auto discovery settings that use WPAD to ensure that all clients get proxy server settings.

CHAPTER 9

Enabling Client Remote Access with ISA Server 2006 Virtual Private Networks (VPNs)

As the widespread adoption of high-speed Internet access and mobile computing becomes commonplace, many organizations are finding that it has become increasingly important to provide remote connectivity services to employees. At the same time, the potential threats posed by unauthorized access using these techniques have increased. It is subsequently critical to be able to allow for the productivity increases that remote access can provide while also maintaining tight security over the mechanism that is used to provide those services.

Many organizations are turning to Virtual Private Network (VPN) solutions to provide these types of capabilities to their remote and roaming users. VPNs allow for encrypted "tunnels" to be created into an organization's network, allowing for resources to be accessed in a secure fashion. ISA Server 2006 includes robust and capable VPN support, enabling organizations to leverage these capabilities in addition to the other capabilities provided by the software.

ISA Server 2006 implements industry-standard VPN protocols to provide secure access to essential data over a public Internet connection, eliminating the need for expensive point-to-point leased connections or modem pools, and with all the security advantages that VPNs provide. In addition, deploying VPNs with ISA allows for the creation of granular rule-based access control through use of ISA's advanced firewall rule capabilities. This gives administrators control over exactly what resource can be accessed by VPN users, which they can do by creating a distinct VPN users network that can be used for the creation of firewall rules.

This chapter focuses on exploring the VPN capabilities of ISA Server 2006. Step-by-step guides are provided for deployment of ISA VPN Client networks using both Point-to-Point Tunneling Protocol (PPTP) and Layer 2 Tunneling Protocol (L2TP), and best-practice design advice is presented. Automatic configuration of client VPN settings with the Connection Management Administration Kit (CMAK) is outlined as well. In addition, deploying VPNs with advanced techniques such as using PKI Certificates, RADIUS authentication, and VPN Quarantine is explored. Site-to-site VPNs for communication between branch offices is covered in a separate chapter, Chapter 10, "Extending ISA Server 2006 to Branch Offices with Site-to-Site VPNs."

Examining ISA Server 2006 VPN Capabilities and Requirements

ISA Server 2006 leverages and significantly enhances the built-in routing and remote access technology that is built into the Windows Server 2003 Operating System. ISA takes these capabilities to the next level, extending them and tying them into the rules-based control provided by ISA. Before you try to understand how to deploy an ISA VPN infrastructure, it is important to look at the general VPN options and requirements.

Understanding ISA Server 2006 VPN Protocols

ISA Server 2006 supports two VPN protocols: Point-to-Point Tunneling Protocol (PPTP) and Layer 2 Tunneling Protocol (L2TP) with Internet Protocol Security (IPSec) encryption. It is important to remember that although both protocols have advantages and disadvantages, the ISA VPN server can support both types of VPN tunnels simultaneously. This type of scenario has several distinct advantages. For example, an organization could provide down-level PPTP VPN client support while performing a staged rollout of the more complex L2TP/IPSec configuration. Another example could be to provide additional security to a smaller division of users that need a higher level of security provided in an L2TP/IPSec VPN, such as users with elevated privileges or human resources employees. This would result in a reduction in costs because the higher cost of purchasing and maintaining certificates, required for L2TP/IPSec, would be limited to fewer users.

Both the PPTP and L2TP protocols are based on the Point-to-Point Protocol (PPP). The technology works by encapsulating IP packets within PPP frames to transmit them securely across a link. If the packets are intercepted, the contents of the frames are unreadable and garbled, making them useless to unauthorized users. Both PPTP and L2TP perform the same basic tunneling functionality by wrapping the PPP frame with additional information required to route the data across the Internet to the remote VPN server. The remote VPN server receives the packet, removes the wrapper, and delivers the packet to the destination, essentially creating a virtual tunnel, such as the one shown in

Figure 9.1. The encryption provided in both VPN protocols ensures the data is kept private, completing the Virtual Private Network.

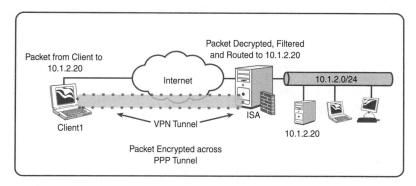

FIGURE 9.1   Examining PPP VPN encryption technology.

Comparing PPTP and L2TP Compression Methods

PPTP and L2TP both use Microsoft Point-to-Point Compression (MPPC) to provide data compression to help reduce the size of the data traveling across the connection. It is important to remember that although the data is compressed, the encryption and additional wrappers added take up a good portion of the available bandwidth, essentially slowing down the application using the connection. This slowdown is typical of encryption technology, and should be taken into account when planning for bandwidth speeds.

Understanding PPTP and L2TP Encryption and Data Security Methods

A PPTP VPN uses Microsoft Point-to-Point Encryption (MPPE) to encrypt the data. MPPE can provide 40-bit, 56-bit, and 128-bit RSA/RC4 encryption. PPTP encrypts only the PPP frame, which is where the data is stored. In a PPTP VPN configuration, it is highly recommended to use the most secure authentication method possible, such as 128-bit encryption. A PPTP VPN has only a single layer protecting the users' credentials. For many organizations, this level of protection is still adequate, when combined with strong domain password policies.

A L2TP/IPSec VPN uses Internet Protocol Security (IPSec) for encryption. IPSec supports the industry standard Data Encryption Standard (DES) and Triple DES (3DES) encryption. IPSec encrypts the entire packet with the exception of an IP header and the IPSec header and trailer. This provides an additional layer of security because the encryption is negotiated before the user authenticates, unlike PPTP, which establishes encryption after the user successfully authenticates and the remaining PPP negotiation is completed. Essentially, user credentials are protected with several secure layers when IPSec encryption is combined with strong authentication methods and strong domain password policies.

An L2TP/IPSec VPN has additional security functionality that comes with the IPSec protocol. Encapsulating Security Payload (ESP) provides this additional security in the form of confidentiality, authentication, integrity, and anti-replay protection.

Comparing PPTP and L2TP Authentication Methods

PPTP and L2TP use the same user authentication methods as discussed in detail later in this chapter, but the L2TP/IPSec VPN provides an additional layer of computer-level authentication. This guarantees that the VPN server and the client workstation establishing the VPN tunnel are who they claim to be.

Additional information regarding PPTP and L2TP can be found by referencing the request for comments (RFCs) that are published describing how they work. RFC 2637, describing PPTP, and RFC 2637, describing L2TP, can be easily found on the Internet Engineering Task Force's (IETF) website, as follows:

http://www.ietf.org/rfc.html

Analyzing VPN Protocol Implementation Issues

A significant technical disadvantage of L2TP is that it can't be easily used behind a Network Address Translation (NAT) device. In other words, if ISA is deployed within the DMZ of an existing firewall that is translated via NAT, or if it is within any private address range of an organization, L2TP encryption cannot be used in most cases. This can also apply to common scenarios such as the VPN client attempting to connect from a private network at a hotel, convention center, coffee shop, or other online location where their traffic is NATed.

It is potentially possible to set up a configuration like this using IPSec NAT Traversal (NAT-T) if the router and/or firewalls between the ISA server and the client support the new NAT-T implementation. It is important to validate this in advance because this could affect a VPN deployment strategy. If the ISA server is directly connected to the Internet as an edge firewall, this issue is moot, and VPN clients can easily use L2TP to connect.

An additional disadvantage to an L2TP/IPSec VPN is the complexity surrounding the implementation of the supporting technology. The IPSec protocol and the required Public Key Infrastructure (PKI) are often considered complex and difficult to understand, let alone implement and support. This means that although a L2TP/IPSec VPN is technically considered to be more secure than PPTP, this security is quickly diminished if the implementation and supportability surrounding the technology are too complex to guarantee they are secured correctly and functioning properly.

Understanding Network Bandwidth Constraints with VPNs

One of the most important aspects to consider when implementing an ISA VPN server is the Internet connection over which the VPN traffic will travel. The available internal bandwidth and the projected additional load VPN communication will add should be calculated to determine whether the existing environment will be suitable. There isn't necessarily a clear-cut method to determine how much Internet bandwidth VPN users will consume while connected to the VPN server, and several factors—including the type of information or applications that the users will access—almost always affect the bandwidth consumption. Generally, existing bandwidth monitoring should be able to give average consumption and availability during specific times. These numbers, along with prototyping the VPN design and expected user load, usually generate reasonably accurate numbers to determine whether the implementation is currently possible under the current conditions.

The roaming users' Internet connection also needs to be taken into consideration. Often factors that influence the overall user experience are beyond an organization's control, such as link speed and reliability while users are in remote locations. These types of aspects should be taken into consideration early in the planning stage.

Preparing Internal Resources for Remote Access

Preparing the internal network infrastructure for remote access is an important process to start well in advance of the actual implementation of the ISA VPN solution. The ISA VPN server, along with the supporting components, should be implemented carefully to avoid errors that could result in security vulnerabilities. The internal resources that remote users will be accessing should also be evaluated to ensure that the proper security layers have been applied and tested to guarantee that the appropriate level of control and management is in place and, most importantly, kept current.

Another aspect of implementing the ISA VPN for remote access is domain password policies and authenticating auditing. Unfortunately, most organizations are slow to adopt biometric scanning devices or even smart cards, and are still relying on archaic user-defined passwords. It is highly recommended to implement strong password policies and authentication auditing to effectively reduce the possibility of anyone quietly slipping into an internal network. ISA VPN solutions support smart card–based authentication, in addition to third-party SecurID two-factor authentication mechanisms, so it is fairly straightforward to include this additional security to an ISA implementation.

Designing an ISA Server 2006 VPN Infrastructure

When designing a VPN infrastructure, there are many important aspects to consider. These considerations are largely based on an organization's current infrastructure and definitive goals. Analyzing and making design decisions around these aspects early on allows for a much more secure and robust VPN implementation, enhancing the overall functionality of the network while providing a positive experience for end users.

Although there are almost unlimited network configuration possibilities, the ISA VPN server is generally involved in two types of scenarios: It is either a member server in a domain or a stand-alone workgroup server separate from a domain. Each configuration is valid and has different advantages; each type of configuration should be evaluated and implemented when appropriate. More about these configurations appears in subsequent sections of this chapter.

Server placement can also affect the VPN protocols that are available, or at least may influence the decision on what protocols to implement. The PPTP protocol supports many different configurations, including being implemented with a private IP address behind a NAT firewall or having a public IP address connected directly to the Internet or within a section of the internal network designed with routable IP addresses, such as the

DMZ. A L2TP/IPSec VPN is best implemented when the ISA server has a public IP address either directly connected to the Internet or within a section of the internal network designed with routable IP addresses, for the NAT-T limitation reasons described in the preceding sections.

Deploying an ISA VPN Server as a Domain Member

There are several advantages when the ISA VPN server is a member of an internal Active Directory domain. These advantages often result in a much lower total cost of ownership and overall simplicity regarding system management and overall maintenance, and are defined as follows:

> ▶ **Group Policy Objects**—Active Directory group policies can be leveraged to create a highly controlled, standardized, and very secure environment by enforcing security settings and security auditing and helping to eliminate human error and repetitive configuration tasks.

> ▶ **Direct Access to Active Directory**—As a member server, ISA can authorize existing groups for remote access and authenticate incoming domain users without the need for a RADIUS server connection and complex remote access policies. Security groups defined in Active Directory can be selected from within the ISA management console, allowing easy-to-use, centralized management of remote access for the entire network.

The process to configure ISA server as a member server is straightforward, consisting of joining the domain and then proceeding with the ISA server installation. For a step-by-step procedure to make the ISA server a domain member, see the section titled "Changing Domain Membership" in Chapter 2, "Installing ISA Server 2006."

Deploying an ISA VPN Server as a Stand Alone Server (Workgroup Member)

There are also a number of advantages, as described in the following list, when the ISA VPN server is not a member of an internal domain. Often it is very important for an organization to apply multiple secure layers between the internal network and remotely accessible systems; this can be accomplished by keeping the ISA VPN server as a stand-alone system located in a DMZ.

> ▶ **Limiting Internal Domain Boundaries**—Many organizations that provide VPN access for remote users or any type of Internet-accessible system feel it is an unacceptable risk to extend the internal domain into the DMZ, and as a result have implemented company policies that prevent such a configuration.

> ▶ **Restrictive Firewall Rules**—When a system in the DMZ is a member of the internal domain, the appropriate ports need to be opened; this would include NetBIOS and the often-exploited RPC ports required to communicate with internal domain controllers. Internal domain controllers are often considered the most critical systems on the network and should not be accessible from the DMZ.

▶ **Limited Access to Active Directory**—By leveraging Microsoft Internet Authentication Service (IAS), which allows for RADIUS authentication against an Active Directory domain, an organization can still leverage its current directory infrastructure to control remote access. The IAS uses the RADIUS protocol to authenticate VPN users' credentials obtained from the ISA VPN server against Active Directory users.

Enabling VPN Functionality in ISA Server

The first step to prepare the ISA server network configuration is to establish relationships between the ISA server networks. As previously mentioned, all VPN clients are pooled together into a logical VPN users network. By itself, however, the VPN users network does not have any type of relationship between the other networks that are set up in ISA Server. A network relationship determines what type of "bridge" will exist between the two environments. It is therefore important to create this type of network relationship in advance of enabling ISA VPN functionality.

Creating Network Relationships for the VPN Users Network

Network relationships, also known as network rules, are automatically created when the Network Template Wizard is used to apply several of the network templates, discussed in detail in Chapter 2. They can be viewed by clicking on the Network Rules tab in the Details pane of the Network node, similar to what is shown in Figure 9.2.

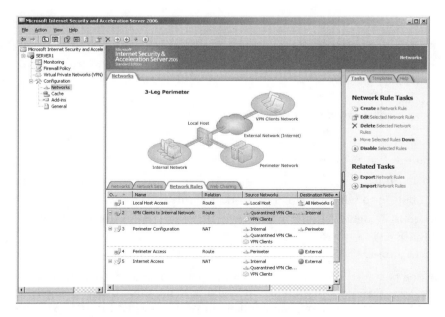

FIGURE 9.2   Viewing VPN users' network rules.

Perform the following steps to set up a standard route relationship:

1. Open the ISA Server 2006 Management Console (Start, All Programs, Microsoft ISA Server, ISA Server Management).

2. Under the Configuration node in the Scope pane, click on the Networks node.

3. Select the Network Rules tab in the Details pane by clicking on it.

4. Click on the link labeled Create a New Network Rule in the Tasks pane.

5. Enter a name for the network rule and then click Next to continue.

6. In the Network Traffic Sources dialog box, click the Add button to add the proper network.

7. Expand the Networks folder in the Add Network Entities dialog box and select the VPN Clients network, similar to what is shown in Figure 9.3. Click Add.

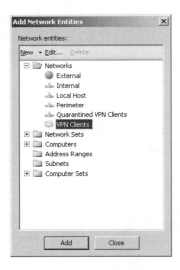

FIGURE 9.3   Creating a network rule for the VPN Clients network.

8. Click Close on the Add Network Entities dialog box.

9. Click Next to continue.

10. Click the Add button to select to which networks the rule will apply.

11. Select the appropriate network, such as the internal network, from the dialog box, click Add, and then click Close.

12. Click Next to continue.

The subsequent dialog box allows for the creation of the type of relationship that will be created between the source and destination network, giving the options shown in Figure 9.4. Select either NAT translation (where external IP addresses such as 12.155.166.151 are translated into internal IP addresses such as 10.10.10.21 automatically) or Route (where the IP addresses of the two networks are linked and made routable through ISA) and continue with the following steps:

1. Click Next to continue.

2. Click Finish when prompted.

3. Review the changes and then click the Apply button at the top of the Details pane to apply the changes and click OK when complete.

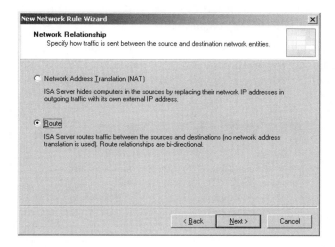

FIGURE 9.4   Establishing the network relationship between networks.

Different network relationships and network rules can be set up between the various networks that are established on the ISA server. The important factor to keep in mind is that the VPN Clients network needs to have some type of relationship set up between the logical network in which the clients are held and the various internal networks at the organization. If this is not done, the VPN clients cannot access any resources at all, even with the proper firewall rules established. The traffic from their network will simply be dropped by the ISA server.

Assigning IP Address Assignment for Remote Users

Remote users that will be establishing a VPN tunnel require an IP address to properly communicate through the tunnel to the internal network. This internal IP address is an additional IP address, separate from the IP address that the user already has configured on the Internet. There are several options available when determining how to assign IP addresses to remote clients:

▶ **Static IP Address from Active Directory**—A static IP address can be configured within the Active Directory user account properties. In most environments, this level of control over who gets an IP address is not required, and could be tedious to configure in a large environment without the use of additional scripting, but it is available if the situation arises.

▶ **Manually Configured Static Address**—The remote client creating the VPN connection can manually configure the IP settings within the connection's properties.

▶ **DHCP IP Address Pool**—The ISA server can be configured to obtain IP addresses from a DHCP server on one of the network interfaces. If a router is between the DHCP server and the ISA VPN server, then a DHCP relay agent is required. It is important to verify that enough available DHCP addresses are available to accommodate the regular load along with the additional VPN users.

▶ **ISA VPN Server IP Address Pool**—The ISA VPN server can provide IP configuration from a static address pool configured within the ISA Server Management Console. It is important to configure enough IP addresses to accommodate the maximum number of concurrent VPN users.

CAUTION

The IP addresses assigned to VPN clients must be on a different subnet than the IP address already configured on their system. For example, many home DSL/cable firewalls come preconfigured to assign the common 192.168.0.x or 192.168.1.x addresses to home computers. If the ISA VPN server was configured to assign addresses in one of these ranges to VPN users, communication would potentially not work correctly and the VPN connection could fail.

Use the following process to configure ISA to provide an IP address from a DHCP server. This configuration is valid only when ISA can communicate with a DHCP server, such as when the internal network is on the same subnet as the DHCP server or a DHCP relay agent. These steps require an internal DHCP server to be in use.

1. Open the ISA Server Management Console and select Virtual Private Networks (VPN) from the Scope pane.

2. Select the VPN Clients tab in the Details pane.

3. Select Define Address Assignments from the Tasks pane.

4. Select the Dynamic Host Configuration Protocol (DHCP) radio button.

5. From the drop-down list, select the interface from which the DHCP server can be reached, as shown in Figure 9.5. Usually this is the internal network interface.

6. Select the Advanced button and review the DHCP-provided DNS and/or WINS settings. This option is helpful if the DNS or WINS addresses provided by the DHCP server are not accessible to VPN users.

7. Select the OK button to close the window.

8. Select the Apply button to apply the new configuration.

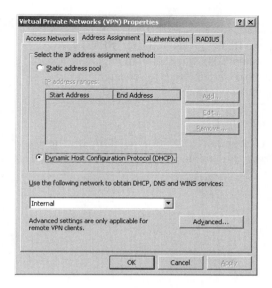

FIGURE 9.5   Setting up DHCP for VPN clients.

Enabling Client VPN Access from the Console

After the network relationships have been established and the IP address assignments have
been defined, the ISA server needs to be configured to support VPN connections. The
following procedure can be used to enable ISA VPN functionality.

1. Open the ISA Server Management Console and select Virtual Private Networks (VPN)
   from the Scope pane.
2. Select the VPN Clients tab in the Details pane.
3. Select Enable VPN Client Access from the Tasks pane.
4. Select the Apply button to apply the new configuration, and then click OK.

When the Apply button is pressed, the process starts the built-in Routing and Remote
Access service and applies the default configuration. If the ISA server is a domain member,
it also attempts to contact a domain controller in the domain to establish itself as a
Routing and Remote Access Server (RRAS).

> **NOTE**
>
> Enabling VPN Client access starts the Routing and Remote Access Server (RRAS) service on the ISA server and sets it to start up automatically. It is therefore important to be sure that this functionality has not been disabled via the Security Configuration Wizard of Windows Server 2003 SP1 or via an Active Directory Group Policy Object.

After it is enabled, the VPN Client access can be turned on and off by clicking on the Configure VPN Client Access link and unchecking the Enable VPN Client Access check box, as shown in Figure 9.6.

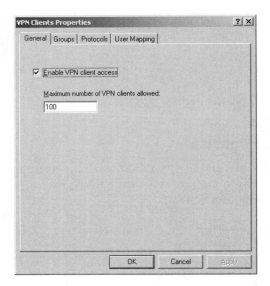

FIGURE 9.6   Establishing network relationships.

Assigning Routes to Remote Users

Often VPN users will need to access many different subnets when connected to the network though a VPN tunnel. There are several options when it comes to the routing configuration for remote VPN users:

▶ **Configure the default route on the client**—The Windows VPN client is configured to change the default gateway on the remote user's system to point to the ISA server when a connection is established. This setting basically routes all traffic to the ISA VPN server. This setting is recommended for a much higher level of security because the VPN clients are using the internal ISA server to reach the Internet and are subject to the configured firewall policies. This also prevents the possibility of another system on the same network as the VPN client from routing traffic to the internal network.

▶ **Use CMAK to modify the routing table**—If routing all information through the ISA server is not desirable, the Connection Manager Administration Kit (CMAK) can be used to configure and deploy a wide array of custom client settings, including custom routing tables to be used when the VPN tunnel is established.

▶ **Manually assign static routes**—Although probably more tedious and complicated than most endusers can handle, it is possible to manually add static routes to the remote client workstation, and then of course manually remove them when the VPN connection has ended.

The settings to configure the default route on the client system along with the CMAK are covered in detail later in this chapter.

Authenticating VPN Users

The placement of the ISA VPN server ultimately governs how user accounts are accessed during authentication. The following authentication methods are available:

▶ **Authenticating directly against Active Directory**—As previously stated, if the ISA VPN server is installed as a domain member server, users can be authenticated directly against the internal Active Directory domain without any additional configuration.

▶ **Implement RADIUS Authentication**—A RADIUS server, such as Microsoft's IAS, included with both the Windows 2000 Server and Windows Server 2003, can allow the stand-alone ISA VPN server to authenticate users against the internal domain. This service is very useful when the ISA VPN server has been implemented in a DMZ configuration. The configuration of IAS is covered in detail later in this chapter.

▶ **Authenticate against local users**—It is possible to configure local users on the ISA VPN server. This type of configuration is usually not recommended in a production environment, but may be acceptable in specific lab scenarios.

When the ISA server is a member of an internal domain, the following process can be used to select the desired groups of users allowed to establish a VPN connection. This task requires that a local or domain group already be created.

1. Open the ISA Server Management Console and select Virtual Private Networks (VPN) from the Scope pane.
2. Select the VPN Clients tab in the Details pane.
3. Select Configure VPN Client Access from the Tasks pane.
4. Select the Groups tab.

5. Select the Add button, enter the name of each group that is to be allowed remote access, click OK, and each of the selected groups will be added to the list, similar to what is shown in Figure 9.7.

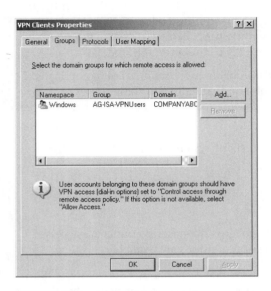

FIGURE 9.7   Adding AD groups for remote access.

6. Click the OK button to close the window.

7. Select the Apply button to apply the new configuration, then click OK.

Working with and Creating Rules for the VPN Clients Network

Even after VPN access has been established, it is still necessary to create firewall rules to allow VPN clients to access specific resources. By default, this type of access is not granted. ISA was designed to be "secure by default," and require administrators to specifically define the type of access that VPN users would have into the network.

Some of the network templates, when applied, create default rules that allow VPN clients access into the network. If one of these templates has not been applied, or if specific granular access for clients is required, the following steps can be performed to allow the VPN Clients network to have access to the internal network:

1. From the ISA Server Management Console, click on the Firewall Policy node in the Scope pane.

2. From the Tasks pane, click on the link labeled Create New Access Rule.

3. Enter a descriptive name for the access rule, such as "Allow VPN Clients Full Access to Internal Network," and click Next.

4. Under Rule Action, select Allow and click Next.

5. Under the setting to which protocols the rule applies, select All Outbound Traffic and click Next.

6. On the subsequent dialog box, source network(s) for the rule can be created. Click the Add button.

7. From the Add Network Entities dialog box, expand the Networks node and click on the VPN Clients network. Click Add when selected.

8. Click Close and then click Next.

9. The subsequent dialog box allows for the destination network to be chosen. Click the Add button.

10. Expand the Networks node and click on the internal network to select it. Click Add and then Close.

11. Under the User Sets dialog box, keep the default at All Users and click Next.

12. Review the rule settings in the confirmation dialog box, similar to what is shown in Figure 9.8. Click Finish when complete.

13. Click the Apply button at the top of the Details pane and then click OK.

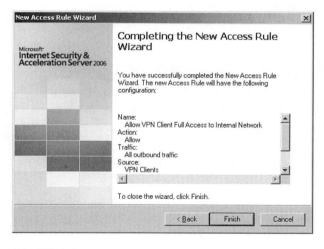

FIGURE 9.8   Finalizing a firewall rule for VPN clients.

NOTE

Using this approach, granular rules can be established to allow VPN clients access to only specific internal resources. This is often recommended over providing full network access to VPN clients. This way, if someone's account is compromised by an unauthorized user, that user can access only a small number of services, rather than the entire network.

Utilizing RADIUS Authentication for VPN Connections

In many cases, it may not be feasible to grant the ISA server domain membership. In these cases, ISA can still perform authentication of VPN users using the industry-standard Remote Access Dial-Up Service (RADIUS). Microsoft's Internet Authentication Service (IAS), which provides for RADIUS authentication against Active Directory user accounts, is included with the Windows 2000 Server and Windows Server 2003. This, in terms of a Microsoft-based network, allows stand-alone servers to authenticate domain users without requiring that they be domain members. For additional information on the RADIUS protocol, please review RFC 2865 on the IETF website, as follows:

http://www.ietf.org/rfc.html

NOTE

Any RADIUS-compliant software, including third-party offerings, can be used by ISA to authenticate users. This can be a useful way to extend ISA to take advantage of existing investment within an organization.

Installing the Internet Authentication Service (IAS) for Active Directory RADIUS Support

IAS can be installed on a member server or domain controller running on Windows 2000 Server or Windows Server 2003. The following procedure can be used to set up IAS on both a Windows 2000 server and a Windows 2003 server:

CAUTION

IAS should never be installed on the ISA server itself, but rather on an internal member server or domain controller.

1. Open the Add or Remove Programs menu from within the Control Panel of the server designated to host IAS.
2. Select the Add/Remove Windows Components button.

3. When the Windows Components Wizard window opens, scroll down to locate the Networking Service component section.

4. Highlight the Networking Services component, and click the Details button. Do not click the check box beside Network Services; this installs every component.

5. On the Networking Service window, check the Internet Authentication Service checkbox, as shown in Figure 9.9.

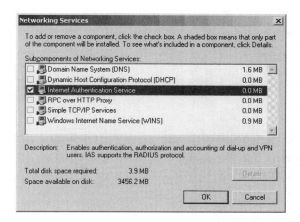

FIGURE 9.9   Installing the Internet Authentication Service (IAS).

6. Click OK to close the Networking Services window. On the Windows Components Wizard window, click Next.

7. When the installation is complete, click Finish to close the window.

Detailing IAS Permissions Required in Active Directory

To successfully authenticate domain users, the IAS server needs rights to read the dial-in properties of user accounts within Active Directory. The process of authorizing the IAS server adds the IAS server account to the RAS and IAS Servers group within the Users container in Active Directory. If users from different domains will authenticate against the IAS server, then the IAS server account must be added to the RAS and ISA server group within the user's local domain. This can be done manually from within Active Directory Users and Computers or scripted with the NETSH or DSMOD utilities.

To successfully register the IAS server by adding the server to the RAS and IAS Server group, the appropriate administrative permissions are required in each domain.

Use the following procedure to authorize the IAS server through the IAS management console:

1. Open the Internet Authentication Service console (Start, Administrative Tools, Internet Authentication Service).

2. Right-click Internet Authentication Service (Local) and select Register Service in Active Directory from the context menu, as shown in Figure 9.10.

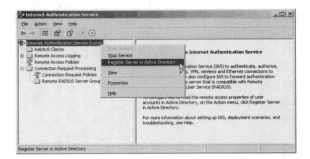

FIGURE 9.10   Registering the IAS in Active Directory.

3. An information dialog box is displayed describing the event. Click the OK button.

4. A warning dialog box is displayed stating that the computer is now authorized to read users' dial-in properties for the domain. Click the OK button.

Setting Up the ISA Server as an IAS Client

IAS needs to be configured to allow the authentication request from the ISA VPN server. The following procedure can be used to set up IAS on both a Windows 2000 server and a Windows 2003 server. The IAS client in this case refers to the ISA VPN server, as it acts as a client for the IAS service.

1. Open the Internet Authentication Service console.

2. Right-click RADIUS Clients and select New RADIUS Client from the context menu.

3. On the Name and Address properties window, enter the friendly name and client address in the fields provided. The friendly name can be any name used to identify the ISA server. The client address can be either the host name or IP address of the internal interface on the ISA server, as shown in Figure 9.11. Click Next to continue.

4. On the Additional Information properties window, select Microsoft from the Client-Vendor drop-down list.

5. Enter and confirm a shared secret in the field provided. This shared secret is entered again at a later point to encrypt the communications between the ISA server and the IAS server.

6. Enable the Request Must Contain the Message Authenticator Attribute option.

7. Click Finish to close the window. The newly configured RADIUS client is displayed in the Details pane.

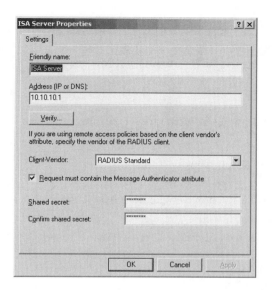

FIGURE 9.11   Setting up the ISA server as an IAS client.

NOTE

The shared secret is used to encrypt specific information sent between the RADIUS server and RADIUS client. The shared secret is also used to verify the integrity of the data and make sure it is not modified during transmission. Because the key is used to encrypt the data between the client and server, it is highly recommended to use a shared secret key with at least 22 characters consisting of a random combination of alphanumeric and special characters, and optimal to use a key with 128 random characters.

Depending on the level of comfort desired, the shared secret should be periodically changed, more often if the network segment between the ISA VPN server and the IAS server is not completely trusted. This ensures that anyone who captures the traffic does not have enough time to crack the key by way of a brute force attack before it has been changed. As an additional level of security, IP Security (IPSec) encryption using machine certificates is recommended.

Establishing IAS Remote Access Policies

After the RADIUS client information has been created, the RADIUS server must be configured to allow VPN connections. IAS allows for the creation of Remote Access Policies that allow specific types of VPN connections to be made. These Remote Access Policies also allow for specific users or groups to be granted access.

> **NOTE**
>
> Whether using domain-based or RADIUS authentication, it is best practice to create an Active Directory group that will be used to grant access to VPN. Granting VPN access then becomes as simple as adding a user as a member of that group.

To create a Remote Access Policy, perform the following from the server running IAS (not the ISA server):

1. Open the IAS Console (Start, All Programs, Administrative Tools, Internet Authentication Service).
2. Right-click the Remote Access Policies node and click New Remote Access Policy.
3. At the Wizard welcome screen, click Next to continue.
4. At the subsequent dialog box, shown in Figure 9.12, select Use the Wizard to Set Up a Typical Policy for a Common Scenario.

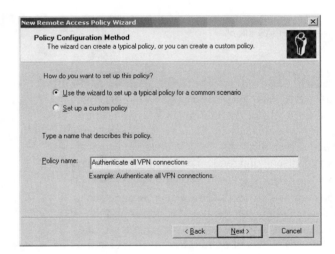

FIGURE 9.12   Creating a Remote Access Policy for RADIUS VPN authentication.

5. Enter a name for the policy, and click Next to continue.
6. From the list of access methods, select VPN and click Next.
7. Under the User or Group Access dialog box, select Group, and then click the Add button.
8. Enter a name of an Active Directory Group whose members will have VPN access and then click OK and then Next to continue.
9. Select the authentication protocols that the policy will support. For security reasons, it is often best to only allow MS-CHAP v2. Click Next to continue.

10. Select the various levels of IPSec encryption that will be supported. Allowing weaker levels of encryption can be a security threat, but can allow for greater compatibility. Click Next to continue.

11. Review the settings and click Finish.

After the Remote Access Policy has been put into place, advanced settings and other modifications can be made to it by double-clicking on the policy itself, enabling the options shown in Figure 9.13 to be displayed.

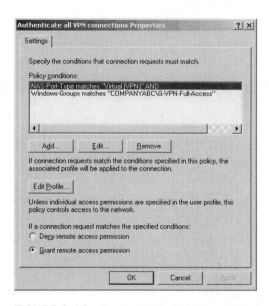

FIGURE 9.13   Reviewing an IAS Remote Access Policy.

Examining RADIUS Message Authentication

The RADIUS server and the RADIUS client communicate only with the designated IP addresses set during the configuring of each device. To prevent IP address spoofing of the client or server during authentication, the message authentication option is enabled. The Message Authenticator attribute specifies that a MD5 hash of the entire authentication message needs to be created, using the shared secret as the key. If the client or server does not calculate the correct value of the Message Authenticator, communication is dropped. For additional information, please review RFC 2869, detailing RADIUS extensions.

Be careful when configuring the RADIUS client address with the hostname of the ISA VPN server. Verifying the IAS server can resolve this name to the internal interface of the ISA VPN server. If the ISA server is a member of the domain, it may have already registered its IP address with the internal Active Directory DNS server. If the ISA server is a stand-alone system, then either a host record needs to be added to the internal DNS server or a record needs to be added to the host file located on the IAS server.

Configuring ISA to Use IAS for Authentication

The first step in the process is to define a list of RADIUS servers available to ISA for authentication. Use the following process to define one or more RADIUS servers. It is recommended to have at least two RADIUS systems for redundancy.

1. Open the ISA Server Management Console.

2. From within the scope pane, expand Configuration, and select the General menu item.

3. Select Specify RADIUS and LDAP Servers from the Details pane.

4. On the RADIUS Servers page, click the Add button.

5. Enter the hostname or IP address of the RADIUS server in the Server Name field.

6. Enter a description in the Server Description field.

7. Click the Change button, and enter and confirm the shared secret, as shown in Figure 9.14. This key must match the key entered on the IAS (RADIUS) server. Click the OK button when complete.

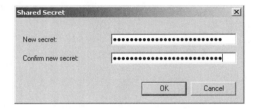

FIGURE 9.14   Defining a RADIUS server shared key in ISA.

8. The default Port and Time-out values are appropriate in most scenarios and can be left as default.

9. Enable the Always Use Message Authenticator check box. Click the OK button to close the Add RADIUS Servers window.

10. Click the OK button to close the RADIUS servers window, and then click the Apply button to save and apply the new changes.

After the list of RADIUS servers has been defined, the VPN configuration can be modified to use RADIUS for authentication. The following process can be used to set the IAS server VPN users will use for authentication:

1. Open the ISA Server Management Console.

2. Select the Virtual Private Networks (VPN) menu item from the Scope pane.

3. Make sure the VPN Clients tab is active in the Details pane, and then select Specify RADIUS Configuration from the Tasks pane.

4. Enable the Use RADIUS for Authentication check box.

5. Click the RADIUS Servers button.

6. From the list of RADIUS servers shown in Figure 9.15, select the RADIUS server created in the previous steps and then press the OK button.

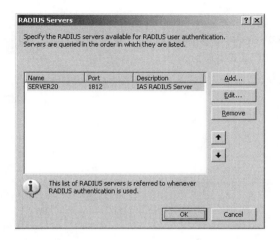

FIGURE 9.15   Modifying RADIUS server settings for VPN client access.

7. Click the OK button, and a warning dialog box then states that if the current setting is applied, all active VPN sessions will be disconnected. Click the OK button to acknowledge the warning.

8. Click the OK button to close the Virtual Private Networks (VPN) Properties window.

9. Click the Apply button to save and apply the configuration.

The effect of the previous steps grays out the Groups option within the VPN configuration. Remote access is now controlled through the Active Directory dial-in policy configuration. From this point, all VPN authentication will use RADIUS unless otherwise reconfigured.

Configuring ISA for Point-to-Point Tunneling Protocol (PPTP) VPN Connections

One of the primary reasons to use the PPTP protocol to establish a VPN connection is the overall "start to finish" simplicity. PPTP connections are fairly straightforward to set up, and provide for a decent level of VPN security. PPTP security is user based, however, which means that if a user's credentials are compromised, access could be obtained by unauthorized users. The most secure VPN connections, however, can be set up using the L2TP protocol, which uses a combination of user and computer authentication. L2TP is described in more detail later in this chapter.

Configuring an ISA VPN Connection to Use PPTP

The following process can be used to enable PPTP VPN support on the ISA VPN server:

1. Open the ISA Server Management Console and select Virtual Private Networks (VPN) from the Scope pane.

2. Select the VPN Clients tab in the Details pane.

3. Select Configure VPN Client Access from the Tasks pane.

4. On the Protocols tab, enable the Enable PPTP check box, as shown in Figure 9.16.

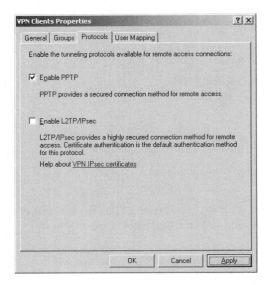

FIGURE 9.16   Configuring an ISA server to use PPTP authentication.

5. Select the OK button to close the window.

6. Select the Apply button to apply the new configuration.

Configuring a Windows XP Professional Client for PPTP Communication

There are two methods for creating VPN connections for clients. The first method is by using the Connection Management Administration Kit (CMAK) to create a custom profile that can be automatically configured on client workstations. This technique is discussed in detail in later sections of this chapter. The second method is a manual method, and can be performed directly on a client workstation with the following procedure:

> **NOTE**
>
> This procedure illustrates how to set up a manual connection on Windows XP Professional. Different operating systems such as Windows 2000 Professional use similar steps, with slight modifications to the process. For security reasons, however, it is recommended to set up client VPN access from Windows XP systems.

1. Log on to the system and Open Network Connections from the Control Panel.

2. Run the New Connection Wizard by clicking on Create a new connection.

3. On the Welcome page, click Next.

4. On the Network Connection Type page, select Connect to the Network at My Workplace and click Next.

5. On the Network Connection page, select Virtual Private Network Connection and click Next.

6. On the Connection Name page, enter the company name or a meaningful description in the field provided and click Next.

7. If there are existing network connections on the workstation, the Public Network page is displayed. Select Do Not Dial the Initial Connection if the client will always have an automatically configured Internet connection; otherwise, select the connection required to establish an Internet connection from the drop-down menu. Click Next to continue.

8. On the VPN Server Selection page, enter the public IP address or Fully Qualified Domain Name (FQDN) of the ISA VPN server, similar to what is shown in Figure 9.17. Click Next to continue.

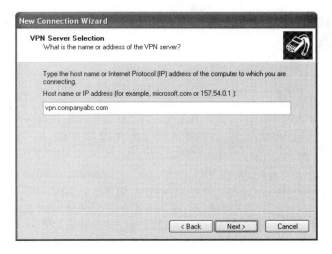

FIGURE 9.17   Setting up a PPTP connection in Windows XP.

9. On the Connection Availability page, select My Use Only if the connection will not be made available to all users that log on to the workstation. For the opposite scenario, select Anyone's Use. Click Next to continue.

10. Click the Finish button to close the window.

Testing the PPTP Connection

At this stage, the test should be able to establish a VPN tunnel to the server. To test the connection, perform the following:

1. From the client's Control Panel, open Network Connections.

2. Double-click on the VPN Connection object created in the preceding step.

3. Enter the username and password of a user that was granted access in the previous steps.

4. Click the Connect button. The default setting in a new configuration is adequate for establishing a PPTP VPN connection.

At this point, the client should make the connection to the ISA VPN server and establish communications with the internal network resources, as specified in the network rules. Note that the client needs to be outside the network to support this. Check the event logs on the IAS server and the ISA VPN server if the connection is not successful.

> **NOTE**
>
> Recall that simply establishing a VPN connection to an ISA server does not automatically grant a client blanket access to the internal network. Firewall and network rules must first be established, as outlined in the previous sections of this chapter.

Creating Layer 2 Tunneling Protocol (L2TP) VPN Connections with ISA

The most secure method of setting up VPN access is to utilize a method that combines both user authentication, such as inputting a username and password, with machine authentication, which involves making sure the computer the user is using is a trusted resource. The advantage to this approach is that even if a user's password is stolen, access is not automatically granted. The Layer 2 Tunneling Protocol (L2TP) with IP Security (IPSec) is the supported method within ISA Server for accomplishing this level of security.

Unfortunately, however, unlike PPTP VPN connections, L2TP VPN tunnels cannot reliably traverse NAT connections. For example, if the ISA server resides on the inside of a packet-filter firewall, such as a PIX firewall, and that firewall provides for a NAT relationship to the ISA server, the L2TP tunnel will fail to be established. L2TP relies on an accurate negotiation between two known addresses.

Recent moves have been made to move to a model known as NAT-T (NAT traversal), which enables this type of access to occur, but this implementation is currently in its infancy, and all routers between source and destination must support its implementation. In the meantime, if a NAT relationship exists between ISA and the clients it supports, PPTP protocol support is the only reliable way to create VPN connections.

If the ISA server holds a public IP address (or if all devices support NAT traversal properly), then L2TP protocol VPN connections can be established. The following process can be used to enable L2TP/IPSec VPN support on the ISA VPN server:

1. Open the ISA Server Management Console and select Virtual Private Networks (VPN) from the Scope pane.

2. Select the VPN Clients tab in the Details pane.

3. Select Configure VPN Client Access from the Tasks pane.

4. On the Protocols tab, enable the Enable L2TP/IPSec check box, as shown in Figure 9.18.

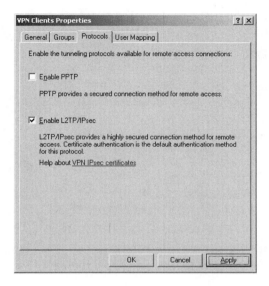

FIGURE 9.18   Enabling L2TP VPN client access.

5. Select the OK button to close the window.

6. Select the Apply button to apply the new configuration.

Configuring an IPSec Pre-Shared Key

Essentially, two options can be used to encrypt the L2TP VPN session. The first option is to use a pre-shared key, which is a manually configured alphanumeric password that is inputted on the server and on all the VPN clients. This creates a secure L2TP IPSec VPN tunnel, but is not considered secure because someone could theoretically uncover the key through social engineering and, when compromised, it must then be manually reset on all clients. The more secure approach is to deploy a PKI infrastructure, which can take more time to set up, but is more inherently secure.

For the purposes of testing an L2TP connection, or to deploy a limited L2TP infrastructure using a pre-shared key, use the following procedure:

1. Open the ISA Server Management Console.

2. Select the Virtual Private Networking (VPN) node from the Scope pane.

3. Click on Select Authentication Methods from the Tasks pane.

4. In the Authentication tab, check Allow Custom IPSec Policy for L2TP Connection.

5. Enter the desired key, similar to the image shown in Figure 9.19.

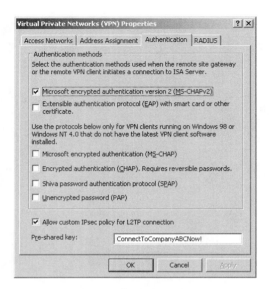

FIGURE 9.19   Entering an IPSec pre-shared key.

6. Press OK to close the window, and then press Apply to save and apply the new configuration.

Configuring a Windows XP Professional Client for an L2TP VPN Connection

The following process can be used to configure a remote Windows XP workstation for standard L2TP communication. For automatic provisioning of this VPN connection, see the later section of this chapter that details the use of the Connection Management Administration Kit (CMAK) to create automatic VPN connections.

1. Log on to the system and open Create a new connection from the Control Panel.
2. Run the New Connection Wizard.
3. On the Welcome page, click Next.
4. On the Network Connection Type page, select Connect to the Network at My Workplace and click Next.
5. On the Network Connection page, select Virtual Private Network Connection, as shown in Figure 9.20, and click Next.
6. On the Connection Name page, enter the company name or a meaningful description in the field provided and click Next.
7. If there are existing network connections on the workstation, the Public Network page is displayed. Select Do Not Dial the Initial Connection in most cases (unless a dial-up modem needs to be connected first). Click Next to continue.

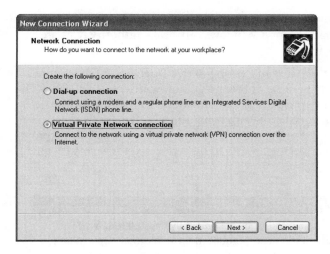

FIGURE 9.20   Configuring a Windows XP Professional client to use an L2TP VPN connection.

8. On the VPN Server Selection page, enter the public IP address or the registered host-name of the ISA VPN server on the Internet. Click Next to continue.

9. On the Connection Availability page, select Anyone's Use. Click Next to continue.

10. Click the Finish button to close the window.

Creating a Public Key Infrastructure (PKI) for L2TP with IPSec Support

As previously mentioned, it is wise to deploy a certificates-based approach to L2TP VPN connections to maintain the highest levels of security and control over VPN access. To deploy this type of environment, a Public Key Infrastructure (PKI) must be set up. PKI provides a mechanism by which individual encrypted certificates are distributed to individual computers to validate their identity.

> **NOTE**
>
> Remember that L2TP/IPSec requires the ISA server's public interface to be directly addressed—not behind any type of Network Address Translation (NAT)—for this type of VPN connection using PKI certificates to take place. The one exception to this case is if the systems providing the network address translation capability are compliant with the recent RFCs for NAT traversal (RFCs 3947 and 3948). Because this is a relatively new technology, it may take a few years for common acceptance of this practice, however.

PKI environments can be set up in a number of ways, with Microsoft and third-party products providing for robust implementations. The Microsoft implementation of PKI is installed on Windows servers and involves the deployment of a Windows certificate authority. The two primary configurations for a Windows certificate authority (CA) are enterprise and stand-alone.

It is recommended that an organization with an existing Active Directory infrastructure implement an enterprise CA primarily because of the integration with Active Directory. By leveraging group policies with the enterprise CA, an administrator can automatically provision certificates to domain members, certificates being the key element in a L2TP/IPSec VPN configuration. With a stand-alone or commercial CA, the certificate provisioning process is manual, requiring a specific process to be performed for each VPN client and server.

NOTE

A PKI design process is complex, and should not be taken lightly. In addition, a Windows certificate authority implementation can be utilized for numerous applications and services in addition to VPN support, so it is recommended that you put careful thought into the design and implementation of a PKI infrastructure.

Installing the Enterprise Root Certificate Authority (CA)

If a PKI infrastructure is not already in place, the Microsoft implementation can be set up and configured in the internal environment. The following steps can be used to install Microsoft Internet Information Services (IIS) and the certificate authority on a domain member. Note that a CA should not be set up on the ISA server itself, and IIS should never be set up on ISA (with the possible exception of the SMTP component of IIS in certain circumstances). IIS is required to support the certificate enrollment website and must be installed on the same system as the CA to provide for web certificate enrollment.

1. Open Add or Remove Programs from the Control Panel.
2. Select the Add/Remove Windows Components button.
3. Click the check box beside Application Server. The check box is enabled, with a gray background, as shown in Figure 9.21. This installs minimal IIS components, perfect for the CA website. Click Next.
4. Press Finish after IIS has been installed to return to the Add or Remove Programs window.
5. Select the Add/Remove Windows Components button.
6. Click the Certificate Services check box.
7. Read the warning dialog box, and then click the Yes button. Click Next.
8. On the CA Type page, select the appropriate option for the environment (enterprise root CA, in most cases). Click Next to continue.

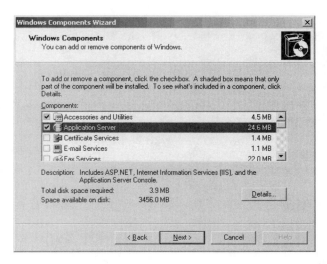

FIGURE 9.21   Installing IIS on a domain member to provide for certificate web enrollment.

9. On the CA Identifying Information page, enter the common name for the CA. This can be any descriptive name. Click Next.

10. On the Certificate Database Settings page, accept the defaults and click Next. For redundancy and scalability, it is recommended to separate the log file from the database.

11. Read the IIS warning dialog box, and then click the Yes button.

12. Read the ASP warning dialog box when it is displayed, and then click the Yes button.

13. Click Finish after the CA has completed the installation.

Configuring the Enterprise Root CA

If using an enterprise certificate authority, and supporting non-domain members, such as an ISA server that is a member of a workgroup, then a template to allow machine certificates should be added and configured to allow provisioning through the web enrollment page. This is common when supporting a mix of domain members and non-domain members.

The following steps can be used to configure the existing enterprise certificate authority with a new computer certificate template.

CAUTION

This process is not required and is not possible with a stand-alone certificate authority because the Client Authentication and Server Authentication certificates are already available by default.

1. From a member server in the domain that has been configured with the enterprise certificate authority in the previous steps (not the ISA server), click Start, Run, type in **CertTmpl.msc**, and press OK.

2. Right-click Computer from the list of available certificates and select Duplicate Template from the context menu.

3. In the properties windows, enter a descriptive name in the Template Display Name field.

4. On the Request Handling tab, enable the Allow Private Key to Be Exported check box, as shown in Figure 9.22.

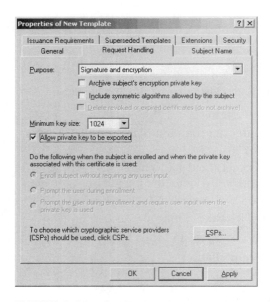

FIGURE 9.22   Configuring the enterprise certificate authority.

5. On the Subject Name tab, select Supply in the Request.

6. On the Security tab, review the security. By default, only administrators can enroll new systems; this responsibility can be delegated if required.

7. Click the OK button to save the changes and close the window.

CAUTION

The previous steps enable machine certificates to be issued through the web enrollment page, using the default settings. This is required when certificates need to be installed on non-domain members. It is highly recommended to research and configure the remaining options as required by company policy.

Now that the template has been created, it must be added to the list of templates available to the enterprise CA. The following process can be used to accomplish this:

1. Open the Certification Authority management console (Start, Administrative Tools, Certification Authority).

2. Expand the CA, right-click Certificate Templates, and select New, Certificate Template to Issue from the context menu.

3. Select the certificate template created in the previous steps and click OK to continue.

The enterprise certificate authority is now ready to provision machine certificates through web enrollment.

Requesting a Certificate for the ISA VPN Server

The process of requesting a certificate from a private internal certificate authority or a public certificate authority generally follows the same principles when the ISA server has been implemented as a stand-alone workgroup member.

Before starting the certificate enrollment process, it is important to add the certificate server to the trusted Internet security zone of the web browser on the ISA server. In addition, there must not be any rules set up on the ISA server that block access from the local host to the web server with the CA installed on it.

The following process can be used to request a certificate for the ISA server. This can be performed from the system that will have the certificate installed on it, but that is not a requirement. If this is performed on a different system, after the certificates have been created, they need to be exported and then imported to the correct system.

> **NOTE**
>
> For this process to work properly, the certificate web enrollment server must be accessible via ISA's system policy rules, which normally restrict the ISA server's capability to read web pages on servers. For more information on the system policy, refer to Chapter 5, "Deploying ISA Server 2006 as a Firewall."

6

The following procedure can be used to create the initial certificate request:

1. From the ISA server, open Internet Explorer, and browse to the certificate web enrollment page. By default, this is http://<certificate server>/certsrv.

2. Select the Request a Certificate task.

3. Select Advanced Certificate Request.

4. Select Create and Submit a Request to This CA.

5. From the Certificate Template drop-down, select Configuring the Enterprise Root CA.

6. Enter the name of the ISA VPN server for which the certificate is being issued in the field provided. This name must match the actual machine name. Fill in the remaining descriptive details as needed.

7. Make sure the Mark Keys as Exportable check box is enabled.

8. Enable the Store Certificate in the Local Computer Certificate Store option.

9. Click the Submit button.

10. Click Yes to acknowledge the Potential Scripting Violation dialog box.

11. On the Certificate Issued page, click Install This Certificate.

12. Click Yes to acknowledge the Potential Scripting Violation dialog box.

A certificate has now been installed in the system's local computer certificate store. The process to move this certificate to another system is discussed later in this chapter.

Requesting a Certificate for the VPN Client

The same process can be used to generate a certificate for a VPN client. Although a certificate can be generated for both a member and a non-member, it is not recommended to configure domain members this way. It is much more efficient to configure the group policy autoenrollment, which automatically distributes the proper certificates to computers that are members of an Active Directory domain. To manually add the certificate to the client, perform the following steps:

1. From the VPN client, open Internet Explorer, and browse to the certificate web enrollment page. By default, this is http://<certificate server>/certssrv.

> **NOTE**
>
> The VPN client must access the web enrollment page from a network that has access to it—that is, is not being blocked by a firewall. Because web enrollment is a particularly sensitive service, it is not common to make it available through the Internet or through untrusted networks.

2. Select the Request a Certificate task.

3. Select Advanced Certificate Request.

4. Select Create and Submit a Request to This CA.

5. From the Certificate Template drop-down, select Configuring the Enterprise Root CA.

6. Enter the name of the VPN client. This name must match the actual machine name. Fill in the remaining descriptive details as needed.

7. Make sure that Mark Keys as Exportable is enabled.

8. Enable the Store Certificate in the Local Computer Certificate Store option.

9. Click the Submit button.

10. Click Yes to acknowledge the Potential Scripting Violation dialog box.

11. On the Certificate Issued page, click Install This Certificate.

12. Click Yes to acknowledge the Potential Scripting Violation dialog box.

A certificate for the VPN client has now been installed in the local computer certificate store of the VPN client. The process to move this certificate to another system is discussed later in this chapter.

Downloading the CA Certificate

After the client(s) and ISA Server have been enrolled and a certificate has been generated, it must then be downloaded and added to the Trusted Root Certification Authorities local store on each device.

An advantage to using an enterprise CA is that the CA certificate is automatically added to the local certificate store on all domain members; only non–domain members are required to add the certificate. A stand-alone CA certificate is added to the local certificate store on domain members only if it is installed on a domain controller. Otherwise, this certificate needs to be added to all systems that will establish a L2TP/IPSec VPN tunnel.

1. Open Internet Explorer, and browse to the certificate web enrollment page. By default, this is http://<certificate server>/certssrv.

2. Select Download a CA Certificate, Certificate Chain, or CRL.

3. Select Download CA Certificate, and save the file to removable media.

This file is not required to be protected and can be freely distributed via any method including email. This is only the CA's public key—not the private key. For example, many commercial CAs' public keys are distributed with Internet Explorer.

Exporting and Importing Certificates

If all the certificates were created through the certificate enrollment page, either with the enterprise CA or the stand-alone CA, from the same computer, they must then be exported to removable media and imported into the local certificates store.

To view the local certificate store on a client or a server, a Microsoft Management Console (MMC) session must be set up. Follow the steps outlined here to perform this function:

1. Click Start, Run, type MMC, and click OK.

2. Select File, Add/Remove Snap-in.

3. Click the Add button.

4. Select Certificates from the snap-in list, as shown in Figure 9.23, and then click Add.

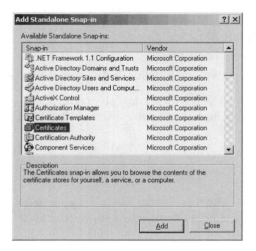

FIGURE 9.23   Adding the Certificates MMC snap-in.

5. Select Computer Account, click Next, then Finish.

6. Select Certificates from the snap-in list and click Add.

7. Select My User Account, click Finish, and then click Close.

8. Save the MMC.

One MMC console can be set up to manage all the different systems that require certificates. This option is usually not available because the VPN server is protected with a firewall, so the certificates may have to be transferred on portable, erasable media.

CAUTION

The certificates that are to be exported contain both the private and public key. It is extremely important to make sure the process that is used to transfer the certificates from one system to another is secure and the media is destroyed afterward. Compromising the private key can render the encryption used in the VPN tunnel useless. In many cases, this transfer takes place at a trusted location, such as a laptop staging area of a help desk, to avoid compromise of the key.

To export the certificate, perform the following steps:

1. From the system where the certificate web enrollment form was created, open the MMC (Start, Run, MMC.exe).

2. Navigate to Certificates (Local Computer) from the Scope pane.

3. Navigate to Personal, Certificates.

4. Right-click the first certificate that was created. This should be the name of the ISA VPN server, with the intended purposes listed as Server Authentication. Select All Tasks, Export from the context menu.

5. On the Welcome page, click Next.

6. On the Export Private Key page, select Yes, Export the Private Key, and click Next.

7. On the Export File Format page, make sure the Enable Strong Protection option is enabled. Click Next.

8. On the Password page, type and confirm a strong password. This should be a random combination of alphanumeric and special characters. Click Next.

9. On the File to Export page, browse to the location of the removable media to which the file will be saved, and click Next.

10. On the Completion page, click Finish.

Repeat the previous process for each of the server and client certificates created. Use the following process to import the certificates to the required systems.

1. Insert the removable media in the ISA VPN server or VPN client system.

2. Open the MMC created in the previous process.

3. Expand Certificates (Local Computer) from the Scope pane.

4. Right-click on Personal and select All Tasks, Import.

5. On the Welcome page, shown in Figure 9.24, click Next.

FIGURE 9.24   Importing client certificates.

6. On the File to Import page, browse to locate the certificate created for the ISA VPN server. Click Next.

7. Enter the password in the field provided and enable the option to mark the key as exportable.

8. On the Certificate Store page, the Personal store should already be selected. Click Next.

9. On the Completing page, click Finish.

10. Right-click on Trusted Root Certificate Authorities and select All Tasks, Import.

11. On the Welcome page, click Next.

12. On the File to Import page, browse to locate the CA certificate previously saved. Click Next.

13. The Trusted Root Certificate Authorities should already be the selected store. Click Next to continue.

Repeat the entire process of importing the certificate and the CA certificate for the remaining VPN servers and client systems.

Using Active Directory Autoenrollment

When VPN clients are members of the internal domain and a PKI infrastructure has been deployed, the easiest and most secure method to get certificates on a workstation is through the process of group policy autoenrollment. The autoenrollment process automatically requests and maintains a certificate for the computers and servers.

As beneficial as autoenrollment may be, many prerequisites must be in place for it to work. These prerequisites are as follows:

▶ All VPN clients must be Windows XP Professional.

▶ The AD domain must be running Windows Server 2003 functional level (Native Mode).

▶ The certificates must be provisioned from a CA server running Windows Server 2003 Enterprise or Data Center Edition.

If these prerequisites are satisfied, the following process can be used to configure autoenrollment.

NOTE

The following steps describe autoenrollment configuration steps using the Group Policy Management Console (GPMC) tool, which is a downloadable add-on to Windows Server 2003. Although the same settings can be accomplished with the built-in tool, it is highly recommended to download and install GPMC. It greatly extends the management capabilities of group policies. The tool can be downloaded at the following URL:

http://www.microsoft.com/windowsserver2003/gpmc/default.mspx

1. Open the GPMC tool (Start, Administrative Tools, Group Policy Management).

2. Either create and link a new group policy or edit an existing group policy.

3. Expand Computer Configuration and choose Windows Settings, Security Settings, Public Key Policies from the Scope pane.

4. Double-click on Autoenrollment Settings.

5. On the Autoenrollment Settings Properties windows, enable Enroll Certificates Automatically and enable both check boxes to renew and update certificates, as shown in Figure 9.25. Click OK.

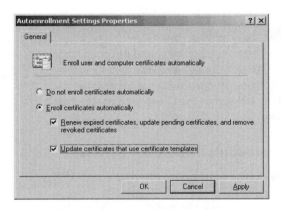

FIGURE 9.25   Configuring AD certificate autoenrollment.

6. Right-click Automatic Certificate Request Settings from the Scope pane. Select New, Automatic Certificate Request from the context menu.

7. On the Welcome page, click Next.

8. On the Certificate Template page, select Computer, and then click Next.

9. On the Completing page, click Finish.

The machine requests the certificate during login or during the next group policy refresh cycle. Use the GPUPDATE.EXE command to refresh the group policy. The simplest method to invoke the autoenrollment process is just to restart the system. Look for event 19, from source autoenrollment, in the event log of the local system to see whether the process was successful. The Certificates snap-in can also be used to view the newly acquired certificate on the client, and the Certification Authority console can be used to view newly provisioned certificates.

Using the Connection Manager Administration Kit (CMAK) to Automate VPN Client Deployment

To assist administrators in the deployment of multiple VPN client configuration settings, Microsoft offers a tool called the Connection Manager Administration Kit (CMAK). This tool, installed as an option on a Windows Server 2003 system (or downloaded for older versions of the OS), allows for custom profiles to be generated and then easily distributed to VPN clients via an executable file.

For example, the CMAK allows administrators to configure complicated VPN connection settings, such as protocol support, VPN server IP address, encryption methods, and more advanced options, and easily distribute them via email or other methods to clients. This greatly simplifies the deployment of a VPN infrastructure that uses ISA Server.

> **NOTE**
>
> If L2TP/IPSec VPNs will be created, using the CMAK helps to automate the connection settings, but does not distribute necessary client certificates. Methods listed in previous sections of this chapter, such as web enrollment of certificates or, preferably, Active Directory autoenrollment, must be run in addition to the CMAK profiles, to allow clients to connect using L2TP/IPSec VPN tunnels.

Installing the Connection Manager Administration Kit (CMAK)

To set up CMAK, it must first be installed as a component on an internal server in the domain. It should not normally be set up on an ISA server: It is not good practice to install unnecessary tools or services on an ISA server itself. To install the CMAK, perform the following steps on the internal member server:

1. Click Start, Control Panel, Add or Remove Programs.
2. Click Add/Remove Windows Components.
3. Scroll down and select the Management and Monitoring Tools component by clicking on the text of the box. Do not check the box or it installs all subcomponents. After it is selected (highlighted), click the Details button.
4. Check the box labeled Connection Manager Administration Kit, as shown in Figure 9.26. Click OK to continue.
5. Click Next to continue.

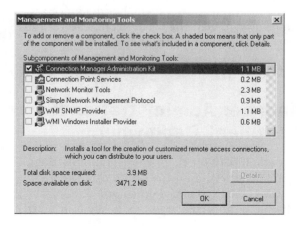

FIGURE 9.26   Installing the Connection Manager Administration Kit (CMAK).

6. Insert the Windows Server 2003 CD if prompted and click OK.

7. Click Finish to finalize the CMAK installation.

Creating CMAK Profiles for Client Deployment Automation

After the CMAK is installed on a member server, individual, unique CMAK profiles can be compiled by running through the steps of a CMAK wizard. The wizard allows for a wide variety of options, but this example focuses on setting up CMAK for a simple VPN connection.

1. Open the CMAK (Start, Administrative Tools, Connection Manager Administration Kit).

2. At the wizard start screen, click Next to continue.

3. Select New Profile from the Service Profile Selection list and click Next to continue.

4. Enter a name for the service, and a filename for the executable, such as what is shown in Figure 9.27. Click Next to continue.

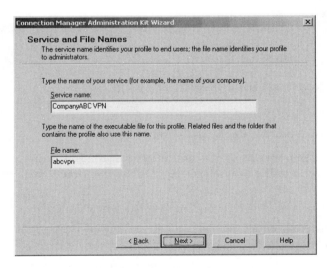

FIGURE 9.27   Creating a CMAK VPN profile.

5. Under the realm name, select Do Not Add a Realm Name to the User Name (a realm name is not normally required, unless multiple ISPs are used for access), and click Next to continue.

6. Under Merging Profile Information, the opportunity to import access numbers and existing phone book information from other profiles is available. For a new profile, leave the fields blank and click Next to continue.

The subsequent dialog box, labeled VPN Support and shown in Figure 9.28, is critical. In it, the Fully Qualified Domain Name (FQDN) of the ISA server or its public IP address can be entered and will be automatically set up when the profile is installed. In addition, an option to allow VPN users to choose from multiple servers is listed. This can prove to be valuable if setting up multiple VPN presences across different geographic areas, for example.

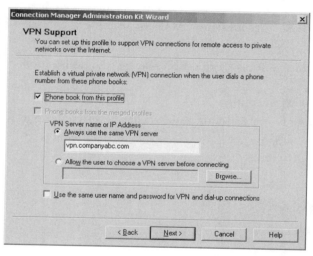

FIGURE 9.28   Entering VPN Support information into a CMAK profile.

To continue with the CMAK VPN profile process, do the following:

1. Check the box labeled Phone Book from this profile, and then enter the FQDN or public IP address of the ISA server into the field labeled Always Use the Same VPN Server. Click Next to continue.

2. Under the VPN Entries dialog box, press the New button to create a new entry.

3. Enter a descriptive name for the entry under the General tab, and review the options under the TCP/IP Settings and Security tab.

The General tab of the New VPN Entry dialog box has two additional options. The Disable File and Printer Sharing option, which affects only Windows NT, 2000, and XP systems, restricts clients from sharing files or printers while they are connected, which may be desired in some cases. The Enable Clients to Log On to a Network option affects only down-level Windows 9x clients, and is normally left checked.

The Security tab of the VPN Entry dialog box, shown in Figure 9.29, is particularly important. This tab allows for the configuration of the type of protocol and encryption support the connection will utilize.

Under the Security tab, the option to utilize advanced and/or basic settings for the VPN connection are listed. Advanced Security options are relevant only for Windows 2000,

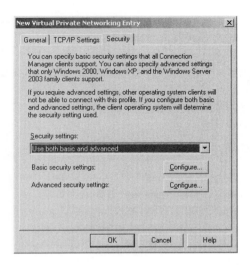

FIGURE 9.29   Examining the Security tab of the New VPN Entry dialog box.

2003, and XP systems, and can be used by only them. Consequently, if the option for Use Advanced Security Settings is selected in the Security Settings drop-down box, only those types of clients can connect. The Basic security settings apply only to down-level clients, and selecting Use Basic Security Settings from the drop-down box allows for only settings that all clients can use. This effectively dilutes the security options available and is not recommended. Selecting Use Both Basic and Advanced from the drop-down box, however, enables the client OS to determine which settings to use.

Clicking on the Configure tab under the Basic Security Settings tab enables down-level OS protocol options to be specified, which are limited to basic PPTP and L2TP settings.

The Advanced Security Settings (click on the second Configure button) enable authentication methods to be selected. Take particular care to select only those forms of authentication that provide the greatest amount of security that can be supported by the clients themselves. Ideally, this involves forcing encryption using L2TP only, with MS-CHAP v2 as the only authentication method, as shown in Figure 9.30.

The TCP/IP Settings tab can be used to manually assign DNS and WINS servers to VPN clients. This is often handled by internal DHCP servers, so it is not always necessary to fill in these fields. The setting labeled Make This Connection the Client's Default Gateway is important because it can increase the security of your VPN client configuration by forcing the client to send all traffic through the ISA server. This limits the client's capabilities to circumvent organizational security by making sure it complies with all security policies and rules while it is connected to the internal network.

To continue with the configuration process, do the following:

1. Using the options discussed as a guide, select the appropriate settings from the New Virtual Private Networking Entry dialog box and click OK when finished.

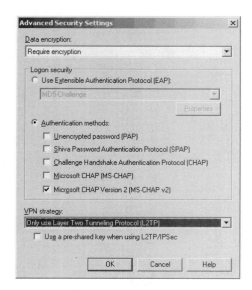

FIGURE 9.30   Viewing Advanced Security Settings for an ISA VPN entry in CMAK.

2. Click Next to continue.

3. The subsequent dialog box allows for the import of a phone book for dial-up. In this case, as a simple VPN connection profile without dial-up options is being created, uncheck the Automatically Download Phone Book Updates option and leave the remaining fields blank. Click Next to continue.

4. The subsequent dialog box dictates the creation of a dial-up networking entry. This must be created, but will be disabled in later stages of this setup because it is not needed in the case of a simple VPN connection profile (one that does not require dialing into RAS servers first before tunneling in through VPN). Click the New button to create this.

5. Enter a descriptive name, accept all defaults, and click OK.

NOTE

The CMAK requires this dial-up networking entry to be created because originally most VPNs were set up by remote users dialing in via modems to a modem pool at an organization. In today's modern infrastructure, however, it is more common to have VPN clients gain remote access directly over the Internet from high-speed or other ISP dial-up connections. It is important to keep this in mind because this example illustrates the latter scenario, and the dial-up networking entry that is created here is essentially discarded in later steps.

6. Click Next at the Dial-up Networking Entries dialog box.

7. Under the Routing Table Update dialog box, accept the default of Do Not Change the Routing Tables and click Next to continue.

8. Under the Automatic Proxy Configuration dialog box, select the default Do Not Configure Proxy Settings and click Next to continue.

The Custom Actions dialog box, shown in Figure 9.31, allows for custom batch files, executables, and other content to be executed upon connection. This provides for a range of capabilities, such as the running of scripts to provide for VPN Quarantine, described in detail in the next section of this chapter.

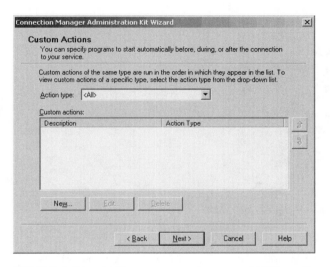

FIGURE 9.31   Adding custom actions to a CMAK profile.

To continue with the configuration, do the following:

1. Click Next at the Custom Actions dialog box.

2. Leave the default graphic as the one illustrated and click Next to continue.

3. Leave the phone book graphic at the default and click Next to continue.

4. Leave the default icons the same and click Next to continue.

5. Notification area shortcuts provide for additional options to be added to the toolbar on the clients. Leave the default of no additional items and click Next.

6. Use the default help file and click Next.

7. For the Support Information field, enter information useful to the client, such as "For support, call 1-800-555-5555." Click Next to continue.

8. The subsequent dialog box enables the Connection Manager client to be installed along with the profile. This may be necessary for some clients that do not have the updated software, so it is common to check this box. Click Next to continue.

9. If a custom license agreement has been created, it can be entered in the subsequent dialog box. If not, click Next to continue.

10. The Additional Files option allows for extra files to be included in the profile. These files may be necessary for certain functionality or login scripts to work properly, such as with VPN Quarantine scripts. Add any files as necessary, using the Add button as shown in Figure 9.32, and click Next to continue.

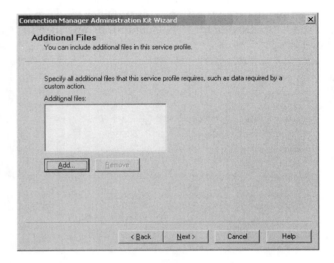

FIGURE 9.32   Specifying additional files for a CMAK profile.

11. Check the Advanced Customization option on the next dialog box and click Next to continue.

As previously mentioned, this connection is for VPN access only, and is not being set up to dial any phone entries first. The Advanced Customization dialog box, shown in Figure 9.33, allows for this option to be set. To turn off the dial-up option, perform the following steps:

1. Under file name, select <nameofyourprofile>.cms, where nameofyourprofile is the executable name that was originally entered at the start of the wizard.

2. Under section name, choose Connection Manager.

3. Under Key name, choose Dialup.

4. Under Value, enter the number 0.

5. Click the Apply button to save the settings.

6. Click Next to continue.

7. Click Finish when the profile has been created and the Finish dialog box is displayed.

At this point, the executable to automate the VPN connection settings has been generated and can be distributed to clients via email or other methods. If settings change, the wizard must be re-run and the profile executable redistributed to all clients.

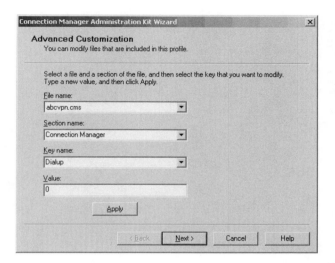

FIGURE 9.33   Customizing the Advanced options of the CMAK profile.

Deploying the Custom CMAK Profile on a Windows XP Client

After the custom CMAK profile has been compiled into an executable and made available to clients (through email, ftp, web download, or removable media), it can be installed and utilized. Installation of the executable is simple and straightforward, and involves the following steps:

1. From the client, and while logged in as a local administrator, double-click on the CMAK executable that was created by the CMAK.

2. Click OK when asked if wanting to install the package.

3. Select to make the connection available for My Use Only and click OK.

4. After installing, the connection screen, shown in Figure 9.34, is displayed. Enter the appropriate information and click Connect.

The connectoid should then connect the client via the settings that were established in the CMAK and on the ISA server. At this point, the client is subject to any of the rules that have been set up to govern the VPN Clients network.

Enabling ISA Server 2006 VPN Quarantine

ISA Server 2006 takes advantage of the Windows Server 2003 Routing and Remote Access (RRAS) service capability to enable Quarantine support for remote users. In a nutshell, what this means is that the ISA server allows clients to be scrutinized via custom scripts for their adherence to specific criteria, such as whether they have anti-virus software installed, or what security patches they have applied. This can help to prevent VPN clients from connecting if they are potential security risks, as many home computers and other non-managed systems can prove to be.

FIGURE 9.34   Connecting from a VPN client configured with a CMAK profile.

Installing the Remote Access Quarantine Service (RQS)

To support VPN Quarantine, the Remote Access Quarantine Service (RQS) must first be installed on the ISA server. This service was not released with the original code of Windows Server 2003, but has been added with Windows Server 2003 Service Pack 1. If Windows Server 2003 Service Pack 1 is not applied, it must be installed as a component of the Windows Server 2003 Resource Kit Tools (http://go.microsoft.com/fwlink/?linkid=30956), updated to a version supported by ISA (http://go.microsoft.com/fwlink/?linkid=30896), and then further extended via specialized scripts (http://www.microsoft.com/downloads/details.aspx?FamilyId=3396C852-717F-4B2E-AB4D-1C44356CE37A&displaylang=en). Of course, simply installing Windows Server 2003 SP1 is the best and most straightforward course of action to provide for VPN Quarantine capabilities.

On the ISA server (running under Windows Server 2003 SP1), perform the following steps to install the Remote Access Quarantine Service:

1. Click Start, Control Panel, Add or Remove Programs.

2. Click Add/Remove Windows Components.

3. Scroll down and select Networking Services by clicking on the text only. Do not check the box or it installs all subcomponents. When selected (highlighted), click the Details button.

4. Check the box for Remote Access Quarantine Service, as shown in Figure 9.35. Click OK.

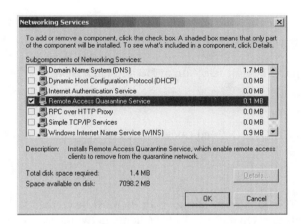

FIGURE 9.35   Installing the Remote Access Quarantine Service.

5. Click Next to continue.

6. Insert the Windows Server 2003 Media if prompted. Click OK.

7. Click the Finish button when complete.

Configuring the RQS Protocol Definition in ISA

To support VPN Quarantine, the Remote Access Quarantine Service Protocol definition must first be established on the ISA server. To set this up, perform the following steps:

1. From the ISA Server Console, click on the Firewall Policy node in the Scope pane.

2. Select the Toolbox tab from the Tasks pane.

3. In the Toolbox, expand the Protocols box by clicking on the down arrow.

4. Select New, Protocol.

5. When the wizard pops up, enter **RQS** as the definition of the protocol.

6. Under the Primary Connection Information dialog box, click the New button.

7. Enter TCP, Outbound, and 7250 for the From and To fields, as shown in Figure 9.36. Click OK when complete.

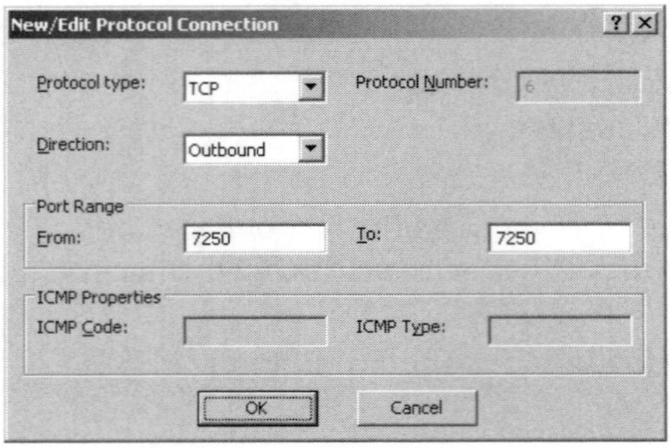

FIGURE 9.36   Defining the RQS protocol.

8. Click Next to continue.

9. Under Secondary Connections, keep the default selection at No and click Next.

10. Click Finish at the final dialog box.

11. Click the Apply button to save the changes.

The RQS protocol is now displayed under the User-Defined node of the Protocols toolbox and can be used to generate rules.

Configuring RQS Rules for ISA

To finalize the configuration of RQS for VPN Quarantine support, a rule must be created to allow the protocol from the VPN Clients and Quarantined VPN Clients networks to the Local Host (the ISA server). To set this up, perform the following steps:

1. From the ISA Server Management Console, select the Firewall Policy node from the Scope pane.

2. In the Tasks pane, select the Tasks tab and then click the Create a New Access Rule link.

3. Enter **Allow Network Quarantine**, or some similar name, in the Access Rule Name field and click Next to continue.

4. Under Action, select Allow and click Next.

5. Under Protocols, select that the rule applies to Selected protocols.

6. Click the Add button to add the protocols.

7. Under the Add Protocols dialog box, expand User-Defined and select RQS, as shown in Figure 9.37. Click Add and then Close.

8. Click Next to continue.

9. Under Access Rule Sources, click the Add button.

10. Expand Networks, select the Quarantined VPN Clients network, and click Add.

11. Select the VPN Clients network as well and click Add.

12. Click Close and Next to continue.

FIGURE 9.37   Adding the RQS protocol to the VPN quarantine access rule.

13. Under Access Rule Destinations, click the Add button.

14. Expand Networks and click on Local Host. Click Add, Close, and Next to continue.

15. Accept the default of All Users and click Next.

16. Click Finish to complete the rule creation, as shown in Figure 9.38.

17. Click the Apply button to save the configuration.

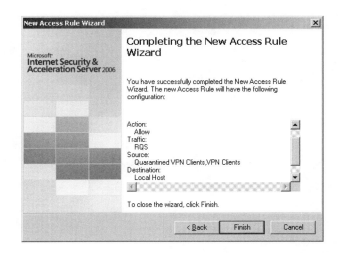

FIGURE 9.38   Finalizing RQS rule creation for VPN Quarantine support.

Enabling VPN Quarantine in ISA

The last step on the server side of VPN quarantine setup is the actual step of enabling VPN quarantine capabilities on the ISA server itself. To set this up, perform the following steps:

CAUTION

Enabling VPN quarantine support automatically assumes all VPN clients are suspect, and potentially disables certain functionality based on the rules that are configured. It is therefore important to ensure that the proper client configuration has been enabled that will take clients out of quarantine, or run the risk of crippling all incoming VPN clients unless quarantine is turned off.

---

1. From the ISA Management Console, click on the Networks subnode under the Configuration node in the Scope pane.
2. Select the Networks tab in the Details pane.
3. Double-click on the Quarantined VPN Clients network.
4. Select the Quarantine tab.
5. Check the Enable Quarantine Control box.
6. Click OK after the warning pops up.

The Quarantine tab, shown in Figure 9.39, allows for the option to quarantine based on ISA Server policies, the method described here, or via RADIUS policies, which may be required in certain circumstances. In addition, the option to disconnect users that don't pass quarantine is offered. In some cases, limited support to a smaller range of network services may be desired for VPN clients in quarantine, so this option is not always checked.

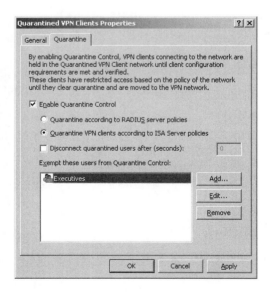

FIGURE 9.39   Enabling VPN Quarantine on the ISA server.

Finally, exempt users or groups can be specified based on ISA User Sets, which can parse AD, RADIUS, or SecurID group membership. This allows for exemptions to Quarantine to be established for choice groups of VPN clients. To add clients, make changes to the Quarantine tab as necessary, then click OK, and Apply.

Customizing a CMAK Package for VPN Quarantine

The clients in a VPN Quarantine configuration must be addressed to properly implement this type of solution. A special script or set of scripts that makes use of the RSC.exe client-side component of the Remote Access Quarantine Service must be run on the clients as they connect to allow them to pass quarantine checks. This type of scripting can be complex, but sample scripts can be downloaded from Microsoft at the following URL:

http://www.microsoft.com/downloads/details.aspx?FamilyID=a290f2ee-0b55-491e-bc4c-8161671b2462&displaylang=en

> **NOTE**
>
> Because of the complexity of the URL, it may be easier to simply search the Internet for VPN Quarantine Sample Scripts.EXE, which should lead directly to the link.

The most straightforward way to deploy a custom VPN Quarantine script to clients is by embedding the script in a CMAK profile. The steps for creating this profile are described in the previous section of this chapter that focuses on CMAK specifically. Follow the procedure outlined in that section, but add two more procedures. In the first procedure, a custom action must be defined that kicks off the Quarantine script that was written as follows:

1. At the Custom Actions Dialog box of the CMAK Profile wizard, which was previously shown in Figure 9.31, click New.
2. Enter a Description, such as "Quarantine Check."
3. Click the Browse button to locate the Batch file that was created and click the Open button when it has been found.
4. Under Parameters, enter the following:

   %DialRasEntry% %TunnelRasEntry% 7250 %Domain% %UserName% Version1
5. Under Action type, select Post-Connect from the drop-down list.
6. Select All Connections under the Run This Custom Action For field.
7. Check both boxes at the bottom of the dialog box, as shown in Figure 9.40.
8. Click OK to save the custom action.
9. Continue with the CMAK Profile setup.

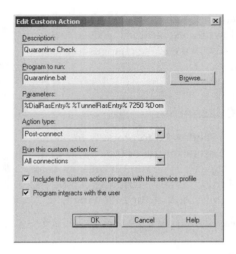

FIGURE 9.40   Creating a CMAK custom action to embed a Quarantine script into a client profile.

The second change to the CMAK process that is required for VPN client quarantine is embedding the RQC.exe file into the custom profile. This file provides for quarantine functionality at the client level. To add this to the profile, follow the same procedure outlined in the CMAK section of this chapter, make the change to the Custom Action mentioned earlier, and perform the following procedure:

1. At the Additional Files dialog box of the CMAK Wizard, previously shown as Figure 9.32, click the Add button.

2. Select the RQC.exe file (normally located in the \Program Files\Cmak\Profiles\<ProfileName> folder) and click Open.

3. Add any remaining files, such as VBS scripts that are referenced by the particular script. When they are all added, such as what is shown in Figure 9.41, click Next and continue the CMAK profile creation process as previously described.

NOTE

For more details on the scripting process for the RQC client, reference the Microsoft white paper at the following URL:

http://www.microsoft.com/resources/documentation/WindowsServ/2003/all/techref/en-us/Default.asp?url=/Resources/Documentation/windowsserv/2003/all/techref/en-us/rqc_remarks.asp

Or, simply search for "Rqc.exe: Remote Access Quarantine Client."

After these two additional procedures have been added to a CMAK profile, the VPN Quarantine scripting support will be added to the VPN network connectoid that is set up when the clients run the CMAK executable.

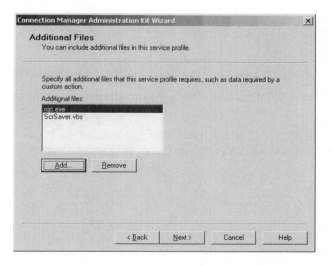

FIGURE 9.41   Adding files for VPN Quarantine script support of a CMAK profile.

Summary

The capability to use a straightforward and robust method for securely accessing internal organization assets is one of the key selling points to ISA Server 2006. ISA's VPN capabilities are what make this type of access possible, offering multiple configuration methods with PPTP or L2TP protocol support available. In addition, ISA's Application-layer filtering support for VPN users, even after they have authenticated, further extends the security of remote user access. A properly designed VPN solution using ISA Server 2006 therefore extends the productivity of an environment without unnecessary security risks.

Best Practices

▶ Use a very strong RADIUS shared secret key comprising a random set of alpha, numeric, and symbols. The key length should be between 22 and 128 characters and it should be changed periodically.

▶ When configuring the ISA VPN server, be sure to check for alerts both in the ISA Management console and in the server's event log. The RRAS service often logs descriptive messages.

▶ Use the IPSec pre-shared key to verify VPN communication during troubleshooting; this will help identify a problem with network or certificates. Refrain from using the pre-shared key in production environments to minimize security risks.

▶ Deploy two-factor authentication methods such as SecurID or smart cards using EAP authentication whenever possible. This provides for secured L2TP/IPSec VPN encryption.

▶ Simplify a PKI Certificate deployment through the AD autoenrollment when possible.

▶ Use the Connection Management Administration Kit (CMAK) to simplify client VPN rollout.

▶ Use Layer 2 Tunneling Protocol (L2TP) with IP Security (IPSec), instead of the Point-to-Point Tunneling Protocol (PPTP), to secure VPN connections whenever possible.

CHAPTER 10

Extending ISA 2006 to Branch Offices with Site-to-Site VPNs

In addition to providing for rich Application-layer firewall capabilities and content-caching acceleration abilities, ISA Server 2006 also sports robust Virtual Private Network (VPN) capabilities. ISA's VPN options allow for traffic between systems to be encrypted and sent across untrusted networks such as the Internet. This allows for rich VPN client support, such as what is illustrated in Chapter 9, "Enabling Client Remote Access with ISA Server 2006 Virtual Private Networks (VPNs)."

In addition to supporting standard VPN client functionality, ISA Server 2006 also allows for site-to-site VPNs to be created, enabling an organization to eschew expensive dedicated WAN links over cheaper Internet connections, without sacrificing any security in the process.

This chapter focuses on site-to-site VPN deployment scenarios that use ISA Server 2006. It includes step-by-step information on how to set up site-to-site VPNs with various protocols, such as the Point-to-Point Tunneling Protocol (PPTP) and the Layer 2 Tunneling Protocol (L2TP). In addition, using IPSec Tunnel Mode for integration of ISA Server 2006 with third-party VPN solutions is covered.

Understanding Branch-Office Deployment Scenarios with ISA Server 2006

ISA Server 2006's site-to-site VPN capabilities are powerful, and give network and security architects a great deal more flexibility in designing an organization's network. To fully

understand what is possible with ISA, it is important to understand what type of deployment scenarios ISA supports.

Extending the Network Without WAN Links or Unnecessary Complexity

The traditional method of extending a network to a remote location was to order a
secured, dedicated wide area network (WAN) link from one of the Telecom providers. These
links were always available, dedicated to the company itself, and relatively expensive.

With the rise of the Internet, organizations found that they could purchase and maintain
much bigger "pipes" of bandwidth to the Internet from their remote locations, and transmit data between their various network locations over the Internet. The big downside to
this was that the traffic was subject to snooping by unauthorized personnel; the Internet
itself was untrusted from the organization's perspective.

This was one of the factors that led to the development and rise of Virtual Private
Networks (VPNs), a concept that enables the traffic sent between disparate networks to be
encrypted and then tunneled across the untrusted networks. If the data packets are intercepted, the interceptor is not able to decipher the contents of the message itself. On the
other end, however, the traffic is decrypted and accepted by the remote host, as shown in
Figure 10.1.

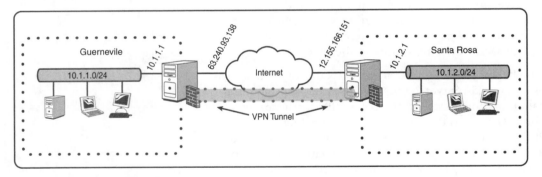

FIGURE 10.1   Understanding VPN concepts.

Controlling and Filtering Traffic Across WAN Segments

One of the additional advantages to deploying ISA Server 2006 site-to-site VPNs is the
capability to create specific rules to govern traffic sent between VPN networks. ISA Server
2006 sees the remote sites as individual network elements, which are then subject to
inspection and Application-layer filtering. This is in contrast to ISA 2000 functionality,
which did not scan site-to-site VPN traffic at the Application layer.

Understanding Site-to-Site VPN Capabilities and Options

ISA Server 2006 site-to-site VPNs are versatile in that they allow for multiple authentication methods and encryption protocol support. For example, the following protocols are supported for encryption of the site-to-site VPN traffic:

▶ **Point-to-Point Tunneling Protocol (PPTP)**—PPTP encryption uses the point-to-point protocol (PPP) to encrypt the packets with a single layer of user-based authentication. This type of encryption is simple to set up but is not as secure as other mechanisms.

▶ **Layer 2 Tunneling Protocol (L2TP)**—L2TP encryption uses IP Security (IPSec) to provide for user-level as well as machine-level authentication, providing for multiple layers of encryption for the packets. It is the most secure mechanism of encrypting site-to-site VPN traffic.

▶ **IPSec Tunnel Mode**—IPSec Tunnel-Mode encryption support was added to ISA Server 2006 to enable ISA to interface with non-Microsoft third-party VPN solutions. Using this type of VPN tunneling, an encrypted tunnel can be set up between ISA and other third-party vendors that may already be deployed at remote locations.

Understanding RADIUS Authentication Options for Site-to-Site VPN Connections

In addition to supporting Windows-based authentication for VPN connections, ISA Server 2006 supports authentication against a remote authentication dial-in user service (RADIUS) authentication infrastructure. This can be useful for environments that have an existing RADIUS environment deployed and that want to take advantage of that environment for authentication of the site-to-site VPN connections.

Outlining a Site-to-Site VPN Scenario

For the exercises in this chapter, a site-to-site VPN connection is made between two ISA servers, one in the San Francisco location and the other in the Toronto location, as illustrated in Figure 10.2.

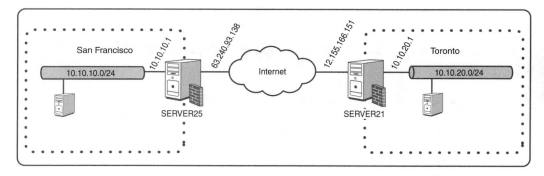

FIGURE 10.2   Examining the site-to-site VPN scenario illustrated in this chapter.

Although the actual network design may be different, the concept is the same. After it is established, a site-to-site VPN connection enables clients in the local network to access resources in the remote network as if they were local.

> **NOTE**
>
> The IPSec Tunnel Mode scenario is the only one that differs slightly from this model:
> The remote server is not an ISA server, but a third-party VPN box.

Important Points to Consider

ISA Server 2006's Site-to-Site VPN Connection wizard is greatly improved over the one provided with ISA Server 2004. The wizard walks through the entire scenario, and allows for the configuration of network rules and access rules. That said, there are still a few areas that can trip up administrators who attempt to set up the connection. It is important to keep these factors in mind when preparing to set up a site-to-site VPN network:

▶ The name of the Local VPN User accounts must exactly match the name of the site created in the wizard. If it doesn't match, it will fail to connect. So, in the scenario we are examining, this means that the ISA server in San Francisco will have a local user account named Toronto, and the ISA server in Toronto will have a local user account named SanFrancisco.

▶ Setting up the initial VPN Connection can be challenging to troubleshoot as there aren't obvious logs created. Check the Windows Event Viewer for RRAS events that would indicate issues. Monitor the connection within the Monitoring node and the Sessions tab.

▶ The site-to-site VPN connection is created by the servers using local accounts to connect via standard VPN client methods. This means that all VPN client considerations must be in place, including a method for giving the client's IP addresses, and enabling client access on the server.

▶ The Security Configuration Wizard (SCW) for Windows Server 2003, which can lock down an ISA server, has a default setting that disables local accounts from being used. If this is set, the VPN site-to-site connection will fail and it will not be obvious why. Run the SCW to see the current config.

Preparing ISA Servers for Site-to-Site VPN Capabilities

Because ISA Server 2006 is first and foremost a security server, many pieces of ISA functionality are disabled by default. This is true for VPN functionality as well. All VPN options, including site-to-site VPN capabilities, must be physically enabled before VPN connections can be made. In short, enabling site-to-site VPN access between two sites involves the following high-level steps:

1. Define the IP Address Assignment.

2. Enable VPN client access. This must be performed as the servers use local user accounts on each server to initially create the VPN connection.

3. Create local VPN user accounts on both servers, and enable dial-in access for those accounts.

4. Run through the Site-to-Site VPN wizard to configure all necessary networks, network rules, and access rules.

5. Repeat the steps on the remote server.

Each of these steps is explained further in the following sections of this chapter.

Defining Address Assignments

When connecting to the remote network, an ISA server needs to be given an IP address in that network, similar to how a standard VPN client would connect to that server. Usually a local DHCP server is available to provide addresses. If a local DHCP server is not available, a static pool of IP addresses can be used.

> **TIP**
>
> If a static pool of addresses is to be used for the VPN connection, they must first be excluded from the local site network definition. If they are not, ISA complains that the static addresses fall within the range of an existing network.

In this scenario, because the DHCP service is running in both the Toronto and San Francisco networks, DHCP is used to assign IP addresses to the site-to-site VPN connections via the following procedure:

1. Open the ISA Server Management Console.

2. Select Virtual Private Networks (VPN) from the Scope pane.

3. Select the Remote Sites tab from the Details pane.

4. Select Define Address Assignments from the Tasks pane.

5. Select Dynamic Host Configuration Protocol (DHCP), as shown in Figure 10.3.

6. Ensure that the internal network is chosen for the location of DHCP, DNS, and WINS services and click OK.

7. Click Apply and OK to save the changes.

8. Repeat on the remote ISA server.

Enabling VPN Client Access

Even though the VPN access that will be set up is for site-to-site VPNs, the server must have VPN client access enabled first. The ISA server views the VPN connection from the remote server as a VPN client itself and authenticates as a local user account to create the initial connection. The following procedure must be followed on both servers:

1. Open the ISA Server Management Console.

2. Select the Virtual Private Networks (VPN) node from the Scope pane.

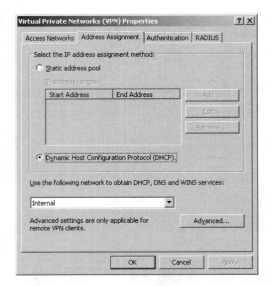

FIGURE 10.3   Defining DHCP as the address assignment method for VPN clients.

3. Select the VPN Clients tab in the Details pane.

4. In the Tasks tab of the Tasks pane, click on the link for Configure VPN Client Access.

5. Check the box labeled Enable VPN Client Access, as shown in Figure 10.4.

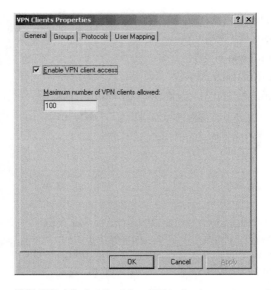

FIGURE 10.4   Enabling VPN client access on the ISA server.

6. Select the Protocols tab from the VPN Clients Properties window and check the boxes for PPTP and L2TP/IPSec. (If only one authentication method is needed, only choose that one. L2TP/IPSec is recommended as it is more secure.)

7. Select Apply, Apply, and OK to save the changes.

8. Repeat the steps on the remote server.

Creating VPN User Accounts on Both Servers

After VPN client access has been enabled, local user accounts must be created on each of the VPN servers. These user accounts will be used by the remote ISA server to authenticate the VPN connection and to gain dial-in access rights. To create this user account, do the following:

1. On the local ISA server, Open Computer Management (Start, Administrative Tools, Computer Management).

2. Select Local Users and Groups from the tree.

3. Select Users.

4. Right-click on Users and select New User.

5. Enter the name of the user, such as Toronto (the user name needs to exactly reflect the name of the remote site when it is created), as shown in Figure 10.5.

6. Enter and confirm the password.

7. Select Password Never Expires.

8. Click Create.

FIGURE 10.5   Creating a VPN user account.

10

> **NOTE**
>
> Remember that the user account must exactly match the name of the remote site. In our example, the San Francisco server has a local user account named Toronto, which matches the name of the remote site. In Toronto, the server has a local account named SanFrancisco, which matches the name of the site defined on that server.

After an account is created, the user must then be granted the proper dial-in access rights. If this step isn't taken, the site-to-site VPN connection creation fails. To enable this, do the following:

1. Double-click on the newly created user.
2. Select the Dial-in tab.
3. Select Allow Access, as shown in Figure 10.6.
4. Click OK.
5. Repeat the user creation and dial-in access steps on the remote server.

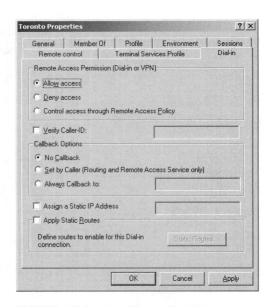

FIGURE 10.6   Enabling dial-in VPN user access.

Selecting the Correct VPN Interface

In most site-to-site VPN scenarios, the ISA server has two NICs: an internal NIC and external NIC. In this case, the VPN is established with the external NIC.

This may not always be true, however, such as if the ISA server has more than two NICs or is part of a hub-and-spoke VPN topology. To configure on what interface the ISA server can establish VPN communication, perform the following steps:

1. Open the ISA Server Management Console.
2. Select Virtual Private Networks (VPN) from the Scope pane.
3. Right-click Virtual Private Networks (VPN), and select Properties from the context menu.
4. Under the Access Networks tab, select the External network, as shown in Figure 10.7.
5. Click OK, Apply, and OK to save the changes.

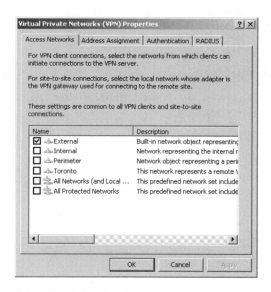

FIGURE 10.7   Configuring Access Networks.

Choosing Between Authentication Mechanisms

After the initial preparation steps have been taken, the decision on which protocol to be used to set up the site-to-site VPN tunnel must be reached. To recap, this involves choosing between the following options:

▶ PPTP

▶ L2TP

▶ IPSec Tunnel Mode

The subsequent sections of this chapter cover setting up each type of protocol access.

10

Configuring a Point-to-Point Tunneling Protocol (PPTP) Site-to-Site VPN Between Two Remote Offices

A Point-to-Point Tunneling Protocol (PPTP) VPN connection is the most straightforward to set up and configure, and doesn't require an existing public key infrastructure (PKI) to be put into place, or some of the complex configuration options of the IPSec Tunnel Mode. On the flip side, PPTP VPN connections are the least secure of the three options.

The following section details the steps involved in setting up a site-to-site VPN connection via PPTP. If selecting to use L2TP or IPSec Tunnel Mode, skip this section and proceed directly to the subsequent sections, "Configuring a Layer 2 Tunneling Protocol (L2TP) Site-to-Site VPN Connection Between Two ISA Servers in Remote Sites" or "Configuring ISA 2006 to Integrate with Third-Party VPN Tunnel Products."

Creating a PPTP Site-to-Site VPN Connection

The first step in setting up a PPTP site-to-site VPN connection is to configure the remote site network definition. To do this, perform the following steps:

1. Open the ISA Server Management Console.
2. Select the Virtual Private Networks (VPN) node from the console tree.
3. Select the Remote Sites tab from the Details pane.
4. Select Create VPN Site-to-Site Connection from the Tasks pane.
5. Enter the name of the connection in the Network Name field; for example, enter **Toronto** and click Next.
6. Select Point-to-Point Tunneling Protocol (PPTP), as shown in Figure 10.8, then click Next.
7. Click OK when prompted about needing to create a remote user account.
8. Enter the IP address of the external interface of the remote ISA server (for example, 12.155.166.151), and then click Next.
9. Check the box labeled Local Site Can Initiate Connections to Remote Site Using These Credentials.
10. Enter the username, domain name, and password of the local user account in the remote site that was created in the previous steps and click Next. For our example, we enter a username of SanFrancisco, domain name of SERVER11 (the local server account in Toronto), and the password we used to create the account on the remote server.

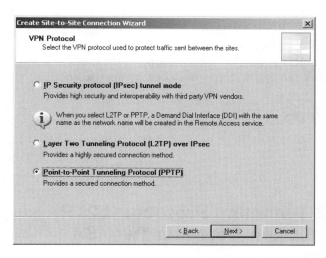

FIGURE 10.8   Using the PPTP protocol to define a remote site network.

11. Add the network ranges of the remote network. In this example, we use 10.10.20.0 as the starting address and 10.10.20.255 as the ending address.

12. Select to create a network rule specifying a route relationship and enter a descriptive name (the default is generally OK). Click Next to continue.

13. Select to create an allow access rule. Use the default name or enter a custom descriptive name for the rule. Select which protocols to allow for the access rule. In this example, we are opening the tunnel to all traffic, so we select the drop-down box and choose All Outbound Traffic. Click Next to continue.

14. Click Finish, Apply, and OK to save the changes.

15. Repeat the procedure on the remote site server. Be sure to change the user account (in our example, we would choose the SERVER1\Toronto account so that the remote server can connect using the local account).

NOTE

Remember that the remote ISA server is governed by the VPN client settings on the local ISA server, and the local ISA server is governed by the VPN client settings on the remote ISA server.

10

Testing the Connection

At this point, the PPTP tunnel is in place. The wizard will have created a network definition, an access rule, and a network rule. If all things have been done properly, the traffic will now be routed between the networks. Test by pinging resources from one network to another.

You will be able to monitor the VPN site sessions by clicking on the Monitor Site Sessions link under the Remote Sites tab of the VPN node.

If it's necessary to change the Tunnel Mode from PPTP to L2TP or IPSec Tunnel Mode, the rule has to be reconfigured.

Configuring a Layer 2 Tunneling Protocol (L2TP) Site-to-Site VPN Connection Between Two ISA Servers in Remote Sites

The most secure encryption method for setting up a site-to-site VPN connection involves creating a L2TP-encrypted tunnel. This option, although slightly more complex, is the preferred connection method when possible. The steps outlined in this section assume that a PPTP tunnel has not yet been created. If it has, it must be reconfigured.

> **NOTE**
>
> L2TP VPN connections are supported only between Windows-based VPN servers, such as ISA Server 2004/2006, Windows Server 2003 RRAS, or Windows 2000 RRAS.

Deciding Between Shared Key and PKI

There are two different options to be considered when establishing L2TP VPN tunnels. The options are outlined as follows:

- **Certificates-Based Encryption**—The most secure method of encryption involves the use of x509 certificates within a public key infrastructure (PKI) environment. Using certificates-based encryption allows for both machine-level and user-level controls that are used to encrypt the connection, so that a nearly unbreakable tunnel is established.

- **Shared Key**—An alternative to PKI-based encryption involves the use of a shared key, which is a static line of text that is entered in both servers and that allows for the VPN connection to be encrypted. Although more secure than PPTP, it is not as secure as a certificates-based L2TP VPN.

Each of these options is outlined in more detail in the following section of this chapter.

Configuring a PKI Infrastructure for PKI-Based Certificate Encryption

If choosing to use a PKI certificates-based infrastructure, there must be one in place already, or one can be set up and configured in an environment. Windows Server (2000/2003) itself has the built-in capabilities to allow for a PKI-based certificate authority (CA) to be set up in an environment through the creation of either a stand-alone CA or an Enterprise CA. For more information on each of these options, see Chapter 9, "Enabling Client Remote Access with ISA Server 2006 Virtual Private Networks (VPNs)."

For this example, an Enterprise Root certificate authority is set up and enabled. This has the added advantage of enabling certificates to be configured automatically on domain members. To install the Enterprise CA and distribute certificates to the ISA servers, follow the steps outlined in Chapter 9 in the section titled "Creating a Public Key Infrastructure (PKI) for L2TP with IPSec Support."

Requesting a Certificate for the ISA VPN Server

If the local ISA server is a domain member in a domain with an Enterprise CA installed, issuing a certificate to the server itself is relatively straightforward through the following procedure:

> **NOTE**
>
> If using a pre-shared key or the PPTP protocol, this step is unnecessary because certificates will not be used.

1. Click Start, Run, type **mmc**, and click OK.
2. Click File, Add/Remove Snap-in.
3. Click the Add button.
4. Select Certificates and click Add.
5. Select Computer Account and click Next.
6. Select Local Computer and click Finish, Close, and OK.
7. Expand the Certificates MMC Console to display Console Root—Certificate (Local Computer) and Personal.
8. Right-click on Personal and choose All Tasks, Request New Certificate.
9. Click Next at the welcome wizard.
10. Select Computer from Certificate Types and click the Advanced check box. Click Next to continue.
11. Leave the default at Microsoft RSA SChannel Cryptographic Provider and click Next to continue.

10

12. Select the local Enterprise Certificate Authority, such as what is shown in Figure 10.9, and click Next to continue.

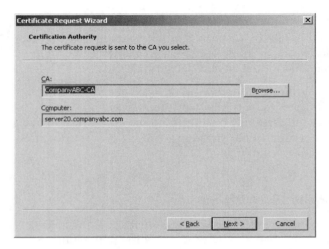

FIGURE 10.9   Creating a certificate request for the ISA server.

13. Enter a friendly name for the certificate, such as ISA Computer Certificate, and click Next to continue.

14. Click Finish.

If the ISA server is not a domain member, it instead must receive the certificate through the web-based enrollment methods described in the section of Chapter 9 titled, "Configuring the Enterprise Root CA."

In either case, certificates from the same CA must be installed on both ISA servers in each location, either through domain-based enrollment or through the web-based enrollment mechanisms.

Creating an L2TP/IPSec Site-to-Site VPN Connection

The first step in setting up a L2TP site-to-site VPN connection is to configure the remote site network definition. To do this, perform the following steps:

1. Open the ISA Server Management Console.

2. Select the Virtual Private Networks (VPN) node from the console tree.

3. Select the Remote Sites tab from the Details pane.

4. Select Create VPN Site-to-Site Connection from the Tasks pane.

5. Enter the name of the connection in the Network Name field; for example, enter **Toronto** and click Next.

6. Select Layer 2 Tunneling Protocol (L2TP) over IPSec and then click Next.

7. Click OK when prompted about needing to create a remote user account.

8. Enter the IP address of the remote ISA server (for example, 192.168.10.253), and then click Next.

9. Check the box labeled Local Site Can Initiate Connections to Remote Site Using These Credentials.

10. Enter the username, domain name, and password of the local user account in the remote site and click Next. In this example, we would enter the SERVER11\SanFrancisco account information to match the local server name in Toronto and the account created there locally.

11. At the subsequent dialog box, shown in Figure 10.10, the option for entering a pre-shared key is given. If a PKI certificates-based model is chosen, this step can be skipped; otherwise, come up with a pre-shared key from scratch (any alphanumeric pattern) and enter it (it is entered on the remote server as well) and click Next.

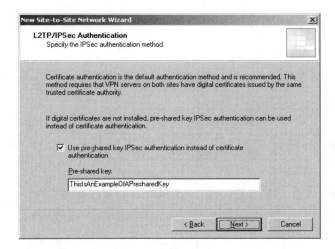

FIGURE 10.10   Entering an L2TP pre-shared key.

12. Add the network ranges of the remote network. In this example, we use 10.10.20.0 as the starting address and 10.10.20.255 as the ending address.

13. Select to create a network rule specifying a route relationship and enter a descriptive name (the default is generally OK). Click Next to continue.

14. Select to create an allow access rule. Use the default name or enter a custom descriptive name for the rule. Select which protocols to allow for the access rule. In this example, we are opening the tunnel to all traffic, so we select the drop-down box and choose All Outbound Traffic. Click Next to continue.

10

15. Click Finish, Apply, and OK to save the changes.

16. Repeat the procedure on the remote site server.

After the L2TP remote site networks have been created on each server, test the connectivity between sites and monitor site session traffic by clicking the Monitor Site Sessions link in the Tasks pane. Traffic will appear under the Sessions tab of the Monitoring node, as shown in Figure 10.11.

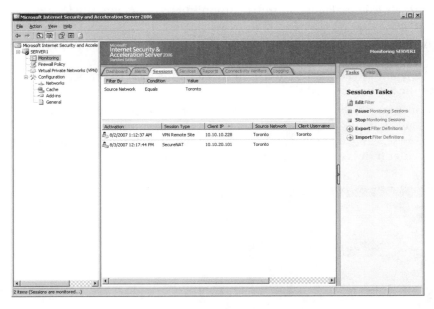

FIGURE 10.11   Monitoring site-to-site VPN traffic.

Configuring ISA 2006 to Integrate with Third-Party VPN Tunnel Products

If the remote network is connected to a non-Microsoft third-party VPN product, the IPSec Tunnel Mode option is the only protocol that can be supported. Fortunately, using IPSec Tunnel Mode to set up a remote site network is relatively straightforward.

Setting Up an IPSec Tunnel Mode VPN Connection

As with L2TP over IPSec protocol methods, IPSec in Tunnel Mode can be set up to use either certificates-based authentication or shared-key methods. The same security concepts apply for this scenario as well, and the pre-shared key is inherently less secure than a certificates-based approach. That said, certain third-party products may only support shared key, and ISA supports either implementation.

Configuring the Third-Party VPN Site

To use the IPSec Tunnel Mode to define a remote site, perform the following steps on the local ISA server:

1. Open the ISA Server Management Console.

2. Select the Virtual Private Networks (VPN) node from the console tree.

3. Select the Remote Sites tab from the Details pane.

4. Select Create VPN Site-to-Site Connection from the Tasks pane.

5. Enter the name of the connection in the Network Name field; for example, enter **Toronto** and click Next.

6. Select IP Security Protocol (IPSec) Tunnel Mode, as shown in Figure 10.12, and click Next to continue.

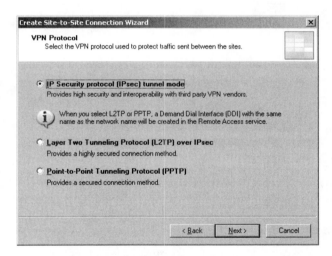

FIGURE 10.12   Creating an IPSec Tunnel Mode remote site for third-party VPN support.

7. Enter the remote IP address of the VPN third-party gateway and enter the local VPN gateway IP address. Click Next to continue.

8. On the IPSec Authentication page, enter whether to use certificates or a pre-shared key for authentication. In this example, a pre-shared key is entered. Click Next to continue.

9. Add the network ranges of the remote network by clicking the Add Range button. For example, use 10.10.20.0 as the starting address and 10.10.20.255 as the ending address. Click Next to continue.

10. Select to create a network rule specifying a route relationship and enter a descriptive name (the default is generally OK), as shown in Figure 10.13. Click Next to continue.

10

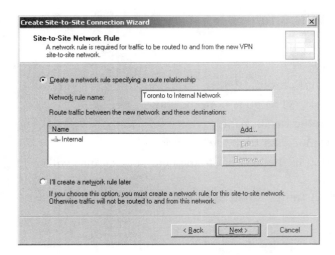

FIGURE 10.13   Creating a network rule for the VPN connection.

11. Select to create an allow access rule. Use the default name or enter a custom descriptive name for the rule. Select which protocols to allow for the access rule. In this example, we are opening the tunnel to all traffic, so we select the drop-down box and choose All outbound traffic. Click Next to continue.

12. Click Finish, Apply, and OK to save the changes.

Configuring the Third-Party VPN Server

After ISA has been configured with the information of the remote site VPN server, that server then needs to be configured to recognize ISA as a VPN gateway as well. This process varies between the various VPN products, so it is recommended to consult the documentation of the product in question on how to set up an IPSec Tunnel back to the ISA server.

As with PPTP and L2TP connections, network and firewall rules must be set up between the newly configured networks to make sure that traffic can properly flow between them.

Summary

ISA Server 2006's site-to-site VPN capabilities allow organizations to extend the Application-layer filtering capabilities of ISA Server to remote sites, extending a network without the need for expensive and cumbersome WAN connections. In addition, ISA's broad support for multiple encryption protocols and authentication methods allows for support of existing third-party VPN products, enabling ISA to co-exist with existing security infrastructure more easily.

Best Practices

▶ Use L2TP over IPSec certificates-based encryption when possible for site-to-site VPN tunnels.

▶ Be careful not to disable local user account access when using the Security Configuration Wizard (SCW) or this will disable site-to-site VPN access.

▶ The commands `NETSH ras set tracing * enabled` and `NETSH ras set tracing * disabled` can be used to enable and disable RRAS tracing.

▶ Check the Windows Application Event log to view RRAS-specific information that may not be listed in the ISA logs.

▶ The command `netsh ipsec dynamic set config ikelogging 1` can be used to turn on IKE logging. The log file is located in `C:\WINDOWS\debug\oakley.log`. The command `netsh ipsec dynamic set config ikelogging 0` can be used to turn off IKE logging.

▶ Use L2TP encryption with PKI certificates whenever possible, rather than PPTP or L2TP with shared key.

10

CHAPTER 11

Understanding Client Deployment Scenarios with ISA Server 2006

There is much confusion about the concept of ISA clients. For many administrators, the concept of a client often conjures up images of software components that constantly need updating, overwriting operating system files, and clients requiring constant maintenance. In addition, confusion around whether a client software piece is required for ISA Server has led many organizations to shy away from deploying ISA Server.

The truth is that ISA Server itself supports three unique types of clients (excluding the VPN client), two of which do not require any software components to be installed. The fact that, by default, an ISA server does not require any client software or client licensing plays very well in ISA Server's favor: The impact and risk of installing ISA Server into an environment is low.

Of course, the fact that ISA does not require the full client does not mean that it is not useful in certain cases. It allows for a much greater level of control and security over an environment. The powerful ISA client allows for user-level authentication and access control, as well as complex protocol support and other advanced features.

This chapter provides an outline of the three types of ISA clients: the SecureNAT client, the Web Proxy client, and the full ISA client. A fourth type of client, the VPN client, is briefly described. Deployment scenarios covering ISA clients are outlined and illustrated. In addition, step-by-step installation and configuration information for the ISA Software client are described.

Outlining Client Access with ISA Server 2006

It is somewhat of a misnomer to describe ISA clients as "clients" in the traditional software sense. In reality, a single ISA client can appear to be all three types of ISA clients to the server itself. In a sense, each client is really defined more by how it uses the ISA server rather than what is on the client machine itself. To understand this concept, it is important to understand what constitutes each one of the types of clients and how ISA views client traffic.

Defining the ISA Firewall Client

ISA Server 2006 comes with a full-blown ISA client software component that can be installed on all workstations. The full ISA Software client provides for the following capabilities:

- ▶ **Per-User Rules Configuration and Logging**—One of the biggest advantages to the Firewall client is its capability to authenticate the client traffic and have the ISA server determine not only from what IP address the client is coming, but also from what Active Directory user account it originated. This allows for the creation of per-user or per-group firewall policy rules, enabling administrators to restrict access to specific applications, networks, and other resources on a per-user basis. This information is also logged in ISA, so that per-user reports on such things as per-user website usage and security audits can be performed.

- ▶ **WinSock Application Support**—The Firewall client works directly with the Windows Sockets (Winsock) drivers to provide for rich support for applications written to take advantage of WinSock functionality.

- ▶ **Complex Protocol Support**—The Firewall client is capable of handling complex protocol definitions in ISA Server, including those that make use of secondary protocols as part of their definition.

TIP

As with any piece of software, the Firewall client requires occasional updates on all the systems. For example, the 2006 version of the software includes a newer version of the Firewall client than ISA 2004 included. For security and functionality reasons, it is therefore important to keep the software up to date, using software such as Systems Management Server (SMS) 2003 or other software management software.

Defining the SecureNAT Client

The second defined client type in ISA Server 2006 is the SecureNAT client, which is essentially any IP client that can be physically routed to the ISA server in one manner or another. This includes any type of client with a TCP/IP stack that is forced to send its traffic through the ISA server.

For example, a simple network with a single internal subnet that has the ISA server's internal IP address listed as the default gateway for that subnet would see all client requests from that network as SecureNAT client traffic, as shown in Figure 11.1.

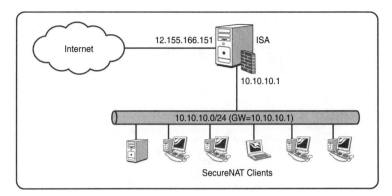

FIGURE 11.1   Understanding SecureNAT clients in a simple network configuration.

The SecureNAT client scenario could also apply to more complicated networks with multiple subnets and routers, provided that the routes defined in the network topology route traffic through the ISA server, as shown in Figure 11.2.

SecureNAT clients are the easiest to work with: They do not require any special configuration or client software. On the flip side, it is not possible to authenticate SecureNAT clients automatically or to determine individual user accounts that may be sending traffic through the ISA server. SecureNAT clients can be controlled only through the creation of rules that limit traffic by IP address or subnet information.

> **NOTE**
>
> SecureNAT client support requires an ISA server to have more than one network interface because the traffic must flow through the server from one network to the next. This disallows a unihomed (single NIC) ISA server from handling SecureNAT or Firewall clients. A unihomed server can handle Web Proxy clients only (for forward- or reverse-proxy support).

Defining the Web Proxy Client

A Web Proxy client is a client connection that comes from a CERN-compatible browser client such as Internet Explorer or Firefox. Web Proxy clients interact directly with the proxy server capabilities of ISA Server 2006, and relay their requests off the ISA server, which operates as a content-caching solution to the clients. This enables commonly downloaded content to be stored on the ISA Proxy server and served up to clients more quickly. For more information on this concept, see Chapter 8, "Deploying ISA Server 2006 as a Content Caching Server."

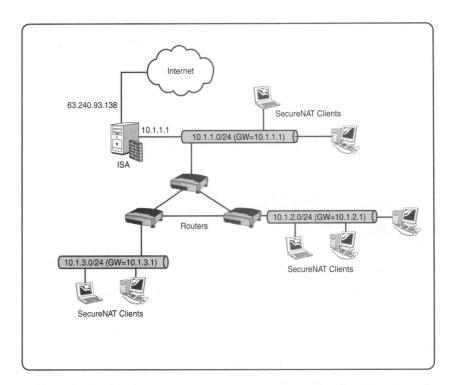

FIGURE 11.2   Understanding SecureNAT clients in a complex network configuration.

> **NOTE**
>
> It is very common to have Web Proxy clients also displayed as SecureNAT or Firewall clients in the ISA Server monitoring tools. This is because, fundamentally, the description of a Web Proxy client simply refers to the web browser–based application traffic that comes from a SecureNAT or Firewall client.

Outlining the VPN Client

Technically speaking, ISA Server recognizes a fourth type of client: Virtual Private Network (VPN) clients. A VPN client is a client system that remotely establishes an encrypted tunnel to an ISA server. For more information on VPN clients and for deployment scenarios involving them, see Chapter 9, "Enabling Client Remote Access with ISA Server 2006 Virtual Private Networks (VPNs)."

Preparing an ISA Environment for the Firewall Client

By default, ISA Server 2006 does not automatically enable an environment for support and installation of the Firewall client component. Specific steps must be taken to enable systems on a network to utilize the Firewall client. Understanding these prerequisites and how the installation of the Firewall client can be automated can help to ease the administration of the Firewall client.

Making the Firewall Client Software Available

The first step in enabling support for the Firewall client is to set up a networked share location that contains the binaries for the Firewall client itself. ISA Server 2004 used to include an installation option known as the Firewall Client Share, which would automatically set up a share on a server that would store the binaries. This is no longer the case, as Microsoft didn't want to encourage administrators to set up file shares on security devices such as ISA servers. More traditional methods of making the installation media available to users, such as placing it in a standard file share or distributing it via a software distribution tool such as SMS, are recommended.

Enabling or Disabling Downlevel Client Support

A default installation of ISA Server 2006 will only allow the most recent 2006 version of the Firewall client to connect to it. This latest version of the client encrypts all communications between the client and the server and is highly recommended. In certain cases, downlevel support for ISA 2004 or earlier clients is needed. If this is the case, the setting for toggling on or off support for downlevel clients can be found by clicking on the Define Firewall Client Settings link in the General node of the ISA Management Console. The checkbox shown in Figure 11.3 controls this setting.

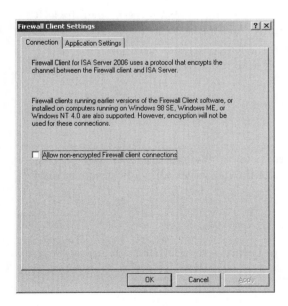

FIGURE 11.3   Changing global Firewall client settings.

Using DHCP to Configure ISA Server for Auto Detection

Creating the ISA Client Installation Share is only one step in the automation and distribution of the ISA client. To fully automate deployment, the network must be configured to know which server is the ISA server. This process is accomplished through the publishing of a record in either the Dynamic Host Configuration Protocol (DHCP) environment or the Domain Name System (DNS) environment, or both, depending on the needs of the environment.

This information is published in either DHCP or DNS via a Web Proxy auto discovery (Wpad) file. With this file published on the server, and with auto discovery enabled on the ISA server (described in the next section of this chapter), the Firewall clients, when installed, automatically detect which IP address is associated with the ISA server, which can be used to automate the way that the ISA client configures the proxy server settings for the system.

> **TIP**
>
> If both DHCP and DNS auto discovery are enabled, the requesting client attempts to use DHCP first, and, that failing, attempts DNS. It may be useful to enable both because some clients may not resolve the DHCP Wpad entry, but instead use the DNS entry.

Assuming that a DHCP server has already been set up in the internal network, use the following steps to set up client auto discovery through DHCP:

1. From the internal server that is running DHCP (not the ISA server), open the DHCP Console (Start, All Programs, Administrative Tools, DHCP).
2. Right-click on the name of the server in the left pane, and select Set Predefined Options.
3. Click the Add button.
4. Enter **Wpad** for the name of the option, and then enter a data type of **String**, a code of **252**, and a description.
5. Click OK.
6. In the String field, enter a value of **http://10.10.10.1/wpad.dat**, as shown in Figure 11.4 (where 10.10.10.1 is the IP address of the ISA server; a DNS host name can be used as well if it is configured).
7. Click OK.
8. Close the DHCP Console.

With this setting enabled, every Firewall client that receives a DHCP lease can set its proxy settings to point to ISA Server.

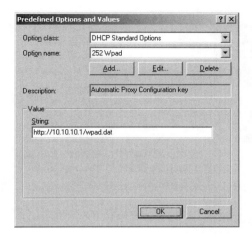

FIGURE 11.4   Creating DHCP WPad entries for automatic client configuration.

> **NOTE**
>
> The biggest downside to DHCP auto discovery is that clients must have local adminis-
> trator rights on their machines to have the proxy server setting changed via this tech-
> nique. If local users do not have those rights, then DNS auto discovery should be used
> instead of, or in combination with, DHCP auto discovery.

Configuring Proxy Client Auto Discovery with DNS

The Domain Name System (DNS) is also a likely candidate for auto discovery information
to be published. Using a Wpad entry in each forward lookup zone where clients need
proxy server settings configured is an ideal way to automate the deployment of the
settings.

Assuming DNS and a forward lookup zone is set up in an environment, auto discovery can
be enabled through the following technique:

1. Log in with admin rights to the DNS server.
2. Open the DNS Console (Start, All Programs, Administrative Tools, DNS).

A host record that corresponds with ISA is required, so it is necessary to set up one in
advance if it hasn't already been configured. To create one, right-click on the forward
lookup zone and select New Host (A). Enter a name for the host (such as
isa.companyabc.com) and the internal IP address of the ISA server and click Add Host.
This host name will be used in later steps. After the host record is created, the CNAME
record for Wpad needs to be created by following these steps:

1. While in the DNS Console, right-click the forward lookup zone where the setting
   will be applied and click New Alias (CNAME), as shown in Figure 11.5.

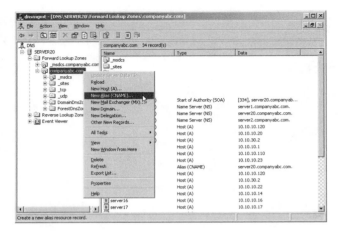

FIGURE 11.5   Creating a DNS Wpad entry for ISA client automatic configuration.

2. For the alias name, enter **Wpad**, and enter the Fully Qualified Domain Name that corresponds to the Host record that was just created (for example, isa.companyabc.com).

3. Click OK to save the CNAME record.

This technique enables all Internet Explorer clients that are configured to use the forward lookup zone in DNS to automatically configure their proxy server information, which can be highly useful in automating the deployment of the proxy configuration for the ISA Firewall clients (and other clients on the network).

Enabling Auto Discovery from ISA Server

After Wpad entries have been created to ease in the proxy server settings, auto discovery of the ISA server itself must be enabled on a per-network basis. To enable this functionality, do the following:

1. On the ISA server, open the ISA Server Management Console.

2. From the Console, click on Configuration, Networks in the console tree.

3. In the Details pane, select the Networks tab.

4. Right-click the network where auto discovery is to be enabled (for example, the internal network) and click Properties.

5. Select the Auto Discovery tab.

6. Check the box for Publish Automatic Discovery Information, as shown in Figure 11.6, and click OK.

7. Click Apply in the Details pane and click OK.

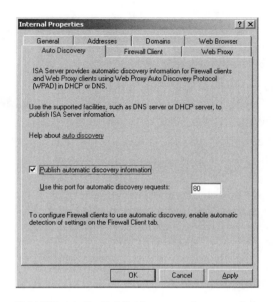

FIGURE 11.6   Publishing auto discovery information for ISA Server Firewall clients.

Installing the ISA Firewall Client

After the necessary server configuration is complete, the actual client software can be installed. There are several different installation options, as follows:

- ► Manual installation

- ► Unattended installation

- ► Automatic group policy installation

Each of these installation options has its particular pros and cons, as described in this section.

NOTE

If older versions of the ISA client are installed, they should be upgraded to match the version that corresponds to the server version itself. Conversely, the ISA client version for ISA Server 2006 cannot connect to downlevel Proxy Server 1.x/2.x servers; the type of traffic required is considered to be a security risk.

The prerequisites to installing the Firewall client are as follows:

- ► Any supported 32-bit version of Windows (client versions recommended)

- ► No ISA Server Management Console software installed

Manually Installing the ISA Firewall Client

The most straightforward way to install the Firewall client is to simply run through the `Setup.exe` GUI. To install the client this way, do the following:

1. From the ISA Firewall client media or file server location where it is copied to, run `setup.exe` by double-clicking on it.

2. At the welcome screen, click Next to continue.

3. Select I Accept the Terms in the License Agreement and click Next to continue.

4. At the Destination Folder dialog box, accept the default path and click Next to continue.

5. From the subsequent dialog box, shown in Figure 11.7, choose whether to Automatically Detect the Appropriate ISA Server Computer or specifically define where the ISA server is. In this case, because the auto detection was previously configured, select to automatically detect and click Next to continue.

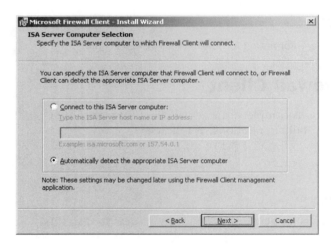

FIGURE 11.7   Installing the ISA Firewall client.

6. Click Install to begin the file copy.

7. Click Finish to end the wizard.

Using Unattended Setup Scripts to Deploy the ISA Firewall Client

The ISA Client `setup.exe` can be automated as part of installation via a batch process, a login script, or a software distribution program. Through a particular set of command-line options, the entire process can be made completely non-interactive and automated. For example, the following command sequence installs the Firewall client:

```
setup.exe /v"SERVER_NAME_OR_IP=EnterNameofISAServer ENABLE_AUTO_DETECT=
1 REFRESH_WEB_PROXY=1 /qn"
```

Figure 11.8 illustrates this, run from the command line of a client.

FIGURE 11.8   Installing the Firewall client from the command prompt.

In the figure, server1 is the name of the ISA server, ENABLE_AUTO_DETECT=1 turns on the automatic detection of the ISA server, and REFRESH_WEB_PROXY=1 turns on automatic configuration of the Web Proxy info.

Deploying the Firewall Client via Active Directory Group Policies

The most efficient and automated approach to ensuring that the Firewall client is deployed and updated on a regular basis is to use Active Directory Group Policy Objects (GPOs), which allow for software installation and customization of various Registry and system settings automatically. Group policies can be applied to all workstations in a domain, or to a subset of systems. To create this type of GPO in an Active Directory domain, do the following:

CAUTION

For this type of group policy, where Firewall client software will be deployed, it is not recommended to deploy the GPO to all systems on a network, but rather to a limited subset, such as all workstations. Be sure to test the GPO on a sample OU first as well.

1. From a domain controller in the internal network, open ADUC (Start, All Programs, Administrative Tools, Active Directory Users and Computers).
2. From the console tree, drill down to the Organizational Unit where the GPO will be applied (such as a Workstations OU), right-click, and choose Properties.
3. Select the Group Policy tab, then click on the New button.

TIP

If the Group Policy Management Console (GPMC) is installed, it needs to be opened and the GPO created directly from it. The GPMC greatly extends the capabilities of AD Group Policy administration and is highly recommended. It can be downloaded from Microsoft at the following URL:

http://go.microsoft.com/fwlink/?linkid=21813

4. Enter a descriptive name for the GPO and click OK.

5. Expand the GPO to Computer Configuration, Software Settings, Software Installation.

6. Right-click Software Installation and choose New, Package.

7. In the File Name field, enter the UNC path of the MSI installer file, such as \\servername\sharename\ms_fwc.msi and click OK.

8. From the Deploy Software dialog box, choose Assigned and click OK. The GPO should look similar to what is shown in Figure 11.9.

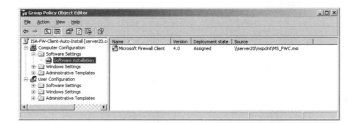

FIGURE 11.9   Reviewing the ISA Firewall client GPO settings.

9. Close the GPO Editor.

With the GPO in place, all computer accounts in the OU to which it applies will have the ISA Firewall client software automatically installed. With the auto-setup options previously described, the configuration can also be automated, making it seamless to the end user.

Working with the ISA Firewall Client

The ISA Firewall client, after it is installed, shows in the client's System Tray (near the clock). If it is right-clicked, as shown in Figure 11.10, it can be configured or disabled, if the proper local administrative rights are configured for the logged-in user.

FIGURE 11.10   Viewing the ISA Firewall client tray icon.

Getting Familiar with the Firewall Client Functionality

Right-clicking on the Firewall client icon and choosing Configure produces two sets of options, as illustrated in Figure 11.11.

This is the only level of configuration that can be done from the client itself, and is mainly limited to enabling or disabling the client, changing how the ISA server is detected, and setting whether web browser settings are automatically detected and changed.

FIGURE 11.11   Configuring ISA Firewall client settings.

Modifying Rules for Firewall Clients

After the Firewall client is deployed, the real desired functionality becomes available on the ISA server itself: the capability to create per-user rules and configurations. From the ISA Server console, individual rule elements can be locked down to be accessible from only particular users, via the Users tab under Access Rules.

NOTE

Per-user firewall rule configuration is limited to Access rules, and is not available for server-based publishing rules.

To illustrate this concept, the following steps will modify an existing rule that allows web browsing access to the Internet only to members of the AD Group called Management:

1. From the ISA Server Management Console, choose Firewall Policy from the console tree.
2. In the Details pane, double-click on the rule to be modified. (For information on how to create firewall policy rules, refer to Chapter 5, "Deploying ISA Server 2006 as a Firewall.")
3. Select the Users tab, click on All Users, and click Remove.
4. Click the Add button on the top field.
5. Under User Sets, click New.
6. At the Welcome dialog box, enter a name for the User Set—such as Management—and click Next.

7. Under the Users dialog box, click Add, Windows Users and Groups.

8. Click the Locations button and select Entire Directory, and then click OK.

9. Enter Management into the Object Names field and click Check Names to Resolve, and then click OK.

10. At the dialog box shown in Figure 11.12, click Next to continue.

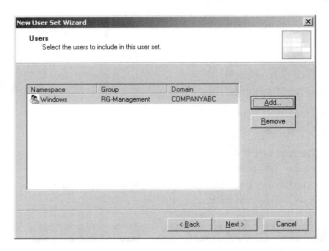

FIGURE 11.12   Modifying firewall policy rules using user authentication.

11. Click Finish.

12. Click Close, OK, Apply, and OK to save the changes.

Summary

By itself, ISA Server 2006 supports a wide variety of client access mechanisms and contains a rich feature set from the server side alone. Through the use of software-less client access such as with the SecureNAT client and the Web Proxy client, ISA can secure network traffic and provide for caching and reverse-proxy capabilities right out of the box.

In addition to these capabilities, ISA also supports the deployment of the full ISA Firewall client, which provides unprecedented control over a firewall environment, allowing for per-user configuration and login mechanisms, complex protocol support, and Winsock application support. The addition of the Firewall client to an ISA Server environment provides additional value-added functionality without the need for additional licensing.

Best Practices

▶ Install the Firewall client if needing to specify per-user firewall policies or logging.

▶ Remove or upgrade legacy Firewall clients when using ISA Server 2006.

▶ In non-Microsoft, mixed environments, or environments that may not need an additional software component installed on workstations, use the SecureNAT and Web Proxy clients.

▶ Use the Firewall client along with custom protocol definitions if needing to support complex secondary protocols for an application.

▶ Automate the installation of the Firewall client with AD group policy objects, if utilized, and place auto discovery information in the network to automate the installation and configuration of the clients.

PART III

Securing Servers and Services with ISA Server 2006

CHAPTER 12

Securing Outlook Web Access (OWA) Traffic

One of the most common reasons for deploying ISA Server 2006 is for securing Microsoft Exchange Outlook Web Access (OWA) sites from access from the Internet. ISA Server 2006 contains unprecedented capabilities to secure and protect an OWA server with its reverse-proxy capabilities, forms-based authentication support, and end-to-end SSL encryption capabilities.

This chapter focuses on the best-practice approaches to securing Outlook Web Access sites with ISA Server 2006. Specific step-by-step examples of setting up OWA with SSL encryption and forms-based authentication are presented. The examples in this chapter focus on a deployment scenario with ISA as an edge firewall. Examples of securing Outlook Web Access in Exchange Server 2003 and Exchange 2007 are both outlined and explained.

The common scenario of ISA as a unihomed reverse-proxy system in the DMZ of an existing firewall, used to secure OWA and other services, is covered in Chapter 7, "Deploying ISA Server as a Reverse Proxy in an Existing Firewall DMZ." That said, many of the tasks illustrated in this chapter apply to that scenario as well, and informational notes are given if the DMZ scenario differs from what is illustrated.

Enabling Secure Sockets Layer (SSL) Support for Exchange Outlook Web Access

One of the most common resources that is secured with ISA Server is Exchange Outlook Web Access (OWA). OWA is a web-based email access method that displays a Microsoft Exchange mailbox, calendar, contacts, public folders, and the like in a web-based interface, such as the one shown in Figure 12.1.

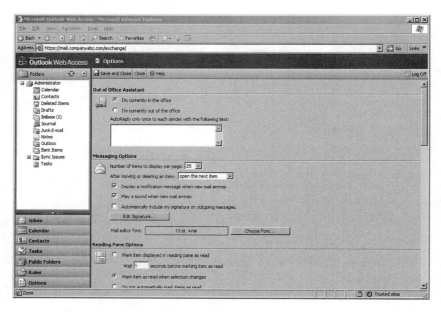

FIGURE 12.1   Examining Outlook Web Access.

OWA was available as an option in Exchange 5.5, and became a standard component in Exchange 2000. The latest iteration of the product, available in Exchange Server 2003, provides for a rich, functional, mailbox-access mechanism, with many of the same features as the full-function Outlook client.

Traffic to and from an OWA server uses the web-based Hypertext Transfer Protocol (HTTP) to communicate with both client and server. The upside to using this protocol is that the OWA server can be accessed from any client on the Internet that supports the HTTP protocol.

The downside to OWA access with the HTTP protocol is that the traffic is sent in clear text, easily readable to any third party that intercepts the traffic sent across untrustworthy networks.

Fortunately, the HTTP protocol can be encrypted with a technology known as Secure Sockets Layer (SSL), which scrambles the packets sent between client and server by using a set of keys tied to an SSL certificate installed on the OWA server, such as what is illustrated in Figure 12.2. This certificate ensures the identity of the server itself, and allows the traffic to be virtually uncrackable, particularly if strong 128-bit encryption is used.

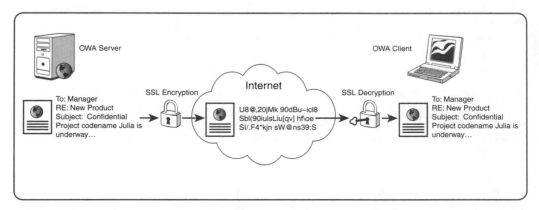

FIGURE 12.2   Examining SSL encryption for OWA traffic.

The upshot of this discussion is that it is vital, and almost always necessary, to secure OWA-based traffic using digital SSL certificates. It is less and less common to run into OWA implementations that are not secured with SSL, and this chapter focuses on deploying and securing OWA sites that use SSL to encrypt the traffic.

Installing a digital certificate on the Exchange OWA server, and later on ISA itself, involves a two-step process. In the first step, the certificate request must be generated from the OWA server and sent to a certificate authority. Secondly, the certificate authority must then verify the identity of the site and send a certificate back to the organization to be installed on the OWA server. The key to this process is to either use a third-party certificate authority such as Verisign or Thawte to provide the certificates, or to install and configure an internal enterprise certificate authority. Each of these processes is described in more detail in the subsequent sections of this chapter.

> **NOTE**
>
> If a digital certificate is already installed and configured on an OWA server, this section can be skipped, and the reader can proceed directly to the section on securing OWA with ISA Server titled "Securing Exchange Outlook Web Access with ISA Server 2006."

Understanding the Need for Third-Party CAs

By and large, the most common approach to securing an OWA server with SSL is to buy a certificate from a third-party certificate authority such as Verisign, Thawte, or one of many other enterprise certificate authorities. These companies exist as a trusted third-party vendor of digital identity. Their job is to validate that their customers are really who they say they are, and to generate the digital certificates that validate this for digital communications that require encryption, such as SSL.

For example, if CompanyABC wishes to create a certificate to install on its OWA server, it sends the certificate request to the third-party certificate authority (CA), who then follows up by researching the company, calling the CompanyABC employees, and conducting interviews to determine the validity of the organization. Based on the information obtained from this process, the third-party CA then encrypts the certificate and sends it back to CompanyABC, which then installs it on its server.

Because the third-party CA is registered on nearly all the web browsers (the most common ones always are), the client automatically trusts the CA and, subsequently, trusts the certificate generated by CompanyABC. It is because of this seamless integration with the majority of the world's browsers that third-party enterprise CAs are commonly utilized.

Internal certificate authorities, built and maintained by the internal IT branch of an organization, are more cost effective. Expensive third-party certificates (which can run up to $1000 a year per certificate in some cases) can be eschewed in favor of internally generated certificates. This also gives an organization more flexibility in the creation and modification of certificates. Windows Server 2003 includes the option of installing an enterprise certificate authority on an internal server or set of servers, giving administrators more options for SSL communications. The biggest downside to an internal CA is that, by default, not all browsers have the required certificate patch that includes the internal CA as part of the default installation, and therefore receive the error illustrated in Figure 12.3 when accessing a site secured by this certificate.

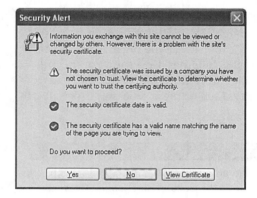

FIGURE 12.3   Viewing a common SSL certificate error.

The only way to avoid this type of error message from appearing is to add the internal CA to the client's list of trusted root authorities, which can be a difficult prospect if OWA access is to be made available to browsers around the world. An enterprise certificate authority is automatically trusted by domain members, which can make this easier for an organization to deploy, but can still limit the deployment of a seamless solution. It is this limitation that sometimes stops organizations from installing their own CAs.

Either third-party CA certificate generation or internal CA generation is required for SSL support on OWA. These deployment options are illustrated in the subsequent sections of this chapter.

Installing a Third-Party CA on an OWA Server

If a third-party certificate authority will be used to enable SSL on an OWA server, then a certificate request must first be generated directly from the OWA server. After this request has been generated, it can be sent off to the third-party CA, who then verifies the identity of the organization and sends it back, where it can be installed on the server.

If an internal CA will be utilized, this section and its procedures can be skipped, and readers can proceed directly to the subsequent section, "Using an Internal Certificate Authority for OWA Certificates."

> **NOTE**
>
> Although it is not a direct part of ISA Server, having an SSL-protected OWA server is the first step in protecting traffic to the OWA server, and is therefore illustrated in this chapter. It is possible to secure an OWA server without using SSL, through basic HTTP securing techniques, but it is highly recommended to use SSL where possible.

To generate an SSL certificate request for use with a third-party CA, perform the following steps:

1. From the OWA server (not the ISA server), open IIS Manager (Start, All Programs, Administrative Tools, Internet Information Services [IIS] Manager).

2. Under the console tree, expand SERVERNAME (local computer), Web Sites, and right-click the OWA virtual server (typically named Default Web Site), and then click Properties.

3. Select the Directory Security tab.

4. Under Secure Communications, click the Server Certificate button.

5. At the welcome page, click Next to continue.

6. From the list of options displayed, select Create a New Certificate and click Next to continue.

7. From the Delayed or Immediate Request dialog box, select Prepare the Request Now, But Send It Later and click Next.

8. Type a descriptive name for the certificate, such as what is shown in Figure 12.4, leave the Bit Length at 1024, and click Next to continue.

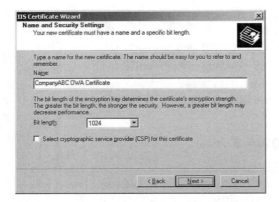

FIGURE 12.4   Generating an SSL certificate request for an OWA virtual server.

9. Enter the name of the organization and what organizational unit will be associated with the certificate. These fields will be viewable by external users, and should accurately reflect the organizational structure of the requestor. Click Next to continue.

10. Enter a common name for the OWA website in the form of the Fully Qualified Domain Name (FQDN). An example of this would be mail.companyabc.com. Click Next to continue.

> **NOTE**
>
> If the OWA site will be made accessible from the Internet, the common name of the site needs to be made accessible from the Internet via a DNS A record.

11. Enter the appropriate information into the Geographical Information dialog box, such as State, City, and Country. Abbreviations are not allowed. Click Next to continue.

12. Enter a filename for the certificate request, such as `C:\owacert.txt`, and click Next to continue.

13. On the Request File Summary dialog box, review the summary page for accuracy and click Next to continue.

14. Click Finish to end the Web Server Certificate Wizard.

After the certificate request has been generated, the text file, which will look similar to the one shown in Figure 12.5, can then be emailed or otherwise transmitted to the certificate authority via its own individual process. Each CA has a different procedure, and the exact steps need to follow the individual CA's process. After an organization's identity has been proven by the CA, it sends back the server certificate, typically in the form of a file, or as part of the body of an email message.

FIGURE 12.5   Viewing a certificate request file.

The certificate then needs to be installed on the server itself. If it was sent in the form of a .cer file, it can be imported via the process described in the following steps. If it was included in the body of an email, the certificate itself needs to be cut and pasted into a text editor such as Notepad and saved as a .cer file. After the .cer file has been obtained, it can be installed on the OWA server through the following process:

1. From the OWA server (not the ISA server), open IIS Manager (Start, All Programs, Administrative Tools, Internet Information Services [IIS] Manager).

2. Under the console tree, expand SERVERNAME (local computer), Web Sites, and right-click the OWA virtual server (typically named Default Web Site), and then click Properties.

3. Select the Directory Security tab.

4. Under Secure Communications, click the Server Certificate button.

5. At the welcome page, click Next to continue.

6. From the Pending Certificate Request dialog box, select Process the Pending Request and Install the Certificate and click Next to continue.

7. Enter the pathname and filename where the .cer file was saved (the Browse button can be used to locate the file), and click Next to continue.

8. Click Finish to finalize the certificate installation.

At this point in the process, SSL communication to the OWA server can be allowed, but forcing SSL encryption requires more configuration, which is outlined in the later section titled "Forcing SSL Encryption for OWA Traffic."

Using an Internal Certificate Authority for OWA Certificates

If a third-party certificate authority is not utilized, an internal CA can be set up instead. There are several different CA options, including several third-party products, and it may be advantageous to take advantage of an existing internal CA. If none is available, however, one can be installed on an internal (non-ISA) Windows Server 2003 system in an organization.

Installing an Internal Certificate Authority On a domain member (not the ISA server) server or, more commonly, on a domain controller, the certificate authority component of Windows Server 2003 can be installed using the following procedure:

> **NOTE**
>
> This procedure outlines the process on a Windows Server 2003 system. It is possible to install and configure a CA on a Windows 2000 system, through a slightly different procedure.

1. Click on Start, Control Panel, Add or Remove Programs.
2. Click on Add/Remove Windows Components.
3. Check the box labeled Certificate Services.
4. At the warning box, shown in Figure 12.6, click Yes to acknowledge that the server name cannot be changed.

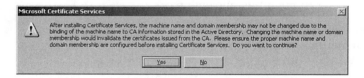

FIGURE 12.6   Installing a local certificate authority.

5. Click Next to continue.

From the subsequent dialog box, shown in Figure 12.7, select what type of certificate authority is to be set up. Each choice of CA type has different ramifications, and each one is useful in different situations. The following is a list of the types of CAs available for installation:

▶ **Enterprise root CA**—An enterprise root CA is the highest-level certificate authority for an organization. By default, all members of the forest where it is installed trust it, which can make it a convenient mechanism for securing OWA or other services within a domain environment. Unless an existing enterprise root CA is in place, this is the typical choice for a home-grown CA solution in an organization.

▶ **Enterprise subordinate CA**—An enterprise subordinate CA is subordinate to an existing enterprise root CA, and must receive a certificate from that root CA to work properly. In certain large organizations, it may be useful to have a hierarchy of CAs, or the desire may exist to isolate the CA structure for OWA to a subordinate enterprise CA structure.

▶ **Stand-alone root CA**—A stand-alone root CA is similar to an enterprise CA, in that it provides for its own unique identity and can be uniquely configured. It differs from an enterprise CA in that it is not automatically trusted by any forest clients in an organization.

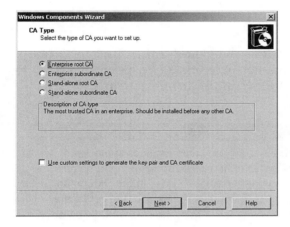

FIGURE 12.7   Selecting a CA type to install.

▶ **Stand-alone subordinate CA**—A stand-alone subordinate CA is similar to an enterprise subordinate CA, except that it is not directly tied or trusted by the forest structure, and must take its own certificate from a stand-alone root CA.

After choosing the type of CA required, continue the CA installation process by performing the following steps:

1. In this example, an enterprise certificate authority is chosen. Click Next to continue.
2. Enter a common name for the certificate authority, such as what is shown in Figure 12.8. Click Next to continue.

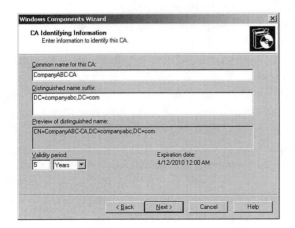

FIGURE 12.8   Entering a common name for the certificate authority.

3. Enter locations for the certificate database and the database log (the defaults can normally be chosen) and click Next to continue.

4. Click Yes when warned that the IIS Services will be restarted.

5. Click Finish after the installation is complete.

Installing an Internal Certificate on the OWA Server   After the internal CA is in place, the OWA server can automatically use it for generation of certificates. To use an internal CA to generate and install a certificate on an OWA server, use the following technique:

CAUTION

The following procedure requires the ISA server to be a domain member of the forest where the enterprise certificate authority is installed. If the ISA server is not a domain member, such as in the scenarios where ISA is a stand-alone server in the DMZ of an existing firewall, the enterprise CA cannot be accessed directly. Instead, the certificate must be installed either through use of a third-party CA or from the internal CA via web auto-enrollment. The procedure for installing an enterprise CA certificate on a stand-alone ISA server via web auto-enrollment is covered in Chapter 7.

---

1. From the OWA server (not the ISA server), open IIS Manager (Start, All Programs, Administrative Tools, Internet Information Services [IIS] Manager).

2. Under the console tree, expand SERVERNAME (local computer), Web Sites, and right-click the OWA virtual server (typically named Default Web Site), and then click Properties.

3. Select the Directory Security tab.

4. Under Secure Communications, click the Server Certificate button.

5. At the welcome page, click Next to continue.

6. Select Create a New Certificate and click Next to continue.

7. From the Delayed or Immediate Request dialog box, select Send the Request Immediately to an Online Certification Authority and click Next to continue.

8. Enter a name for the certificate, such as CompanyABC OWA Certificate, leave the bit length at 1024, and click Next to continue.

9. Enter the Organization and Organizational Unit name, keeping in mind that they should accurately reflect the real name of the requestor. Click Next to continue.

10. Enter the Fully Qualified Domain Name (FQDN) of the OWA server, such as mail.companyabc.com.

11. In the Geographical Information dialog box, enter an unabbreviated State, City, and Country and click Next to continue.

12. Specific the SSL port (443 is the default) that the server is to use and click Next to continue.

13. Under the Choose a Certification Authority dialog box, shown in Figure 12.9, select the CA that was set up in the previous steps and click Next to continue.

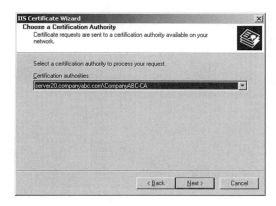

FIGURE 12.9   Installing a local CA certificate on an OWA server.

14. Review the request in the Certificate Request Submission dialog box and click Next to continue.

15. Click Finish when complete.

After installation, the certificate can be viewed by clicking on the View Certificate button of the Directory Services tab under the Virtual Server properties.

After SSL is placed on a server, SSL encryption is made available on the OWA server. If the enterprise certificate authority was installed in an Active Directory domain, then all the domain members will include the internal CA as a trusted root authority and connect to OWA via SSL with no errors. External or nondomain members, however, need to install the enterprise CA into their local trusted root authorities to avoid the error message described in the previous section.

Forcing SSL Encryption for OWA Traffic

After either a third-party or a local internal certificate has been installed on an OWA server, it is typical to then set up the OWA server to force SSL traffic, rather than allow that traffic to use the unencrypted HTTP protocol. This is especially necessary given the fact that most users simply connect to the OWA server from their browser by typing in the name of the server, such as mail.companyabc.com, which defaults to the unencrypted http:// prefix, rather than the encrypted https:// prefix. To solve this problem, SSL encryption must be forced from the OWA server via the following procedure:

1. On the OWA server (not the ISA server), open IIS Manager (Start, All Programs, Administrative Tools, Internet Information Services [IIS] Manager).

2. Navigate to Internet Information Services, Websites, OWA Web Site (usually named Default Web Site).

3. Right-click on the Exchange virtual directory (under the OWA virtual server) and choose Properties.

4. Choose the Directory Services tab.

5. Under Secure Communications, click the Edit button.

6. From the Secure communications dialog box, shown in Figure 12.10, check the boxes for Require Secure Channel (SSL) and Require 128-bit Encryption.

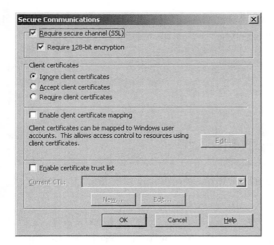

FIGURE 12.10   Forcing SSL encryption on the Exchange virtual directory.

7. Click OK, OK.

8. Repeat the process for the Public virtual directory.

NOTE

Although it may seem like it is better to force SSL on the entire site, it is not actually required, and can also interfere with some of the functionality that may be needed, such as automatic redirection of users, covered in the next section of this chapter. The Exchange and Public virtual directories are the only default directories that should have their information encrypted. That said, other directories used for ActiveSync, OMA, and RPC over HTTP should also be secured with SSL.

Customizing and Securing an OWA Website from Internal Access

Before Outlook Web Access can be secured with ISA, it should pass through a series of internal securing procedures. This helps to mitigate the risk of internal attack against the OWA server, and prepares it for being further secured with ISA Server. The following section deals with best-practice methods to optimize and secure the OWA site with standard Windows and Exchange methods. After the site is secured in this fashion, the ISA specific mail publishing rules can be applied.

Redirecting Clients to the Exchange Virtual Directory   By default, any clients that access an OWA implementation by simply typing in the name of the server, such as mail.companyabc.com, do not gain access to OWA, as the full patch to the Exchange virtual directory (for example, http://mail.companyabc.com/exchange) must be entered. For external access through ISA, methods to automate this process are described later, but for internal access (without using ISA), a simple trick automates this procedure. To set up the automatic redirection to the Exchange virtual directory, perform the following steps on the OWA server:

1. On the OWA server, open IIS Manager (Start, All Programs, Administrative Tools, Internet Information Services [IIS] Manager).

2. Navigate to SERVERNAME, Web Sites.

3. Right-click on the OWA virtual server (usually Default Web Site) and choose Properties.

4. Select the Home Directory tab.

5. Change the setting under the heading The Content for This Resource Should Come From to A Redirection to a URL, and enter **/exchange** into the Redirect To field, as shown in Figure 12.11.

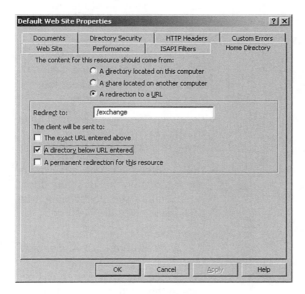

FIGURE 12.11   Setting the OWA virtual server to automatically use the exchange virtual directory.

6. Check the check box labeled A Directory Below URL Entered.

7. Click OK.

8. When prompted about inheritance overrides, click OK.

9. Restart the IIS Services by right-clicking on the name of the server in IIS Manager and choose All Tasks, Restart IIS.

10. Click OK to complete the restart of IIS.

With the automatic redirect in place, the OWA server is configured to automatically add the /exchange to the URL that the user enters.

Summarizing OWA Virtual Server Settings   It is sometimes difficult to keep track of the particular SSL and authentication settings that constitute best practice OWA design. Consequently, Table 12.1 is provided to give administrators a quick glance at best-practice OWA virtual server and virtual directory settings. This table is meant to be used as a general guideline for organizations seeking a laundry list of standard settings.

TABLE 12.1   OWA Virtual Server Settings

Virtual Directory	SSL	Authentication	Notes
Root (at the virtual server level)	Not enabled	Anonymous only	▶ Change home directory redirect to URL /exchange. ▶ Check the check box for A Directory Below this One under the Home Directory tab.
Exadmin	Not enabled	Integrated Windows authentication	▶ Notused for remote access; only needed to allow for public folders to be displayed when the local Exchange System Manager tool is accessed from the server.
Exchange	Required	Basic only	▶ Create custom 403.4 error to point to URL of /owa_redirect/owahttps.asp.
ExchWeb	Required	Anonymous	▶ Note that enabling only anonymous connections on this directory does not decrease security because the files themselves are secured.
Iisadmpwd	Required	Basic only	▶ Used to enable the Change Password feature in OWA, disabled by default in Exchange Server 2003. See the step-by-step examples in the section titled "Enabling the Change Password Feature in OWA Through an ISA Publishing Rule."
Microsoft-Server-ActiveSync	Required	Basic only	▶ Special considerations exist for OWA servers that are not dedicated front-end servers. See Chapter 13.
OMA	Required	Basic only	▶ Special considerations exists for OWA servers that are not dedicated front-end servers. See Chapter 13.

TABLE 12.1   OWA Virtual Server Settings

Virtual Directory	SSL	Authentication	Notes
ExchDAV	Not enabled	Integrated Windows server authentication	▶ Used only when OWA is also a back-end database server and the front-end components also run on the same server. This is for supporting OMA and EAS in this configuration, referenced in Chapter 13. ▶ Configure it to deny all connections except the local OWA server's IP address (for security reasons).
Public	Required	Basic only	▶ Used for public folder access.
Rpc	Required	Basic only	▶ Used for RPC over HTTPS communications. See Chapter 13 for information on how to configure this.

NOTE

Table 12.1 lists a full spectrum of potential virtual directories that an OWA server may use. Depending on what is installed and/or enabled, they may or may not be present on a particular OWA virtual server. The subsequent chapter of this book, Chapter 13, "Securing Messaging Traffic," has detailed information on setting up some of these features, such as OMA, RPC-HTTP, and ActiveSync.

CAUTION

Service packs and hotfixes can have the effect of erasing custom changes made in IIS Manager, including SSL and Authentication settings on virtual directories. One of the first things that should be done after applying patches or service packs should be to double-check these settings and validate functionality.

Securing Exchange Outlook Web Access with ISA Server 2006

As previously mentioned, OWA is one of the most commonly secured services that ISA servers protect. This stems from the critical need to provide remote email services while at the same time securing that access. The success of ISA deployments in this fashion gives tribute to the tight integration Microsoft built between its ISA product and Exchange product.

An ISA server used to secure an OWA implementation can be deployed in multiple scenarios, such as an edge firewall, an inline firewall, or a dedicated reverse-proxy server. In all these scenarios, ISA secures OWA traffic by "pretending" to be the OWA server itself, scanning the traffic that is destined for OWA for exploits, and then repackaging that traffic and sending it on, such as what is illustrated in Figure 12.12.

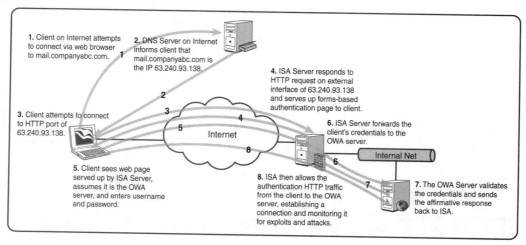

FIGURE 12.12   Explaining OWA publishing with ISA Server 2006.

NOTE

There are a few differences in setup and configuration of a deployment scenario where ISA is in the DMZ of an existing firewall. These scenarios are discussed in more detail in Chapter 7.

ISA performs this type of OWA securing through a mail publishing rule, which automatically sets up and configures a listener on the ISA server. A listener is an ISA component that listens to a specific IP address and port combination for traffic, and processes that traffic for the requesting client as if it were the actual server itself. For example, an OWA listener on an ISA server would respond to OWA requests made to it by scanning them for exploits and then repackaging them and forwarding them on to the OWA server itself. Using listeners, the client cannot tell the difference between the ISA server and the OWA server itself.

ISA Server is also one of the few products that has the capability to secure web traffic with SSL encryption from end to end. It does this by using the OWA server's own certificate to re-encrypt the traffic before sending it on its way. This also allows for the "black box" of

SSL traffic to be examined for exploits and viruses at the Application layer, and then re-encrypted to reduce the chance of unauthorized viewing of OWA traffic. Without the capability to scan this SSL traffic, exploits bound for an OWA server could simply hide themselves in the encrypted traffic and pass right through traditional firewalls.

Exporting and Importing the OWA Certificate to the ISA Server

For ISA to be able to decrypt the SSL traffic bound for the Exchange OWA server, ISA needs to have a copy of the certificate used on the OWA server. This certificate is used by ISA to decode the SSL packets, inspect them, and then re-encrypt them and send them on to the OWA server itself. For this certificate to be installed on the ISA server, it must first be exported from the OWA server, as follows:

1. From the OWA server (not the ISA server), open IIS Manager (Start, All Programs, Administrative Tools, Internet Information Services [IIS] Manager).

2. Navigate to Internet Information Services, SERVERNAME (local computer), Web Sites.

3. Right-click on the OWA virtual server (typically named Default Web Site) and choose Properties.

4. Choose the Directory Security tab.

5. Click View Certificate.

6. Click the Details tab.

7. Click Copy to File.

8. At the wizard, click Next to begin the export process.

9. Select Yes, Export the Private Key, as shown in Figure 12.13, and click Next to continue.

10. Select to include all certificates in the certification path and also select to enable strong protection, then click Next to continue.

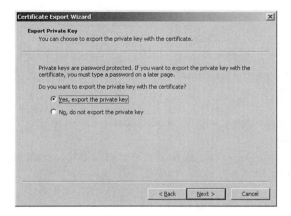

FIGURE 12.13   Exporting the SSL private key.

11. Type and confirm a password and click Next to continue.

12. Enter a file location and name for the file and click Next.

13. Click Finish.

After the .pfx file has been exported from the OWA server, it can then be imported to the ISA server via the following procedure:

> **CAUTION**
>
> It is important to securely transmit this .pfx file to the ISA server and to maintain high security over its location. The certificate's security could be compromised if it were to fall into the wrong hands.

1. From the ISA server, open the MMC console (Start, Run, mmc.exe, OK).

2. Click File, Add/Remove Snap-in.

3. Click the Add button.

4. From the list shown in Figure 12.14, choose the Certificates snap-in and click Add.

FIGURE 12.14   Customizing an MMC Certificates snap-in console for import of the OWA certificate.

5. Choose Computer Account from the list when asked what certificates the snap-in will manage and click Next to continue.

6. From the subsequent list in the Select Computer dialog box, choose Local Computer (the Computer This Console Is Running On) and click Finish.

7. Click Close and OK.

After the custom MMC console has been created, the certificate that was exported from the OWA server can be imported directly from the console via the following procedure:

1. From the MMC Console root, navigate to Certificates (Local Computer), Personal.

2. Right-click the Personal folder and choose All Tasks, Import.

3. At the wizard welcome screen, click Next to continue.

4. Browse for and locate the .pfx file that was exported from the OWA server. The location can also be typed into the file name field. Click Next when located.

5. Enter the password that was created when the certificate was exported, as illustrated in Figure 12.15. Do not check to mark the key as exportable. Click Next to continue.

FIGURE 12.15   Installing the OWA certificate on the ISA server.

6. Choose Automatically Select the Certificate Store Based on the Type of Certificate, and click Next to continue.

7. Click Finish to complete the import.

After it is in the certificates store of the ISA server, the OWA SSL certificate can be used as part of publishing rules.

NOTE

If a rule that makes use of a specific SSL certificate is exported from an ISA server, either for backup purposes or to transfer it to another ISA server, then the certificate must also be saved and imported to the destination server, or that particular rule will be broken.

Creating an Outlook Web Access Publishing Rule

After the OWA SSL has been installed onto the ISA server, the actual ISA mail publishing rule can be generated to secure OWA via the following procedure:

> **NOTE**
>
> The procedure outlined here illustrates an ISA OWA publishing rule that uses forms-based authentication (FBA) for the site, which allows for a landing page to be generated on the ISA server to preauthenticate user connections to Exchange. This forms-based authentication page can be set only on ISA, and must be turned off on the Exchange server itself to work properly. Therefore, this particular rule does not configure the ancillary services of OMA, ActiveSync, and RPC over HTTP. If FBA is not used, these services can be installed as part of the same rule. See Chapter 13 on OMA, ActiveSync, and RPC over HTTP for more info on how to do this.

1. From the ISA Management Console, click once on the Firewall Policy node from the console tree.
2. From the Tasks tab in the Task pane, click on the link titled Publish Exchange Web Client Access.
3. Enter a name for the rule (such as OWA) and click Next to continue.
4. From the Select Services dialog box, shown in Figure 12.16, select the version of Exchange from the drop-down box, then check the box for Outlook Web Access. In this example, Exchange Server 2007 OWA is being secured. Click Next to continue.

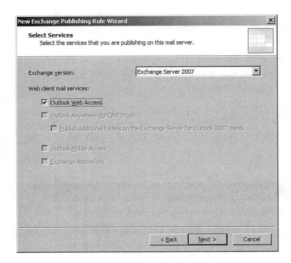

FIGURE 12.16   Selecting an Exchange OWA version to publish.

5. At the Publishing Type dialog box, choose whether to publish a single OWA server or multiple servers (load balancing). If a single server, choose the first option and click Next.

6. From the Server Connection Security dialog box, shown in Figure 12.17, choose whether there will be SSL from the ISA server to the OWA server. Because end-to-end SSL is recommended, it is preferred to select the first option, to use SSL. Click Next to continue.

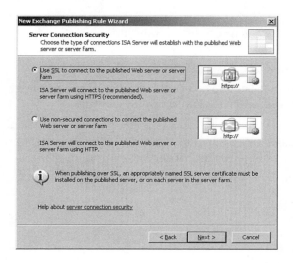

FIGURE 12.17   Selecting to secure traffic between ISA and the OWA server using SSL.

7. Enter the Fully Qualified Domain Name (FQDN) of the OWA server on the next dialog box. This should match the external name referenced by the client (for example, mail.companyabc.com). Click Next to continue.

CAUTION

For an SSL-based OWA rule to work, the FQDN entered in this dialog box must exactly match what the clients will be entering into their web browsers. If it does not match, the host header for the SSL traffic from the ISA server to the Exchange OWA server changes, which causes an upstream chaining error when the site is accessed. It is also very important that the ISA server is able to resolve the FQDN to the internal OWA server, and not to an outside interface. This may involve creating a hosts file to redirect the ISA server to the proper address or by using a different internal DNS zone (split-brain DNS).

8. Under the Public Name Details dialog box, select to Accept Request for This Domain Name (Type Below) and enter the FQDN of the server into the Public Name field (for example, mail.companyabc.com). Click Next to continue.

9. Under the Web Listener dialog box, click the New button, which invokes the New Web Listener Wizard.

10. In the welcome dialog box, enter a descriptive name for the web listener (for example, OWA SSL Listener with FBA) and click Next.

11. Under Client Connection Security, select to require SSL connections with clients. This is highly recommended to secure usernames, passwords, and communications from others on the Internet. A certificate installed on the ISA server per the procedure listed previously is needed. Click Next to continue.

12. Under the IP Addresses dialog box, check the box to listen from the external network, and then click Next to continue.

13. At the Port Specification dialog box, uncheck Enable HTTP, then check Enable SSL.

14. Click on the Select Certificate button to locate the certificate installed in the previous steps, select it from the list displayed, and click OK to save the settings.

15. Click Next to continue.

16. Under the Authentication Settings dialog box, shown in Figure 12.18, select what type of authentication to use. For this example, HTML Form Authentication (FBA) is chosen.

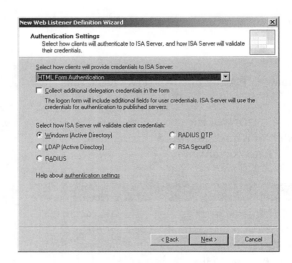

FIGURE 12.18   Enabling FBA on the OWA listener.

17. Under the Single Sign On Settings, you have the option to have this listener used for access to multiple sites, using SSO to logon only once. To enable SSO (you don't have to use it right away), enter the authentication domain name in the form of ".companyabc.com" (without the quotes; don't forget the preceding dot). Click Next to continue.

18. Click Finish to complete the Listener Wizard.

19. While still on the Select Web Listener dialog box, with the new listener selected, click the Edit button.

20. Select the Connections tab.

21. Under the Connections tab, shown in Figure 12.19, check the box for HTTP, and select to redirect all HTTP connections to HTTPS. This will allow all HTTP requests to be automatically redirected to HTTPS.

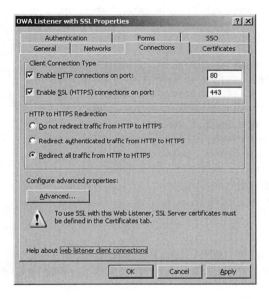

FIGURE 12.19   Automatically redirecting from HTTP to HTTPS.

22. Click on the Forms tab. If deciding to allow users to change their passwords through OWA, check the boxes under the Password Management section. Note that password change through OWA must still be enabled in OWA for this to work.

23. Click OK to save the settings to the listener. Click Next when back at the Select Web Listener page.

24. Under Authentication Delegation, choose Basic Authentication from the drop-down box, since we are using Basic over SSL to the OWA server. Click Next to continue.

25. Under the User Sets dialog box, accept the default of All Authenticated Users, and click Next to continue.

26. Click Finish to complete the wizard.

27. Click OK to confirm that further publishing steps may be required.

28. Click the Apply button at the top of the Details pane.

29. Click OK to acknowledge that the changes are complete.

At this point, the ISA server is set up to reverse proxy the OWA traffic and scan it for Application-layer exploits. Note that with ISA Server 2004, the automatic HTTP to HTTPS redirection was not possible, and additional rules needed to be created to handle the redirection. Fortunately, this is not the case in 2006, and automatic redirection is a new and highly useful feature.

Double-click on the newly created rule in the Details pane, and look through the tabs to see the options created in the rule. Check each of the tabs, and be careful about making changes as one small error can make the rule not work.

CAUTION

It is important not to be confused by some of the options listed under the tabs of the individual publishing rule itself. Some of the options may seem to be necessary, but end up breaking the rule itself. If testing a different scenario, be sure to export it out to an XML file for backup purposes before making changes. ISA publishing rules need to be set up "just so," and minor changes to the rules can break the rules, so it is useful to save the specific rule so that it can be restored in the event of a problem. See Chapter 18, "Backing Up, Restoring, and Recovering an ISA Server 2006 Environment," for step-by step instructions on exporting individual rules.

To double-check, the following is a standard rule for publishing OWA that is known to work. Some of your specifics may vary, but use this list as a guide for troubleshooting any issues (see Table 12.2).

Applying Strict HTTP Filter Settings on the OWA Rule

By default, any new rule that is created only restricts the traffic using that rule to the global settings on the server. For each publishing rule, however, it is recommended to apply more strict HTTP filtering settings to match the type of traffic that will be used. For Exchange Outlook Web Access and other Exchange Services, see the table published at the following Microsoft URL:

http://www.microsoft.com/technet/isa/2004/plan/httpfiltering.mspx

Note that while the article was written for ISA 2004, the filtering settings apply to 2006 as well.

Enabling the Change Password Feature in OWA Through an ISA Publishing Rule

If publishing OWA using Exchange Server 2003, by default, Exchange does not display the Change Password button in Outlook Web Access. This option was previously made available by default in Exchange 2000 OWA, so many administrators may be looking to provide for this same functionality.

TABLE 12.2   Sample ISA Rule for OWA

Rule Tab	Settings
General tab	Defaults (Enable)
Action tab	Defaults (Allow)
From tab	Defaults (from anywhere)
To tab	Server field=mail.companyabc.com (hosts file points this to OWA server; make sure virtual server is set to Basic Auth)
	Forward original host header (checked)
	Requests come from ISA Server
Traffic tab	Defaults (128-bit grayed-out)
Public Name tab	Websites and IP addresses=mail.companyabc.com
Paths tab	External Path=<same as internal> Internal=/public/*
	External Path=<same as internal> Internal=/Exchweb/*
	External Path=<same as internal> Internal=/Exchange/*
	External Path=<same as internal> Internal=/OWA/*
Bridging tab	Redirect requests to SSL port (checked), 443 entered
Users tab	Defaults (All authenticated users)
Schedule tab	Defaults (Always)
Link translation	Defaults (Apply link translation to this rule)
Listener tab	General=OWA listener name
	Networks=External (if inline or edge firewall; if unihomed in DMZ, choose internal network)
	Connections= (HTTP=Enabled-80, HTTPS=Enabled-443, Redirect all traffic from HTTP to HTTPS)
	Certificates=mail.companyabc.com (this has to be installed in the local machine cert store)
	Authentication=HTML Form Authentication, Windows (Active Directory)
	Forms=Defaults
	SSO=Enabled, .companyabc.com

The Change Password button was removed to provide for a higher degree of default security in Exchange Server 2003, particularly because the Exchange 2000 Change Password feature was highly insecure in its original implementations. Fortunately, however, the Exchange Server 2003 Change Password option in OWA was recoded to operate at a much lower security context, and is subsequently much safer. Despite this fact, however, this functionality must still be enabled, first on the Exchange server, and then on the ISA server itself.

Enabling the Change Password Feature on the OWA Server   Enabling the Change Password feature on the Exchange OWA server involves a three-step process: creating a virtual directory for the password reset, configuring the virtual directory, and modifying the Exchange server registry to support the change. To start the process and create the virtual directory, perform the following steps:

1. From the OWA server, open IIS Manager (Start, All Programs, Administrative Tools, Internet Information Services [IIS] Manager).
2. Right-click the OWA virtual server (typically named Default Web Site) and choose New, Virtual Directory.
3. At the welcome dialog box, click Next.
4. Under Alias, enter **iisadmpwd** and click Next.
5. Enter **C:\windows\system32\inetsrv\iisadmpwd** into the path field, as shown in Figure 12.20 (where C:\ is the system drive), and click Next to continue.

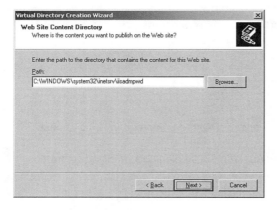

FIGURE 12.20   Creating the IISADMPWD virtual directory.

6. Check the boxes for Read and Run Scripts permissions and click Next.
7. Click Finish.

After it is created, the IISADMPWD virtual directory needs to be configured to use the Exchange Application pool, and also be forced to use basic authentication with SSL (highly recommended for security reasons). To do so, perform the following steps:

1. In IIS Manager, under the OWA virtual server, right-click the newly created iisadmpwd virtual directory and choose Properties.

2. Under the Virtual Directory tab, in the Application Settings field, choose ExchangeApplicationPool from the drop-down box labeled Application Pool, as shown in Figure 12.21.

FIGURE 12.21   Modifying the IISADMPWD virtual directory.

3. Choose the Directory Security tab, and click Edit under Authentication and Access Control.

4. Uncheck Enable Anonymous Access, and check Basic Authentication.

5. Click Yes to acknowledge the warning (SSL will be used, so this warning is moot).

6. Click OK to save the authentication methods changes.

7. Under Secure Communications, click the Edit button.

8. Check the boxes for Require Secure Channel (SSL) and Require 128-bit Encryption and click OK twice to save the changes.

After the virtual directory has been created, a registry change must be made to allow password resets to take place. To do this, perform the following steps:

1. Click Start, Run, type in **regedit.exe**, and click OK.

2. Navigate to My Computer\HKEY_LOCAL_MACHINE\SYSTEM\CurrentControlSet\ Services\MSExchangeWEB\OWA.

3. Look for the DWORD value labeled DisablePassword, as shown in Figure 12.22, double-click on it, enter 0 in the value data field, and click OK. Entering 0 forces changes to be made in SSL, which is highly recommended.

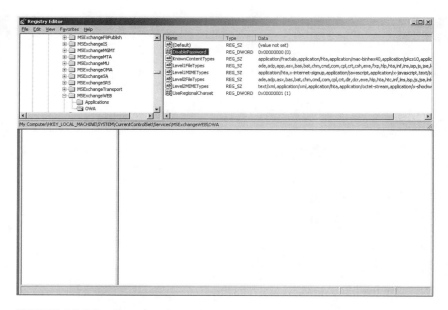

FIGURE 12.22   Changing the registry to support password resets.

4. Back in IIS Manager, restart IIS by right-clicking on the server name in IIS Manager and choosing All Tasks, Restart IIS, and then click OK.

Modifying the ISA OWA Publishing Rule to Support the Change Password Feature   After the Change Password feature has been enabled on the OWA server, the existing ISA OWA publishing rule must be modified to support the change, if it hasn't been already. To enable this, do the following from the ISA console:

1. From the ISA server, open the ISA Management Console (Start, All Programs, Microsoft ISA Server, ISA Server Management).
2. Navigate to the Firewall Policy node in the console tree.
3. Double-click on the OWA rule.
4. Select the Path tab.
5. Click Add.
6. For the path, enter /**iisadmpwd**/*, as shown in Figure 12.23.
7. Click OK, OK, Apply, and OK to save the changes.

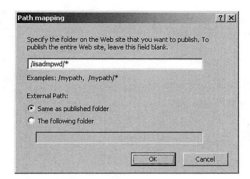

FIGURE 12.23   Allowing change password functionality in an ISA OWA publishing rule.

Summary

Outlook Web Access is a powerful tool that, when properly utilized, allows for a broad array of functionality that can increase productivity. Along with the productivity increases, however, comes the risk associated with exposing internal corporate assets to the Internet. Fortunately, ISA Server 2006 allows for unprecedented securing techniques to make OWA implementations safer and more productive.

Best Practices

- ▶ Use ISA to reverse-proxy web-based mail products, such as Outlook Web Access, whenever possible.

- ▶ Use a second external IP address, DNS host, and certificate if forms-based authentication for OWA is required to co-exist with OMA, ActiveSync, and RPC-HTTP.

- ▶ Use Secure Sockets Layer (SSL) encryption whenever possible to secure Outlook Web Access.

- ▶ Use forms-based authentication where possible to secure access and prevent unauthenticated traffic from touching the Exchange server.

- ▶ Secure an OWA virtual server with the settings described in Table 12.1.

CHAPTER 13

Securing Messaging Traffic

Messaging has moved from the realm of a "nice to have" service to a business-critical application that serves as the communications lifeblood for many organizations. It no longer is acceptable for email services to be unavailable for lengthy periods of time or for performance from the email system to be slow and unresponsive. At the same time, the demands for new and better methods of getting to email keep increasing, putting additional strain on messaging administrators who are tasked with providing secure, reliable access.

In tandem with the growth of the capabilities and reach of messaging are the security concerns associated with providing access to these resources. Along with the need to provide for "anytime, anywhere" access to email comes the risks of opening up the messaging environment to prying eyes.

In response to these threats, ISA Server 2006 provides for a comprehensive set of tools to secure messaging platforms, with built-in knowledge to inspect and protect mail traffic to and from email systems through advanced Application-layer filtering and publishing rules.

This chapter focuses on the best-practice approaches to securing email-related services (other than OWA) with ISA Server 2006. Specific step-by-step examples of using ISA to secure OMA, SMTP, MAPI, POP, IMAP, RPC over HTTP, and ActiveSync are illustrated and defined. Outlook Web Access (OWA) deployment scenarios are covered in Chapter 12, "Securing Outlook Web Access (OWA) Traffic." The examples in this chapter focus on a deployment scenario with ISA as an edge firewall or inline firewall to an additional firewall product, though the HTTP filtering scenarios can be accomplished with a unihomed ISA server in the DMZ of a firewall.

Understanding the Need for Secure Mail Access

Electronic mail systems were originally designed without a great deal of security in mind, and were essentially a convenient way to send messages from one system to another through a common medium. Eventually, however, messaging systems become a common target for hacking and exploit attempts, and organizations were forced to make a decision between opening up a messaging system to increased security threats, or closing it down and sacrificing the increased productivity that remote access could provide them.

Some of the original designs for allowing access did not necessarily take security in mind, and they subsequently suffered from security breaches and attacks. During the time that messaging was not of large consequence, this may have been brushed off, but modern communications require a high degree of confidentiality and accountability, which these platforms did not provide. Indeed, auditors and governmental regulations such as HIPAA, Sarbanes-Oxley, and others stipulated that these methods of remote access be secured or shut down, which many were, greatly affecting productivity.

Weighing the Need to Communicate Versus the Need to Secure

The security versus productivity realities of modern messaging provided the backdrop to the development of ISA Server 2006's security capabilities. These capabilities enable many organizations to provide for secured, auditable access to their messaging environments. This helps to satisfy the governmental and industry compliance concerns that plagued some of the past messaging access methods.

Outlining ISA Server 2006's Messaging Security Mechanisms

As a backdrop to these developments, ISA Server 2006 was designed with messaging security in mind. A great degree of functionality was developed to address email access and communications, with particularly tight integration with Microsoft Exchange Server built in. To illustrate, ISA Server 2006 supports securing the following messaging protocols and access methods:

- ▶ Simple Mail Transport Protocol (SMTP)
- ▶ Message Application Programming Interface (MAPI)
- ▶ Post Office Protocol (POP3)
- ▶ Internet Message Access Protocol (IMAP4)
- ▶ Microsoft Exchange Outlook Web Access (OWA,) with or without forms-based authentication (FBA)
- ▶ Microsoft Exchange Outlook Mobile Access (OMA)
- ▶ Exchange ActiveSync

▶ Remote Procedure Call over Hypertext Transfer Protocol (RPC over HTTP/HTTPS), recently renamed as "Outlook Anywhere"

▶ Third-party web-based mail access using Hypertext Transfer Protocol and/or Secure Sockets Layer (SSL) encryption

Securing each of these types of messaging access methods and protocols is detailed in subsequent sections of this chapter. For web-related mail access with OMA and ActiveSync, it may be wise to review Chapter 12; this chapter deals with integrating OMA and ActiveSync with existing OWA deployments.

Configuring ISA Server 2006 to Support OMA and ActiveSync Access to Exchange

The Outlook Mobile Access (OMA), Exchange ActiveSync, and Remote Procedure Call over Hypertext Transport Protocol (RPC over HTTP) services are similar to Outlook Web Access (OWA) in that they all use web protocols to provide access to mail resources. Each of these services provides for unique methods of access to an Exchange server, as follows:

▶ **Outlook Mobile Access (OMA)**—OMA allows web-enabled phones and other mobile devices to have access to mailbox resources via a simple, streamlined interface that displays only simple text. OMA is only available with Exchange 2003; support for it has been deprecated in Exchange 2007.

▶ **Exchange ActiveSync (EAS)**—Exchange ActiveSync allows ActiveSync-enabled phones, such as those running Windows Mobile, to synchronize content remotely with the Exchange server wirelessly or while docked to a workstation. This combined with the "direct push" functionality of Exchange Server 2003 SP2 or Exchange 2007 allows ActiveSync-enabled devices to have full real-time send and receive capabilities, similar to that offered by products such as RIM Blackberry devices.

▶ **Outlook Anywhere / RPC over HTTP(S)**—Outlook Anywhere (previously named RPC over HTTP) is an extremely useful method of accessing Exchange servers from Outlook 2003/2007 clients anywhere in the world. It uses secure SSL-encrypted web communications between the client and the server. Outlook Anywhere can be used in conjunction with Cached mode on Outlook 2003/2007 to offer instant available access to up-to-date email, calendar info, and other mail data whenever a roaming laptop is connected to a network that has SSL access back to the Exchange server, which typically covers most networks on the Internet.

OMA and ActiveSync can be enabled in an Exchange organization relatively easily: All that's required is that a box be checked. RPC over HTTP access is more complex, however, and is described in the upcoming section of this chapter, titled "Configuring ISA Server to Secure RPC over HTTP(S) Traffic."

Specific requirements to enabling these types of mail access mechanisms must be taken into account. Getting a better understanding of how these access methods can be secured with ISA is therefore important.

Enabling and Supporting OMA and ActiveSync on an Exchange 2003 OWA Server

Enabling OMA and ActiveSync is a relatively straightforward process, but one that requires that certain special steps be taken in particular circumstances. Particular attention needs to be taken when SSL is used and when Exchange front-end servers are not. First and foremost, the Exchange Mobile Services must be enabled in an Exchange organization.

Enabling OMA and ActiveSync in Exchange System Manager   OMA and EAS can be enabled in an Exchange organization by an Exchange administrator via the following procedure:

1. On any Exchange server in the organization, open Exchange System Manager (Start, All Programs, Microsoft Exchange, System Manager).
2. Navigate to Global Settings, Mobile Services.
3. Right-click on Mobile Services and choose Properties.
4. Check the boxes for ActiveSync and OMA, as shown in Figure 13.1. Enable partial or full access to the services by checking some or all of these check boxes. Click the Help (question mark) for more info on the options.

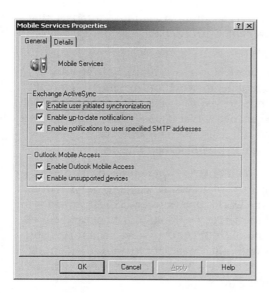

FIGURE 13.1   Enabling OMA and EAS in an Exchange 2003 organization.

5. Click OK to save the changes.

Enabling or Disabling OMA and EAS on a Per-Mailbox Basis   By default, all mailbox-enabled users in an Exchange organization have OMA and EAS individually enabled. If OMA and EAS access needs to be disabled for an individual user, or to verify that it is indeed enabled for that user, the individual setting can be found on the Exchange Features tab of an individual user account in Active Directory, as shown in Figure 13.2.

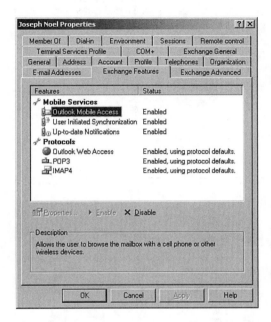

FIGURE 13.2   Validating OMA and EAS per-mailbox settings.

Supporting OMA and ActiveSync on an OWA Server Configured as a Back-End Mailbox Server   One of the most misunderstood and confusing topics with OMA and EAS has to do with how to enable mobile services on an Exchange OWA server that operates both as an Exchange SSL-enabled OWA server and an Exchange mailbox server. In these cases, mobile services fail to work properly, with error messages such as Synchronization failed due to an error on the server... or Currently your mailbox is stored on an older version of Exchange Server.... To understand why these error messages occur, and how to fix them, it is important to understand how EAS and OMA access mail resources, and how specific SSL or forms-based authentication settings can break this.

A standard IIS virtual server for web-based mail access uses specific virtual directories to make calls into the Exchange database. For example, the /exchange virtual directory is used to display individual mailboxes; the /public virtual directory is used for public folders; and the /exchweb virtual directory is used for mailbox maintenance tasks, such as rule configuration and out-of-office settings. When Secure Sockets Layer (SSL) encryption is forced on an OWA server, however, the /exchange and /public directories are modified to force all connections made to them to use SSL only.

Now, this is all fine when OWA is the only web-based access mechanism used. OWA users negotiate SSL encryption and open a secured tunnel directly to the secured virtual directories. Figure 13.3 illustrates this concept.

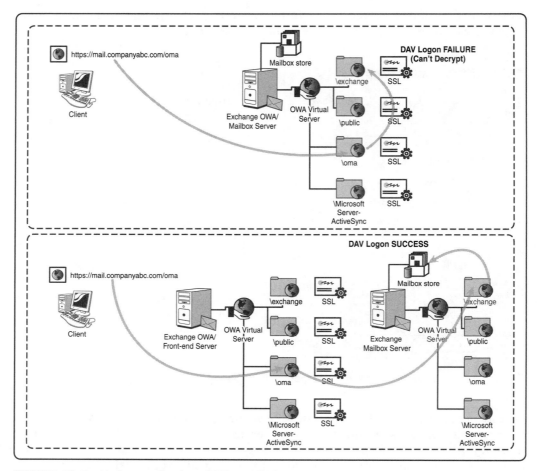

FIGURE 13.3   Understanding how OMA and EAS work.

OMA and EAS, however, work in a different way. They have their own virtual directories (/oma and /Microsoft-Server-ActiveSync). As a throwback to the origins of OMA and EAS (which were previously part of a separate product called Mobile Information Server), the server decrypts the OMA and EAS traffic, then opens up a DAV logon from the Exchange server itself to the /exchange virtual directory on the server where the mailboxes for that user are located. The problem arises when the /exchange directory on the server with the mailbox is encrypted via SSL. The DAV logon cannot establish an encrypted session with the virtual directory, and communications fails.

For environments with front-end servers, this is not a problem because the DAV calls are made to the back-end server with the user's mailbox on it. Because front-ends can only communicate to back-end servers over the HTTP protocol, an Exchange back-end mailbox server would not be configured with SSL anywhere on the virtual server, and OMA and EAS would not have a problem accessing the mailboxes.

For many organizations, however, a single Exchange server is the only system in place, and it performs the duties of both an Exchange front-end and back-end server. These organizations may require the use of SSL or forms-based authentication, and subsequently encrypt the /exchange virtual directory, breaking OMA and EAS traffic.

The solution to this problem is to configure a separate virtual directory for mobile services that has the same functionality as the /exchange virtual directory, but without SSL enabled on it. If the Registry is modified, the Exchange server makes the DAV call to this additional virtual server instead. To avoid having users bypass SSL encryption on the server, this virtual directory must be configured to allow only the local OWA server to access it and to deny connections from other IP addresses. To start the process, the configuration of the /exchange virtual directory must first be saved to an XML file, so it can be used to make a copy of itself. To do this, perform the following steps:

> **CAUTION**
>
> Remember, the entire ExchDAV procedure is necessary only if the environment is configured with a single Exchange server. If front-ends are used, this procedure is not necessary and can interfere with the default front-end/back-end topology.

1. On the Exchange server, start IIS Manager (Start, All Programs, Administrative Tools, Internet Information Services (IIS) Manager).
2. Expand SERVERNAME (local computer), Web Sites, and choose the OWA Web Site (usually Default Web Site).
3. Right-click on the /exchange virtual directory and choose All Tasks, Save Configuration to a File.
4. Enter a filename and a path to which the XML file should be saved. As an optional security precaution, a password can be entered to encrypt the XML file. Click OK.

After the XML file has been created, it can be imported as part of a new virtual directory via the following process:

1. Right-click the OWA virtual server (Default Web Site) and choose New, Virtual Directory (from file).
2. Type the path of the XML file created in the previous steps, as shown in Figure 13.4, and click Read File.
3. Select the Exchange configuration and click OK.
4. When prompted that the virtual directory still exists, select Create a New Virtual Directory, enter **ExchDAV** as the alias, and click OK.
5. Enter the password entered when exporting the file (if prompted).

Now the virtual directory is in place, and the authentication and IP restriction parameters can be inputted. To do this, proceed as follows:

1. Right-click the ExchDAV virtual directory and choose Properties.
2. Select the Directory Security tab and click on the Edit button under the Authentication and Access Control section.

3. Check only Integrated Windows Authentication and Basic Authentication; leave everything else unchecked and click OK.

4. Under Secure Communications, click the Edit button.

5. Make sure that SSL is not enabled (uncheck the boxes for Require Secure Channel if they are checked) and click OK.

6. Under IP Address and Domain Name Restrictions, click the Edit button.

7. Configure all connections to be denied by changing the setting to Denied Access. Enter an exception for the local Exchange server by clicking Add and entering the IP address of the local server, as shown in Figure 13.5.

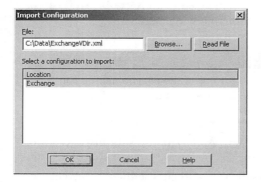

FIGURE 13.4   Importing the Exchange virtual directory to an XML file.

FIGURE 13.5   Locking down the ExchDAV folder so that only the local server can initiate DAV logon calls for OMA and EAS.

8. Click OK and OK to save the changes

The final step to set this up on the Exchange server is to edit the Registry to point mobile services DAV logons to the ExchDAV virtual directory. To do this, follow this procedure:

1. Open regedit (Start, Run, regedit.exe, OK).

2. Navigate to HKEY_LOCAL_MACHINE\SYSTEM\CurrentControlSet\Services\ MasSync\Parameters.

3. Right-click the Parameters folder, and select New, String Value.

4. Enter **ExchangeVDir** as the name of the value.

5. Double-click on ExchangeVDir and enter /**ExchDAV** as the Value data; click OK to save the changes. The setting should look like what is shown in Figure 13.6.

6. Close Registry Editor, and restart IIS from IIS Manager (right-click the Servername and choose All Tasks, Restart IIS, OK).

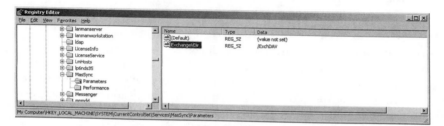

FIGURE 13.6   Configuring the Registry settings for the ExchDAV changes.

> **NOTE**
>
> For more information on this particular solution, reference Microsoft KB Article #817379 at the URL:
>
> http://support.microsoft.com/kb/817379/EN-US/

Supporting Mobile Services in ISA When Using Forms-Based Authentication for OWA

For environments that have Outlook Web Access configured to use forms-based authentication through ISA, there is somewhat of a catch-22 in regard to enabling OMA, ActiveSync, and RPC-HTTP (commonly referred to as the *Exchange mobile services*). The problem arises from the fact that the listener that the FBA-enabled OWA site uses must be the only listener that can be bound to the IP address and port where it is assigned, and that the mobile services cannot support FBA authentication tied to the listener that they use.

To illustrate with a hypothetical situation, say that CompanyABC hosts an OWA presence on the Internet that corresponds to mail.companyabc.com. In this scenario, DNS lookups to this address correspond to 63.240.93.138. CompanyABC's ISA server, which owns the 63.240.93.138 IP address, is configured with an HTTPS listener that corresponds to that IP address and answers to all HTTPS requests sent to it.

The problem arises when OMA, RPC-HTTP, and/or ActiveSync traffic need to be sent through the same connection. It fails because the traffic sent to the virtual directory for these mobile services cannot understand FBA authentication. Fortunately, however, there is a workaround for this, but it involves installing and configuring an additional IP address on the external interface of the ISA server. This IP address is then used by ISA to create an additional listener that uses basic authentication (encrypted via SSL), which is supported by OMA and ActiveSync.

Avoiding Dual Authentication Approaches

If forms-based authentication is not utilized directly on the ISA server, this problem does not exist, and the OMA and ActiveSync publishing rules can be configured as part of the same OWA publishing rule itself, or a new rule can be configured to use the same listener. In this scenario, the additional IP address, DNS A record, and additional certificate are no longer necessary; standard SSL-encrypted basic authentication can be used. The downside is that the increased security and functionality of FBA is lost and the user is prompted with the standard Username/Password dialog box.

The only additional requirement is that this traffic be directed to an additional DNS namespace, such as http://mail2.companyabc.com, so that it can be configured to point the external A record for mail2 to the different external IP address. Of course, this requires installing a separate certificate for the additional presence, which may add additional cost to the environment, depending on whether third-party CAs are used. To finish the example, in this case, CompanyABC would install and configure a certificate for mail2.companyabc.com and associate all non-FBA traffic with that particular FQDN.

This solution provides a less than elegant, but fully supported solution to the problem of enabling OMA, ActiveSync, and OWA with FBA at the same time.

TIP

If it is not feasible to obtain an additional external IP, DNS name, and certificate, the fallback solution to the problem would be to simply use standard basic authentication with OWA. This would allow all services, including OWA, OMA, ActiveSync, and RPC over HTTPS, to be enabled on the same virtual server and with the same ISA rule.

Deploying Multiple OWA Virtual Servers

To make things more complex, an ISA rule that uses SSL to access OMA across a different listener requires an Exchange server to have a different web "identity," so that it can use the new certificate name (for example, mail2.companyabc.com). There are a few ways to do this, but the most straightforward way is to configure an additional virtual server on the Exchange OWA server. This configuration can also be used in other scenarios, such as the following:

▶ A need exists to have an SSL-secured OWA (for external clients) in addition to a standard HTTP OWA (for internal clients).

▶ Different SSL OWA web presences need to be implemented (such as mail.companyabc.com, mail2.companyabc.com, mail.companyxyz.com) with unique certificates.

▶ OWA with forms-based authentication and OWA without FBA need to be allowed.

▶ OWA with FBA through ISA, and OWA with FBA directly to Exchange, need to be set up.

Fortunately, these scenarios can be accommodated on the OWA server through the creation of additional OWA virtual servers that are associated with a different IP address on the OWA server.

Once again, as previously mentioned, this step can be avoided if basic authentication (without FBA) is used for OMA and EAS and the main OWA publishing rule includes support for the \oma and \Microsoft-Server-ActiveSync paths.

Adding IP Addresses to an OWA Server   To start the process of configuring the OWA server to support the second certificate for OMA-EAS, a second IP address needs to be added to the OWA server. Follow these steps:

1. From the OWA server, click Start, Control Panel, Network Connection, then locate the OWA NIC from the list, right-click it, and choose Properties.
2. On the General tab, double-click Internet Protocol (TCP/IP).
3. Click the Advanced button.
4. Under IP Settings, click Add.
5. Enter the additional IP address and its corresponding mask and click Add.
6. Add any additional IP addresses to the dialog box.
7. Click OK three times to save the settings.

Before a new virtual server can be created, the original OWA virtual server must be configured to use the first IP address, rather than all the IP addresses on the server (the default setting). To change this, do the following:

1. Open IIS Manager.
2. Right-click the original OWA virtual server (often called Default Web Site) and choose Properties.
3. Under IP Address, change the drop-down box to display only the first IP address on the server and click OK.

Creating an Additional OWA Virtual Server   After additional IP addresses have been added, they can be used to create the additional OWA presence. After it is created, the additional OWA presence can be individually configured from the original virtual server, enabling an administrator to have two or more instances of OWA running on the same server. This procedure should be performed in Exchange System Manager, not in IIS Manager. To set up an additional virtual server on the OWA server, do the following:

1. On the OWA server, open Exchange System Manager (Start, All Programs, Microsoft Exchange, System Manager).
2. Expand ORGNAME (Exchange), Administrative Groups, ADMINGROUPNAME, Servers, SERVERNAME, Protocols, HTTP.
3. Right-click the HTTP folder and choose New, HTTP Virtual Server.

4. Enter a descriptive name in the Name field, and change the IP address to match the additional IP address added to the server in the previous steps.

5. Select the Access tab and click the Authentication button.

6. Change the authentication settings to allow only basic authentication and clear Integrated Windows Authentication. Click OK twice when finished making changes.

After the virtual server is created, the virtual directories for Exchange need to be created. To do this, perform the following steps:

1. Right-click the newly-created virtual server and choose New, Virtual Directory.

2. Enter **Exchange** for the name, and leave the default path as Mailboxes for SMTP domain, as shown in Figure 13.7.

FIGURE 13.7   Creating a second instance of the Exchange virtual directory.

3. Change the authentication settings under the Authentication button to support basic authentication and click OK, OK.

4. Right-click the virtual server again and choose New, Virtual Directory.

5. Enter a name of **Public** in the Name field, and choose Public Folder under Exchange Path, set the Access Authentication to Basic Only (no Integrated for the rest of the virtual folders), and then click OK, OK.

6. Right-click the virtual server again and choose New, Virtual Directory.

7. Enter a name of **oma** in the Name field and choose Outlook Mobile Access under Exchange Path. This time, authentication does not need to be changed because it is inherited from the root. Click OK.

8. Right-click the virtual server again and choose New, Virtual Directory.

9. Enter a name of **Exchange-Server-ActiveSync**, and choose Exchange ActiveSync under the Exchange Path field. No need to change authentication, so click OK.

10. Restart IIS by right-clicking the server name and choosing All Tasks, Restart IIS and clicking OK.

The capability to create multiple virtual servers for an OWA server gives a great deal of flexibility in supporting a heterogeneous environment that requires different types of authentication mechanisms, access methods, and certificate identities.

Assigning a Second SSL Certificate to the New OMA-EAS Virtual Server   Before SSL can be enabled for the new virtual server, an SSL certificate must be installed and enabled on the site. In addition, the virtual directories must be configured to require SSL. Follow the steps in Chapter 12, in the section that is titled "Enabling Secure Sockets Layer (SSL) Support for Exchange Outlook Web Access," to create the new certificate (for example, mail2.compa-nyabc.com). The only additions to the steps in Chapter 12 are to ensure that the OMA and EAS virtual directories are configured to force SSL, and the Exchange virtual directory is configured *not* to force SSL, per the reasoning described in the section of this chapter titled "Supporting OMA and ActiveSync on an OWA Server Configured as a Back-End Mailbox Server."

After the certificate is installed, it must be exported and imported to the ISA server, via the same procedure described in Chapter 12, in the section "Exporting and Importing the OWA Certificate to the ISA Server." Only then can an additional ISA rule be configured with a separate listener for non-FBA traffic.

Assigning a New IP Address on the ISA Server for the Additional Web Listener

The first step to enabling support for OMA and ActiveSync on an ISA server that supports OWA with FBA is to add an additional IP address to the ISA server for the additional listener to attach itself to. To do this, perform the following steps on the ISA server:

> **NOTE**
>
> If the ISA server is directly connected to the Internet, an additional public IP address needs to be obtained directly from the Internet Service Provider (ISP) to support this process. In addition, the additional DNS A record must be registered for the new name-space.

1. From the ISA server, click Start, Control Panel, Network Connection, then locate the external NIC from the list, right-click it, and choose Properties.

2. On the General tab, double-click Internet Protocol (TCP/IP).

3. Click the Advanced button.

4. Under IP Settings, click Add.

5. Enter the additional IP address (see the previous note about obtaining an additional public IP) and its corresponding mask and click Add.

6. Click OK three times to save the settings.

Setting Up an Outlook Mobile Access (OMA) and ActiveSync Publishing Rule

After the necessary IP prerequisites and listener requirements have been satisfied, the OMA and ActiveSync publishing rule can be created.

As an initial cleanup step, the original OWA rule that was created via the procedure outlined in Chapter 12 needs to be modified to use only the first IP address, and not all IP addresses on the server (the default). To set this up, do the following:

1. In the Details pane of the ISA Console, double-click on the OWA rule previously created via the steps in Chapter 12.
2. Select the Listener tab.
3. Click Properties.
4. Select the Networks tab.
5. Double-click on the external network.
6. Select to listen for requests on specified IP addresses, select the primary IP address of the ISA server, and click Add, similar to what is shown in Figure 13.8.
7. Click OK, OK, OK, Apply, and OK to save the changes.

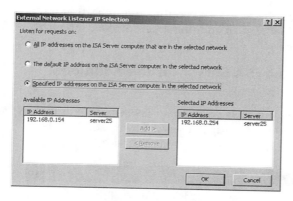

FIGURE 13.8   Modifying the OWA rule to use only the primary IP address on the server.

After setting the primary OWA rule to use only the IP associated with the FBA traffic, the following process can be used to set up the OMA-EAS rule in ISA:

1. Open the ISA Management Console and select the Firewall Policy node from the console tree.
2. In the Tasks tab of the Tasks pane, click the link for Publish Exchange Client Web Access.
3. Enter a descriptive name for the rule, such as Exchange Mobile Services, and click Next.
4. Select Exchange Server 2003 from the drop-down list shown in Figure 13.9 and check the boxes for RPC/HTTP, Outlook Mobile Access, and Exchange ActiveSync.

5. Select to publish a single web site or load balancer and click next to continue. If there is more than one web front-end servers for Exchange, ISA will be able to load balance the traffic by selecting to publish a server farm. In this example, a single server is published.

6. Select to use SSL to connect to the server, as shown in Figure 13.10. Click Next to continue.

7. Enter the mail server name (that is, mail2.companyabc.com). Make sure the host name is addressable from the ISA server and that it points to the secondary IP of the OWA server. Click Next to continue.

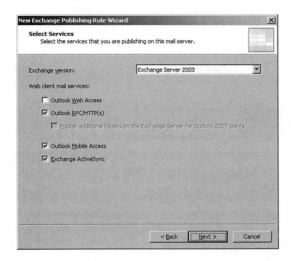

FIGURE 13.9   Setting up an OMA-EAS ISA publishing rule.

FIGURE 13.10   Selecting to use SSL to connect to the OWA server.

8. Enter the FQDN again (for example, mail2.companyabc.com) under the Public Name Details tab and click Next to continue.

9. Under Web Listener, click New.

10. Enter a descriptive name for the web listener into the name field and click Next.

11. Check to require secured SSL connections with clients and choose Next.

12. Check to listen for requests from the External network and click the Select IP addresses button.

13. Select Specified IP Addresses on the ISA Server Computer in the selected network, and choose the secondary IP address configured in the previous steps. Click Add when selected and click OK.

14. Click Next to continue.

15. Select to use a single certificate for the listener and click on Select Certificate to add it.

16. Choose the EMS certificate from the list (that is, mail2.companyabc.com) and click Select. Click Next to continue.

17. Under Authentication Settings, shown in Figure 13.11, select HTTP Authentication and check Basic. This will allow for the use of SSL with basic authentication. Click Next to continue.

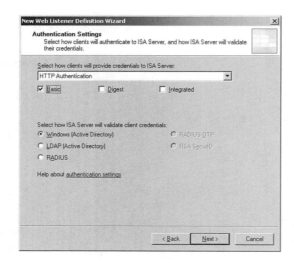

FIGURE 13.11   Configuring the EMS listener.

18. At the SSO page, click Next to continue (SSO cannot be enabled on a listener without FBA).

19. Click Finish to create the new listener.

20. From the Select Web Listener dialog box, click Edit.

21. Select the Connections tab.

22. Check the box to enable HTTP connections, and configure HTTP to HTTP Redirection, as shown in Figure 13.12. This will allow for all HTTP traffic to be automatically redirected to HTTPS traffic. Click OK to save.

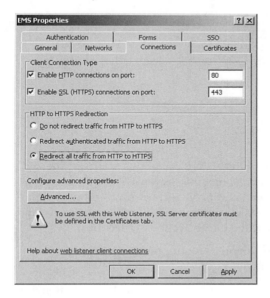

FIGURE 13.12   Configuring the EMS listener to redirect traffic from HTTP to HTTPS.

23. Click Next to continue.

24. Select Basic Authentication from the Authentication Delegation dialog box and click Next.

25. Keep the default at All Authenticated Users and click Next.

26. At the completion screen, click Finish.

27. Click Apply and OK to save the changes to ISA.

> **NOTE**
>
> The concept described in this section could easily be extended to create multiple presences for an organization, depending on the type of service being set up—for example, owa.companyabc.com, oma.companyabc.com, eas.companyabc.com, rpc.companyabc.com, pop.companyabc.com, imap.companyabc.com, and the like. The only limitation is the number of IP addresses and certificates that can be created.

Configuring ISA Server to Secure RPC over HTTP(S) Traffic

The techniques used to configure publishing rules for RPC over HTTP(S) are slightly different techniques than those used with the OWA, OMA, and ActiveSync publishing rules, but the basic idea is still the same: to provide for reverse-proxied HTTP(S) access through the ISA server, to secure the traffic sent back to Exchange. Before RPC over HTTP(S) can be secured with ISA Server, it must first be enabled in the Exchange topology.

NOTE

Client support of RPC over HTTP requires Outlook 2003 to be running on Windows XP SP2 (or Windows XP SP1 with the KB Article #331320 patch installed) or higher. The KB article can be found at the following URL:

http://support.microsoft.com/kb/331320

Installing the RPC over HTTP Proxy

The RPC over HTTP service requires the use of an RPC-HTTP proxy that assists in the management of RPC-HTTP requests to the Exchange mailbox server. This Proxy is normally installed on an Exchange front-end server, but can also be installed on a single all-in-one Exchange server that acts as both the back-end and front-end server, if special Registry changes are made to that server, as described in the following sections.

To install the RPC over HTTP service on the front-end or all-in-one back-end server, perform the following steps:

1. From the Exchange front-end or all-in-one back-end server, go to Start, All Programs, Add or Remove Programs.
2. Click the button for Add/Remove Windows Components.
3. Scroll down and select Networking Services by clicking once on the name (not the check box) and then clicking the Details button.
4. Check the box next to RPC over HTTP Proxy, as shown in Figure 13.13. Click OK.
5. Click Next to continue.
6. Click Finish when complete.

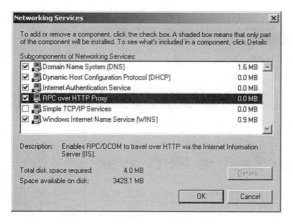

FIGURE 13.13   Installing the RPC over HTTP Proxy service.

Configuring RPC over HTTPS on an Exchange Back-End Server

After the networking service for RPC over HTTP has been installed, the Exchange server must be configured to act as an RPC over HTTP back-end server. In the case of the all-in-one Exchange server, where there is no unique front-end server and a single Exchange server acts as the primary mailbox and OWA server for the enterprise, this configuration is performed on the Exchange server where the RPC over HTTP networking service was installed, and must be followed by the Registry change outlined in following sections.

In deployment scenarios where there are separate front-end and back-end servers, the back-end server must first be configured as an RPC over HTTP back-end, followed by configuration of the front-end server as an RPC-HTTP front-end. To configure the back-end server for RPC over HTTP, do the following:

> **NOTE**
>
> The scenarios outlined in this book assume that Exchange Server 2003 Service Pack 1 is installed. SP1 adds a lot of configuration enhancements, including a much more simplified RPC over HTTP configuration. It is not recommended to use RPC over HTTP on pre-SP1 Exchange Server 2003 implementations, and the scenarios presented in this book will not be accurate without SP1 installed.

1. From the Exchange back-end mailbox server, open ESM by clicking on Start, All Programs, Microsoft Exchange, System Manager.
2. Navigate to ORGANIZATIONNAME (Exchange), Administrative Groups, ADMIN-GROUPNAME, Servers.
3. Right-click on the back-end server and click Properties.
4. Select the RPC-HTTP tab (if it doesn't appear, it probably means that Exchange Server 2003 Service Pack 1 is not installed).
5. Select RPC-HTTP Back-End Server from the list.
6. Click OK if warned that there are no RPC-HTTP front-end servers in the organization.
7. Click OK to save the changes.
8. When prompted with a warning message, select OK to change the ports automatically.
9. Click OK to acknowledge that the role change will not be effective until reboot.
10. Reboot the server (when feasible to do so).

Configuring RPC over HTTPS on an Exchange 2003 Front-End Server

As previously mentioned, deployment scenarios involving separate hardware for Exchange front-end servers and Exchange back-end servers require the front-end server or servers to be configured as RPC over HTTP front-ends. In single all-in-one server deployments, this step can be skipped and the Registry change outlined in the next section of this chapter should instead be run.

That said, the following procedure enables an Exchange Server 2003 SP1 front-end server to act as a proxy for RPC-HTTPS traffic:

1. From the Exchange back-end mailbox server, open ESM by clicking on Start, All Programs, Microsoft Exchange, System Manager.
2. Navigate to ORGANIZATIONNAME (Exchange), Administrative Groups, ADMIN-GROUPNAME, Servers.
3. Right-click on the front-end server and click Properties.
4. Select the RPC-HTTP tab.
5. Select RPC-HTTP Front-End Server from the list and click OK.
6. Reboot the server to complete the changes.

Modifying the Registry to Support a Single-Server Exchange RPC over HTTP Topology

As previously mentioned, if there is not a dedicated front-end server in the RPC-HTTP topology, then a special Registry change needs to be performed on the all-in-one Exchange server. To make this change, do the following:

CAUTION

Be sure that the Registry change is made to only back-end servers that do not have any front-end RPC-HTTP servers in the environment. This procedure is meant only for Exchange servers that serve dual roles as both front-end and back-end servers.

---

1. On the all-in-one Exchange front-end/back-end server, open the Registry editor (Start, Run, cmd.exe, regedit.exe).
2. Navigate through the console tree to HKEY_LOCAL_MACHINE\Software\Microsoft\Rpc\RpcProxy.
3. Right-click the ValidPorts entry, and then click Modify.
4. In the Edit String field, under Value Data, type in the following and click OK, as shown in Figure 13.14:

   SERVERNAME:6001-6002;*server.companyabc.com*:6001-6002;

   SERVERNAME:6004;*server.companyabc.com*:6004;

   (Where SERVERNAME is the NetBIOS name of the server and server.companyabc.com is the FQDN of the server as it will appear for RPC services.)
5. Close Registry Editor.

CAUTION

It is critical to match the FQDN entered into this Registry with the FQDN that will be used from the Internet for RPC over HTTP traffic. This may or may not be different from the FQDN used for OWA, depending on whether a different namespace is used so as to allow forms-based authentication, as described in Chapter 12.

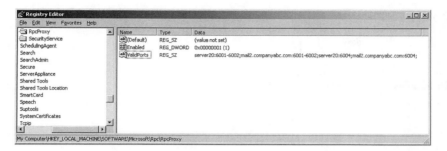

FIGURE 13.14   Entering the Registry change for RPC-HTTP support on an all-in-one Exchange front-end/back-end server.

Creating the RPC Virtual Directory on the Proper Virtual Server

In certain scenarios, such as when a separate virtual server has been created for non–forms-based authentication traffic, the RPC virtual directory needs to be exported from the default OWA virtual server to the secondary virtual server, such as in the scenarios described in this chapter. To export and import this setting, do the following:

> **NOTE**
>
> This procedure needs to be followed only if multiple OWA virtual servers have been created, and the RPC traffic will be directed at the one that doesn't currently have the \rpc virtual directory.

1. From the OWA server, open IIS Manager (Start, All Programs, Administrative Tools, Internet Information Services [IIS] Manager).
2. Navigate to SERVERNAME, Web Sites, Default Web Site (or the name of the primary OWA virtual server).
3. Right-click the RPC virtual directory listed under the OWA website and select All Tasks, Save Configuration to a File.
4. Enter **rpc** as the filename and a local patch and click OK.
5. Right-click the secondary virtual server and choose New, Virtual Directory (from file).
6. Enter the path and name of the XML file that was exported, and click the Read File button. Select RPC from the list, as shown in Figure 13.15, and click OK.
7. Right-click the server name and choose All Tasks, Restart IIS, then click OK to confirm.

Securing RPC over HTTPS Servers with an ISA Publishing Rule

Securing an RPC over HTTPS proxy server involves publishing the RPC virtual directory as part of a publishing rule. This is typically done on the rule where OMA and ActiveSync have been set up, unless forms-based authentication is used, and then it is typically enabled on the standard OWA rule.

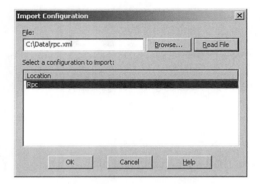

FIGURE 13.15   Importing the RPC virtual directory to a secondary virtual server.

> **CAUTION**
>
> Once again, it is important to note that RPC over HTTP cannot utilize a listener on a rule that uses forms-based authentication. Instead, it must utilize a basic authentication-enabled listener. Consult the previous sections for more information on this.

The Exchange Web Client Access publishing wizard in ISA 2006 allows for RPC/HTTP to be enabled automatically when creating a rule. If it wasn't enabled when the wizard was run, a rule can retroactively be enabled for RPC/HTTP access via the following steps:

1. From the ISA Server Console, select the Firewall Policy node.
2. Double-click on the rule that will be modified (typically the OMA-EAS rule previously set up, or the OWA rule if FBA is not used).
3. Select the Paths tab and click the Add button.
4. Enter /**rpc**/* and click OK.
5. Click OK, Apply, and OK to save the changes.

> **NOTE**
>
> For access to an internal RPC over HTTP topology over the Internet, the server's host name must be published via external DNS so that it can be propagated across the Internet and made available for lookups.

Setting Up an Outlook 2003 Profile to Use RPC over HTTP

The final step involved with enabling RPC over HTTP support for clients is to configure the client Outlook 2003 mail profiles to use it as a service. First, ensure that Windows XP Service Pack 2 (or the hotfix for RPC over HTTP previously mentioned) is installed, along with the Outlook 2003 client. After it is verified, a mail profile can be created via the following procedure:

> **NOTE**
>
> Unfortunately, the profile cannot be set up remotely, or at least not without RPC access to the Exchange server to create the initial connection. The initial creation of the profile itself should be performed on the internal network, or somewhere with standard RPC access (essentially full network access) to the Exchange server. After it has been set up for the first time and all mail has been synchronized, it can then be sent out into the field indefinitely. The upside to this is that the initial synchronization of the offline folder settings, which can be quite extensive, can be done on a fast local network segment.

1. From the Outlook 2003 client (connected to the internal network, with full access to the Exchange server), click Start, Control Panel.
2. Double-click on the Mail item (switching to Classic view may be required to see it).
3. Click Show Profiles.
4. At the General tab, select either Always Use This Profile (if this is the only mail server that will be set up as part of a profile), or Prompt for a Profile to Be Used. Click Add.
5. Enter a name for the profile, such as Exchange-RPC-HTTP.
6. Select Add a New E-mail Account and click Next.
7. Select Microsoft Exchange Server from the list shown in Figure 13.16 and click Next.
8. Enter the local name of the back-end mailbox server, such as server20, and make sure that Use Cached Exchange Mode is checked.

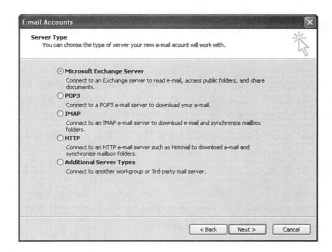

FIGURE 13.16   Configuring an RPC over HTTP–enabled Outlook profile.

9. Enter the name of the mailbox that will be set up (for example, the user's username or full name) and click More Settings.

10. Select the Security tab and check the box for Always Prompt for User Name and Password.

11. Select the Connection tab and check the box for Connect to My Exchange Mailbox Using HTTP, then click the Exchange Proxy Settings button.

12. Using the Exchange Proxy Settings dialog box, enter the FQDN of the external name of the RPC-HTTP topology, such as mail2.companyabc.com (which corresponds to the ISA listener for basic authentication). Check the box to Mutually Authenticate the Session, and enter **msstd:serverfqdn** (for example msstd:mail2.companyabc.com). Change the proxy authentication settings to basic authentication, as shown in Figure 13.17.

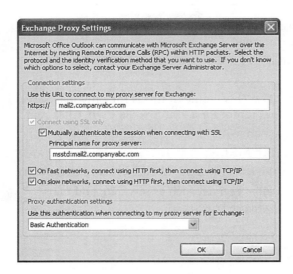

FIGURE 13.17   Reviewing Exchange proxy settings for the RPC-HTTPS Outlook profile.

13. To force RPC over HTTP for all connections, select the box labeled On Fast Networks, Connect Using HTTP First, Then Connect Using TCP/IP. If this is not checked, MAPI is attempted first when the connection to the server is fast. Click OK twice.

14. The username and Exchange server should be underlined at this point; click Next to continue.

15. Click Finish and then click OK.

Outlook needs to be opened and the mailbox synchronized with the client at this point. After the full mailbox data has been copied locally, the system is free to roam around on the Internet, wherever HTTPS access back to the ISA server is granted.

Securing Exchange MAPI Access

The Message Application Programming Interface (MAPI) has traditionally been used for communications between the client and an Exchange server. This type of traffic is highly functional, but can pose a security threat to an Exchange server because it requires the use of the dangerous Remote Procedure Call (RPC) protocol, which has become notorious through recent exploits that take advantage of the open nature of the RPC protocol to take over services on poorly coded services.

In the past, organizations have been handcuffed by the fact that blocking RPC requires blocking a huge range of ports (all dynamic ports from 1024 to 65,536, plus others) because of the dynamic nature in which RPC works. Blocking RPC access to an Exchange server was not feasible either. This type of block would also block client access through MAPI, effectively crippling email access to an Exchange server.

ISA Server 2006 greatly simplifies and secures this process through its capability to filter RPC traffic for specific services, dynamically opening only those ports that are negotiated for use with MAPI access itself. This greatly limits the types of exploits that can take advantage of an Exchange server that is protected with MAPI filtering techniques.

Configuring MAPI RPC Filtering Rules

To configure an ISA server to filter and allow only MAPI access across particular network segments, use the following technique:

1. From the ISA Console, navigate to the Firewall Policy node in the console tree.
2. In the Tasks tab, click on the link for Publish Mail Servers.
3. Enter a name for the rule, such as MAPI Access from Clients Network, and click Next.
4. Select Client Access from the list of access types and click Next.
5. Check the box for Outlook (RPC), as shown in Figure 13.18, and click Next to continue.
6. Enter the IP address of the Exchange server that is to be published and click Next.
7. Select from which networks the rule will listen to requests, and click Next to continue.
8. Click Finish, Apply, and OK.

To set up more advanced MAPI filtering, examine the Traffic tab of the rule that was created and click on the Properties buttons, and finally choose the Interfaces tab. Advanced settings, such as which UUIDs to allow, can be found here, as shown in Figure 13.19.

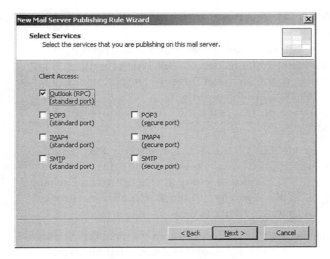

FIGURE 13.18   Enabling a MAPI filtering rule.

FIGURE 13.19   Examining advanced MAPI filtering.

Deploying MAPI Filtering Across Network Segments

Where MAPI filtering really shines is in scenarios where the ISA server is used to protect a server's network from the client's network in an organization, similar to what is shown in Figure 13.20.

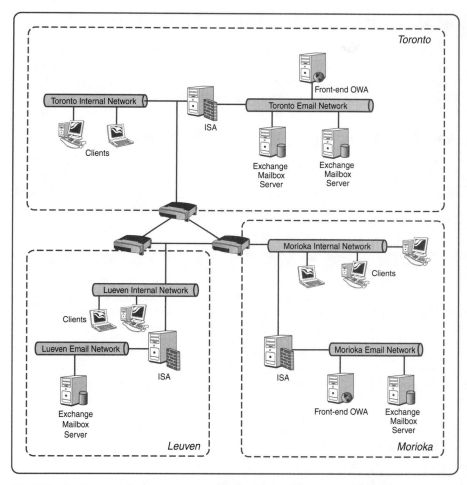

FIGURE 13.20   Isolating and securing an Exchange environment behind an internal ISA firewall.

In these scenarios, the ISA server acts as an Exchange firewall, providing secured mail, OWA, POP, and any other necessary services to the ISA server through a secured, Application-layer filtered environment. This type of deployment scenario is very useful for organizations that want to reduce the exposure to security threats faced from unruly or exploited clients. It allows for a great degree of control over what type of access to an Exchange environment can be set up.

Securing POP and IMAP Exchange Traffic

The ancillary mail services of the Post Office Protocol version 3 (POP3) and Internet Message Access Protocol version 4 (IMAP4) can be secured through an ISA server. This is particularly important for organizations that require support of these legacy protocols; they are less secure than the newer forms of mail access available.

Creating and Configuring a POP Mail Publishing Rule

POP3 servers are secured in ISA through the creation of a special rule that enables ISA to examine all traffic sent to the POP3 server and perform intrusion detection heuristics on it with an advanced POP intrusion detection filter. The POP server does not necessarily need to be a Microsoft server, such as Exchange, but can be run on any POP3-compliant messaging system.

CAUTION

Enable POP support in a messaging environment only if there is no other viable option. POP3 support is less secure than other access methods, and can cause mail delivery and security issues. For example, many POP clients are configured to pull all the mail off the POP server, making it difficult to do disaster recovery of mail data.

Enabling POP3 Access on an Exchange Server   If no existing POP3 server is available, but support for the protocol needs to be enabled, the service can be enabled on an internal Exchange Server 2003 system via the following procedure:

1. On the Exchange server, open the Services MMC Console (Start, All Programs, Administrative Tools, Services).

2. Right-click the Microsoft Exchange POP3 service and choose Properties.

3. Change the Startup Type to Automatic, as shown in Figure 13.21.

4. Click Start to start the service and click OK.

Enabling SSL Support on the POP Virtual Server   Realistically, all POP traffic across an untrusted network such as the Internet should be encrypted as well, using Secure Sockets Layer. This involves installing a certificate onto the POP virtual server.

NOTE

An existing certificate can be used for POP-SSL traffic as well as HTTPS traffic. ISA is intelligent enough to decipher whether the traffic hitting its interface is HTTPS or POP-SSL traffic, and it forwards the requests to the appropriate rule. That said, some organizations do decide to create an additional name (such as pop.companyabc.com) for POP traffic to create a logical separation. Although this is convenient, this is not necessary with ISA.

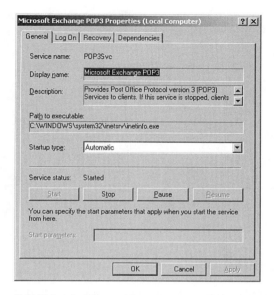

FIGURE 13.21   Enabling POP support on the Exchange server.

To configure the POP virtual server for SSL by using an existing certificate (for example, mail.companyabc.com), do the following:

1. On the Exchange server (or front-end Exchange server), open Exchange System Manager (Start, All Programs, Microsoft Exchange, System Manager).

2. Navigate to ORGANIZATIONNAME, Administrative Groups, ADMINGROUPNAME, Servers, SERVERNAME, Protocols, POP3.

3. Right-click the POP virtual server and select Properties.

4. Select the Access tab.

5. Under Secure Communication, click the Certificate tab.

6. Click Next at the welcome dialog box.

7. Select Assign an Existing Certificate and click Next.

8. Select the certificate desired (for example, mail.companyabc.com) from the list and click Next to continue.

9. Click Next at the summary page.

10. Click Finish.

The final step is to force SSL on the POP virtual server. To do this in the same dialog box, perform the following steps:

1. Click the Communication button.

2. Check Require Secure channel and Require 128-Bit Encryption, and click OK.

3. Click the Authentication button.

4. Clear the button for Simple Authentication and leave Basic Authentication checked. Check the box for Requires SSL/TLS encryption, as shown in Figure 13.22.

5. Click OK.

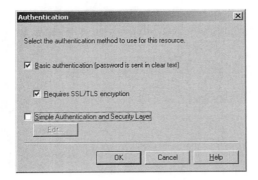

FIGURE 13.22   Forcing SSL on the POP virtual server.

Configuring an ISA POP Filtering Rule   After a POP server has been enabled or established on the internal network, it can be secured via modification of an existing rule or creation of a new rule to secure POP traffic as follows:

1. From the ISA Console, select the Firewall Policy node from the console tree.

2. In the Tasks pane, click the link for Publish Mail Servers.

3. Enter a descriptive name for the rule (for example, POP-SSL Access) and click Next.

4. Select Client Access: RPC, IMAP, POP3, SMTP from the radio box list and click Next.

5. In the Select Services dialog box, select POP3 (secure port) and click Next.

6. Enter the internal IP address of the POP server and click Next.

7. Select to which networks the ISA server will listen by checking the boxes next to them and click Next.

8. Click Finish, Apply, and OK.

Creating and Configuring an IMAP Mail Publishing Rule

The Internet Message Access Protocol (IMAP) is often used as a mail access method for Unix systems and even for clients such as Outlook Express. It also can be secured through an ISA server, using the same rule as a POP rule, or through the configuration of a unique IMAP publishing rule.

Enabling IMAP4 Access on an Exchange Server   If IMAP protocol support is required, but an internal IMAP server is not currently available, Exchange Server 2003 can be configured to provide for IMAP functionality through the following procedure:

1. On the Exchange server, open the Services MMC Console (Start, All Programs, Administrative Tools, Services).

2. Right-click the Microsoft Exchange IMAP4 service and choose Properties.

3. Change the Startup type to Automatic.

4. Click Start to start the service and click OK.

Configuring SSL on the IMAP Virtual Server   As with POP traffic, it is preferable to force SSL encryption for IMAP traffic. The procedure to configure this is very similar to POP SSL configuration and can be done with the following steps:

1. On the Exchange server (or front-end Exchange server), open Exchange System Manager (Start, All Programs, Microsoft Exchange, System Manager).

2. Navigate to ORGANIZATIONNAME, Administrative Groups, ADMINGROUPNAME, Servers, SERVERNAME, Protocols, IMAP4.

3. Right-click the IMAP virtual server and select Properties.

4. Select the Access tab.

5. Under Secure Communication, click the Certificate tab.

6. Click Next at the welcome dialog box.

7. Select Assign an Existing Certificate and click Next.

8. Select the certificate desired (for example, mail.companyabc.com) from the list and click Next to continue.

9. Click Next at the summary page.

10. Click Finish.

The final step is to force SSL on the IMAP Virtual Server. To do this, perform the following steps in the same dialog box:

1. Click the Communication button.

2. Check Require Secure Channel and Require 128-Bit Encryption and click OK.

3. Click the Authentication button.

4. Clear the button for Simple Authentication and leave Basic Authentication checked. Check the box for Requires SSL/TLS Encryption and click OK.

5. Click OK.

Configuring an ISA IMAP Filtering Rule   After the internal IMAP presence has been established, an ISA rule can be created to allow IMAP traffic to the IMAP server. The following procedure outlines this process:

1. From the ISA Console, select the Firewall Policy node from the console tree.

2. In the Tasks pane, click the link for Publish Mail Servers.

3. Enter a descriptive name for the rule (for example, IMAP-SSL Access) and click Next.

4. Select Client Access: RPC, IMAP, POP3, SMTP from the radio box list, as shown in Figure 13.23, and click Next.

5. Under the Select Services dialog box, select IMAP4 (secure port) and click Next.

6. Enter the internal IP address of the IMAP4 server and click Next.

7. Select to which networks the ISA server will listen by checking the boxes next to them and click Next.

8. Click Finish.

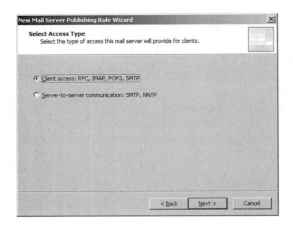

FIGURE 13.23   Setting up an ISA IMAP publishing rule.

Managing and Controlling Simple Mail Transport Protocol (SMTP) Traffic

The Simple Mail Transport Protocol (SMTP) is the second most commonly used protocol on the Internet, after the web HTTP protocol. It is ubiquitously used as an email transport mechanism on the Internet and has become a critical tool for online collaboration.

Unfortunately, SMTP is also one of the most abused protocols on the Internet as well. Unsolicited email (spam), phishing attacks, and email-borne viruses all take advantage of the open, unauthenticated nature of SMTP, and it has become a necessity for organizations to control and monitor SMTP traffic entering and leaving the network.

ISA Server 2006's Application-layer inspection capabilities allow for a high degree of SMTP filtering and attack detection. By default, ISA supports the protocol as part of standard rules and policies.

It does not, however, have built-in intelligence to filter out email-borne viruses. It can, however, be extended with a third-party virus filter product that is designed for use with

ISA Server 2006. The list of these products keeps growing over time, but they can be found at the following URL:

http://www.microsoft.com/isaserver/partners/contentsecurity.mspx

With the addition of one of these third-party extensions to the SMTP filter, the capabilities of ISA Server can be further extended to include enterprise SMTP virus scanning and content filtering.

Enabling Outbound and Inbound SMTP Filtering

Several different varieties of SMTP rules can be set up on the ISA server for SMTP filtering, depending on the type of traffic that will be allowed, such as the following:

▶ **Inbound SMTP filtering**—Inbound SMTP filtering is the most common type of SMTP filtering deployed. The primary security need for organizations with SMTP mail is to secure the anonymous email traffic coming into their networks from the untrusted Internet. At a minimum, inbound SMTP filtering should be enabled.

▶ **Outbound SMTP filtering**—Outbound SMTP filtering is becoming more important. Organizations are finding that they are being held liable for internal employees launching attacks and sending spam (often without their knowledge) to external employees. Filtering and scanning the outbound traffic from a network can help to mitigate these risks.

▶ **Inbound and outbound SMTP filtering**—The best and most secure approach is to deploy an SMTP filtering strategy that makes use of both inbound and outbound SMTP filtering for an environment. This also has the advantage of enforcing SMTP communications through the ISA server itself, rather than opening up any direct communications from internal clients or servers.

Creating an Outbound SMTP Filtering Rule   The different types of rules are set up in similar ways, using the standard ISA rule methodology discussed throughout this book. To set up a rule to allow inbound SMTP filtering (to an internal SMTP server from the Internet), do the following:

TIP

For inbound SMTP filtering to work properly, the MX record on the Internet needs to resolve to the external IP address of the ISA server, either through the public IP address on ISA or through the single IP address, when ISA is configured as a unihomed server in the DMZ of an existing firewall. In these configurations, the extra firewall needs to establish a NAT relationship between the IP address that the public MX record references, and the ISA server IP address.

---

1. From the ISA Console, click on the Firewall Policy node.
2. In the Tasks pane, select the link for Publish Mail Servers.

3. Enter a descriptive name for the publishing rule, such as "Inbound SMTP," and click Next to continue.

4. Select the Server-to-Server Communication radio button from the list and click Next to continue.

5. Select SMTP from the check boxes in the Select Services dialog box, as shown in Figure 13.24, and click Next to continue.

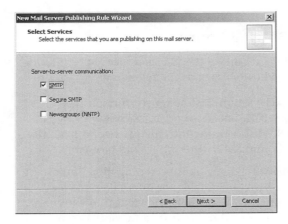

FIGURE 13.24   Setting up an inbound SMTP rule.

6. Enter the IP address of the internal ISA interface (the rule needs to specify that the internal email server can send directly to ISA), and click Next to continue.

7. Select Listen to Requests from the external network and click Next.

8. Click Finish, Apply, and OK to save the changes.

Configuring an Access Rule for the SMTP Server to Forward Outbound Messages   The final step toward configuring ISA to send outbound messages is to allow the actual SMTP traffic from the ISA server to all external mail servers on the Internet. This can be configured with a simple access rule, set up as follows:

1. On the ISA server, open the ISA Console and choose the Firewall Policy node from the console tree.

2. Under the Tasks pane, click the link for Create New Access Rule.

3. Enter a descriptive name, such as SMTP Outbound, and click Next.

4. Select Allow from the rule action list and click Next.

5. Under This Rule Applies To, select Specified Protocols.

6. Click Add under Protocols, then drill down and choose Common Protocols, SMTP, as shown in Figure 13.25. Click Add.

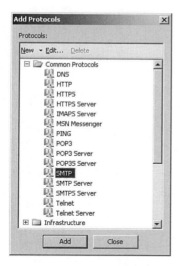

FIGURE 13.25   Adding an SMTP access rule for ISA outbound SMTP traffic.

7. Click Close and Next.

8. Under Access Rule Sources, click Add.

9. Drill down to Networks, and select Internal and click Add, then Close.

10. Under Access Rule Destinations, click Add.

11. Under Networks, select External, and then click Add and Close.

12. Click Next, Next, Finish.

13. Click the Apply button at the top of the Details pane and the OK button to confirm.

Customizing the SMTP Filter

After SMTP rules have been set up to allow the traffic to flow through the ISA server, the ISA SMTP filter can be customized to block specific types of SMTP commands and content. To access the SMTP filter settings on the ISA server, do the following:

1. From the ISA Console, click the Add-ins node in the console tree.

2. Under Application Filters in the Details pane, double-click on SMTP Filter.

3. Examine and configure the settings on the SMTP Filter Properties dialog box, some of which are shown in Figure 13.26.

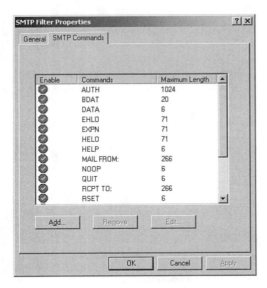

FIGURE 13.26   Configuring SMTP filter settings.

Summary

Messaging is one of the most critical components of an organization's IT structure, and is therefore one of the most obvious candidates to secure. Fortunately, ISA's securing capabilities in this realm are extremely strong, and ISA makes it possible to protect OWA, SMTP, OMA, RPC-HTTP, ActiveSync, POP, and IMAP messaging traffic and protocols, making it a versatile tool in the fight against modern viruses and exploits.

Best Practices

- ▶ Use ISA to reverse-proxy web-based mail products, such as OMA and EAS whenever possible.

- ▶ Use a second external IP address, DNS host, and certificate if forms-based authentication for OWA is required to co-exist with OMA, ActiveSync, and RPC-HTTP.

- ▶ Use POP and IMAP sparingly and only when it can be secured through ISA server and when configured to use SSL encryption.

- ▶ Configure the ISA server to filter both inbound and outbound SMTP traffic where possible.

- ▶ Use a third-party SMTP anti-virus product to further extend the capabilities of ISA's SMTP filtering capabilities.

- ▶ Consider placing Exchange and other messaging servers in a dedicated screened subnet that is secured by an ISA server.

CHAPTER 14

Securing Web (HTTP) Traffic

Although ISA Server 2006 is designed to handle any type of network traffic, it does particularly well in the filtering and securing of the Hypertext Transport Protocol (HTTP), the most common protocol used on the Internet and the transport mechanism for delivering website information, pictures, and video across the Internet.

ISA Server 2006's Application-layer filtering technologies enable organizations to properly secure their outward-facing web services from external attacks such as Code Red, Nimbda, and future HTTP-based exploits yet to be written. Although standard packet filter firewalls are limited to opening a port for HTTP, ISA Server 2006 includes the capability to filter the HTTP traffic by host header, path, content type, HTTP commands, and a whole host of other filter options.

In addition to providing for secure web-filtering options as an edge firewall, ISA Server 2006 also provides for robust reverse-proxy options in the DMZ of an existing firewall, allowing for additional layers of protection and providing for capabilities such as end-to-end SSL encryption, link translation, and more.

This chapter focuses on ISA Server 2006's HTTP securing capabilities. ISA deployment scenarios as an edge firewall and a reverse-proxy server are outlined, and step-by-step guides for securing web servers, SharePoint sites, and other custom web applications are outlined.

Outlining the Inherent Threat in Web Traffic

The Internet provides somewhat of a catch-22 when it comes to its goal and purpose. On one hand, the Internet is designed to allow anywhere, anytime access to information, linking systems around the world together and enabling free exchange of that information. On the other hand, this type of transparency comes with a great deal of risk. It effectively means that any one system can be exposed to every connected computer, either friendly or malicious, in the world.

Often, this inherent risk of compromising systems or information through their exposure to the Internet has led administrators to lock down access to that information with firewalls. Of course, this limits the capabilities and usefulness of the free information-exchange system that web traffic provides. Many web servers need to be made available to anonymous access by the general public, which poses a particular dilemma: Organizations need to place that information online without putting the servers on which the information is placed at undue risk.

Fortunately, ISA Server 2006 provides for robust and capable tools to secure web traffic, making it available for remote access but also securing it against attack and exploit. To understand how it does this, it is first necessary to examine how web traffic can be exploited.

Understanding Web (HTTP) Exploits

It is an understatement to say that the computing world was not adequately prepared for the release of the Code Red virus. The Microsoft Internet Information Services (IIS) exploit that Code Red took advantage of was already known, and a patch was made available from Microsoft for several weeks before the release of the virus. In those days, however, less emphasis was placed on patching and updating systems on a regular basis, as it was generally believed that it was best to wait for the bugs to get worked out of the patches first.

So, what happened is that a large number of websites were completely unprepared for the huge onslaught of exploits that occurred with the Code Red virus, which sent specially formatted HTTP requests to a web server to attempt to take control of a system. For example, the following example URL lists the type of exploits that were performed:

http://www.companyabc.com/scripts/..%5c../winnt/system32/cmd.exe?/c+dir+c:\

This exploit in particular attempts to launch the command prompt on a web server. Through the proper manipulation, viruses such as Code Red found the method for taking over web servers and using them as drones to attack other web servers.

These types of HTTP attacks were a wakeup call to the broader security community. It became apparent that Packet-layer filter firewalls that could simply open or close a port were worthless against the threat of an exploit that packages its traffic over a legitimately allowed port such as HTTP.

HTTP filtering and securing, fortunately, is something that ISA Server does extremely well, and it offers a large number of customization options that enable administrators to have control over the web server's traffic and security.

Securing Encrypted (Secure Sockets Layer) Web Traffic

As the World Wide Web was maturing, organizations realized that if they encrypted the HTTP packets that were transmitted between a website and a client, it would make them virtually unreadable to anyone who might intercept those packets. This led to the adoption of Secure Sockets Layer (SSL) encryption for HTTP traffic.

Of course, encrypted packets also create somewhat of a dilemma from an intrusion detection and analysis perspective because it is impossible to read the contents of the packet to determine what it is trying to do. Indeed, many HTTP exploits in the wild today can be transmitted over secure SSL-encrypted channels. This poses a dangerous situation for organizations that must secure the traffic against interception, but must also proactively monitor and secure their web servers against attack.

ISA Server 2006 is uniquely positioned to solve this problem, fortunately, because it includes the capability to perform end-to-end SSL bridging. Because the SSL certificate from the web server is installed on the ISA server itself, along with a copy of the private key, ISA can decrypt the traffic, scan it for exploits, and then re-encrypt it before sending it to the web server. Very few products on the marketplace do this type of end-to-end encryption of the packets, and fortunately ISA allows for this level of security.

Publishing and Customizing Web Server Publishing Rules

The key to ISA's HTTP filtering functionality revolves around the website publishing rule. What this type of rule does is enable an ISA server to "pretend" to be the web server itself, while secretly passing the packets back to the server via a separate process. This has the added advantage of securing the traffic by not exposing the web servers to direct attack and by forcing them to first overcome the ISA server before they can overcome the web server.

> **NOTE**
>
> Unlike the other types of server publishing rules, ISA does not need to be installed as a multi-homed (multiple NICs) server to take advantage of web publishing rules. Instead, ISA allows for the creation of web-based publishing rules when it is set up as a unihomed server, sometimes set up in the DMZ of an existing packet filter firewall. In fact, this setup is a very common deployment model for ISA because there is a strong demand for systems to provide this type of secured reverse-proxy capabilities. For more information on this deployment model, see Chapter 7, "Deploying ISA Server as a Reverse Proxy in an Existing Firewall DMZ."

All the HTTP-based filtering and functionality is stored within the web publishing rule options, and it is therefore critical to become intimately aware of its capabilities.

Using the Website Publishing Wizard

To secure a web server through ISA Server 2006, a basic website publishing rule must be set up and configured. When this rule is created, it can be modified as necessary to provide for additional filter capabilities and other options. To create a simple rule, follow the instructions outlined in the following steps.

1. From the ISA Server Management Console, click on the Firewall Policy node in the console tree.
2. From the Tasks tab in the Tasks pane, click the link titled Publish Web Sites.
3. Enter a descriptive name for the rule and click Next to continue.
4. Under Action to Take, select Allow and click Next to continue.
5. Under Publishing type, as shown in Figure 14.1, select whether to publish a single site, multiple websites, or an entire server farm. ISA 2006 has a new added feature that allows for load balancing of traffic to a team of web servers. In this example, we are publishing to a single server, so choose to publish a single website and click Next to continue.

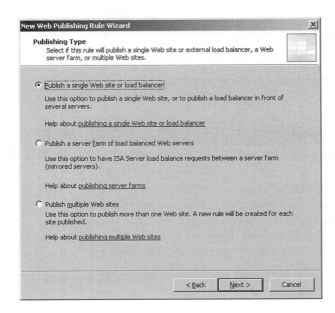

FIGURE 14.1 *Publishing a single website.*

6. Select whether to use SSL to connect to the published web server. Because this specific rule will be for a non-SSL website, we select to use nonsecured connections. Click Next to continue.

7. Under Computer Name or IP Address, enter the Fully Qualified Domain Name (FQDN) and the IP address of the server, as shown in Figure 14.2, using an IP address or name that ISA can use to contact it. For SSL websites, only the FQDN should be entered. The ISA server has to subsequently resolve the FQDN to an internal IP address with a host file or split-brain DNS. In this example, because it is an HTTP rule, the IP address is directly entered. Click Next to continue.

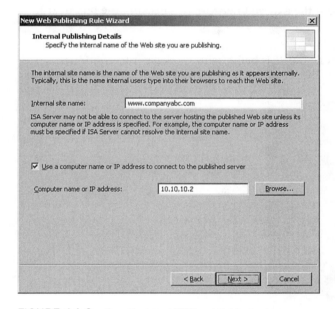

FIGURE 14.2   *Creating an HTTP publishing rule.*

NOTE

It is important to note that the ISA server must be able to address the web server directly via the name or IP address entered, which almost always resolves to a separate IP address than the one that is publicly addressable. In certain cases, it may be necessary to "fool" ISA into resolving a Fully Qualified Domain Name into an internal IP address with a hosts file, so as to preserve the host header information for the connection from end to end. This is particularly the case with SSL-encrypted websites, which fail if the host header is not exactly the same.

---

8. Under Path, enter /* so that the entire site will be published, and click Next to continue.

9. Under Public Name Details, choose to accept requests for This Domain Name, and type it into the Public Name field (for example, www.companyabc.com). Leave the Path as /* and click Next to continue.

10. Under Select Web Listener, click the New button to create a listener for the website traffic.

11. Enter a name for the listener, such as HTTP-WWW-Listener, and click Next

12. At the Client Connection Security dialog box, select to not require SSL connections with clients (an SSL rule would have the opposite setting here) and click Next to continue.

13. Select to listen for requests from the external network by checking the box next to it and clicking Next.

14. Under the Authentication Settings dialog box, shown in Figure 14.3, select No Authentication, since basic HTTP traffic is being sent. Click Next to continue.

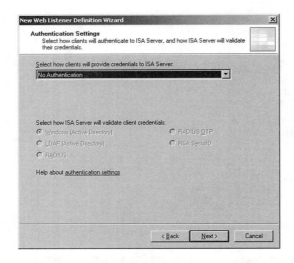

FIGURE 14.3   *Creating an HTTP listener.*

15. At the SSO dialog box, click Next to continue (make no changes, as SSO only applies to forms-based authentication sites).

16. Click Finish to finish creating the web listener.

17. From the next dialog box, review the listener properties, and click Next to continue.

18. From the Authentication Delegation dialog box, select "No delegation, and client cannot authentication directly" from the drop-down box. For this scenario, we are enabling access to an anonymous site, so no authentication is required.

19. Under User Sets, accept the default of All Users and click Next to continue.

20. Click Finish to create the rule.

> **NOTE**
>
> It is important to note that after the server publishing rule is in place, all HTTP requests sent to the website should point to the IP address of the HTTP listener on the ISA server itself. This includes publicly accessible websites, which must register the DNS namespace with an IP address on the external interface of the ISA server.

After it is created, the rule itself should be viewed and the administrator should become aware of the different settings and options available for HTTP filtering, as described in the following sections.

General Tab Options

Double-clicking on the web publishing rule that was created brings up the Properties dialog box, which allows for the configuration of the HTTP filtering settings. The first tab displayed is the General tab, as shown in Figure 14.4.

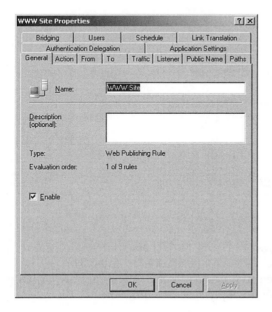

FIGURE 14.4   *Examining the General tab on an ISA web publishing rule.*

The General tab enables the rule to be enabled or disabled with the check box, as well as for the name to be changed and a description added, if necessary.

Action Tab Options

Under the Action tab of the web publishing rule, shown in Figure 14.5, the rule can be set up to either allow or deny traffic. For web publishing rules, this is typically set to Allow. In some circumstances, specific paths of a website, such as the root, or a specific subpath, could be denied and replaced with a custom web page. For example, the root of an Outlook Web Access site could be denied access, and users could be redirected to a custom HTTP error page that automatically redirects the user to the /owa (for Exchange 2007) or /exchange (for Exchange 2000/2003) subdirectories.

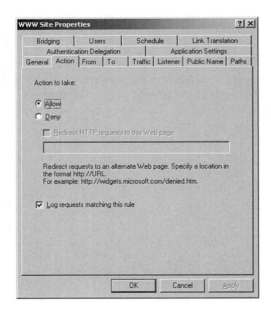

FIGURE 14.5   *Examining the Action tab on an ISA web publishing rule.*

From Tab Options

The From tab of a web publishing rule, as shown in Figure 14.6, enables an administrator to limit the scope of locations from which the traffic will be allowed to come. For example, a rule could be limited to only those users on a particular subnet, or only a specified list of servers. The Add button can be used to apply specific limitations for the rule.

In addition to specifying where the traffic can originate, this tab also enables specific exceptions to be made. For example, if an entire subnet is restricted, specific IP exceptions can be made.

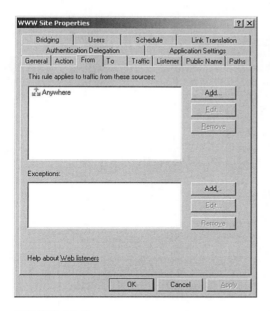

FIGURE 14.6 *Examining the From tab on an ISA web publishing rule.*

To Tab Options

The To tab of a web publishing rule, as shown in Figure 14.7, enables input of information about the particular server that is being published. This includes the FQDN of the server itself, an optional internal IP address, as well as the option to forward the original host header, if necessary.

It may be advantageous to forward the original host header (which takes the form of the FQDN) in cases where specific websites are being restricted by host headers or when a web-based application is expecting host header traffic, such as in SSL scenarios. For HTTP publishing rules, an internal IP address can be entered here; this is a new feature in ISA Server 2006. Although this will work for HTTP rules, it is not recommended for HTTPS rules, as the server will require the full FQDN as part of the traffic.

Another very important option is displayed on this tab: the option determining whether the web traffic sees the traffic as originating on the original client or on the ISA server computer itself. The option to make the traffic appear to come from the original client can help with auditing the traffic and making sure that user access is properly documented. Changing to make all requests come from ISA makes the web server think that the traffic originates from ISA instead. This option is typically more inclusive, and works in multiple scenarios.

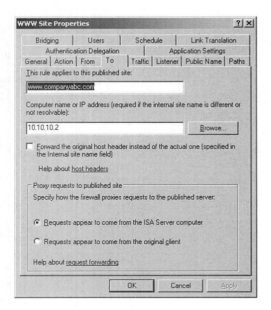

FIGURE 14.7   *Examining the To tab options on an ISA web publishing rule.*

> **CAUTION**
>
> If the ISA server is deployed in unihomed NIC mode in a firewall's DMZ, the only option that will work properly is to have the requests appear to come from the ISA Server Console. Most firewalls do not allow the ISA server to mimic the packets from an untrusted network, and block the traffic itself.

Exploring the Traffic Tab and Filtering HTTP Packets

The Traffic tab, shown in Figure 14.8, looks relatively innocuous, but is actually a launching point to the advanced HTTP filtering options. The basic tab itself shows to what type of traffic the rule applies (HTTP or HTTPS) and provides for the option to inform users to use HTTPS if it is enforced. When using SSL, it also gives the option to require the stronger 128-bit encryption to the traffic, a recommended move in most cases. On some rules, such as HTTP-only publishing rules or FBA rules, these options will be grayed out, as the default values will be used instead.

Filtering HTTP Traffic   To filter the HTTP traffic, click on the Filtering tab and choose Configure HTTP, which allows for the following HTTP filtering options:

- ▶ Maximum Header Length
- ▶ Request Payload Length

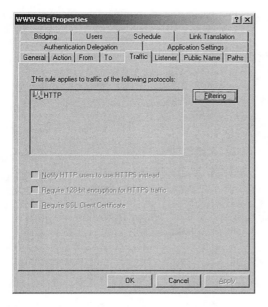

FIGURE 14.8 *Examining the Traffic tab on an ISA web publishing rule.*

► Maximum ULR Length

► Maximum Query Length

► Verify Normalization

► Block High Bit Characters

► Block Responses Containing Windows Executable Content

Customizing Allowed Methods   In addition to these options, the filter definitions also enable specific HTTP methods (such as GET and POST) to be allowed in the particular rule. If specific HTTP methods are restricted, a web server can be made even more secure because many of the exploits take advantage of little-used HTTP methods to gain control of a system. To restrict by a specific HTTP method, perform the following steps while in the Methods tab:

1. Under Specify the Action Taken for HTTP Methods, use the drop-down box to specify to Allow Only Specific Methods.

2. Click the Add button.

3. Enter a name for the HTTP method that will be allowed. For example, enter **GET** (the method is case-sensitive) and click OK.

4. From the dialog box shown in Figure 14.9, click OK to save the changes.

FIGURE 14.9   *Customizing HTTP methods.*

Customizing Extensions   The Extensions tab of the Filtering Rules setting allows only specific types of message attachments to be displayed, such as .mpg files, .exe files, or any other ones defined in this rule. It also allows for the reverse, where all attachments except for specific defined ones are. To accomplish this, choose the option Block Specified Extensions (Allow All Others).

For additional security, the box on this page can be checked to block ambiguous or ill-defined extensions, which can pose a security risk to an ISA server.

Blocking Headers   Specific HTTP headers can be blocked on the Headers tab of the filtering options. This allows for HTTP Request headers or Response headers to be blocked, which can be useful in denying certain types of HTTP headers, such as User-Agent or Server, which define what type of HTTP traffic is being used.

Restricting Signatures   The Signature Restriction tab is one of the most important. It is "ground zero" for filtering of HTTP traffic to scan for specific exploits and viruses, such as the signature that is defined to block the Kazaa file-sharing application, shown in Figure 14.10.

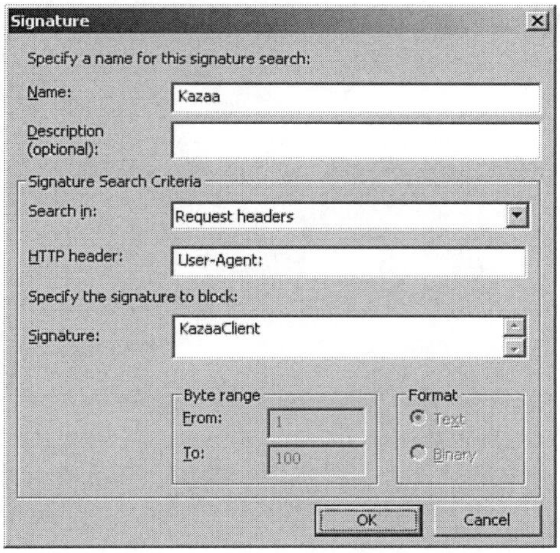

FIGURE 14.10   *Blocking Kazaa HTTP traffic by signature.*

This dialog box is where the majority of the custom filters can be created and applied. Because so many applications and exploits use the HTTP port to tunnel their traffic, it is extremely useful to configure these settings to block malware, scumware, and any other applications that are not approved by the organization. This allows for blocking of signatures from such applications as Instant Messaging, Gnutella, Kazaa, Morpheus, and many more. For a list of signatures that can be blocked, see the following Microsoft URL:

http://www.microsoft.com/technet/isa/2004/plan/commonapplicationsignatures.mspx

NOTE

Although this link applies to ISA Server 2004, the content still applies to ISA Server 2006 as well.

Understanding Listener Tab Configuration Options

The Listener tab of the web publishing tool, shown in Figure 14.11, allows for the customization and creation of various web listeners. A listener is an ISA construct that "listens" for requests made to a specific IP port combination. As soon as the listener receives the traffic, it then processes that traffic back into ISA. Listeners are required for web server publishing rules, and are what enable the ISA server to act as a web server to the requesting client.

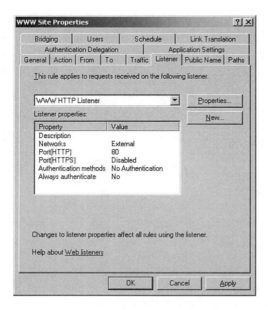

FIGURE 14.11   *Viewing the Listener tab settings.*

The existing listener that was created in the Publishing Rule Wizard can be directly modified if the rule is selected from the drop-down box and the Properties button is clicked. This allows for various settings to be applied, such as the following:

▶ Rule name and description

▶ Which IP address(es) the listener will listen to

▶ Whether SSL or HTTP or both are enabled and whether traffic is redirected from HTTP to HTTPS automatically

▶ What type(s) of authentication methods are available, such as basic, integrated, and forms-based authentication

▶ Whether RADIUS servers are needed

▶ Number of connections allowed and connection timeout

▶ RSA SecureID settings as necessary

Viewing Public Name Options

The Public Name tab on the web server publishing rule, shown in Figure 14.12, enables an administrator to dictate that the traffic to the ISA server travels with a specific public name. For example, it could be stipulated that access to a website such as www.companyabc.com is granted only to requests made to that website, rather than requests to an internal server such as \\server20. If a user tries to access that site from an IP address, that request fails because the web publishing rule is allowing only traffic sent to the www.companyabc.com website in this case.

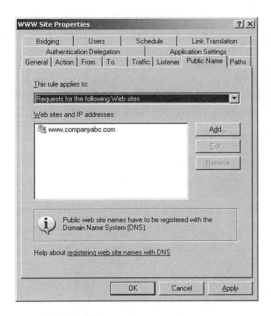

FIGURE 14.12   *Viewing Public Name options.*

When testing a rule, administrators often test via the external IP address, and are frustrated in their efforts as ISA will block that traffic. To enable this type of scenario, the IP address must be added to the Public Name options.

Paths Tab Options

In the Paths tab, shown in Figure 14.13, specific external paths can be mapped to different locations on a web server. For example, it may be helpful to send requests to http://www.companyabc.com to http://www.companyabc.com/public automatically. The Paths tab offers this type of functionality. To add a path to accomplish what this model illustrates, for example, do the following:

1. On the Paths tab of the web publishing rule, click the Add button.
2. Under Path Mapping, enter /**public**/*.
3. Under External Path, select The Following Folder and enter /*.
4. Click OK, Apply, and OK to save the changes.

Exploring Authentication Delegation Options

The Authentication Delegations tab of an ISA web publishing rule, shown in Figure 14.14, displays options for how the ISA server will authenticate to the web server. For anonymous HTTP rules, it can be turned off, as shown in the diagram. For rules that require authentication, authentication can be enabled.

Exploring the Application Settings Tab

The Applications Settings tab, shown in Figure 14.15, allows for a custom forms-based authentication page to be enabled for the published site. The default FBA page may not be desired for the specific rule, and organizations may want their own logo displayed or additional information to be gathered in the form. This tab allows for a connection to that custom page to be made.

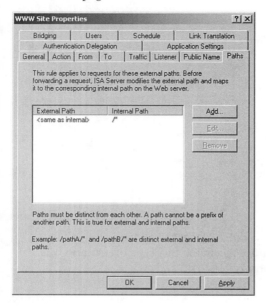

FIGURE 14.13   *Viewing the Paths tab.*

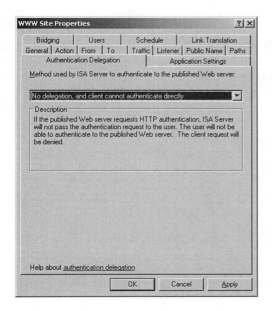

FIGURE 14.14   *Exploring authentication delegation options.*

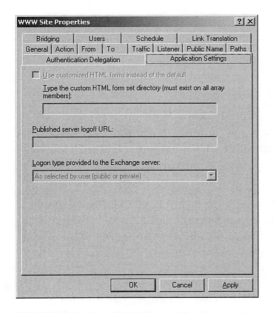

FIGURE 14.15   *Exploring application settings options.*

Exploring the Bridging Tab

The Bridging tab of an ISA web publishing rule, shown in Figure 14.16, gives an administrator the flexibility to send HTTP and/or SSL traffic to different ports on a web server. This concept can help to support those environments that have nonstandard ports set up for their web environments.

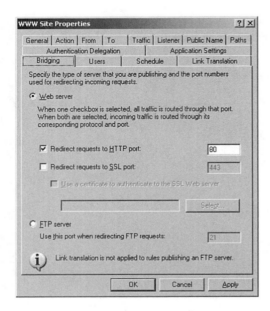

FIGURE 14.16   *Exploring bridging concepts.*

For example, an organization may have set up multiple web servers on an internal web server that has a single IP address. Rather than assign multiple IP addresses to that server, the administrators chose to set up different ports for each virtual server and each website. So, internally, users would have to point to http://site1.companyabc.com:8020 and http://site2.companyabc.com:8030, and so on.

The Bridging option in ISA Server 2006 enables end users to not have to enter in strange port combinations to access websites, and instead relies on the Bridging tab of the rule to direct port 80 traffic to the appropriate ports, such as port 8020 or any other defined port.

Understanding the Users Tab

The Users tab, shown in Figure 14.17, is typically set to All Authenticated Users for a default rule. For most inbound web publishing rules, this is the option that must be chosen for it to work properly. If using pre-authenticated VPN users or Firewall client users, however, distinctions can be made between users by groups.

Outlining Schedule Tab Options

The Schedule tab of a web publishing rule, shown in Figure 14.18, does not require much explanation. Using this tab, an organization can decide at exactly what times the rule will be in effect.

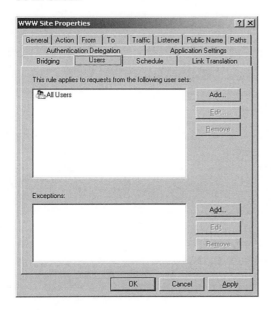

FIGURE 14.17   *Exploring Users tab options.*

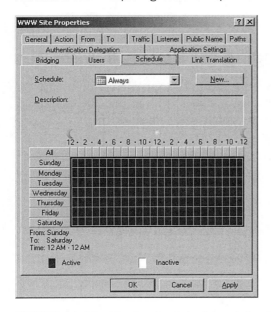

FIGURE 14.18   *Viewing the Schedule tab for the web publishing rule.*

Exploring the Link Translation Tab

The Link Translation tab, shown in Figure 14.19, allows for a great deal of flexibility in searching for unique bits of contents and replacing those bits of content with something else. More information on this is included in the section of this chapter titled "Securing Access to SharePoint Sites with ISA 2006."

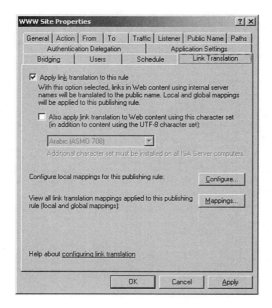

FIGURE 14.19   *Viewing the Link Translation tab for the web publishing rule.*

Configuring SSL-to-SSL Bridging for Secured Websites

As previously mentioned, ISA Server 2006 allows for end-to-end SSL encryption to take place between client and ISA and ISA and Exchange and back. This ensures the integrity of the transaction, and keeps the data secure and encrypted across the entire path.

To set up a scenario like this, however, a Public Key Infrastructure (PKI) must either be in place locally, or a third-party company such as Verisign or Thawte can be used to create the certificate's infrastructure.

Working with Third-Party Certificate Authorities

A good number of organizations rely on third-party certificate authorities (CAs) to issue their certificates. A large advantage to this is that these third-party CAs are generally trusted on the vast majority of client machines on the Internet. This means that the connection to a web server is automatically switched to HTTPS, without any error messages popping up on the client workstation.

Installing a Local Certificate Authority and Using Certificates

For those organizations that choose to manage and handle their own certificate structure, Windows includes a Certificate Server component that can be installed directly on a domain controller. If a private CA is created, issuing certificates is a breeze and costs much less.

On the flip side, client workstations do not, by default, trust an internal CA, so it must be added into their Trusted Sites list. If it is not added, an error message always appears for them when they try to connect to that website.

To install and configure a PKI environment in Windows, follow the procedure outlined in the section on securing SharePoint site access later in this chapter.

Modifying a Rule to Allow for End-to-End SSL Bridging

If SSL support is to be added to an existing web publishing rule, the listener must be modified and extended to include the information on the website's particular certificate. For example, if a web server on the internal network named www.companyabc.com is set up and a certificate is associated with that site, the certificate must be exported out to a PFX file, imported into the ISA server, and then used to modify the listener via the following procedure:

1. In the ISA Management Console, click on the Firewall Policy node.
2. In the Details pane, double-click on the web publishing rule that is to be modified.
3. Go to the Listener tab.
4. Under the listener for the website, click Properties.
5. Select the Connections tab, shown in Figure 14.20, and check the box to enable SSL. You can specify whether to automatically redirect from HTTP to HTTPS as well.
6. Click on the Certificates tab. Select the Select Certificate button, select the certificate that matches the rule, then click Select to select a certificate to apply (a certificate must be installed on ISA for this to work).
7. Click on the certificate that was exported and click OK.
8. Click OK, OK, Apply, and OK to save the changes.

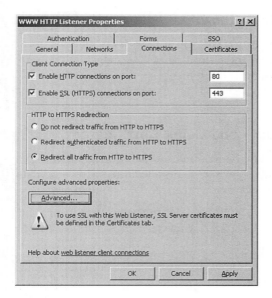

FIGURE 14.20   *Enabling SSL on an ISA listener.*

Securing Access to SharePoint Sites with ISA 2006

Microsoft SharePoint Products and Technologies 2007, including Windows SharePoint Services (WSS) 3.0 and Office SharePoint Server 2007, are fast becoming a preferred choice for collaboration and document management. SharePoint sites themselves compromise one of the more common types of content that are secured by ISA servers. This stems from the critical need to provide remote document management while at the same time securing that access. The success of ISA deployments in this fashion give tribute to the tight integration Microsoft built between its ISA product and the SharePoint 2007 product.

An ISA server used to secure a SharePoint implementation can be deployed in multiple scenarios, such as an edge firewall, an inline firewall, or a dedicated reverse-proxy server. In all these scenarios, ISA secures SharePoint traffic by "pretending" to be the SharePoint server itself, scanning the traffic that is destined for the SharePoint server for exploits, and then repackaging that traffic and sending it on, such as what is illustrated in Figure 14.21.

ISA performs this type of securing through a SharePoint site publishing rule, which automatically sets up and configures a listener on the ISA server. A listener is an ISA component that listens to specifically defined IP traffic, and processes that traffic for the requesting client as if it were the actual server itself. For example, a SharePoint listener on an ISA server would respond to SharePoint HTTP requests made to it by scanning them for exploits and then repackaging them and forwarding them on to the SharePoint server itself. Using listeners, the client cannot tell the difference between the ISA server and the SharePoint server itself.

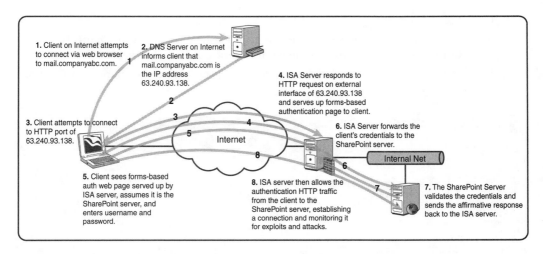

FIGURE 14.21   *Explaining SharePoint site publishing with ISA Server 2006.*

ISA Server is also one of the few products that has the capability to secure web traffic with SSL encryption from end to end. It does this by using the SharePoint server's own certificate to re-encrypt the traffic before sending it on its way. This also allows for the "black box" of SSL traffic to be examined for exploits and viruses at the Application layer, and then re-encepted to reduce the chance of unauthorized viewing of the traffic. Without the capability to scan this SSL traffic, exploits bound for a SharePoint server could simply hide themselves in the encrypted traffic and pass right through traditional firewalls.

This chapter covers one common scenario that ISA server is used for: securing a SharePoint site collection; in this example, "home.companyabc.com" using ISA. The steps outlined here describe this particular scenario, though ISA can also be used for multiple other securing scenarios as necessary.

Configuring the Alternate Access Mapping Setting for the External URL

Before external access can be granted to a site, an Alternate Access Mapping (AAM) must be established for the particular web application. An AAM is a host header value (such as https://portal.companyabc.com, http://server4, https://home.companyabc.com, and so on) that must be consistently applied to the site across all links. If it is not put into place, external clients will not be able to access internal links.

To configure the AAM in this scenario, home.companyabc.com, on a web application, perform the following tasks:

1. Open the SharePoint Central Admin Tool from the SharePoint Server (Start, All Programs, Microsoft Office Server, SharePoint 3.0 Central Administration).

2. Click on the Operations tab.

3. Under the Global configuration options, click the link for Alternate access mappings.

4. Click Edit Public URLs.

5. Enter the https:// AAM needed under the Internet box, as shown in Figure 14.22. In this example, we enter https://home.companyabc.com. Click Save.

6. Review the AAMs listed on the page for accuracy, then close the SharePoint Central Admin tool.

FIGURE 14.22   *Configuring Alternate Access Mappings.*

Installing an SSL Certificate on a SharePoint Server

It is generally well accepted that SharePoint content that travels across an insecure network such as the Internet should be encrypted to avoid it being examined by prying eyes. The most common form of encryption for web traffic is by using Secure Sockets Layer (SSL) encryption using Public Key Infrastructure (PKI) X.509 certificates. The certificates themselves reside on the IIS Virtual Servers that have been extended as SharePoint web applications.

If SSL is not already enabled on a SharePoint web application, it must be set up and configured in advance of the procedures outlined later, which describe how to use ISA to filter the SSL traffic destined for the SharePoint server. Use the procedures outlined earlier in this chapter to install and configure an SSL certificate on the SharePoint server.

NOTE

ISA Server 2006 also supports SSL encryption that is not end to end, but rather terminates on the ISA server. ISA can then make a connection to a web application secured with Integrated Windows Authentication. This can be convenient for those organizations that desire to offload SSL from the SharePoint environment.

Exporting and Importing the SharePoint SSL Certificate to the ISA Server

For ISA to be able to decrypt the SSL traffic bound for the SharePoint server, ISA needs to have a copy of this SSL certificate. The certificate is used by ISA to decode the SSL packets, inspect them, and then re-encrypt them and send them on to the SharePoint server itself. For this certificate to be installed on the ISA server, it must first be exported from the SharePoint server, as follows:

NOTE

This procedure assumes that an SSL certificate has already been installed and added to the ISA server, per the process outlined in Chapter 10.

1. From the SharePoint server (not the ISA server), open IIS Manager (Start, All Programs, Administrative Tools, Internet Information Services (IIS) Manager).
2. Navigate to Internet Information Services, SERVERNAME (local computer), Web Sites.
3. Right-click on the virtual server housing the SharePoint web application and choose Properties.
4. Choose the Directory Security tab.
5. Click View Certificate.
6. Click the Details tab.
7. Click Copy to File.
8. At the wizard, click Next to begin the export process.
9. Select Yes, Export the Private Key and click Next to continue.
10. Select to include all certificates in the certification path and also select to enable strong protection and click Next to continue.
11. Type and confirm a password and click Next to continue.
12. Enter a file location and name for the file and click Next.
13. Click Finish.

After the .pfx file has been exported from the SharePoint server, it can then be imported to the ISA server via the following procedure:

> **CAUTION**
>
> It is important to securely transmit this .pfx file to the ISA server and to maintain high
> security over its location. The certificate's security could be compromised if it were to
> fall into the wrong hands.

1. From the ISA server, open the MMC console (Start, Run, mmc.exe, OK).
2. Click File, Add/Remove Snap-in.
3. Click the Add button.
4. From the list shown in Figure 14.23, choose the Certificates snap-in and click Add.

FIGURE 14.23   *Customizing an MMC certificates snap-in console for import of the SharePoint
certificate.*

5. Choose Computer Account from the list when asked what certificates the snap-in
   will manage and click Next to continue.
6. From the subsequent list in the Select Computer dialog box, choose Local Computer:
   (the computer this console is running on) and click Finish.
7. Click Close and OK.

After the custom MMC console has been created, the certificate that was exported from the
SharePoint server can be imported directly from the console via the following procedure:

1. From the MMC Console root, navigate to Certificates (Local Computer), Personal.
2. Right-click the Personal folder and choose All Tasks, Import.
3. At the wizard welcome screen, click Next to continue.
4. Browse for and locate the .pfx file that was exported from the SharePoint server. The
   location can also be typed into the file name field. Click Next when located.

5. Enter the password that was created when the certificate was exported, as illustrated in Figure 14.24. Do not check to mark the key as exportable. Click Next to continue.

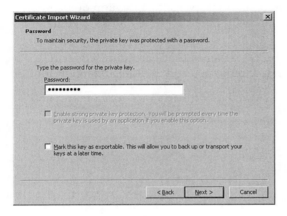

FIGURE 14.24   *Installing the SharePoint certificate on the ISA server.*

6. Choose Automatically Select the Certificate Store Based on the Type of Certificate, and click Next to continue.

7. Click Finish to complete the import.

After it is in the certificates store of the SharePoint server, the SharePoint SSL certificate can be used as part of publishing rules.

> **NOTE**
>
> If a rule that makes use of a specific SSL certificate is exported from an ISA server, either for backup purposes or to transfer it to another ISA server, than the certificate must also be saved and imported to the destination server, or that particular rule will be broken.

Creating a SharePoint Publishing Rule

After the SharePoint SSL has been installed onto the ISA server, the actual ISA SharePoint publishing rule can be generated to secure SharePoint via the following procedure:

> **NOTE**
>
> The procedure outlined here illustrates an ISA SharePoint publishing rule that uses forms-based authentication (FBA) for the site, which allows for a landing page to be generated on the ISA server to pre-authenticate user connections to SharePoint.

1. From the ISA Management Console, click once on the Firewall Policy node from the console tree.

2. Click on the link in the Tasks tab of the Tasks pane labeled Publish SharePoint Sites.

3. Enter a descriptive name for the publishing rule, such as SharePoint publishing rule.

4. Select whether to publish a single website, multiple websites, or a farm of load-balanced servers. In this example, we choose to publish a simple single website. Click Next to continue.

5. Choose whether to require SSL from the ISA server to the SharePoint server, as shown in Figure 14.25. It is recommended to provide end-to-end SSL support for ISA. Click Next to continue.

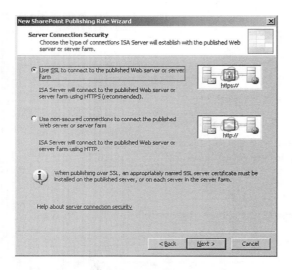

FIGURE 14.25   *Choosing SSL Publishing options.*

6. On the Internal Publishing Details dialog box, enter the site name that internal users use to access the SharePoint server. Examine the options to connect to an IP address or computer name; this gives additional flexibility to the rule. Click Next to continue.

7. Under the subsequent dialog box, enter to accept requests for "This domain name (type below):" and enter the FQDN of the server, such as home.companyabc.com. This will restrict the rule to requests that are destined for the proper FQDN. Click Next to continue.

8. Under Web Listener, click New.

9. At the start of the Web Listener Wizard, enter a descriptive name for the listener, such as SharePoint HTTP/HTTPS Listener, and click Next to continue.

10. Again a prompt is given to choose between SSL and non-SSL. This prompt refers to the traffic between client and SharePoint, which should always be SSL whenever possible. Click Next to continue.

11. Under Web Listener IP addresses, select the external network and leave it at All IP addresses. Click Next to continue.

12. Under Listener SSL Certificates, click on Select Certificate.

13. Select the previously installed certificate, as shown in Figure 14.26, and click the Select button.

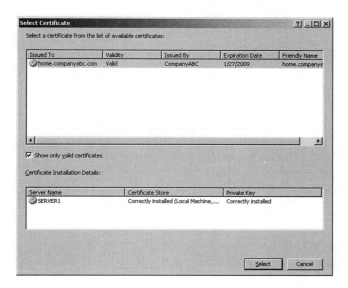

FIGURE 14.26   *Choosing a certificate for the listener.*

14. Click Next to continue.

15. For the type of authentication, choose HTML Form Authentication, as shown in Figure 14.27. Leave Windows (Active Directory) selected and click Next.

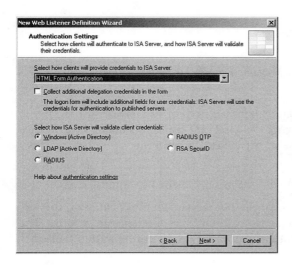

FIGURE 14.27   *Choosing an authentication type for the listener.*

16. The Single Sign On Settings dialog box is powerful—it allows all authentication traffic through a single listener to be processed only once. After the user has authenticated, he or she can access any other service, be it an Exchange OWA server, web server, or other web-based service that uses the same domain name for credentials. In this example, we enter .companyabc.com into the SSO domain name. Click Next to continue.

17. Click Finish to end the Listener Wizard.

18. Click Next after the new listener is displayed in the Web Listener dialog box.

19. Under Authentication Delegation, choose Basic from the drop-down box. Basic is used as SSL is the transport mechanism chosen. Click Next to continue.

20. At the Alternate Access Mapping Configuration Dialog box, shown in Figure 14.28, select that SharePoint AAM is already configured, as we configured the Alternate Access Mapping on the SharePoint server in previous steps.

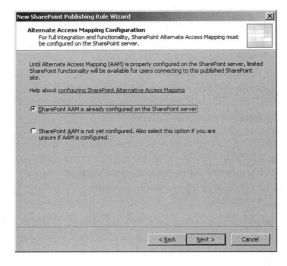

FIGURE 14.28   *Configuring Alternate Access Mapping settings for the SharePoint rule.*

21. Under User Sets, leave All Authenticated Users selected. In stricter scenarios, only specific AD groups can be granted rights to SharePoint using this dialog box. In this example, the default setting is sufficient. Click Next to continue.

22. Click Finish to end the wizard.

23. Click Apply in the Details pane, then click OK when finished to commit the changes.

The rule will now appear in the Details pane of the ISA server. Double-clicking on the rule brings up the settings. Tabs can be used to navigate around the different rule settings. The rule itself can be configured with additional settings based on the configuration desired.

For example, the following rule information is used to configure our basic forms-based authentication web publishing rule for SharePoint:

- ▶ **General tab**—Name: SharePoint; Enabled=checked.

- ▶ **Action tab**—Action to take=Allow; Log requests matching this rule=checked.

- ▶ **From tab**—This rule applies to traffic from these sources=Anywhere.

- ▶ **To tab**—This rule applies to this published site=home.companyabc.com; Forward the original host header instead of the actual one (specified in the Internal site name field)=checked; Specify how the firewall proxies requests to the published server=Requests appear to come from the ISA server.

- ▶ **Traffic tab**—This rule applies to traffic of the following protocols=HTTP,HTTPS; Require 128-bit encryption for HTTPS traffic=checked.

- ▶ **Listener tab**—Listener properties-Networks=External,Port(HTTP)=80,Port(HTTPS)=443,Certificate=home.companyabc.com,Authentication methods=FBA with AD,Always authenticate-No,Domain for authentication=COMPANYABC.

- ▶ **Listener tab, Properties button**—Networks tab=External, All IP addresses; Connections tab—Enabled HTTP connections on port 80, Enable SSL connections on port 443; HTTP to HTTPS Redirection=Redirect authenticated traffic from HTTP to HTTPS; Forms tab=Allow users to change their passwords, Remind users that their password will expire in this number of days=15; SSO tab=Enable Single Sign On, SSO Domains=.companyabc.com.

- ▶ **Public Name tab**—This rule applies to:Requests for the following Web sites=home.companyabc.com.

- ▶ **Paths tab**—External paths=All are set to <same as internal.; Internal paths= /*, /_vti_inf.html*, /_vti_bin/*, /_upresources/*, /_layouts/*.

- ▶ **Authentication Delegation tab**—Method used by ISA Server to authenticate to the published web server=Basic authentication.

- ▶ **Application Settings tab**—Use customized HTML forms instead of the default=unchecked.

- ▶ **Bridging tab**—Redirect requests to SSL port=443.

- ▶ **Users tab**—This rule applies to requests from the following user sets=All Authenticated Users.

- ▶ **Schedule tab**—Schedule=Always.

- ▶ **Link Translation tab**—Apply link translation to this rule=checked.

Different rules require different settings, but the settings outlined in this example are some of the more common and secure ones used to set up this scenario.

Summary

ISA Server 2006 is, without doubt, one of the better web proxy and filtering solutions available today. In addition to providing for edge firewall capabilities, ISA also allows for complete reverse-proxy scenarios with HTTP, allowing for secure publishing of web services. In addition, the Application-layer filtering capabilities of ISA give excellent HTTP filtering capabilities, including locking down specific applications based not on their port numbers but on the actual content of the HTTP packet itself.

Best Practices

▶ Use ISA Server 2006 to secure websites with end-to-end SSL encryption.

▶ Generate custom HTTP filters to handle exploits and viruses as they arise.

▶ Stay on top of new HTTP filter definitions and download and install them as necessary.

▶ Use link translation with SharePoint sites along with Alternate Access Mappings in SharePoint 2007.

CHAPTER 15

Securing RPC Traffic

This chapter covers the specifics of how ISA Server 2006 can be deployed to filter and secure RPC traffic. It focuses on scenarios where ISA Server monitors and secures RPC traffic between various networks segments and WAN links, and includes step-by-step securing techniques for securing RPC traffic and creating custom RPC protocol definitions.

In addition to covering RPC filtering, this chapter also touches on the other types of server publishing rules that are available in ISA and how they can be used to further secure an environment.

Understanding the Dangers of Remote Procedure Call (RPC) Traffic

Of all the protocols on the Internet today, none has gotten more of a bad rap than the Remote Procedure Call (RPC) protocol. RPC is a favorite protocol for programmers because it allows for a high degree of functionality and ease of use. Along with these powerful capabilities, however, come powerful risks. RPC was directly responsible for many of the more common and destructive exploits to traverse the Internet, including the notorious Blaster virus.

RPC exploits and security issues have caused many organizations to severely restrict RPC communications, which has had the unintended effect of diminishing end user productivity. A better, more intelligent method of allowing secured RPC access was necessary.

Fortunately, ISA Server 2006's advanced application-layer filtering abilities enable organizations to take back control over their RPC communications, restricting RPC traffic to conform to only specific types of requests and reducing the overall threat inherent in the services. These types of capabilities position ISA as an excellent gateway product to protect networks not only from external traffic but from internal RPC exploits and viruses as well.

Examining How Remote Procedure Call (RPC) Traffic Works

To understand the basics of the problem, it's important to first understand, at least in outline, the specifics of how the RPC protocol works. RPC is very powerful, and provides programmers with efficiency and enhanced functionality. It is therefore commonly used for many applications and services.

> **NOTE**
>
> The scope of this chapter is not on the intricate programming specifics of RPC, but more information can be found at the following URL:
>
> http://msdn.microsoft.com/library/default.asp?url=/library/en-us/dnanchor/html/rpcank.asp

In short, RPC works by publishing an endpoint mapping port (Port 135) on a server running RPC services. This port is responsible for directing clients to dynamically assigned high-range ports for the services. These ports may be any of the TCP/IP ports in the range of 1024 through 65,536, depending on a random assignment by the RPC endpoint mapping service. The fact that so many ports must be opened to allow RPC is one of the reasons why it has gotten a bad rap in security circles.

Another problem with the way that RPC operates is that it is very chatty, and by default exposes much information about the services that run on the particular server. It doesn't take too much probing of the default RPC endpoint mapping port to retrieve sensitive information about which RPC interfaces are available.

The fact that RPC was so powerful, yet so insecure, brought many organizations face to face with a dilemma: They could allow the RPC access and expose themselves to threats and exploits, or they could block access to it, and limit the productivity advances that IT technologies could provide them. A solution that provided for secure RPC access became necessary, which gave rise to the RPC filtering capabilities of ISA Server.

Outlining RPC Exploits

The world became uniquely acquainted with the power and destructive capabilities of RPC with the release of the Blaster worm a few years back. Blaster took advantage of a Microsoft security hole in the Windows Distributed Component Object Model (DCOM) Remote Procedure Call (RPC) interface, which effectively allowed a remote hacker to use an exposed RPC port to take over a server remotely. These types of exploits take advantage of the fact that a "bare" RPC interface that is opened on a server effectively has all ports from 1024 to 65536 open, leaving a much larger surface area exposed.

Although most RPC traffic is blocked on the Internet today, the real arising problem is that RPC exploits are becoming increasingly common on "trusted" networks, such as internal corporate LANs. Simply clicking on the wrong website and downloading scumware, malware, and viruses from the Internet can turn a client on the network into an attacking host, exposing critical server components to exploit and damage.

Understanding the Need for RPC Filtering Versus RPC Blocking

The reaction to RPC issues in the past has been to block the RPC traffic by disallowing Port 135 between network segments on routers and/or firewalls. This can cause severe problems with internal network traffic because a large quantity of critical network services rely on RPC calls and protocol access. For example, shortly after the Slammer virus was released and wrecked havoc on IT infrastructure, it took months to sort out what routers were blocking necessary functionality such as Active Directory domain controller replication. The initial reaction was to drop all RPC traffic, regardless of whether it was needed or not.

What is needed is a way to secure the RPC protocol itself, by delving further into its functionality than simple Layer 3 packet analysis can. Intelligent Application-layer filtering of the traffic using ISA Server 2006 is one excellent approach to solving this problem.

Securing RPC Traffic Between Network Segments

As outlined, the problem of RPC traffic is most evident between internal network segments. An infected or compromised client in an environment can destroy critical infrastructure through the use of RPC exploits. On the other hand, locking down all RPC port access between network segments severely cripples needed network functionality and makes troubleshooting extremely difficult. Scanning RPC traffic and allowing only acceptable RPC queries is therefore necessary.

Outlining How ISA RPC Filtering Works

ISA Server 2006 secures RPC access through the use of RPC server publishing rules, which scan the RPC traffic for specific universally unique identifiers (UUIDs) and allows only those UUIDs that are associated with that particular service. For example, Figure 15.1 shows some of the UUIDs (referred to as *interfaces*) that are utilized to allow Exchange MAPI traffic, which utilizes RPC.

When the client is restricted to requests made to particular services, it no longer becomes necessary to allow promiscuous queries to be made to the RPC endpoint mapper service on port 135. In fact, when secured through ISA, the endpoint mapper releases very little information about what available services are running, and instead relies on the client itself to issue requests to specific services. This has the effect of greatly reducing the risk that RPC services pose because ISA allows only specially formatted requests, often very benign in nature, as in the case of MAPI.

In addition, at the packet layer, ISA Server 2006's RPC filtering does not require the dynamic ports to remain open. Instead, ISA dynamically negotiates the port between the client and server and opens that port only after the negotiation. This eliminates the need to blindly open multiple ports to get RPC to work properly.

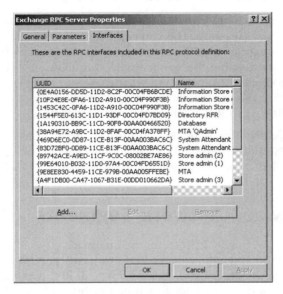

FIGURE 15.1   Examining MAPI UUIDs used in an RPC server publishing rule.

Deploying ISA for RPC Filtering

Of course, aside from reverse proxy of web-related (HTTP, HTTPS) traffic, ISA Server can use server publishing rules, including RPC rules, only if the traffic sent between client and server flows through ISA Server. This requires ISA Server to have multiple network interfaces, and for the client traffic to be routed through it, either because ISA is the default gateway or because the routing traffic is configured to flow through ISA. Through these types of deployment configurations, as shown in Figure 15.2, ISA Server RPC filtering can greatly limit the risk of RPC-based attacks.

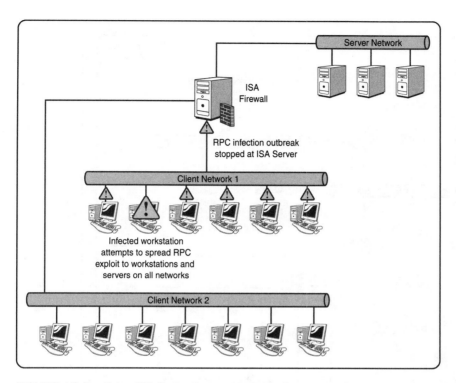

FIGURE 15.2   Using ISA Server to secure network segments.

If a client becomes infected with an RPC-based virus or worm, or if an internal employee uses an RPC exploit to attempt to "hack" a server, this type of deployment scenario effectively contains both.

It is important to note that ISA is very flexible about the method in which it is deployed, and certain other deployment scenarios can take advantage of ISA RPC filtering and other server publishing scenarios. For example, in the scenario illustrated in Figure 15.3, ISA servers are deployed to protect an Exchange server environment, allowing only MAPI and OWA traffic from anywhere else on the network.

Obviously, many other deployment options are available, but it is important to understand the limitations of RPC publishing, and when it is possible to use it or not.

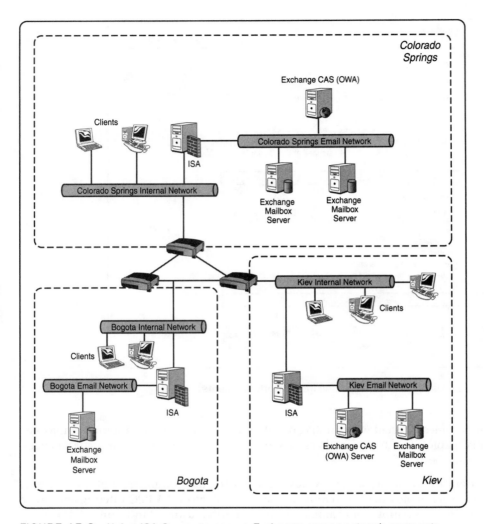

FIGURE 15.3   Using ISA Server to secure Exchange server network segments.

Publishing RPC Services with ISA Server 2006

ISA Server 2006 utilizes a concept of a server publishing rule to protect specific services such as RPC. A server publishing rule enables a specific service on a single server to be published to the clients on a separate network. For example, an Exchange server in a protected Exchange network can have the MAPI RPC service published to the clients in the separate Clients network, making only that service available to them. Or, a DNS server in a Perimeter (DMZ) network could have the DNS service published to clients in an internal network.

Server publishing rules are often confused with ISA Access rules, which enable specific protocols to traverse between networks. There are some fundamental differences between publishing rules and access rules, however, such as the following:

▶ Individual publishing rules can publish only a single server, whereas access rules can allow blanket access to an entire range of systems.

▶ Port translation can be accomplished through server publishing rules, but not access rules.

▶ Certain application filters in ISA Server were designed to work with server publishing rules only, such as the SMTP filter.

▶ Web publishing rules can be used in single-NIC (unihomed) scenarios because the web traffic terminates at the ISA server and is then retransmitted to the actual web server. This is not possible with access rules (or any other non–web-based publishing rules, for that matter).

▶ Access rules cannot be used to grant access to NAT clients; only server rules can be used for this.

Publishing an RPC Service

It is a relatively straightforward process to publish an RPC service in ISA Server 2006. The following step-by-step procedure illustrates how to publish general RPC traffic to a particular server. In this scenario, users on the Internal network need to have full RPC access to a server on the DMZ network, so an RPC server publishing rule is created.

> **CAUTION**
>
> For more secured RPC access, it is best to ascertain which UUIDs will be used and to restrict RPC access to only those interfaces. This process is illustrated in later sections of this chapter. Although less secure than UUID restrictions, using this process to publish RPC to a server is still much more secure than allowing "bare" RPC access to a server. ISA still hides much of the RPC service's promiscuity.

1. From the ISA Management Console, click on the Firewall Policy node in the console tree.

2. Under the Tasks tab in the Tasks pane, click on the link for Publish Non-Web Server Protocols.

3. Enter a descriptive name for the rule and click Next to continue.

4. Enter the IP address of the server that is to be published (remember that you can do only one server for each rule) and click Next to continue.

5. Under Select Protocol, use the drop-down list to select RPC Server (All Interfaces), as shown in Figure 15.4. Click Next to continue.

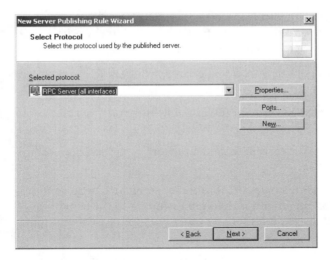

FIGURE 15.4   Creating an RPC server publishing rule.

6. Under which networks to listen to, check which ones are needed (for this example, the Internal network is checked). Click Next to continue.

7. Click Finish, Apply, and OK.

Creating Custom RPC Protocol Definitions

By default, only two types of RPC options are available for RPC-based server publishing rules. The first option is to open all RPC interfaces, which is what was used for the scenario in the previous section. The other defined RPC protocol definition is used for Exchange MAPI access to mailboxes that use RPC. This protocol definition includes all the custom UUIDs that Outlook and Exchange need to communicate over MAPI.

In addition to using the default RPC protocol definitions, custom RPC protocols can be created and used for server publishing rules. If custom definitions are created for RPC, the service can be secured even further to allow only RPC traffic to the UUID services that the rule absolutely needs, rather than open up blanket RPC access.

For example, an RPC protocol definition could be made for Active Directory domain controller replication that uses the UUIDs that are required for replication to take place. Or, a RPC protocol definition could be created to allow access to a system using the Microsoft Management Console (MMC), which uses a different unique ID.

> **NOTE**
>
> To determine which UUID is used by a particular service, the Network Monitor tool can be used to "sniff" the packets that hit a server and determine which UUIDs are necessary. This procedure is covered in later portions of this chapter.

To create a custom RPC protocol definition, do the following:

1. Open the ISA Management Console.
2. Click on the Firewall Policy node in the console tree.
3. Click on the Toolbox tab in the Tasks pane.
4. Click on Protocols to select it from the list of options in the Tasks pane.
5. Click on New, RPC Protocol, as shown in Figure 15.5.

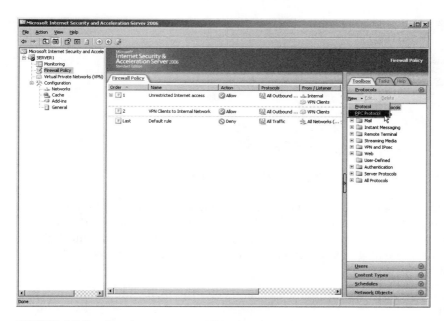

FIGURE 15.5   Creating a custom RPC protocol definition.

6. Enter a descriptive name for the protocol and click Next to continue.
7. In the Select Server dialog box, specific interfaces (UUIDs) from running servers can be viewed and used to create rules. Enter the name of a server to parse and click Next.
8. Under the Server Interfaces dialog box, shown in Figure 15.6, existing UUIDs from existing services running on the server being examined can be used to create the custom definition. Select any UUIDs that the particular service needs to use by checking them and click Next to continue.

NOTE

It is not obvious in many cases which UUIDs are necessary. In certain cases, it may be useful to consult the product documentation to find which interfaces to add.

9. Click Finish, Apply, and OK to save the changes.

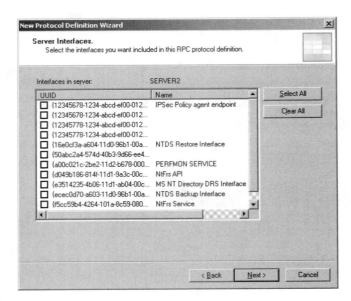

FIGURE 15.6   Adding server interfaces to a custom RPC protocol.

In addition to using existing defined service UUIDs, it is also possible to add them manually to the RPC protocol definition by clicking the Add Interfaces Manually radio button on the Select Server dialog box and clicking Next. This brings up the Adding Interfaces to the Protocol Definition dialog box, which enables custom UUIDs to be added to the RPC protocol definition.

To add the custom UUIDs, click the Add button and enter the UUID into the dialog box shown in Figure 15.7.

UUIDs should be entered enclosed in brackets, and the option for defining whether RPC will manually assign a specific port or dynamically assign one of the high ports is also provided. Click OK and continue with the wizard, adding as many custom UUIDs as necessary for the specific protocol definition.

After they are created, custom protocol definitions can be used specifically for server publishing rules, so that very secure RPC connections can be made to the servers.

Using Network Monitor for Custom RPC

In many cases, it may not be obvious what specific interfaces a particular application uses to connect to another server. This is particularly true with RPC UUIDs, which are not always published in documentation or on the Internet. In cases where custom protocol definitions need to be made for securing the service, but the UUIDs are unknown, using a network packet capture tool is a useful approach for identifying which types of interfaces to allow.

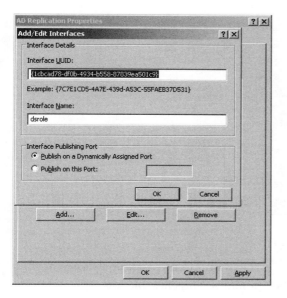

FIGURE 15.7   Manually adding UUIDs to an RPC protocol definition.

Windows Server 2003 includes a free Network Monitor tool that can be installed on any server to monitor the packets that are sent directly to that particular server. It can be installed on a destination server, for example, to identify which RPC interfaces a particular application is using, for example.

Installing Network Monitor

The first step to inspecting the RPC packets and creating a custom rule based on the UUIDs of a service is to install Network Monitor on the server. For the procedure to install Network Monitor on a Windows Server 2003 system, perform the following steps:

> **TIP**
>
> It might be useful to install Network Monitor on an ISA server to assist in troubleshooting problems and monitoring traffic sent to it. It can also be used to determine which types of RPC traffic are hitting ISA's network interfaces, which can be useful for the type of scenario being described as well.

1. Go to Start, Control Panel, Add or Remove Programs.
2. Click Add/Remove Windows Components.
3. Scroll down under Components and click on the text of Management and Monitoring Tools to select it (don't check the box; just click on the text).
4. Click the Details button.
5. Check the box next to Network Monitor Tools, as shown in Figure 15.8. Click OK.

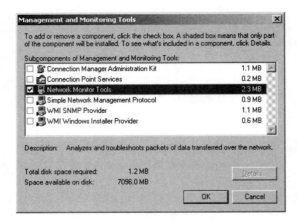

FIGURE 15.8   Installing Network Monitor.

6. Click Next to continue.

7. Enter the Windows Server 2003 media if prompted and click OK.

8. Click Finish.

Using Network Monitor to Scan Traffic for RPC UUIDs

After it has been installed, Network Monitor can be used to take snapshots of the packets that hit the network interfaces that are installed on the server. Looking through these packets can help to identify critical pieces of information, such as which UUIDs are being called for. To start the process, start Network Monitor and capture some data through the following process:

> **NOTE**
>
> During the data capture, the application that is to be tested for UUID transmittal must be run against the server in question. Also, systems with multiple network cards need to choose which network to scan.

1. Open Network Monitor (Start, Administrative Tools, Network Monitor).

2. Click on Capture, Start, as shown in Figure 15.9.

3. After the application has been run, and enough time has passed to capture all the packets that hit the server, click Capture, Stop and View.

After the capture is complete, look through the packet Description for ones that start with c/o RPC Bind: UUID, similar to what is shown in Figure 15.10. Look for each of the UUIDs that were requested by the server, and take note of them for use in the custom RPC protocol definition.

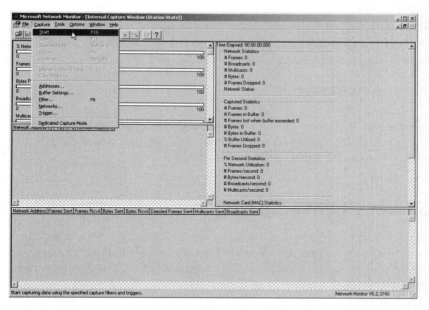

FIGURE 15.9   Capturing packets with Network Monitor.

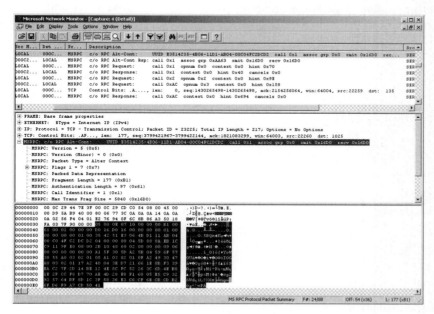

FIGURE 15.10   Looking for RPC UUIDs in Network Monitor traffic.

> **TIP**
>
> Because the UUID needs to be entered without typos, it may be wise to cut and paste the results of Network Monitor into Notepad, so that it can be used later in the creation of the RPC protocol definition.

Using Network Monitor is an excellent way to ascertain what type of traffic an application uses. This information can then be easily translated into a custom filter rule in ISA, further securing the traffic sent between networks protected by ISA servers.

Creating Server Publishing Rules

In addition to the capability to secure RPC traffic and custom-defined services traffic, ISA Server 2006 also contains several other default server publishing rules that can be used to secure commonly used services. It is important to understand what these services are and how they can be secured with ISA Server.

Outlining Default Server Publishing Rules in ISA Server

The list of protocols available by default with server publishing rules is extensive and includes the following:

- DNS Server
- Exchange RPC Server
- FTP Server
- HTTPS Server
- IKE Server
- IMAP4 Server
- IMAPS Server
- IPSec ESP Server
- IPSec NAT-T Server
- L2TP Server
- Microsoft SQL Server
- MMS Server
- NNTP Server
- NNTPS Server
- PNM Server
- POP3 Server
- POP3S Server

- ▶ PPTP Server
- ▶ RDP (Terminal Services) Server
- ▶ RTSP Server
- ▶ SMTP Server
- ▶ SMTPS Server
- ▶ Telnet Server

With the server publishing rule capabilities that ISA possesses, any one of these services can be secured easily behind an ISA server.

Creating a Server Publishing Rule

Just as with an RPC server publishing rule, an ISA server publishing rule is straightforward to set up and configure. The following procedure illustrates how to set up one of these rules. In this case, RDP (Terminal Services) is published from the External network to a server in the Perimeter network via the following steps:

1. Open ISA Server Management Console.
2. Click on the Firewall Policy node from the console tree.
3. In the Tasks tab, click on the link for Publish Non-Web Server Protocols.
4. Enter a descriptive name for the publishing rule and click Next to continue.
5. Enter the IP address of the server that will be published, similar to what is shown in Figure 15.11, and click Next to continue.
6. From the Select Protocol dialog box, select the server protocol that will be published from the list, in this case RDP (Terminal Services) Server, and click Next to continue.

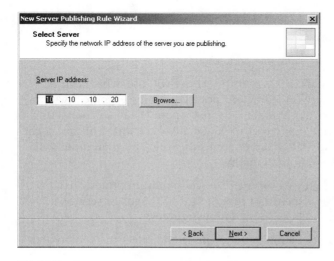

FIGURE 15.11   Publishing an RDP Server with a server publishing rule.

7. Check the box listed for requests from the External network and click Next to continue.

8. Click Finish, Apply, and OK to save the rule.

Defining a Custom Publishing Rule

A good deal of customization can be done on individual server publishing rules and on individual protocols. This enables custom publishing rule scenarios to be implemented and custom protocols to be established. For example, clicking on the Ports button on the Select Protocol dialog box from the server publishing step-by-step provided earlier brings up the dialog box shown in Figure 15.12.

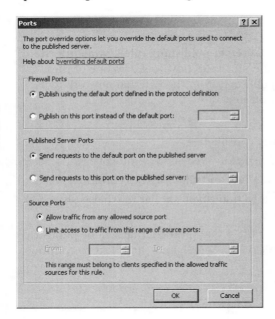

FIGURE 15.12   Customizing server publishing rule port settings.

This dialog box allows for customization of the port the service will use, which can be useful when publishing a known service on a different port. For example, some organizations may want their users to connect to a standard FTP port (port 21) when connecting to a server on the Internet, but to have that server itself actually use a different port such as 2021, for security reasons. Creating an FTP server publishing rule and then modifying these port settings allows for this type of functionality.

In addition, custom protocols can be created for use in server publishing rules. For example, if a particular application used a custom port of TCP 12345 for its service, a custom protocol could be generated in ISA with the following steps:

1. In ISA Admin Console, click on the Firewall Policy node and select the Toolbox tab from the Tasks pane.

2. Click on Protocols.

3. Click New, Protocol.

4. Enter a description for the protocol and click Next.

5. Under the Primary Connection Information field, click the New button.

6. In the New/Edit Protocol Connection dialog box, shown in Figure 15.13, enter the type of protocol (TCP or UDP), the direction that it will use (Outbound for access rules and Inbound for server publishing rules), and the port range that is needed. Click OK when finished.

7. Click Next to continue.

8. At the following dialog box, shown in Figure 15.14, select whether to use secondary connections. Based on the type of application required, secondary connections may be necessary. If not, simply click Next to continue.

9. Click Finish, Apply, and OK to create the protocol.

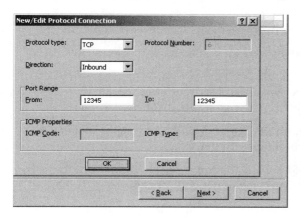

FIGURE 15.13   Defining the port settings for a custom protocol.

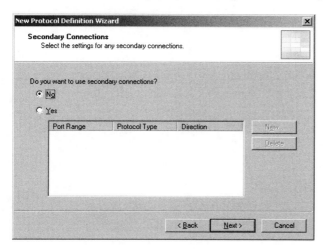

FIGURE 15.14   Choosing whether to use secondary connections for a custom protocol.

Once created, the protocol can be used for either access rules or server publishing rules, depending on the direction defined in the port settings (outbound versus inbound).

Summary

The field of RPC communications promises enhanced productivity and functionality, but it is riddled with the land mines of unsecured RPC traffic. Fortunately, however, ISA Server 2006's RPC filtering functionality enables organizations to take full advantage of RPC's capabilities without needlessly exposing services to the risks associated with RPC traffic.

The ability of an ISA server to inspect individual UUIDs in RPC traffic and allow only those used by specific applications is highly valuable, and can greatly improve the ability to secure a networked environment.

Best Practices

▶ Secure RPC communications across network segments whenever possible.

▶ Create custom RPC protocol definitions to restrict RPC traffic to specific RPC UUID interfaces.

▶ Use server publishing rules to protect servers and services from specific types of traffic, particularly RPC-based traffic.

▶ Install and utilize Network Monitor on ISA Server or on other systems to analyze traffic and create intelligent protocol filters with ISA.

▶ Consider deploying multi-homed ISA servers to protect servers from client traffic by using server publishing rules and isolated server network VLANs.

PART IV

Supporting an ISA Server 2006 Infrastructure

CHAPTER 16

Administering an ISA Server 2006 Environment

The day-to-day operations of an ISA Server 2006 environment are not complex. This said, it is still important to use best-practice techniques to properly maintain, monitor, and administer ISA Server. Fortunately, administration is secured and simplified in ISA Server 2006, allowing for the use of predefined admin roles, customized ISA console access, and wizards that simplify common tasks.

This chapter focuses on defining the role of the ISA administrator and outlining the particular tools that are available to ease in the administration of ISA itself. Best-practice approaches to administering the security and rules of an ISA server are outlined, and step-by-step procedures outlining particular administrative tasks are detailed.

Defining the Role of the ISA Administrator

ISA administrators are defined in different ways, depending on the organization using the product. For smaller environments, the role of the ISA administrator most often falls upon those individuals already tasked with general user administration and server support. Larger organizations may delegate ISA admin tasks to messaging administrators, security admins, or network admins, depending on the factors surrounding the deployment of ISA itself.

Understanding Who Administers the ISA Environment

The fact that ISA can fit into so many roles is a tribute to the diverse range of functionality that the server possesses. For example, the following roles are affected in one way or another with an ISA server:

▶ **Network Administrator**—Network administrators are in charge of shaping network traffic and routing it to proper destinations. Because ISA can act as a router, and is often deployed in that capacity to secure an isolated server or network segment, it often falls upon the network admin's shoulders to understand and potentially administer portions of ISA functionality.

▶ **Messaging Administrator**—Because ISA is so often deployed specifically to secure messaging solutions, particularly Exchange solutions such as Outlook Web Access, the role of administering ISA is often undertaken, at least in part, by messaging administrators.

▶ **Security/Firewall Administrator**—Firewall administrators will be most familiar with ISA itself. ISA uses the familiar concept of firewall rules, security concepts, and the look and feel of the console itself.

It is really not important who eventually takes over administrative control of an ISA server, but what is important is that the important characteristics of the ISA server itself are taken into account. An ISA server acts and performs in a profoundly different way than other servers, particularly other Microsoft servers.

Exploring ISA Administrator Roles

ISA Server 2006 Standard edition comes installed with three predefined Administrator groups, depending on the type of administration that needs to be performed:

▶ **ISA Server Full Administrator**—An ISA Server Full Administrator can perform all ISA Admin tasks, including all firewall, VPN, and content-caching configuration.

▶ **ISA Server Monitoring Auditor**—The ISA Server Monitoring Auditor role can only view and acknowledge alerts, services, and sessions, and cannot configure any of the ISA settings.

▶ **ISA Server Auditor**—The ISA Server Auditor role allows for configuration of specific alerts, viewing log information and creating reports and definitions, and stopping and restarting individual sessions and services.

Each one of these roles can be delegated to individual users or, preferably, to groups of users, through use of ISA Server's Assign Administrative Roles wizard. First, however, best-practice security precautions and a controllable and auditable access mechanism should be deployed before the wizard is run.

Deploying a Role-Based Access Control Model for ISA Server 2006

For many years, Microsoft has provided for ease of administrative delegation in its products, for better or for worse. Unfortunately, however, this concept has been misused and abused and generally misunderstood. Too often, access is simply granted ad hoc, and to individual users, resulting in a mess of security permissions, orphaned SIDs, and potential security risks.

What is needed is a best-practice strategy for securing access to resources, including ISA Server itself. Ideally, this strategy should involve granting access only when a person's role dictates that he should be allowed access to that resource. For example, if Susan is an accountant, then it would stand to reason that she should not have access to Human Resources file servers. What should happen is that the role of Accountant should be defined, and the resources that the role needs to perform that job should also be defined.

Exploring the Concept of Active Directory Access Groups and Role Groups

A best-practice approach that utilizes role-based access control for ISA Server 2006 Administration, and administration of an IT environment in general, can be deployed in a relatively straightforward approach, using Active Directory groups to delegate administration and to define membership in particular roles.

This administrative concept logically divides groups into two types, as follows:

▶ **Access Groups**—Access groups are Active Directory groups that are created to control a certain level of access that is granted to a particular resource, such as a file share, printer, server, or any other network resource. For example, a group could be created called AG-ISAFullAdmins that would be granted Full Admin rights to an ISA server. For the most efficient replication and application, these types of groups are typically Domain Local groups.

▶ **Role Groups**—Role groups are Active Directory groups whose members share the same roles within an organization. These groups are then added into the membership of an access group to allow the members of that role to have the type of access they need to do their job. An example of a role group would be RG-IT-SecurityAdmins, which would be added as a member of the AG-ISAFullAdmins access group. Role groups are best created as Active Directory Global groups.

NOTE

The terms *access group* and *role group* are not official Microsoft terms, but are useful descriptors to help understand this concept.

Illustrating a Role-Based Access Approach

To illustrate this concept, take fictional CompanyABC. CompanyABC has several job types within the company, such as the following:

▶ Human Resources Officer

▶ Marketing Analyst

▶ Accountant

▶ Information Technology Engineer

▶ Manager

▶ Security Admins

▶ IT Helpdesk

▶ Salesperson

In Active Directory, global groups were created at CompanyABC to correspond to each of these groups, such as the following:

▶ RG-HROfficers

▶ RG-MarketingAnalysts

▶ RG-Accountants

▶ RG-ITEngineers

▶ RG-Managers

▶ RG-IT-SecurityAdmins

▶ RG-IT-Helpdesk

▶ RG-Salespersons

CompanyABC spent the time auditing what each role needed to access. They determined different types of access requirements for each role. For example, they determined that the Security Admins required full control of the ISA infrastructure, whereas the Helpdesk needed only to monitor ISA, as well as to perform multiple other tasks within the organization. Access groups were created and directly given the particular rights on the resources through use of the various Administrative Control wizards. For example, the following access groups were created for ISA:

▶ AG-ISA-FullAdmins

▶ AG-ISA-MonitoringAuditors

▶ AG-ISA-Auditors

To allow the Security Admins to be full ISA Admins, the RG-IT-SecurityAdmins group was added as a member of the AG-ISA-FullAdmins group. For the Helpdesk resources to monitor ISA, they were added into the AG-ISA-MonitoringAuditors group.

With this type of model in place, when a new employee comes into the organization into a particular role, or when an employee changes his role, only the role group membership needs to be changed, which automatically grants access to the resources that job requires. It also makes it very easy to audit administrative access to an environment.

This concept is very useful for administering an ISA server environment, and can also be extended for use with the administration of other components in an environment.

> **NOTE**
>
> For ISA servers that are not domain members, local groups on the ISA server can be used in the same type of capacity. The only downside to this type of configuration is that it becomes more difficult to scale this configuration because groups and users have to be duplicated between individual servers.

Delegating and Customizing Administrative Access to the ISA Console

After a best-practice model is developed for controlling access to an ISA server through role-based access control, those groups can then be created and delegated access to an ISA server. Groups can either be created in Active Directory, if the ISA server is a domain member, of local groups can be created for workgroup member servers.

Creating Active Directory Groups for Admin Access

If an Active Directory environment is utilized, creation of the access groups for delegation of ISA administration is straightforward. It is recommended to create the three groups to correspond with the three levels of ISA Administration. To create a group, do the following:

> **NOTE**
>
> The following procedure illustrates the creation of AD groups in a Windows Server 2003 environment. The procedure is slightly different on a Windows 2000 server.

1. On an Active Directory domain controller, open Active Directory Users and Computers (ADUC) by clicking Start, All Programs, Administrative Tools, Active Directory Users and Computers.

2. In ADUC, drill down through the console tree and locate the Organizational Unit where the group is to be created. Right-click that OU (the default is the Users container, if no other OU has been specified) and select New, Group.

3. Enter a descriptive group name (with the same name entered into the pre–Windows 2000 field) and enter the group scope and type, similar to what is shown in Figure 16.1. For an access group, select Domain Local and Security and click Next.

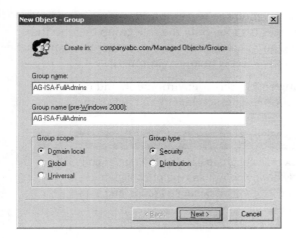

FIGURE 16.1   Creating an AD group for ISA administration.

4. Do not check to create an Exchange email address if prompted, and click Next.

5. Click Finish to create the group.

6. Add groups as necessary, using the concepts illustrated in the previous sections of this chapter as a guide.

Creating Local Server Users and Groups for Admin Access

On an ISA server that is not a domain member, users and groups can be created to serve the same purpose. To create local user accounts on the ISA server, do the following:

1. On the ISA server, click on Start, All Programs, Administrative Tools, Computer Management.

2. In the Computer Management console tree, click on Local Users and Groups and expand to the Users folder.

3. Right-click the Users folder and select New User.

4. Enter a username, full name, description, and password, as shown in Figure 16.2. Do not select to change password at next logon, and click Create to continue.

5. Enter any other users as necessary, using the same process.

After the user accounts have been created, groups can be created to control access to the ISA console. To create local groups on an ISA server, do the following:

1. On the ISA server, click on Start, All Programs, Administrative Tools, Computer Management.

2. In the Computer Management console tree, click on Local Users and Groups and expand to the Groups folder.

3. Right-click the Groups folder and select New Group.

4. Enter a descriptive name for the group and a description. Click Add to add the local user or users created in the earlier steps, as shown in Figure 16.3.

FIGURE 16.2   Creating a local user account for ISA administration.

FIGURE 16.3   Adding a local ISA group for administrative access.

5. Add members and click Create when finished.

6. Repeat as necessary to create additional local groups.

Delegating Admin Access to ISA Server

After the proper groups have been created, they can be granted proper administrative rights in ISA Server. To start this process, perform the following steps:

1. From the ISA Management Console, click on the server name in the console pane.

2. In the Tasks tab of the Tasks pane, click the link labeled Assign Administrative Roles.

3. From the Assign Roles tab, click the Add button.

4. Use the Browse button to locate the group created earlier, such as
   COMPANYABC\AG-ISA-FullAdmins, select the role that matches the group, such as
   what is shown in Figure 16.4, and click OK.

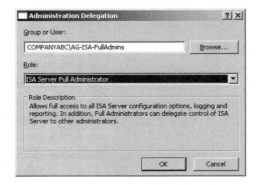

FIGURE 16.4   Delegating administrative roles in ISA.

5. Click Add again and follow the same process for any other groups that will be delegated access to the ISA server. Eventually, after the proper groups have been added, the
   Delegate Control dialog box will look similar to Figure 16.5. Click Next to continue.

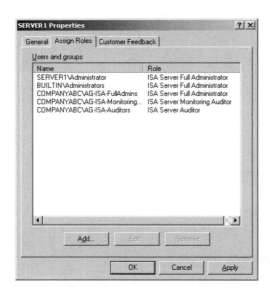

FIGURE 16.5   Reviewing newly added administrative delegation roles.

6. Click OK to end the process.
7. Click Apply and then click OK to save the changes to ISA.

After these procedures are complete, granting administrative access to an ISA server is as straightforward as adding the proper user account (or the appropriate role group) into the access group.

Administering an ISA Server Remotely

From the console of the ISA server, those who have been delegated privileges to administer an ISA box can after the administrative delegation wizard has been run. In many cases, however, remote access to ISA is necessary. Because ISA is a firewall, this presents particular challenges. ISA is configured to drop anything that hasn't been specifically set up for access.

Setting up access to ISA remotely is subsequently a two-step process. In the first step, either remote access via Remote Desktop Protocol (RDP) must be enabled, or the ISA Management Console must be installed on the remote host. The second step involves configuring the ISA rules to specifically allow remote administration from remote hosts.

Installing the ISA Server Management Console

If remote administration using the thin client–based Remote Desktop Protocol (RDP) is not available, administration of ISA Server 2006 can be accomplished via installation of the ISA Management Console itself. The console is essentially a Microsoft Management Console (MMC) snap-in, which can be physically installed on any one of the following operating systems:

▶ Windows Server 2003, Standard or Enterprise

▶ Windows XP Workstation

▶ Windows 2000 Workstation, Server, or Advanced Server

> **CAUTION**
>
> It is not always best practice to install remote ISA Administration Consoles for two reasons. First off, the console software needs to be kept at the same service pack level as the ISA server itself. Secondly, MMC access to the ISA server needs to be granted, which can be more impactful than standard RDP. For these reasons, it is preferable to set up access through RDP when possible.

On a remote host, the full ISA Management Console can be installed via the following steps:

1. Insert the ISA Server 2006 media into the drive (or run `autorun.exe` from a network location where the ISA files are located).
2. Click on the link for Install ISA Server 2006.
3. Click Next to continue.
4. Select I Accept and click Next to continue.

5. Enter a username, organization name, and the product serial number and click Next to continue.

> **NOTE**
>
> If Windows XP Professional is being used, there may be an additional prompt that says the version of ISA cannot be installed on this version of Windows. Because only the Admin Console is being installed, this dialog box can be ignored and Next can be clicked. If using a supported OS, a prompt is offered to perform either a custom or a standard setup, choose the Custom setup, and click Next.

6. Select Custom from the Setup Type dialog box and click Next.

7. From the Custom Setup dialog box, select to install only the ISA Server Management component, as shown in Figure 16.6. Make sure the other components are not selected by clicking them and selecting This Feature Will Not Be Available. Click Next to continue.

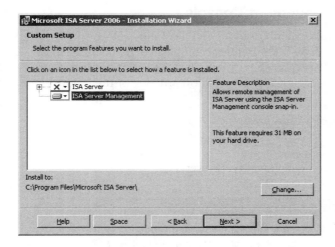

FIGURE 16.6   Installing the ISA Server Management Console.

8. Click Install to begin the installation process.

9. Click Finish to end the process.

After installation, the ISA Server Console should be brought to the same service pack level as the ISA server itself.

After it is installed, the ISA Server System Policy must be modified to allow the MMC Console access from the particular workstation. To do this, perform the following steps:

1. From the physical ISA Server Console, expand the Console tree to show SERVER-NAME, Firewall Policy.

2. Under the Tasks tab in the Tasks pane, click on Edit System Policy.

3. Scroll down to Remote Management, Microsoft Management Console and click on the text.

4. Ensure that the box for Enable is checked and select the From tab.

5. Double-click on Remote Management Computers in the dialog box shown in Figure 16.7.

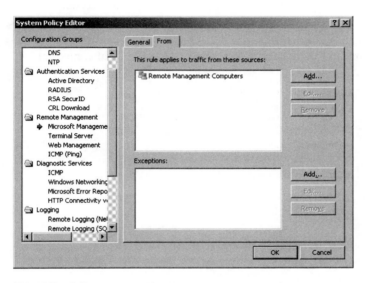

FIGURE 16.7   Allowing ISA Server management from a remote machine.

6. Click Add, Computer.

7. Enter a name for the remote console machine, an IP address, and a description, as shown in Figure 16.8, and click OK.

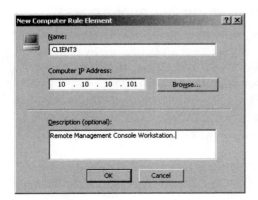

FIGURE 16.8   Creating a Computer object from which to allow remote access.

8. Click OK, OK, Apply, and OK to save the changes.

The final step is to configure the remote console to connect to a specific ISA server. To do this, perform the following steps on the remote console machine:

1. Open the newly installed ISA Management Console (Start, All Programs, ISA Server Management).

2. From the console tree, right-click on Microsoft Internet Security and Acceleration Server 2006 and click Connect To.

3. In the Connect To dialog box, shown in Figure 16.9, select to connect to Another Computer, enter the computer name, and select either to use the local credentials or another set of credentials. Click OK.

4. Navigate and administer the ISA server as needed.

FIGURE 16.9   Configuring the remote console to connect to an ISA server.

Configuring an ISA Server for Remote Desktop Protocol Access

The preferred ISA Administration route is through the use of the Remote Desktop Protocol (RDP), which provides for thin-client access to the desktop of an ISA server. By default, this type of administration is installed on any Windows Server 2003 system, but it needs to be enabled to function properly. RDP allows for up to two thin-client sessions and one console session to operate simultaneously, which enables multiple administrators to access and administer ISA simultaneously.

To enable RDP functionality on an ISA server, perform the following steps:

1. On the ISA server, click Start, Control Panel, System.

2. Select the Remote tab.

3. Check the box for Enable Remote Desktop on This Computer, as shown in Figure 16.10.

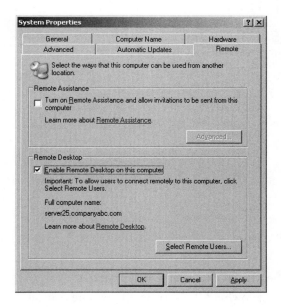

FIGURE 16.10   Enabling RDP on an ISA server.

4. Click OK when warned about local accounts not having passwords.

5. Click OK to save the changes.

After it is enabled, RDP also has to be allowed via System Policy rules, in a similar fashion to the MMC Console System Policy rules. To set this up, do the following:

> **CAUTION**
>
> It is not common or advised to allow RDP directly to the ISA server from an untrusted network such as the Internet. This opens ISA to attacks and password-cracking attempts.

1. From the physical ISA Server Console, expand the Console tree to show SERVER-NAME, Firewall Policy.

2. Under the Tasks Tab in the Tasks pane, click on Edit System Policy.

3. Scroll down to Remote Management, Terminal Server and click on the text.

4. Make sure the Enable box is selected, as shown in Figure 16.11, and click the From tab.

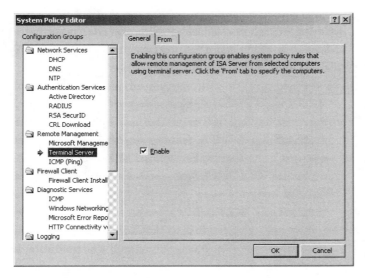

FIGURE 16.11   Enabling RDP access to an ISA server.

5. Under the From tab, double-click on the Remote Management Computers.

6. If already added in the previous steps on allowing MMC access, the remote console will already be in this list. If not, it can be added by clicking Add, Computer and adding the name and IP address of the remote computer. Click OK, OK, Apply, and OK to save the changes.

Working with ISA Server 2006 Lockdown Mode

ISA Server 2006 has a new feature known as lockdown mode, which enables an ISA server to continue to function in a limited capacity when the firewall service has crashed or has not been enabled yet. This is an important feature to understand when administrating an ISA server.

Administering and Understanding Lockdown Mode

Lockdown mode enables administrators to access and troubleshoot an ISA server, in addition to allowing internal clients to continue to have external network access in the event of a problem with ISA Server, while at the same time disabling external network access rules. This has the effect of keeping critical network access intact, while protecting the internal network from denial of service (DoS) or other attacks.

Triggering and Resetting ISA Lockdown Mode

Putting ISA Server 2006 into lockdown mode can be triggered by various mechanisms, based on the sensitivity of the environment and the rules of the organization. For example, a highly sensitive organization prone to major hacking attempts could configure an ISA server to block all inbound access to the organization when specific types of attacks or port scans take place.

To change the parameters for when a server enters lockdown, click on the Configure Alert Definitions link under the Tasks Tab of the Alerts tab in the Monitoring node of the console. This enables the alert definitions, shown in Figure 16.12, to be shown and modified.

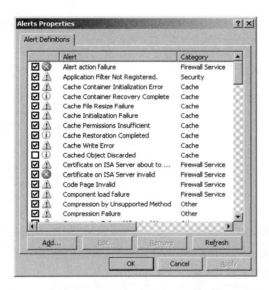

FIGURE 16.12   Configuring alert definitions.

For example, the default setting for the Log Failure alert, which can be viewed by double-clicking on the entry in the dialog box, is to take the action of stopping the firewall service, putting the server into lockdown mode. The setting can be set via the Actions tab, as shown in Figure 16.13.

Configuring the alert settings helps to set thresholds for when a server enters lockdown mode. To take a server out of lockdown mode, simply restart the firewall service.

Performing Advanced ISA Administration

Occasionally, ISA administrators need to perform specific advanced administrative actions, such as renaming an ISA server within the console and administering multiple ISA servers at the same times. These techniques are important to understand, even if just at the conceptual level.

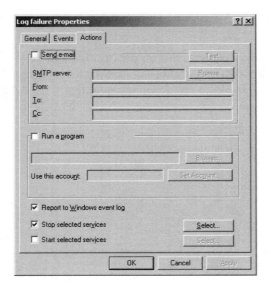

FIGURE 16.13   Setting the alert actions.

Renaming an ISA Server in the Console

An ISA server cannot be renamed unless the server itself is reinstalled, which can cause problems in certain circumstances when the name of the server is required to change, either through corporate mergers or other restructuring. Fortunately, the name can be changed in the console if necessary, through the following procedure:

1. From the ISA Server Console, right-click the server's name in the console tree and choose Properties.

2. Enter a new name for the server in the name field, shown in Figure 16.14, and click OK.

3. Click the Apply button and click OK.

Administering Multiple ISA Servers

The ISA Server Console is capable of administering multiple ISA servers in an environment easily. Those servers only need to be added directly into the console. The only consideration in these circumstances is that the user account used to access each of the ISA servers ideally should be identical. If not, the administrator is required to authenticate each individual user when the server itself is accessed. To add an additional ISA server to the console, do the following:

1. From the ISA Server Console, right-click on the very top item, labeled Microsoft Internet Security and Acceleration Server 2006, and choose Connect To, as shown in Figure 16.15.

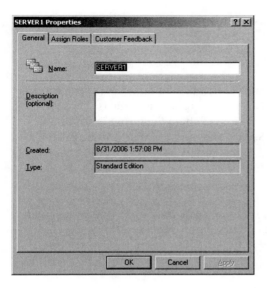

FIGURE 16.14   Renaming an ISA server in the console.

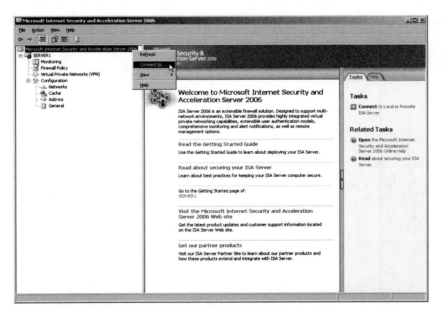

FIGURE 16.15   Adding multiple ISA servers to an ISA Admin Console.

2. Select Another Computer (Remote Management) from the list, and enter the name
of the computer.

3. Select whether to use the same credentials or different credentials (enter them as necessary) and click OK.

Summary

Administration of an ISA server is relatively straightforward, assuming the proper controls have been put into place to restrict console access to the proper individuals. Through the use of an auditable, controlled access mechanism such as that which role-based access controls can give, access to administer an ISA Server 2006 environment can be easily controlled and monitored.

Best Practices

▶ Use the concept of role-based access control to delegate administrative access to an ISA server and to other network resources.

▶ Use the Remote Desktop Protocol (RDP) to administer an ISA server when possible, rather than using the ISA Administrator MMC Console remotely.

▶ Use the lockdown mode functionality of an ISA server to protect it from attacks and denial of service attempts.

▶ Create groups to correspond with each of the ISA administrative roles, such as ISA Full Administrator, ISA Basic Monitoring, and ISA Extended Monitoring.

CHAPTER 17

Maintaining ISA Server 2006

By and large, ISA Server 2006 does a great job in keeping itself in working order with a fairly low amount of maintenance required. As with any complex system, however, getting the most out of an ISA Server implementation requires that certain best-practice procedures be performed on a regular basis. These procedures can range from simple daily tasks such as checking the ISA admin console for alerts and updates, to complex issues such as performing operating system, ISA, and hardware upgrades.

This chapter focuses on the best-practice maintenance procedures that should be performed to keep ISA Server 2006 in top shape. Guides and checklists for ISA maintenance are included, and step-by-step maintenance procedures are outlined.

Understanding the Importance of a Maintenance Plan for ISA

It is sometimes difficult to keep ahead of this type of schedule, so developing a custom maintenance plan for ISA Server is recommended. It should include the types of tasks that should be run on ISA on a daily, weekly, monthly, quarterly, and yearly basis. A task list of this type can also be beneficial for audits and compliance with governmental regulations such as those stipulated by Sarbanes-Oxley, Gramm-Leach-Bliley, HIPAA, and others. Having this type of paper trail to ISA maintenance can help to assure auditors that due diligence is being performed and security measures are being taken.

Keeping Ahead of Updates and Patches

Software is constantly being changed, with features added, bugs fixed, and improvements made. At the same time, malicious computer hackers are constantly probing software for holes and exploits, modifying techniques, and attacking in numbers. For these reasons, it is critical to keep an ISA Server system updated with the recent security patches and fixes on a regular basis to minimize the threat posed by these types of systems.

ISA itself is often the first or second line of defense for an organization, bearing the brunt of attacks and exploit maneuvers, so it is doubly important to maintain it with the latest in security patches and updates.

Taking a Proactive Approach to Security Maintenance

Unfortunately, there is no "cruise control" button on an ISA server that can be pressed after it is put into place to automatically keep it up to date, patched, and monitored. Because of the sensitive nature of the server, it is unwise to turn on automatic updates and/or automatic patching solutions. This leaves it squarely in the hands of the ISA administrator to take a proactive approach to security maintenance, heading off potential exploits and attacks before they occur.

In reality, nearly all security vulnerabilities that have arisen in modern business environments, such as Code Red, Nimda, and SQL Slammer, had patches available before the outbreak of the exploit or virus. If a proactive maintenance plan had been in place for many of the servers that were affected by these exploits, the extent of the damage would have been limited. This underscores some of the reasons for developing a solid ISA maintenance plan.

NOTE

It is important to point out that although ISA is run on the Windows operating system, a vast majority of the hotfixes and patches that are generated to address exploits in Windows do not affect ISA servers. ISA servers by default drop most traffic and ignore the types of requests across which exploits normally travel. This makes the "surface area" of an ISA server quite small, in comparison with a standard Windows server. That said, it is still important to keep the ISA Server OS up to date and patched to avoid any potential for a failure in ISA programming.

Understanding ISA Server's Role in an IT Maintenance Plan

ISA Server itself is typically only a small component in an IT organization and encompasses a small portion of the total IT environment. The maintenance plan and procedures generated for ISA should take this into account, and should dovetail with existing maintenance plans and documentation. If existing maintenance documentation is not readily available, or never was created, then the ideal time for creating an omnibus IT maintenance plan would be when the ISA plan is drawn up.

Updating ISA's Operating System

The most commonly updated portion of ISA Server is ISA's operating system, which is Windows Server 2003. Any of several methods can be used to patch the Windows operating system, as follows:

- **Manual Patching**—The traditional way of patching Windows has been to download and install patches to the server itself. In highly secure ISA scenarios, where access to the Internet or internal systems cannot be granted or obtained, this may be the only feasible approach to patching.

- **Windows Update**—Windows Update is a Microsoft website that allows for detection of installed patches and provides for automated installation of the necessary Windows patches. Windows Update must be manually invoked from the server console itself, and must be made available through ISA system policy rules.

- **Microsoft Update**—Microsoft Update is the evolution of Windows Update, as it can detect and install not only Windows updates, but updates for most Microsoft products, including ISA Server. If the Windows Update approach is used for patch management, it is highly recommended to use Microsoft Update, as it will detect and install all relevant patches.

- **Automatic Updates Client**—The Automatic Updates client uses the same type of technology as Windows Update/Microsoft Update, but automates the transfer of patches and updates. It can be configured to use Microsoft servers or internal Windows Server Update Services (WSUS) servers. This method is an unorthodox way to update an ISA server. It is generally preferred to manually control when a server is patched and rebooted.

- **Windows Server Update Services (WSUS)**—A Windows Server Update Services (WSUS) server pushes administrator-approved updates to clients and servers on a network, using the Automatic Updates client and on a predefined schedule.

- **Other Patch Push Technology**—Other patch push technologies for updating clients and servers such as ISA allow for patches and updates to be automatically pushed out on a scheduled basis. This includes technologies such as Systems Management Server (SMS) 2003. In general, these types of technologies are not used with an ISA server.

Manually Patching an ISA Server

Given the fact that it is often not viable to automatically update and reboot a critical system such as ISA, the most common approach to ISA Server Patch management involves manually installing and patching an ISA server on a controlled basis. Given the large number of server updates that Microsoft releases, this may seem like a rather onerous task. In reality, however, only a small number of these patches and updates apply to ISA server itself, so one of the tasks of the administrator is to validate whether an ISA server requires a specific patch or not.

For example, a patch that addresses a WINS server vulnerability would not apply to an ISA server that is not running that particular service. In reality, because ISA is locked down to not respond to any type of traffic other than those that are specifically defined, only a small number of the patches that are produced need to be run on an ISA server.

In general, a patch may need to be applied on the ISA server if it addresses a vulnerability in the following Windows components:

▶ The kernel of the operating system.

▶ Any part of the TCP/IP stack.

▶ The Remote Routing and Access Service (RRAS), if VPN capability is enabled on the ISA server.

▶ Any other service turned or identified as enabled during the Security Configuration Wizard (SCW) that is run during the setup of the server. See Chapter 2, "Installing ISA Server 2006," for this procedure.

NOTE

If in doubt, it is best to install the patch after testing it in a lab environment. If it is not a critical patch, it may be wise to wait until a designated maintenance interval and then install the cumulative patches that have come out so far.

Verifying Windows/Microsoft Update Access in the ISA System Policy

ISA Server System Policies control whether or not the Local Host network (effectively the ISA server itself) is allowed access to certain websites. The System Policy controls whether or not ISA can ping servers on the internal network, whether it can contact NTP servers to update its internal clock, and any other type of network access, including whether the server can access external websites such as Windows Update or Microsoft Update.

The default web policy blocks most websites from direct access from ISA, and enabling the ISA server to access specific sites must be manually defined in the System Policy. To allow for automatic updates via the Windows Update website, ISA grants the Local Host network access to the windowsupdate.com website. If this setting has been changed, or if access to additional websites is required, the System Policy must be updated. It is therefore important to know the location of this policy and how to modify it. To view this setting, perform the following steps:

1. From the ISA Management Console, right-click on the Firewall Policy node in the console tree and select Edit System Policy.

2. Under the Configuration Groups pane on the left, scroll down to Various, Allowed Sites, and select it by clicking on it once.

3. Select the To tab on the right pane.

4. Under This Rule Applies to Traffic Sent to These Destinations, double-click on System Policy Allowed Sites.

5. Under the System Policy Allowed Sites Properties, shown in Figure 17.1, ensure that *.windowsupdate.com and *.microsoft.com sites are entered.

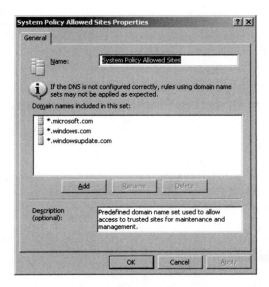

FIGURE 17.1   Modifying System Policy Allowed Sites settings.

6. Add additional sites as necessary, such as third-party hardware or software vendor sites, by using the New button and entering in the site in the same format as the existing sites.

7. Click OK twice when changes are done.

8. Click the Apply button, and then click OK to save the changes to ISA.

Working with Windows Update to Patch the Operating System

Utilizing the Windows Update (or preferably the Microsoft Update) websites gives a greater degree of control to updating an ISA server, while at the same time making it easier for an administrator to determine what patches are needed. Assuming the Windows Update site has been added to the System Policy Allowed Sites group, as described in the previous section, using this technique to patch an ISA server is straightforward. Windows Update can be invoked easily by clicking on the built-in link at Start, All Programs, Windows Update.

For step-by-step instructions on using Windows Update to patch an ISA server, see Chapter 2.

Managing ISA Server Updates and Critical Patches

In addition to operating system updates, the ISA application itself may require patching. This involves installing and configuring an ISA Standard Edition server with the latest service pack for ISA, in addition to checking the ISA website at Microsoft for updates to ISA. Up-to-date information on patch availability for ISA Server 2006 can be found at the following URL:

http://www.microsoft.com/isaserver/downloads/2006.asp

In addition, it may be helpful to review the ISA Server community boards on such websites as http://www.isaserver.org, http://www.isatools.org, and http://www.msisafaq.de for updates and issue troubleshooting on a regular basis. Reviewing the real-world deployment issues and questions on these sites can be an important part of maintaining an ISA server.

Prototyping ISA Server Patches Before Updating Production Equipment

In general, it is always good practice to prototype the deployment of patches for an ISA system before they are installed on a production system. A spare ISA server in a lab environment is an ideal candidate for this type of deployment. In addition, a robust backup and restore plan for ISA, in the event of an installed patch taking a server down, should be developed. For more information on backing up and restoring ISA, see Chapter 18, "Backing Up, Restoring, and Recovering an ISA Server 2006 Environment."

Performing Daily Maintenance

The processes and procedures for maintaining Windows Server 2003 systems can be separated based on the appropriate time to maintain a particular aspect of Windows Server 2003. Some maintenance procedures require daily attention, whereas others may require only quarterly checkups. The maintenance processes and procedures that an organization follows depend strictly on the organization; however, the categories described in the following sections and their corresponding procedures are best practices for organizations of all sizes and varying IT infrastructures.

Certain maintenance procedures need to be performed more often than others. The procedures that require the most attention are categorized into the daily procedures. Therefore, it is recommended that an administrator take on these procedures each day to ensure system reliability, availability, performance, and security. These procedures are examined in the following four sections.

Monitoring the ISA Dashboard

The ISA Server dashboard, shown in Figure 17.2, allows for a quick all-encompassing view of what is going on with the ISA server. The dashboard contains areas for showing alerts, current sessions, reports, monitored services, and connectivity verifiers, all on one screen. As part of daily maintenance, reviewing the ISA dashboard for alerts and other problems is recommended to allow for proactive management of the ISA environment.

For more information on monitoring ISA Server, see Chapter 19, "Monitoring and Troubleshooting an ISA Server 2006 Environment."

Checking Overall Server Functionality

Although checking the overall server health and functionality may seem redundant or elementary, this procedure is critical to keeping the system environment and users working productively.

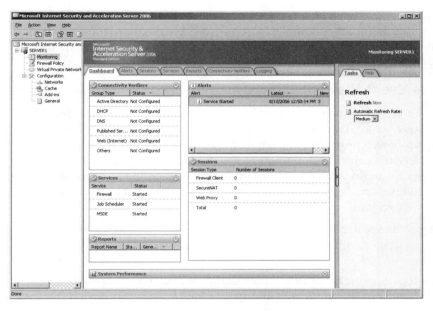

FIGURE 17.2   Monitoring the ISA dashboard.

Some questions that should be addressed during the checking and verification process are the following:

▶ Can users access published servers and services?

▶ Can VPN connections be made?

▶ Is Internet access time especially slow?

Verifying Backups

To provide a secure and fault-tolerant organization, it is imperative that a successful backup, done either with backup software or through ISA config exports, be performed each night. In the event of a server failure, the administrator may be required to perform a restore from tape. Without a backup each night, the IT organization is forced to rely on rebuilding the ISA server without the data. Therefore, the administrator should always back up servers so that the IT organization can restore them with minimal downtime in the event of a disaster. Because of the importance of the tape backups, the first priority of the administrator each day needs to be verifying and maintaining the backup sets, or ensuring that the XML export completed successfully.

If disaster ever strikes, the administrators need to be confident that an individual server or array can be recovered as quickly as possible. Successful backup mechanisms are imperative to the recovery operation; recoveries are only as good as the most recent backups.

Although Windows Server 2003's NTBackup backup program does not offer alerting mechanisms for bringing attention to unsuccessful backups, many third-party programs do. In addition, many of these third-party backup programs can send emails or pages if backups are successful or unsuccessful. In addition, exporting out ISA configuration information using automated scripts, such as the one described in Chapter 18, can help ensure the recoverability of an ISA server.

Monitoring the Event Viewer

The Windows Event Viewer, shown in Figure 17.3, is used to check the System, Security, and Application logs on a local or remote ISA server. These logs should not be confused with the ISA firewall or web proxy logging, which log network traffic through the ISA server. Rather, the Event Viewer logs information specific to the server itself, and its functionality. These logs are an invaluable source of information regarding the operation of the underlying Windows structure of ISA. The following event logs are present for Windows Server 2003 systems:

▶ **Security log**—The Security log captures all security-related events that are being audited on a system. Auditing is turned on by default to record success and failure of security events.

▶ **Application log**—Specific application information is stored in the Application log. This information includes services and any applications that are running on the server.

▶ **System log**—Windows Server 2003–specific information is stored in the System log.

All Event Viewer events are categorized as informational, warning, or error.

Some best practices for monitoring event logs include the following:

▶ Preferably, using a proactive monitoring tool with built-in intelligence to collect, filter, and alert on ISA-specific events. This includes the Microsoft Operations Manager (MOM) 2005 product, which is described in more detail in Chapter 19. Note that the MOM product is currently undergoing a rename to System Center Operations Manager.

▶ Understanding the events that are being reported.

▶ Archiving event logs frequently.

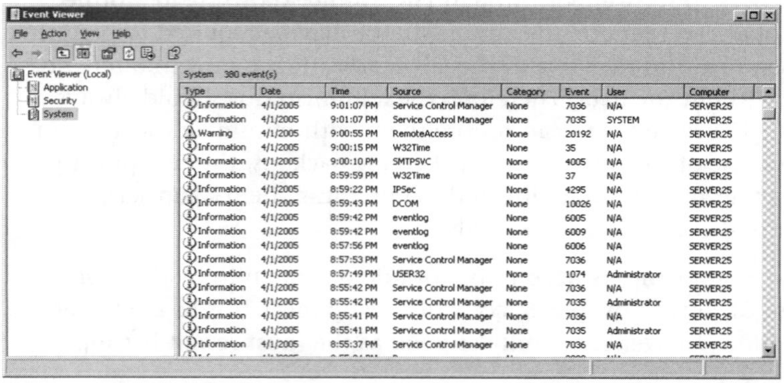

FIGURE 17.3   Examining the Event Viewer.

To simplify monitoring hundreds or thousands of generated events each day, the administrator should use the filtering mechanism provided in the Event Viewer. Although warnings and errors should take priority, the informational events should be reviewed to track what was happening before the problem occurred. After the administrator reviews the informational events, she can filter out the informational events and view only the warnings and errors.

To filter events, do the following:

1. Start the Event Viewer by clicking Start, All Programs, Administrative Tools, Event Viewer.
2. Select the log that is to be filtered.
3. Right-click the log and select View, Filter.
4. In the log properties window, shown in Figure 17.4, select the types of events to filter.
5. Optionally, select the time frame in which the events occurred. Click OK when finished.

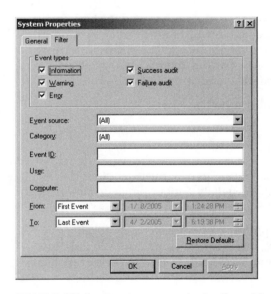

FIGURE 17.4   Filtering events in the Event Viewer.

Some warnings and errors are normal because of bandwidth constraints or other environmental issues. The more the logs are monitored, the more familiar the messages become and the easier it is to spot a problem before it affects the user community.

17

> **TIP**
>
> The size of the log files may need to be increased to support the number of log files that are produced by the system. This is particularly true if failure events are logged in the security log.

Performing Weekly Maintenance

Maintenance procedures that require slightly less attention than daily checking are categorized in a weekly routine and are examined in the following section. These tasks should be performed on a regular weekly basis, such as on Monday morning or another convenient time.

Checking for Updates

As previously mentioned, updates and patches to the Windows operating system that ISA uses and the ISA software itself are constantly being produced. It is wise to check for updates to these components, using the techniques described in the earlier sections. In addition, it may be good practice to sign up for a service such as the Microsoft Security Notification Service, which sends emails when new patches and updates have been released. More information on this program can be found at the following URL:

http://www.microsoft.com/technet/security/bulletin/notify.mspx

Checking Disk Space

Although the disk capacity of an ISA system can appear to be virtually endless, the amount of free space on all drives should be checked daily. Serious problems can occur if there isn't enough disk space.

Running out of disk space can be a particular problem for ISA servers. ISA logging can chew up a good portion of available disk space, and setting a cache drive can also leave less room for OS components. It is critical to monitor this, however, to prevent problems including, but not limited to, the following:

- Application failures
- System crashes
- Unsuccessful backup jobs
- Service failures
- The inability to audit
- Degradation in performance

To prevent these problems from occurring, administrators should keep the amount of free space on an ISA server to at least 25%.

Verifying Hardware

Hardware components supported by Windows Server 2003 are typically reliable, but this doesn't mean that they'll run continuously without failure. Hardware availability is measured in terms of mean time between failures (MTBF) and mean time to repair (MTTR). This includes downtime for both planned and unplanned events. These measurements provided by the manufacturer are good guidelines to follow; however, mechanical parts are bound to fail at one time or another. As a result, hardware should be monitored weekly to ensure efficient operation.

Hardware can be monitored in many different ways. For example, server systems may have internal checks and logging functionality to warn against possible failure, Windows Server 2003's System Monitor may bring light to a hardware failure, and a physical hardware check can help to determine whether the system is about to experience a problem with the hardware.

If a failure has occurred or is about to occur, having an inventory of spare hardware can significantly improve the chances and timing of recoverability. Checking system hardware on a weekly basis provides the opportunity to correct an issue before it becomes a problem.

TIP

One of the major advantages that ISA has over many of the other hardware firewalls is the fact that it can be installed and run on any standard Intel-based server hardware. This makes it much easier to swap out hardware components if they fail. It is therefore advantageous to use the same standard hardware configuration as other systems to set up ISA Server. For example, many organizations that use a common 1U rack-mounted server model for their Active Directory domain controllers, Exchange Client Access servers, MOM monitoring servers, and other systems can easily set up ISA on the same 1U standard, making it easier to swap out hardware and components if necessary.

Archiving Event Logs

The three event logs on all ISA servers can be archived manually or with the use of a utility such as MOM 2005. The event logs should be archived to a central location for ease of management and retrieval.

The specific amount of time to keep archived log files varies on a per-organization basis. For example, banks or other high-security organizations may be required to keep event logs up to a few years. As a best practice, organizations should keep event logs for at least three months.

Performing Monthly Maintenance

It is recommended to perform the tasks examined in the following sections on a monthly basis.

Maintaining File System Integrity

The physical disks on which ISA runs should be tested for file system–level integrity on a monthly basis with a utility such as CHKDSK. CHKDSK, included with Windows Server 2003, scans for file system integrity and can check for lost clusters, cross-linked files, and more. If Windows Server 2003 senses a problem, it runs CHKDSK automatically at startup.

To run CHKDSK maintenance on an ISA server, do the following:

1. At the command prompt, change to the partition that will be checked (for example, C:\).
2. Type **CHKDSK** without any parameters to check only for file system errors, as shown in Figure 17.5.

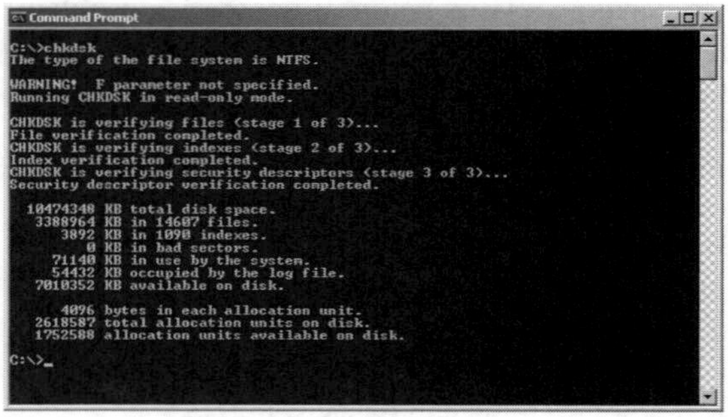

FIGURE 17.5   Running the CHKDSK utility on ISA Server disks.

3. If any errors are found, run the CHKDSK utility with the /f parameter to attempt to correct the errors found.

CAUTION

If errors are detected, it is important to back up the system and perform the changes (using the /f switch) during designated maintenance intervals because there is an inherent risk of system corruption when CHKDSK is used in write mode. Without the switch, however, CHKDSK can be run as often as desired.

Testing the UPS

An uninterruptible power supply (UPS) can be used to protect the system or group of systems from power failures (such as spikes and surges) and keep the system running long enough after a power outage so that an administrator can gracefully shut down the system. It is recommended that an administrator follow the UPS guidelines provided by the manufacturer at least once a month. Also, monthly scheduled battery tests should be performed.

Validating Backups

Once a month, an administrator should validate backups by restoring the backups to a server located in a lab environment. This is in addition to verifying that backups were successful from log files or the backup program's management interface. A restore gives the administrator the opportunity to verify the backups and to practice the restore procedures that would be used when recovering the server during a real disaster. In addition, this procedure tests the state of the backup media to ensure that they are in working order and builds administrator confidence for recovering from a true disaster.

ISA Server XML Export files can be validated if they are imported on test ISA servers in a lab environment. This activity can be performed on a monthly basis so that administrators become familiar with the process and are also provided with a current copy of the production ISA server(s) in a lab environment.

Updating Automated System Recovery Sets

Automated System Recovery (ASR) is a recovery tool that should be implemented in all Windows Server 2003 environments. It backs up the system state data, system services, and all volumes containing Windows Server 2003 system components. ASR replaces the Emergency Repair Disks (ERDs) used to recover systems in earlier versions of Windows.

After building a server and any time a major system change occurs, the ASR sets (that is, the backup and floppy disk) should be updated. Another best practice is to update ASR sets at least once a month. This keeps content in the ASR sets consistent with the current state of the system. Otherwise, valuable system configuration information may be lost if a system experiences a problem or failure.

To create an ASR set, do the following:

1. Open Windows Server 2003's NTBackup utility by choosing Start, All Programs, Accessories, System Tools, Backup.
2. Click Advanced Mode link from the first screen in the Backup or Restore Wizard.
3. Click the Automated System Recovery Wizard button.
4. Click Next in the Automated System Recovery Preparation Wizard window.

17

5. Select the backup destination, as shown in Figure 17.6, and then click Next to continue.

6. Click Finish.

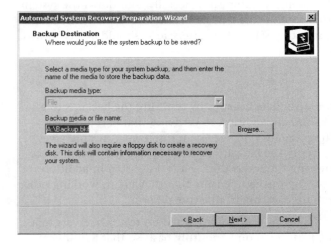

FIGURE 17.6   Using the ASR tool.

NOTE

This process may take a while to complete, so be patient. Depending on the performance of the system being used and the amount of information to be transferred, this process could take several minutes to a few hours to complete.

Updating Documentation

An integral part of managing and maintaining any ISA environment is to document the network infrastructure and procedures. The following are just a few of the documents that should be considered for inclusion in an ISA environment:

- ▶ Server build guides
- ▶ Disaster recovery guides and procedures
- ▶ Checklists
- ▶ Configuration settings
- ▶ Change configuration logs
- ▶ Historical performance data
- ▶ Special user rights assignments
- ▶ Special application settings

As systems and services are built and procedures are ascertained, document these facts to reduce learning curves, administration, and maintenance.

It is not only important to adequately document the ISA environment, but it's often even more important to keep those documents up to date. Otherwise, documents can quickly become outdated as the environment, processes, and procedures change with business changes.

For more information on documenting an ISA environment, see Chapter 20, "Documenting an ISA Server 2006 Environment."

Performing Quarterly Maintenance

As the name implies, quarterly maintenance is performed four times a year. Areas to maintain and manage on a quarterly basis are typically fairly self-sufficient and self-sustaining. Infrequent maintenance is required to keep the system healthy. This doesn't mean, however, that the tasks are simple or that they aren't as critical as those tasks that require more frequent maintenance.

Changing Administrator Passwords

Local administrator passwords should, at a minimum, be changed every quarter (90 days). Changing these passwords strengthens security measures so that systems can't easily be compromised. In addition to changing passwords, other password requirements such as password age, history, length, and strength should be reviewed.

This is particularly important for ISA servers that are not domain members because the local accounts on the system provide the only access into the environment.

Audit the Security Infrastructure

Security is the cornerstone of ISA Server functionality, and it is critical to validate that an ISA server is secure. This validation should be performed no less than every quarter, and can also be useful in satisfying third-party IT environment audits that may be dictated by governmental or industry compliance.

Security audits can be performed via traditional checks of security procedures and infrastructure, such as the following:

- ▶ Who has administrative access
- ▶ The physical security of the servers
- ▶ The presence of procedural documentation
- ▶ Firewall policy based on role-based access controls
- ▶ Existence and maintenance of audit and firewall logs

In addition to validating security in this way, third-party hacking and intrusion tools can be used to validate the effective security of an ISA server. These tools are constantly being used "in the wild" on the Internet, and it can be advantageous for an organization to use the latest tools to test the robustness of the current ISA configuration.

Gather Performance Metrics

It is often the case that an ISA server, when first deployed, can easily handle the traffic that it processes, but then slowly become more and more overloaded over time. This can be true particularly for servers that start their lives with limited roles, such as a reverse-proxy server only, but then over time take on additional roles such as VPN server, content-caching server, or edge firewall. It is therefore important to monitor the performance of an ISA server on a quarterly basis, using a utility such as the Performance Monitor (perfmon), shown in Figure 17.7.

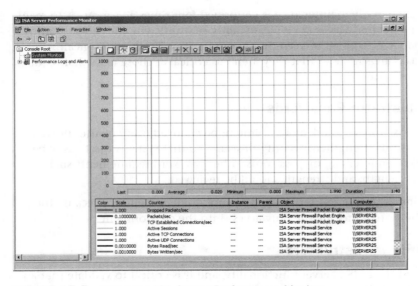

FIGURE 17.7   Using the ISA Server Performance Monitor.

If regular monitoring of the ISA server indicates that the system is getting overloaded, it can be retrofitted with additional memory, more processors, faster disks, or multiple servers that are added into the environment.

Reassess Goals and Objectives

As is often the case with IT solutions, a project's goals and objectives may change over time. ISA may have been deployed for a limited role—for example, to satisfy a certain need. Later on, however, other functionality that ISA can provide may become necessary. It can be quite advantageous to reevaluate goals and objectives on a quarterly basis to see whether any of the additional functionality that ISA provides can satisfy them.

The reason this reassessment is important for an environment is because in many cases, an ISA server that has been deployed simply sits in one place, doing its job, and the fact that it can be utilized for other functionality often is overlooked. Organizations may go out and purchase expensive SSL/VPNs, intrusion-detection solutions, or content-caching products to satisfy newly identified needs, without realizing that a product that is currently deployed can fill those needs easily.

Summary

ISA Server 2006 was written to perform well without regular fine-tuning. Indeed, these capabilities are almost too good, as many ISA servers subsequently become neglected in favor of other "squeaky wheels" in an IT organization. For the best reliability and security of an ISA environment, however, it is important to follow best-practice maintenance guidelines to ensure that ISA continues to provide for the best performance.

Maintaining a checklist of ISA maintenance daily, weekly, monthly, and quarterly procedures, and integrating these tasks into an overarching maintenance plan for an IT environment, can go a long way to achieving the goal of a well-run and well-behaved environment.

Best Practices

▶ Include ISA maintenance procedures into a broader organization-wide plan that includes checklists and step-by-step procedures.

▶ Sign up for automatic notification of new security patches and updates with a service such as the Microsoft Security Notification Service.

▶ Test all patches and updates in an isolated prototype lab environment before deploying them on production ISA servers.

▶ Use third-party hacking tools to audit the security of an ISA environment on a quarterly basis.

▶ Keep free disk space on server volumes above 25%.

▶ Use manual or Microsoft Update methods to update the Windows operating system on an ISA server.

▶ Consider the use of a tool such as Microsoft Operations Manager (MOM) 2005/Systems Center Operations Manager 2007 to archive and report on ISA event logs.

17

CHAPTER 18

Backing Up, Restoring, and Recovering an ISA Server 2006 Environment

One of the most overlooked but necessary tasks for a security implementation such as ISA Server is performing regular backups of key system functionality. Even more important is the capability to quickly recover and restore that functionality in the event of system malfunction or failure. Although it is one of the most important features, this is often overlooked in many other security products, with disastrous consequences in some cases. Fortunately, however, ISA Server 2006 includes robust and capable methods of backing up and restoring ISA configuration or individual policy elements.

This chapter focuses on the export and import capabilities of ISA Server 2006 and how they can be leveraged to back up and restore ISA Server environments. Methods of automating scripting for these types of backups are covered, and information is provided pertaining to export and import of individual ISA rules and/or components.

Understanding ISA Server's Backup and Recovery Capabilities

ISA Server 2006 provides a flexible backup and recovery toolset that enables the entire configuration set, as well as individual elements, to be backed up or exported. Those elements can then be restored or imported back to the same firewall on the same machine or to another firewall on another machine.

The big advantage to this type of process is that a full system and OS backup is not required to restore the configuration of an ISA server. Instead, a small, Extensible Markup Language (XML) text-formatted file is all that is necessary, facilitating a wide degree of flexibility in backup and restore approaches.

Using Export and Import Functionality to Simplify Recovery

Using the export and import features of ISA Server 2006 makes it possible to preserve and recover individual components of the firewall installation. In case of a problem with a specific and known component of the system, importing the component from a trusted export is all that's necessary to restore the firewall.

Backing Up Individual ISA Components

Individual ISA components can be backed up with the export functionality built into the product. The following components can be exported:

- ▶ Entire ISA configuration
- ▶ All networks or an individual network
- ▶ All network sets or an individual network set
- ▶ All network rules or an individual network rule
- ▶ All web-chaining rules or an individual web-chaining rule
- ▶ All policy rules or an individual policy rule
- ▶ System policy
- ▶ All connectivity verifiers or an individual verifier
- ▶ Monitoring filter definitions
- ▶ All cache rules or an individual cache rule
- ▶ All content download jobs or an individual content download job
- ▶ VPN client configuration
- ▶ Remote site definition

Components that have been exported in this manner can be imported into the same firewall for recovery purposes or into another firewall for configuration purposes (cloning, mass distribution, migration from ISA Standard to Enterprise Edition or vice versa, and so on).

If the components selected for export include confidential information (user credentials, pre-shared keys or secrets, and so on), a password is required for export. This password is used to encrypt the sensitive information in the export file and is required for importing the file.

Exporting ISA Settings for Backups

One of the major improvements in ISA Server 2006 over older versions of the software is the capability to back up individual or complete ISA settings to a simple text file in Extensible Markup Language (XML) format for easy import into other servers. This functionality gives administrators much more flexibility to export individual rules or other ISA elements and then import them into additional servers or use them to restore a server.

Exporting Individual Sets of Rules

ISA Server export is not limited in scope, but can be used to export out individual rules, entire rule sets, or other specific functionality on a server. These configuration sets can subsequently be imported back into ISA Server or onto another ISA Server configuration. This includes export and import of rules and configuration from ISA Server 2006 Standard Edition to ISA Server 2006 Enterprise Edition. The advantages to this functionality are immediately obvious because individual customized elements can be backed up easily and restored at will.

To export all the firewall policy rules, perform the following steps:

1. In the ISA Server Management Console, select Firewall Policy in the console tree on the left.
2. Make sure that the Tasks tab is visible in the Tasks pane.
3. Under Related Tasks, choose Export Firewall Policy.
4. Click Next at the welcome wizard.
5. Check the box to export confidential information, enter a password, and click Next to continue.

> **NOTE**
>
> If confidential information is exported, a password is assigned to the exported file for encryption purposes. That password is required to import the file.

18

6. Enter the full path of the file to be exported and click Next, then click Finish.
7. The export process displays the dialog box shown in Figure 18.1 while it is processing. After the export completes, click OK.

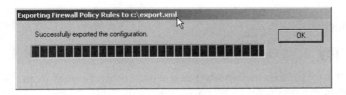

FIGURE 18.1   Exporting ISA settings.

CAUTION

Because the exported files contain sensitive information that could potentially compromise a network or system, they should be protected and stored in a safe location and deleted when they are no longer needed.

Backing Up the Entire ISA System Config to an XML File

A firewall's entire configuration can be exported for disaster protection reasons, as well as to assist with the configuration of a large number of ISA servers. Because the system policy rules are often server specific, you can export the entire server configuration with the system policy rules by using the Export feature.

To perform a backup of the ISA configuration, with all system policy rules and custom-configured rules (often used for disaster protection and recovery), perform the following steps:

1. In the ISA Server Management Console, right-click the server name in the selection tree on the left.
2. Select Export (Back Up), as shown in Figure 18.2.

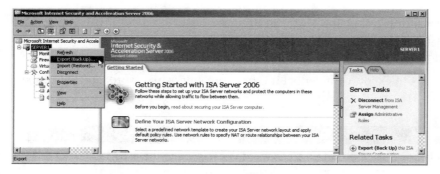

FIGURE 18.2   Backing up the ISA server configuration.

3. Click Next at the welcome wizard.
4. Check to Export confidential information; enter a password twice. If desired, select to export user permission settings as well. Click Next to continue.
5. Enter a name for the backup file and a backup location for the file. Click Next.
6. Click Finish.
7. After the backup completes, click OK.

Exporting the System Policy

The specific system policy of an ISA server can be exported as a separate component from individual firewall policy rules. This can be useful in scenarios where individual customization of the system policy on a specific ISA server needs to be exported to a separate server or backed up. To back up the system policy, perform the following actions on the ISA server:

1. From the ISA Console, click on the Firewall Policy node in the Console pane.
2. In the Tasks tab of the Tasks pane, click on the Export System Policy link under the heading System Policy Tasks.
3. Click Next on the welcome screen.
4. At the Export Preferences dialog box, as shown in Figure 18.3, check the box to encrypt the information and then enter a password twice. Click Next to continue.

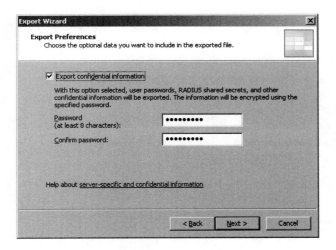

FIGURE 18.3   Backing up the system state.

5. Enter the full path and the name of the file and click Next to continue.
6. Click Finish, and then click OK when complete.

Exporting URL Sets

URL sets can be used to limit traffic destinations based on URLs. Because it is often very labor intensive to manually enter in these sets of URLs, it is often ideal to manually export and import them between ISA servers. To export all URL sets on a server, perform the following steps:

1. In the ISA Server Management Console, select Firewall Policy in the console tree.
2. Make sure that the Toolbox tab is visible in the Tasks pane.

3. Select the Network node and right-click on URL Sets. Select Export All, as shown in Figure 18.4.

FIGURE 18.4   Exporting URL sets.

4. The Export Configuration dialog box now appears. Click Next.
5. Check the box to export confidential information and enter in password information. Click Next.
6. Enter a full path and name of the XML file and click Next to continue.
7. Click Finish and then click OK when the wizard is complete.

If individual URL sets need to be exported, a similar procedure can be used to do so:

1. In the ISA Server Management Console, select Firewall Policy under the server name in the selection tree on the left.
2. Make sure that the Toolbox tab is visible on the right action bar.
3. Select the Network Objects bar and expand URL Sets. Right-click the URL set to be exported (URL sets must be previously established for this procedure to work) and select Export Selected.
4. The Export wizard now appears. Click Next.

5. Choose whether to export confidential information and if so, provide a password that will be used to encrypt the confidential information. Click Next.

6. Enter a filename for the export file. Click Next.

7. Click Finish.

The automatic import and export of URL sets can greatly ease the administrative burden of managing lists of websites for specific ISA rules and configuration.

Importing ISA Settings for Restores

Just as easily as information can be exported from ISA Server, it can be imported back in. The portability and flexibility that this type of process gives ISA administrators greatly eases the administrative burden associated with managing settings such as firewall rules, URL sets, and general ISA configuration.

Importing Individual ISA Components

To import individual ISA components, use the Import entry in the Tasks pane. This option allows for individual elements, such as network rules, firewall rules, URL sets, or other ISA components to be restored or transferred to other servers. To perform the import, do the following:

> **NOTE**
>
> If an exported rule contains information about a rule that utilizes a particular Secure Sockets Layer certificate, that certificate must also be exported and imported into the destination server.

1. Select the configuration screen for the component to be imported. Depending on which component is to be imported, this could be the Firewall Policy node, Networks node, Monitoring node, or Cache node.

2. Make sure that the Tasks tab is visible in the Tasks pane.

3. Select the Import component, labeled based on the type of import, such as Import Cache Rules, Import Firewall Policy, and the like.

4. Click Next to start the wizard.

5. Browse to and select the XML configuration file to be imported.

6. If server-specific information is to be imported, check the box on the subsequent dialog box shown in Figure 18.5. This would normally be the scenario if the same server was being restored. If, however, the information is being exported to a different server, the box would normally not be checked. Click Next to continue.

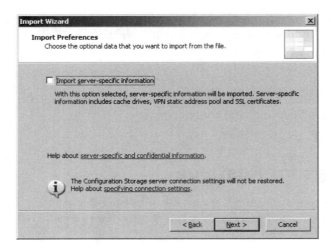

FIGURE 18.5   Importing individual ISA elements.

7. If user permission settings are selected (this option is available only if the selected file was exported with user permission settings), enter the password required to decrypt the information and click Next.

8. Click Finish.

9. When the import process completes, click OK.

Importing Entire ISA Configs

The entire configuration of an ISA server can be imported onto a server to clone a configuration to another server, restore a server to a prior state, or assist with disaster recovery. After following the steps previously outlined to export the configuration, perform the following to import that information:

> **CAUTION**
>
> Running the Import wizard allows for two options; the first option is to Import, or merge the information with the existing ISA information. The second option is to Overwrite, which will remove all previous information on the ISA server. Be cautious when choosing because the Overwrite option cannot be reversed after the settings have been applied.

1. Right-click on the server name in the navigation tree. Select Import (Restore).

2. Click Next at the welcome screen.

3. Enter the file path and name and click Next to continue.

4. On the next dialog box, shown in Figure 18.6, select whether to import or overwrite the current settings, taking to mind that the Overwrite option will permanently remove current settings. Click Next to continue.

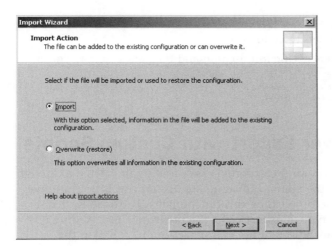

FIGURE 18.6   Running the Import wizard.

5. At the subsequent dialog box, click Yes to confirm that you are aware of the over-write nature of the import process.

6. Select the configuration file to be imported.

7. Configure options for importing user permission settings and cache drive settings as appropriate.

8. If user permission settings are selected (this option is available only if the selected file was exported with user permission settings), enter the password required to decrypt the information and click OK.

NOTE

If the configuration was exported with certificate information and is then imported into a computer with different certificates, the firewall service fails to start. To correct this problem, export the original certificate(s) and import them to the new computer.

Importing URL Sets

As previously mentioned, it is highly valuable to be able to import specific URL sets, which can be used to limit traffic destinations based on URLs. Through mass import and export, the administrative overhead associated with importing lists of URLs is greatly decreased.

To import all URL sets from the export XML file that was previously created, perform the following steps:

1. In the ISA Server Management Console, select Firewall Policy under the server name in the selection tree on the left.

2. Make sure that the Toolbox tab is visible on the right action bar.

3. Select the Network Objects bar and right-click on URL Sets. Select Import All.

18

4. At the welcome dialog box, click Next to continue.

5. Select the file containing URL sets to be imported.

6. Select whether to import server-specific information and then click Next to continue.

7. Click Finish.

8. Click OK at the conclusion of the import.

Automating ISA Server Export with Custom Scripts

Although the entire ISA configuration can be exported easily to a single XML file through the use of the export functionality, the method to automate this process is not intuitive, and there are no built-in tools for accomplishing this functionality. Fortunately, it is relatively straightforward to script this type of export using the predefined FPC scripting object. More information on the capabilities of the FPC object can be found at the following URL:

http://msdn2.microsoft.com/en-us/library/Aa489786.aspx

Creating and Deploying an ISA Server Automatic Export Script

Scripting expertise and a knowledge of the FPC object make it possible to create scripts to automate the export of specific ISA functionality. This can be extremely useful for many organizations because it takes the manual effort out of ISA server backup, making it more likely that a full backup will exist for an ISA server.

Listing 18.1 is an example of a WSF file that automates the export of the entire ISA configuration to a local or network location.

LISTING 18.1   ISA Configuration Export Job

```
<?xml version="1.0" ?>
<package>
 <job id="isaexport">
  <runtime>
    <description>
**************************************************************
ISA Configuration Export Job
**************************************************************
    </description>
      <named name="path" helpstring="The UNC or file path to which you want to
      export the configuration report to." type="string" required="1" />
      <named name="silent" helpstring="Runs script in silent mode." type="simple"
      required="0" />
    <example>
Example:
cscript isaexport.wsf /path:"\\remoteserver\sharename"
cscript isaexport.wsf /path:"c:\isabackups"
```

```vbscript
    </example>
  </runtime>
  <form>


  </form>
  <script language="VBScript">
<![CDATA[
'=====================================================================
' Comments about the script
'=====================================================================
' This script uses the FPC object to produce an export of an ISA
' configuration. As currently written, this script can be run only on
' the local ISA server from which the configuration is being
' exported. However, if the FPC object is used in conjunction
' with the FPCArray object, the script can be modified to produce a
' script that would allow for a centralized backup of all ISA servers
' in an organization. For more information about the FPC object,
' please see the following URL:
'
' http://msdn.microsoft.com/library/default.asp?url=/library/en-us
' /isasdk/isa/fpc_object.asp
'
' Please note that in all cases, usage of the FPC object is limited
' to a server that has ISA 2004/2006 or greater installed on it.
'
'=====================================================================
' Check args
'=====================================================================
If WScript.Arguments.Named.Exists("path") = FALSE Then
  WScript.Arguments.ShowUsage()
  WScript.Quit
End If

Dim WSHNetwork, objXML
Dim strPath
Dim strFileName
Dim dtmThisMinute, dtmThisHour
Dim dtmThisDay, dtmThisMonth, dtmThisYear

Set WSHNetwork = CreateObject("WScript.Network")
Set objXML = CreateObject("Msxml2.DOMDocument")

strPath = WScript.Arguments.Named("path")
```

```
dtmThisMinute = PadDigits(Minute(Now), 2)
dtmThisHour = PadDigits(Hour(Now), 2)
dtmThisDay = PadDigits(Day(Now), 2)
dtmThisMonth = PadDigits(Month(Now), 2)
dtmThisYear = Year(Now)

strFileName = WSHNetwork.ComputerName & "-" & dtmThisYear & "-" & dtmThisMonth
& "-" &_
        dtmThisDay & "-" & dtmThisHour & "-" & dtmThisMinute & ".xml"

'====================================================================
' Get export
'====================================================================
Dim objFPC
Dim objArray

' Here an instance of the FPC object is created.
Set objFPC = WScript.CreateObject("FPC.Root")

' Here, the GetContainingArray method is used, thereby obtaining an instance of the
' IFPCArray interface that represents an array that contains the
' current ISA server's configuration.
Set objArray = objFPC.GetContainingArray

' Here, using the Export method dumps the configuration for the ISA server
' into the XML object that was created.
objArray.Export objXML, 0

objXML.Save(strPath & "\" & strFileName)

If WScript.Arguments.Named.Exists("silent") = FALSE Then
  WScript.Echo("Finished export to " & strPath & "\" & strFileName)
End If


'====================================================================
' Functions
'====================================================================
' This function is used to pad date variables that contain only one
' digit.
Function PadDigits(n, totalDigits)
  If totalDigits > len(n) then
    PadDigits = String(totalDigits-len(n),"0") & n
  Else
    PadDigits = n
  End If
End Function
```

```
]]>
  </script>
 </job>
</package>
```

Note that the file can be modified as necessary to add additional variables, and to allow for functionality such as remote backup of servers or entire server arrays.

This particular script is run from the command line, and, after it is completed, automatically exports out the ISA configuration to the remote or local destination chosen, as shown in Figure 18.7.

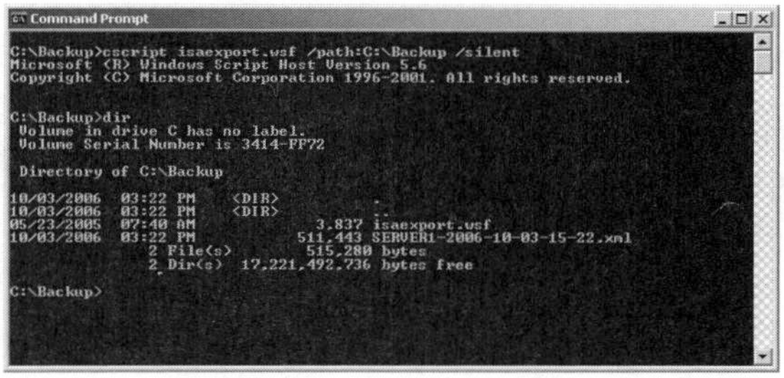

FIGURE 18.7   Running the custom automated ISA backup script.

> **NOTE**
>
> This code, as well as other snippets of code relevant to ISA Server 2006 that are referenced in this book, can be downloaded from the Sams Publishing website by searching for the book, then clicking on the Downloads link associated with the title.

Scheduling the Automatic ISA Export Script

The biggest advantage to using a script such as the one illustrated is that it can be scheduled to run weekly, daily, or even hourly backups of the ISA configuration with little overhead to the server itself. Scheduling the script to run automatically can be done with the Windows Task Scheduler service, which can be configured to run particular programs, executables, or batch files on a regular basis.

With this particular script, the Task Scheduler can be configured to run a batch file that contains the string of commands that it needs, such as the following:

```
cscript isaexport.wsf /path:C:\Backup /silent
```

This batch file simply executes the script, telling it to run silently and instructing it to export the configuration out to the C:\Backup folder. It should reside in the same folder on the ISA server as the WSF script that was created. The last step to automating this process would be to configure the Task Scheduler service to run this batch file on a regular basis.

18

NOTE

The Task Scheduler service must be running for this procedure to work properly. If the service is set to Disabled, creation of the task produces errors, and the tasks fail to run. This is often the case if the Security Configuration Wizard has been run against the server. To enable this functionality, set the service back to Automatic and start it on the ISA server.

To use the Task Scheduler to automate the ISA Configuration backups with the batch file and script, follow this procedure:

1. Go to Start, Control Panel, Scheduled Tasks, Add Scheduled Task.

2. Click Next at the Intro dialog box.

3. Click Browse to locate the batch file.

4. Browse through the folder hierarchy to locate the WSF script. When it has been located, click once on it to select it and then click Open.

5. Enter a name for the task and how often it should run, such as what is shown in Figure 18.8. Click Next.

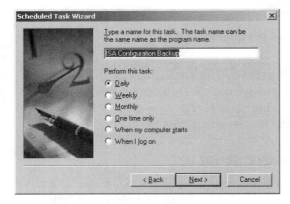

FIGURE 18.8   Scheduling an automated backup script to run on a daily basis.

6. Select a time, how often to perform the task, and a start date, and click Next.

NOTE

At the subsequent dialog box, the credentials of a user with ISA admin rights must be entered. In addition to rights to the local ISA box, this account must have the capability to save the XML config file to the location that is specified when the script is run. Because it is desirable to automate the backup of the script to a location not on the server, it might be wise to have it written to a file server on the internal network. If this is not feasible, it can be written to the local drive, as long as the system is backed up to tape or other removable media, so that it can be recovered quickly.

7. Add the username and password per the guidelines in the note, and click OK.

8. Click Finish.

If a simple yet effective schedule to automate ISA exports is set up, it becomes much easier to recover an ISA server from an up-to-date copy of the configuration.

Restoring an ISA Server from the ISA Export Script

One of the advantages to a model such as this is that up-to-date backups of all the ISA-specific settings on a server are exported on a daily (or more often) basis. If a server "dies," restoring that server can involve simply importing the config file to another cold-standby server that is installed with ISA Server 2006. In addition, the XML can be ported to any other server that is installed with ISA Server 2006, so many different recovery scenarios are possible.

For specific step-by-step instructions on how to use the XML file generated by this type of script to restore the ISA config file, reference the previous section of this chapter titled, "Importing Entire ISA Configs."

Using Traditional Backup and Restore Tools with ISA Server 2006

"Traditional" backup utilities, such as Veritas Backup Exec, ArcServ, CommVault, or even the built-in NTBackup utility, can be used to back up ISA Server 2006. These types of backup solutions do entire system backups, rather than ISA-specific backups such as XML exports, and can be useful for restoring information such as server-installed certificates and customized user settings on a server.

> **NOTE**
>
> Full-system backups done with third-party utilities are often used in addition to ISA export functionality to provide for multiple layers of backup and restore protection.

Backing Up and Restoring the ISA Server Operating System and Components

Each version of backup software has specific steps that are used to back up and restore system components. These procedures should be followed per the specific instructions provided by the product. If a third-party product is not available, the built-in NTBACKUP product that ships with Windows Server 2003 can be used. This product provides for full server backup and restore capabilities, only with a few less options than the enterprise third-party backup software available. To use NTBackup to back up an ISA server, perform the following steps:

1. Click Start, Run, and then type **NTBackup** and click OK.

2. If NTBackup has never been run before, a wizard starts. If the wizard does not start, click Backup Wizard (Advanced) from the Welcome tab.

3. When the prompt asks what will be done, select Back Up Files and Settings and click Next.

4. At the subsequent dialog box, shown in Figure 18.9, select All Information on This Computer and click Next.

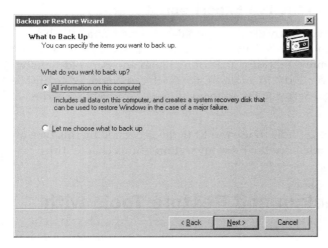

FIGURE 18.9   Using NTBackup to back up an ISA server.

5. When prompted where to place the backup file, click the Browse button and select the folder on the server or in a remote location to which the backup file will be saved. After the folder has been selected, click Save and then click Next to continue.

6. Review the information and click Finish.

7. Click Close after the backup has completed.

Restoring the information on an ISA server follows a similar procedure. If specific files need to be restored, for example, the NTBackup program can be run from the same ISA server. If, on the other hand, an entire server needs to be restored from scratch, the process is slightly different. The following high-level steps are involved with this process. A full rebuild of the ISA server, followed by a restore using the BAK backup file previously created, is necessary. Because of the complexity of this process, it is highly recommended to use the XML export and import procedures to restore ISA server whenever possible.

Summary

The backup and restore capabilities of ISA Server 2006 are vastly superior to the capabilities of its predecessors. The capability to export and import individual ISA elements, such as firewall rules, URL sets, or entire ISA configurations, gives administrators the flexibility to design straightforward and robust restore strategies. No ISA design is complete without some type of disaster recovery plan, and it is therefore fortunate that ISA Server 2006 was designed with its backup and restore capabilities.

Best Practices

▶ Use the Export and Import feature to back up individual ISA elements so that they can be ported easily to other ISA servers.

▶ Back up the ISA configuration after making network changes, rule base changes, system policy changes, firewall policy changes, or admin rights changes.

▶ To facilitate restoring a server to its original configuration, it is recommended to back up the firewall configuration immediately after installation.

▶ Automate daily backups of ISA server by using a script that takes advantage of the FPC scripting object.

▶ Back up certificates, used for publishing rules, in addition to ISA configuration.

▶ Incorporate ISA servers into an overall disaster recovery plan.

CHAPTER 19

Monitoring and Troubleshooting an ISA Server 2006 Environment

Some of the best security solutions suffer from the same problem. They offer great capabilities and functionality, but lack available tools to assist administrators with troubleshooting and monitoring of their environment.

Fortunately, the ISA development team took this into account and built in a series of robust and capable monitoring and logging tools. ISA logging, for example, provides live or archived views of network traffic that hits the ISA server, enabling administrators to make intelligent troubleshooting decisions and to have access to all pertinent information, without requiring anyone to wade through long, complex, and hard-to-manage log files.

This chapter focuses on understanding the monitoring and troubleshooting capabilities of ISA Server. It details ISA tools that are used to monitor a network environment, and provides step-by-step guides on how to use them to troubleshoot. Specific information on using Microsoft Operations Manager (MOM) 2005 or System Center Operations Manager 2007 to monitor ISA Server 2006 are also presented and discussed.

Outlining the Importance of ISA Monitoring and Logging

Without a log of what is happening on an ISA server, ISA's functionality is a real "black box," with no way to understand what is happening with the traffic, what type of errors may be occurring, or whether the server is overwhelmed or underpowered. It therefore becomes important to understand what types of tools and capabilities ISA possesses to enable the configuration to be modified as necessary and to help administrators adapt to evolving threats.

Logging for Governmental and Corporate Compliance

In addition to the troubleshooting capabilities inherent in the monitoring options in ISA Server 2006, logging access to protected resources can also help to establish an audit trail of who accessed which resources. Putting controls in place to secure and control access to network resources is also a central aspect of many governmental compliance rules that have come into the spotlight recently, such as Sarbanes-Oxley and HIPAA.

ISA provides for accurate, manageable, and auditable logging, which enables organizations to create custom reports on specific types of network activities, in response to specific threats or as a result of requested audits. This type of functionality makes it ideally suited for modern business, which requires a strict record of activities.

Taking a Proactive Approach to Intrusion Attempts

In today's risky computing atmosphere, caution simply cannot be thrown to the wind. Organizations need to be proactive in monitoring intrusion attempts by looking for activities such as port scans, authentication failures, and outright service-level attacks. If these types of activities are not proactively monitored and dealt with, they can turn into serious security issues. Fortunately, ISA Server 2006 allows for automatic detection of many forms of intrusion attempts, providing greater peace of mind.

Configuring ISA Logging and Monitoring

Most of the monitoring and logging functionality in ISA Server is provided in the Monitoring node of the console tree, as shown in Figure 19.1.

This node is the jumping-off point for the individual ISA monitoring and logging activities, and includes tabs in the Details pane for activities such as setting alerts, generating reports, monitoring sessions and services, and logging traffic. Before delving into the capabilities of each of these tools, it is important to properly set up the ISA Server Monitoring environment, using a best-practice approach.

Delegating ISA Monitoring Settings

In addition to the ISA Full Administrator, ISA Server 2006 also provides for unique roles that provide for unique monitoring capabilities. These roles are as follows:

- **ISA Server Monitoring Auditor**—An ISA Server Monitoring Auditor has the ability to view existing dashboards and session information setup.

- **ISA Server Auditor**—An ISA Server Auditor has all the rights of a Monitoring Auditor, with the added capabilities to create alert definitions, custom dashboards, and other monitoring customizations.

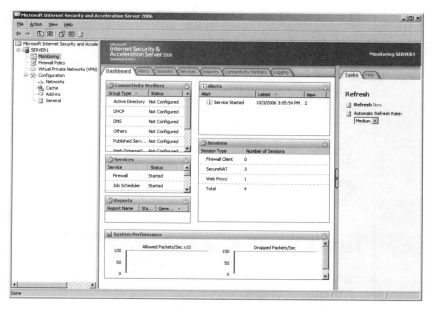

FIGURE 19.1   Viewing the ISA Monitoring node.

If administration of the monitoring aspect of ISA Server is required, then it becomes necessary to delegate these roles to individual users or, preferably, groups. To delegate control of ISA Auditing to a group, for example, follow these steps:

1. From the ISA Administration Console, click on the server name in the console tree to select it.

2. In the Tasks tab of the Tasks pane, click on Assign Administrative Roles.

3. Under the Assign Roles tab, click Add.

4. Enter the group name (or click Browse to locate) that will be used, such as COMPANYABC\AG-ISA-Auditor, choose ISA Server Auditor from the list of roles, as shown in Figure 19.2, and click OK.

5. Click Next to continue.

6. Click Finish, Apply, and OK.

Understanding the ISA Advanced Logging Service

ISA Server 2006 logging is comprised of two unique types of logs as follows:

▶ Firewall logging

▶ Web Proxy logging

Each one of these logging services is independently controlled and can be enabled and configured differently.

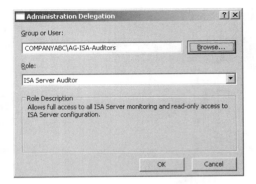

FIGURE 19.2   Delegating ISA Server Monitoring rights.

TIP

In general, it is best practice to configure ISA logs to reside on a separate logical drive from the operating system, but it is not required. There is no effective performance increase from having them on a separate physical drive.

The logs themselves can be stored in three unique formats, as shown in Figure 19.3 and listed as follows:

▶ **MSDE database**—The Microsoft Data Engine (MSDE) format allows for SQL-type database functionality without SQL licensing or operations costs. Although MSDE

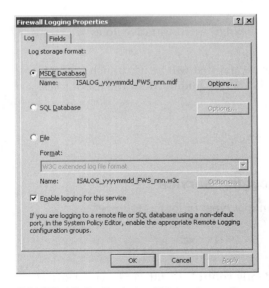

FIGURE 19.3   Exploring ISA logging options.

has a 2GB limit for the database files, ISA creates new files as necessary for logging, and the entire sum of logs can be searched when logging and troubleshooting.

▶ **File**—File-based logging saves the ISA logs to a W3C text-based format, which is often used when the ISA logs need to be parsed by third-party products.

▶ **SQL database**—The SQL database option enables an ISA server to log all the logging information to a SQL Server 2000/2005 server in the organization.

For the most advanced logging, either the MSDE or the SQL database logging component must be configured properly.

Installing the ISA Advanced Logging Service

If not already installed on an ISA server (it is one of the default installation options), ISA Server 2006 advanced logging can be set up via the Add/Remove programs process on an ISA server. Simply insert the ISA media and perform the following steps:

1. Click Start, Control Panel, Add or Remove Programs.

2. From the list of installed programs, select Microsoft ISA Server 2006 and click Change/Remove.

3. Click Next at the Welcome dialog box.

4. Select Modify from the dialog box shown in Figure 19.4 and click Next.

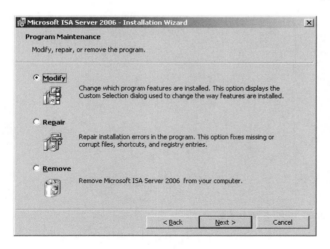

FIGURE 19.4   Adding the Advanced Logging component to ISA.

5. Under Firewall Services, drill down to Advanced Logging, left-click, and choose This Feature, and All Subfeatures, Will Be Installed on Local Hard Drive. Click Next to continue.

6. Click Install.

7. Click Finish when complete.

Configuring Firewall Logging

Firewall logging can be enabled and configured on the ISA server through the Logging tab in the Details pane of the ISA Monitoring node. For example, the following step-by-step procedure enables ISA Firewall logging to write up to 10GB of firewall logs to the D:\ drive, and to enable logging of all potential fields:

1. From the ISA Management Console, click on the Monitoring tab from the console tree.
2. Select the Logging tab in the Details pane.
3. Under the Tasks tab in the Tasks pane, click the link for Configure Firewall Logging.
4. Select MSDE Database and ensure that Enable Logging for This Service is checked. Click the Options button.
5. Under the location for the ISA logs, enter the folder path manually by selecting This Folder and entering the full path, as shown in Figure 19.5.

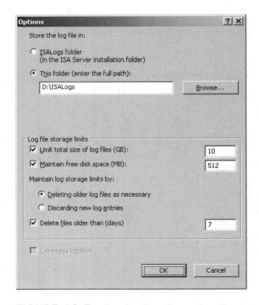

FIGURE 19.5   Configuring firewall policy logging options.

6. Under Log File Storage Limits, select to limit total size of log files to 10GB, and to maintain 512MB of free space. Click OK.
7. Select the Fields tab.
8. Click the Select All button.
9. Click OK, Apply, and OK to save the changes.

Configuring Web Proxy Logging

Web Proxy logging is very similar to Windows Firewall logging, but deals specifically with logging requests made from Web Proxy clients, whereas the firewall logs deal with SecureNAT clients. The same options exist for configuring Web Proxy logging, and the same basic procedure applies. It is important to note that the number of fields that are available for the Web Proxy logging service, as shown in Figure 19.6, differs from the Firewall Proxy fields.

FIGURE 19.6   Configuring SMTP Screener Logging components.

Logging ISA Traffic

One of the most powerful troubleshooting tools at the disposal of ISA administrators is the logging mechanism, which gives live or archived views of the logs on an ISA server, and allows for quick and easy searching and indexing of ISA Server log information, including every packet of data that hits the ISA server.

> **NOTE**
>
> Many of the advanced features of ISA logging are available only when MSDE or SQL databases are used for the storage of the logs.

Examining ISA Logs

The ISA logs are accessible via the Logging tab in the Details pane of the Monitoring node, as shown in Figure 19.7. They enable administrators to watch, in real time, what is happening to the ISA server, whether it is denying connections, and what rule is being applied for each Allow or Deny statement.

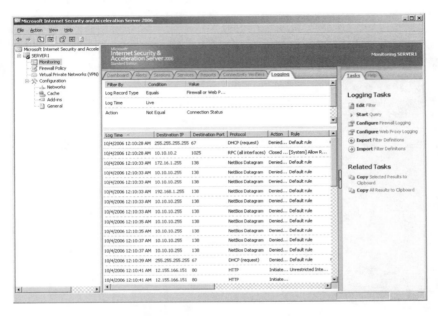

FIGURE 19.7   Examining ISA logging.

The logs include pertinent information on each packet of data, including the following key characteristics:

- ▶ **Log Time**—The exact time the packet was processed.

- ▶ **Destination IP**—The packet's destination IP address.

- ▶ **Destination Port**—The destination TCP/IP port, such as port 80 for HTTP traffic.

- ▶ **Protocol**—The specific protocol that the packet utilized, such as HTTP, LDAP, RPC, or others.

- ▶ **Action**—What type of action the ISA server took on the traffic, such as initiating the connection or denying it.

- ▶ **Rule**—Which particular firewall policy rule applied to the traffic.

- ▶ **Client IP**—The IP address of the client that sent the packet.

- ▶ **Client Username**—The username of the requesting client. Note that this is populated only if the Firewall client is being used.

▶ **Source Network**—The source network from which the packet came.

▶ **Destination Network**—The network where the destination of the packet is located.

▶ **HTTP Method**—If it is HTTP traffic, this column displays the type of HTTP method utilized, such as GET or POST.

▶ **URL**—If HTTP is used, this column displays the exact URL that was requested.

Searching through the logs for specific criteria identified in these columns, such as all packets sent by a specific IP address, or all URLs that match http://mail.companyabc.com, simplifies advanced troubleshooting and monitoring.

Customizing Logging Filters

What is displayed in the Details pane of the Logging tab is a reflection of only those logs that match certain criteria in the log filter. It is highly useful to use the filter to weed out the extraneous log entries that just distract from the specific monitoring task. For example, on many networks, an abundance of NetBIOS broadcast traffic makes it difficult to read the logs. For this reason, a specific filter can be created to show only traffic that is not NetBIOS traffic. To set up this particular type of rule, do the following:

1. From the ISA Administration Console, click on the Monitoring node from the console tree and select the Logging tab in the Details pane.

2. From the Tasks tab in the Tasks pane, click the link for Edit Filter.

3. In the Edit Filter dialog box, change the Filter By, Condition, and Value fields to display Protocol, Not Equal, NetBios Datagram, and click Add to List.

4. Repeat for the NetBios Name Service and the NetBios Session values, so that the dialog box looks like the one displayed in Figure 19.8.

5. Click Start Query.

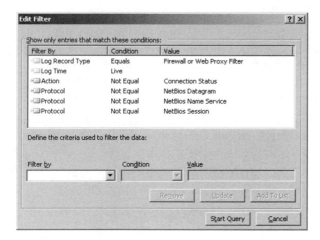

FIGURE 19.8   Creating a custom logging filter.

NOTE

It cannot be stressed enough that this logging mechanism is quite literally the best tool for troubleshooting ISA access. For example, it can be used to tell whether traffic from clients is even hitting the ISA server, and if it is, what is happening to it (denied, accepted, and so on).

Monitoring ISA from the ISA Console

In addition to the robust Logging mechanism, the ISA Monitoring node also contains various tabs that link to other extended troubleshooting and monitoring tools. Each of these tools performs unique functions, such as generating reports, alerting administrators, or verifying connectivity to critical services. It is therefore important to understand how each of these tools works.

Customizing the ISA Dashboard

The ISA dashboard, shown in Figure 19.1, provides for quick and comprehensive monitoring of a multitude of ISA components from a single screen. The view is customizable, and clicking on the Arrow buttons in the upper-right corner of individual components expands or collapses them. All the individual ISA Monitoring elements are summarized here.

TIP

The ISA dashboard is the logical "parking" page for ISA administrators, who can leave the screen set at the dashboard to allow for quick-glance views of ISA health.

Monitoring and Customizing Alerts

The Alerts tab, shown in Figure 19.9, lists all the status alerts that ISA has generated while it has been in operation. It is beneficial to look through these alerts on a regular basis, and acknowledge them when it's no longer necessary to display them on the dashboard. If alerts need to be permanently removed, they can be reset instead. Resetting or acknowledging alerts is as simple as right-clicking on them and choosing Reset or Acknowledge.

Alerts that show up in this list are listed because their default alert definition specified an action to display them in the console. This type of alert behavior is completely customizable, and alerts can be made to perform the following actions:

▶ Send email

▶ Run a program

▶ Report to Windows Event log

▶ Stop Selected Services

▶ Start Selected Services

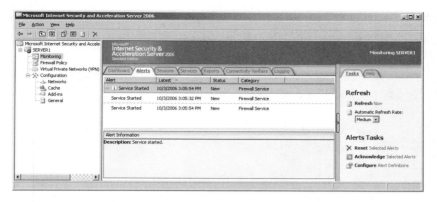

FIGURE 19.9   Viewing the ISA Alerts tab.

For example, it may be necessary to force a stop of the firewall service if a specific type of attack is detected. Configuring alert definitions is relatively straightforward. For example, the following process illustrates how to create an alert that sends an email to an administrator when a SYN attack is detected:

1. From the Alerts tab of the ISA Monitoring node, select the Tasks tab in the Tasks pane.

2. Click the link for Configure Alert Definitions.

3. Under the Alert definitions dialog box, shown in Figure 19.10, choose SYN Attack and click Edit.

4. Choose the Actions tab from the SYN Attack Properties dialog box.

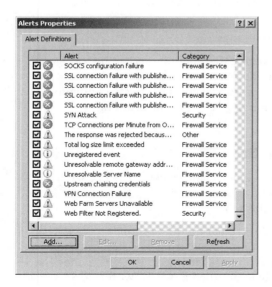

FIGURE 19.10   Creating a custom alert definition.

5. Check the Send E-mail box.

6. Enter the SMTP Server in the organization field, then enter the information in the From, To, and CC fields, similar to what is shown in Figure 19.11.

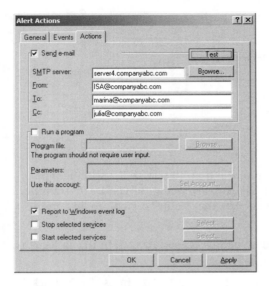

FIGURE 19.11   Modifying a custom alert definition.

7. Click the Test button to try the settings, and then click OK to acknowledge a successful test.

8. Click OK, OK, Apply, and OK to save the settings.

As is evident from the list, a vast number of existing Alert definitions can be configured, and a large number of thresholds can be set. In addition, clicking the Add button on the Alerts Properties dialog box and following the wizard makes it possible to configure customized alerts. This allows for an even greater degree of personalization.

Monitoring Session and Services Activity

The Services tab, shown in Figure 19.12, offers a quick-glance view of the ISA Services: whether they are running and how long they have been up since last being restarted. The services can also be stopped and started from this tab.

The Sessions tab allows for more interaction: Individual unique sessions to the ISA server can be viewed and disconnected as necessary. For example, it may be necessary to disconnect any users who are on a VPN connection if a change to the VPN policy has just been issued. VPN clients that have already established a session with the ISA server are subject to the laws of only the VPN policy that was in effect when they originally

FIGURE 19.12   Monitoring ISA Services.

logged in. To disconnect a session, right-click on it and choose Disconnect Session, as shown in Figure 19.13.

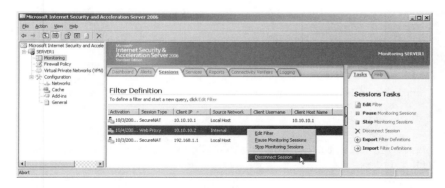

FIGURE 19.13   Disconnecting a session.

Creating Connectivity Verifiers

Connectivity verifiers can be a useful way of extending ISA's capabilities to include monitoring of critical services within an environment, such as DNS, DHCP, HTTP, or other custom services. Connectivity verifiers are essentially a "quick and dirty" approach to monitoring an environment with very little cost because they take advantage of ISA's alerting capabilities and the dashboard to display the verifiers.

For example, the following step-by-step process illustrates setting up a connectivity verifier that checks the status of an internal web server:

1. In the Monitoring tab of the ISA Console, click on the Connectivity Verifiers tab of the Details pane.

2. In the Tasks tab of the Tasks pane, click the Create New Connectivity Verifier link.

3. Enter a name for the connectivity verifier, such as Web Server Verifier, and click Next.

19

4. Under the Connectivity Verification Details dialog box, enter the server FQDN, the Group type (which simply determines how it is grouped on the dashboard), and what type of verification method to use—in this case, an HTTP GET request, as shown in Figure 19.14.

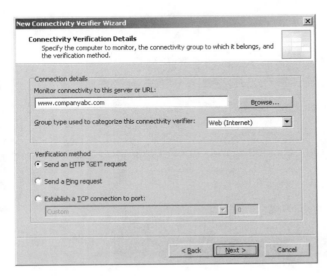

FIGURE 19.14   Configuring an HTTP connectivity verifier.

5. Click Finish.

6. Click Yes when prompted to turn on the rule that allows ISA Server to connect via HTTP to selected servers.

7. Click Apply and OK.

After they are created, connectivity verifiers that fit into the major group types are reflected on the dashboard. Creating multiple connectivity verifiers in each of the common group types can make the dashboard a more effective monitoring tool.

Generating Reports with ISA Server

ISA Server 2006 has excellent reporting capabilities that take advantage of the logging mechanisms in place. By default, a number of useful reports are included in ISA Server, as follows:

▶ **Web Usage Report**—A Web Usage Report illustrates which users and client systems are the top web users, which sites are accessed most often, what types of browsers and operating systems are used, and what types of objects are being accessed.

▶ **Application Usage Report**—The Application Usage Report gives information on which protocols are used most often, what destinations are being used, and what types of client applications and operating systems are used.

▶ **Traffic and Utilization Report**—This report details network traffic by protocol and also indicates how effective the content caching is.

▶ **Security Report**—The Security Report lists users who most often have authorization failures and dropped packets. This can help to triangulate the source of attacks.

▶ **Summary Report**—The Summary Report lists the top information from each type of report and summarizes it into a single report.

The reports are generated in HTML and can be saved to other network locations on a scheduled basis. They can be a very effective tool in discovering useful information about a network.

Customizing Reports

Each one of the default report types can be customized directly from the Tasks tab of the Reports area. Clicking on the Customize links makes available settings such as the ones shown in Figure 19.15. For example, the top users could be modified to display only the top 10, or expanded to include the top 20.

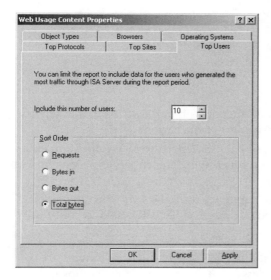

FIGURE 19.15   Customizing report content.

Generating Reports

Generating a report in ISA Server is another straightforward task, which can be kicked off via a wizard process. For example, to create a one-time summary report, do the following:

1. In the ISA Console, select the Monitoring node, then select the Reports tab from the Details pane.

2. From the Tasks tab of the Tasks pane, click the link for Generate a New Report.

3. Enter a descriptive name, such as ISA Summary Report, and click Next.

4. Under the type of content to include, check only Summary, as shown in Figure 19.16, and click Next to continue.

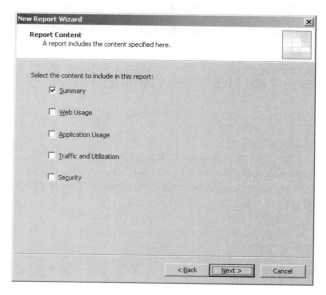

FIGURE 19.16   Creating a summary report.

5. Enter the Start and End Date from which the report will pull data. Note that reports can pull data out of only dates in the past, and not the current date.

6. Under Reports Publishing, check the box to Publish Reports to a Directory and enter a UNC path to which the report is to be saved, entering credentials as necessary to write the file. Click Next to continue.

7. The Send E-mail Notification dialog box enables emails to be sent when the report is generated. This is optional, and is skipped in this example. Click Next to continue.

8. Click Finish.

After creating the report, wait for the report's status to change from Generating to Completed (press F5 to refresh the screen if necessary). To view the report, as shown in Figure 19.17, double-click on the report name in the Details pane.

Scheduling Report Generation

Another great advantage to ISA reports is that they can be scheduled to run daily, weekly, or monthly on a scheduled basis. By automating this type of information, administrators and management can get consistent, updated, useful information on the traffic that ISA is processing.

1. From the Tasks tab of the Tasks pane, click the link for Create and Configure Report Jobs.

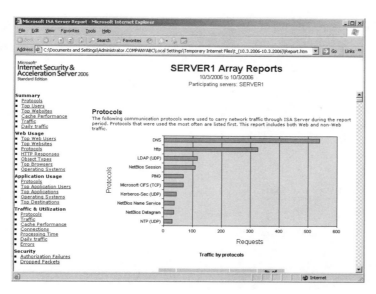

FIGURE 19.17   Viewing a summary report.

2. Click Add.

3. Enter a descriptive Report Job name, such as Weekly ISA Full Report, and click Next.

4. Select which reports are to be included by checking them (all are chosen by default) and click Next.

5. Under Run This Report Job, select Weekly, and choose Sunday as the day, as shown in Figure 19.18.

6. Under Publish Reports to a Directory, check the box and enter a UNC path of a server to which the HTML file should be saved. If credentials are needed, enter them by checking the box to Publish Using This Account. Click Next to continue.

7. Enter email notification information, if desired, and click Next to continue.

8. Click Finish, OK, Apply, and OK.

Monitoring ISA Server 2006 Health and Performance with Microsoft Operations Manager (MOM)

The ultimate monitoring strategy for ISA Server 2006 involves the use of the Microsoft Operations Manager (MOM) 2005 product. MOM 2005 offers an unprecedented level of proactive management and monitoring capabilities that enable administrators to react to problems and recover from them more quickly. An understanding of ISA monitoring concepts is not complete without an understanding of how MOM 2005 can fit into the overall ISA monitoring strategy. Recently, the new version of MOM has been released as Operations Manager (OpsMgr) 2007, which has the same general concepts as MOM 2005, with some advanced monitoring features added.

19

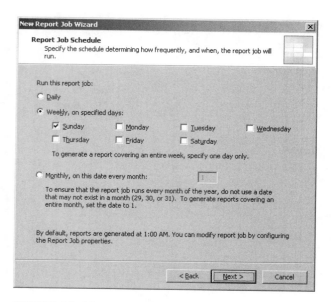

FIGURE 19.18   Scheduling a report.

Taking a Close Look at Microsoft Operations Manager (MOM)

MOM 2005 is the latest version of Microsoft's enterprise monitoring product. Previously owned by NetIQ and then sold to Microsoft, the product has evolved from the MOM 2000 version to the latest, most capable 2005 version.

MOM provides for several major pieces of functionality, as follows:

▶ **Event log consolidation**—MOM agents, deployed on managed systems, forward all event log information to a central MOM SQL Server database, which is managed and groomed by MOM. This data is used for reporting, auditing, and monitoring of the specific events.

▶ **Advanced alerting capabilities**—MOM provides advanced alerting functionality by enabling email alerts, paging, and functional alerting roles to be defined.

▶ **Performance monitoring**—MOM collects performance statistics that can let an administrator know whether a server is being overloaded or is close to running out of disk space, among other things.

▶ **Built-in application-specific intelligence**—MOM management packs are packages of information about a particular application or service, such as DNS, DHCP, Exchange Server, or ISA Server. The Microsoft management packs are written by the design teams for each individual product, and they are loaded with the intelligence and information necessary to properly troubleshoot and identify problems. For example, the ISA Server 2006 management pack knows that Event ID 11005 is a VPN configuration error, and it specifically directs an administrator to the proper location on the web where Microsoft Knowledge Base articles can be used for troubleshooting.

MOM architecture can be complex, but often is as simple as a SQL database running on a server, with another server providing the management server functions of MOM. This type of server is also known as a DCAM server.

Downloading and Extracting the ISA Server 2006 Management Pack for MOM 2005

As previously mentioned, management packs contain intelligence about specific applications and services and include troubleshooting information specific to those services. Shortly after the release of the Enterprise version of ISA Server 2006, Microsoft released a MOM management pack that covers both the Standard and Enterprise versions of both ISA 2000 and ISA Server 2006. This management pack is highly recommended for MOM environments.

To install the ISA Server 2006 management pack on the MOM management server, first download it from the Microsoft ISA Downloads page at the following URL:

http://www.microsoft.com/technet/isa/2006/downloads/default.mspx

To install the management pack on the MOM management server, do the following:

1. Double-click on the downloaded executable.

2. Select I Agree to the License Agreement and click Next to continue.

3. Select a location to which to extract the management pack, such as what is shown in Figure 19.19, and then click Next.

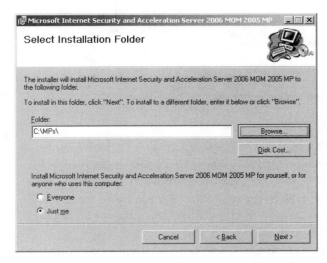

FIGURE 19.19   Extracting the ISA MOM management pack.

4. Click Next again to start the installation.

5. Click Close when the file extraction is complete.

Importing the Management Pack File into MOM 2005

After it is extracted, the following steps can be taken to upload the management pack file directly into the MOM Administrator Console:

1. From the MOM server, open the MOM Administrator Console (Start, All Programs, Microsoft Operations Manager 2005, Administrator Console).

2. Navigate to the Management Packs node.

3. Click the Import/Export Management Packs link, as shown in Figure 19.20.

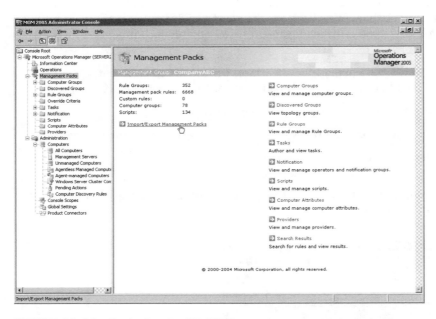

FIGURE 19.20   Beginning the ISA MOM management pack import process.

4. At the Welcome dialog box, click Next to continue.

5. From the Import or Export Management Packs dialog box, select to Import Management Packs and/or reports and click Next to continue.

6. From the subsequent dialog box, type in the folder (or click Browse to locate it) where the files from the previous steps were extracted, select to import management packs only, and click Next to continue.

7. From the Select Management Packs dialog box, select the most updated ISA management pack from the list and check the radio button to Replace Existing Management Pack. Uncheck the button to back up the existing management pack as there isn't one installed. Click Next to continue.

8. Click Finish.

9. After the import has completed, click Close.

Configuring MOM Settings

Because ISA is a firewall, it is very picky about what type of traffic it allows. For this reason, it is best to perform a manual install of the MOM agent on the ISA server. Before this can be done, the MOM global settings need to be modified to allow for manual agent installations. To do so, perform the following steps:

1. From the MOM Administrator Console, navigate to Administration, Global Settings.

2. Double-click on Management Servers.

3. Select the Agent Install tab.

4. Uncheck the box labeled Reject New Manual Agent Installations, as shown in Figure 19.21.

5. Click OK.

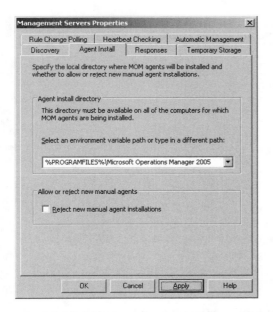

FIGURE 19.21   Configuring MOM agent settings for ISA.

Configuring MOM Global Settings for Non–Domain Member ISA Servers

For ISA servers that are not domain members, there is an additional step that must be undertaken before the MOM agent can be installed successfully. In this scenario, do the following:

CAUTION

Perform these steps only if the ISA server is not a domain member. They downgrade the client/server security in the MOM environment.

---

1. From the Global Settings node in the MOM Admin Console, double-click on the Security tab.
2. On the Security tab, shown in Figure 19.22, uncheck the box for Mutual Authentication Required.

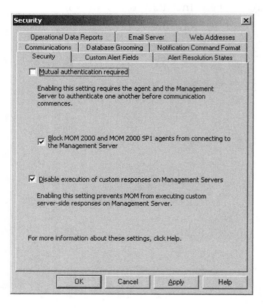

FIGURE 19.22   Configuring MOM security settings for ISA.

3. Click OK.
4. When prompted with the warning about turning off mutual authentication, click OK.
5. Restart the MOM service on all management servers.

Configuring ISA to Allow MOM Communications

1. From the ISA Server Management Console, click on the Firewall Policy node in the console tree.
2. Click the Edit System Policy link in the Tasks tab of the Tasks pane.

3. Under the Remote Monitoring section, select Microsoft Operations Manager.

4. Click the checkbox to enable the configuration group.

5. Select the To tab and click Add under the section This Rule Applies to Traffic Sent to These Destinations.

6. Enter MOM (or a similar name) in the Name column, the IP address of the MOM Management server, and a description if necessary and click OK.

7. In the Add Network Entities dialog, expand Computers, select the MOM server, and click Add and Close.

8. Remove any other entries from the selection box, and then click OK, Apply, and OK to save the changes.

This procedure should be replaced with one using the new MOM system policy rule. This would not require defining any custom protocols. The steps are as follows:

1. From the ISA Server Management Console, click on the Firewall Policy node in the console tree.

2. Click the Edit System Policy link in the Tasks tab of the Tasks pane.

3. Under the Remote Monitoring section, select Microsoft Operations Manager.

4. Click the checkbox to enable the configuration group.

5. Select the To tab and click Add under the section This Rule Applies to Traffic Sent to These Destinations.

6. Enter MOM (or a similar name) in the Name column, the IP address of the MOM Management server, and a description if necessary, as shown in Figure 19.24, and click OK.

7. In the Add Network Entities dialog, expand Computers, select the MOM server, and click Add and Close.

8. Remove any other entries from the selection box, and then click OK, Apply, and OK to save the changes.

Installing the MOM Agent on the ISA Server

After all prerequisites have been satisfied, the actual MOM agent installation on the ISA server can begin. To start the process, do the following:

1. From the MOM 2005 CD (or a network location), double-click on the \i386\MOMAgent.msi file.

2. At the Welcome screen, click Next to continue.

3. At the Destination Folder dialog box, click Next to continue.

4. Enter the Management Group Name and Management Server name; they are listed in the MOM environment. Leave the port unchanged at 1260 and the Agent Control Level at None, as shown in Figure 19.23. Click Next to continue.

19

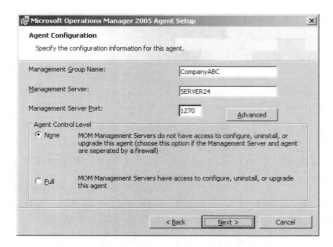

FIGURE 19.23   Manually installing the MOM agent.

5. Select Local System as the MOM Agent Action Account and click Next to continue.
6. Under Active Directory Configuration, select Yes if the ISA server is a domain member, or select No if it is not a domain member. Click Next to continue.
7. Click Install.
8. Click Finish.

After installation, it may be necessary to wait a few minutes before processing the agent installation. After waiting, do the following to process the pending installation request:

1. From the MOM Administrator Console, Expand Administration, Computers, Pending Actions.
2. Look for the Manual Agent Install Request from the ISA server, right-click it, and choose Approve Manual Agent Installation Now, as shown in Figure 19.24.
3. Click Yes to confirm.

Monitoring ISA Functionality and Performance with MOM

After the management pack is installed for ISA and the agent has been installed and is communicating, MOM consolidates and reacts to every event and performance counter sent to it from the ISA server. This information is reflected in the MOM Operations Console, as shown in Figure 19.25.

Performance data for ISA, such as what is shown in Figure 19.26, can also be displayed in MOM. This allows reports and performance metrics to be obtained from ISA.

For more information on MOM 2005, see the Microsoft website at the following URL:

http://www.microsoft.com/mom

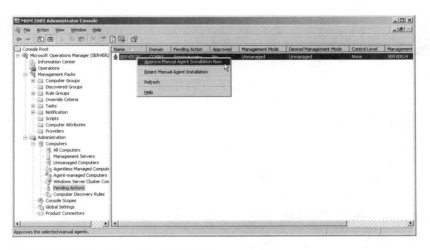

FIGURE 19.24 Approving the MOM agent install.

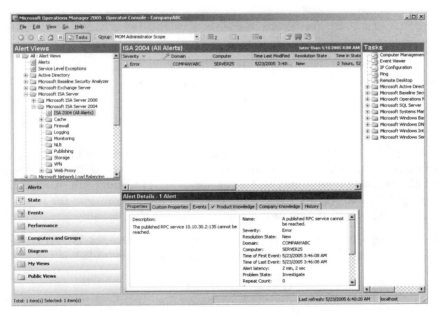

FIGURE 19.25 Viewing ISA alerts.

Monitoring ISA with Windows Performance Monitor (Perfmon)

ISA Server 2006 comes with several predefined performance counters that take advantage of the Windows Performance Monitor (perfmon) utility. These counters can be useful for checking to see whether an ISA server is being overwhelmed. To run the Performance

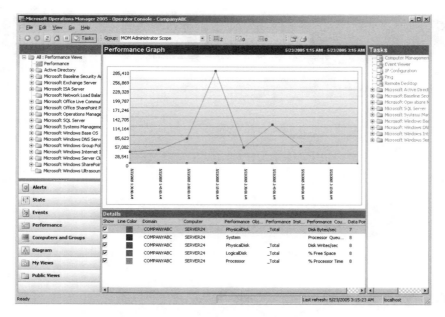

FIGURE 19.26   Viewing server performance in MOM.

Monitor application with preconfigured ISA counters, simply click Start, All Programs, Microsoft ISA Server, ISA Server Performance Monitor.

Summary

The ISA server developers did not disappoint when it came to developing the monitoring and troubleshooting tools made available to administrators. Using advanced logging to an MSDE or SQL database allows for advanced report generation, fast indexing and searching, and real-time logging. ISA alerts, connectivity verifiers, session monitoring, and the ISA dashboard also provide for excellent "out of the box" monitoring functionality.

In addition to monitoring with the ISA tools, Microsoft Operations Manager (MOM) 2005 can allow for proactive management and troubleshooting capabilities in an ISA Server environment.

Best Practices

▶ Use Advanced ISA logging to an MSDE or SQL database to take advantage of the real-time logging and searching capabilities that this type of logging allows.

▶ Use the logging mechanism to troubleshoot connectivity problems and errors with firewall policy rules.

► Reset VPN sessions from the Sessions tab of the Monitoring node if changes are made to the VPN policy.

► Use Microsoft Operations Manager (MOM) 2005 or the more recent System Center Operations Manager 2007 product with the ISA Server 2006 management pack to monitor an ISA Server 2006 environment whenever possible.

► Make use of connectivity verifiers to provide "quick glance" views of critical network services.

Documenting an ISA Server 2006 Environment

One of the most commonly skipped but important tasks in an ISA deployment project is the documentation of the design and functionality elements of an ISA Server environment. It is one thing to deploy an ISA server to address specific needs, but it is quite another to try to decipher why a particular ISA design was put into place or what an ISA server does years after it goes into place. Best practice dictates that the design, implementation, and functionality of an ISA server is incorporated into easy-to-understand and readily available documentation that can be accessed for disaster recovery purposes or during security audits.

This chapter outlines key best-practice documentation techniques that can be used to formalize the design and implementation of an ISA environment. Specific table of contents and document examples are shown, and documentation recommendations are given. In addition, this chapter also includes examples of a custom script that can be created to export firewall policy rules for documentation purposes.

Understanding the Benefits of ISA Server Documentation

Some of the benefits of documentation are immediate and tangible, whereas others can be harder to pin down. The process of putting the information down on paper encourages a level of analysis and review of the topic at hand that helps to clarify the goals and contents of the document. This process should also encourage teamwork and collaboration within the organization, as well as interdepartmental exchange of ideas.

For example, an ISA server maintenance document that details downtime for an individual SMTP publishing rule might be reviewed by the marketing manager who is concerned about the company's capability to send out emails to the existing and potential client base during the scheduled periods of downtime. The CIO or IT director should review the document as well to make sure that the maintenance process meets his or her concerns, such as meeting an aggressive service-level agreement (SLA).

Consequently, documentation that has specific goals, is well organized and complete, and goes through a review or approval process should contribute to the overall professionalism of the organization and its knowledge base. The following sections examine some of the other benefits of professional documentation in the ISA Server environment.

Using Documentation for Knowledge Management

Quite simply, proper documentation enables an organization to better organize and manage its data and intellectual property. Rather than having the company's policies and procedures in a dozen places, such as individual files for each department or, worst of all, in the minds of many individuals, consolidating this information into logical groupings can be beneficial.

A design document that details the decisions made pertaining to an ISA Server 2006 deployment project can consolidate and summarize the key discussions and decisions, as well as budgetary concerns, timing issues, and the like. In addition, there will be one document to turn to if questions emerge at a later date.

Similarly, if a service-level agreement is created and posted where it can be accessed by any interested parties, it should be very clear what the network users can expect from the ISA server infrastructure in terms of uptime or prescheduled downtimes.

A document that describes the specific configuration details of a certain server or type of server might prove to be very valuable to a manager in another company office when making a purchasing decision. The documents also must be readily available so that they can be found when needed, especially in the case of disaster recovery documents. Also, it's handy to have them available in a number of formats, such as hard copy, in the appropriate place on the network, and even via an intranet.

CAUTION

It is important to find a balance between making sure the documentation is readily available and making sure that it is kept completely secure. ISA Server documentation contains particularly sensitive information about the security structure of an environment. Placement of ISA documentation is therefore key: It should be kept in locations that are readily accessible in the event of an emergency, but that also are highly secured.

By simply having these documents available and centralizing them, an organization can more easily determine the effects of changes to the environment and track those changes. Part of the knowledge-management process needs to be change management, so that although the information is available to everyone, only authorized individuals can make changes to the documents.

Using Documentation to Outline the Financial Benefits of ISA

Proper ISA Server documentation can be time consuming and adds to infrastructure and project costs. It is often difficult to justify the expense of project documentation. However, when the documents are needed, such as in maintenance or disaster recovery scenarios, it is easy to determine that creating this documentation makes financial sense. For example, in an organization where downtime can cost thousands of dollars per minute, the return on investment (ROI) on disaster recovery and maintenance documentation is easy to calculate. Likewise, in a company that is growing rapidly and adding staff and new servers on a regular basis, tested documentation on server builds and administration training can also have immediate and visible benefits.

Well thought-out and professional design and planning documentation should help the organization avoid costly mistakes in the implementation or migration process, such as buying too many server licenses or purchasing too many servers.

Baselining ISA with Document Comparisons

Baselining is a process of recording the state of an ISA Server 2006 system so that any changes in its performance can be identified at a later date. Baselining also pertains to the overall network performance, including WAN links, but in those cases, special software and tools (such as sniffers) may be required to record the information.

An ISA Server 2006 system baseline document records the state of the server after it is implemented in a production environment and can include statistics such as memory utilization, paging, disk subsystem throughput, and more. This information then enables the administrator or appropriate IT resource to determine how the system is performing in comparison to initial operation.

Using Documentation for ISA Troubleshooting

Troubleshooting documentation is helpful both in terms of the processes that the company recommends for resolving technical issues, and in documenting the results of actual troubleshooting challenges. Often companies have a database and trouble-ticket processes in place to record the time a request was made for assistance, the process followed, and the results. This information should then be available to the appropriate support staff so they know the appropriate resolution if the problem comes up again.

Organizations may also choose to document troubleshooting methodologies to use as training aids and also to ensure that specific steps are taken as a standard practice for quality of service to the user community.

20

Understanding the Recommended Types of Documentation

There are several main types of documentation, including the following:

- ▶ Historical/planning (who made which decision)
- ▶ Support and maintenance (to assist with maintaining the hardware and software on the network)
- ▶ Policy (service-level agreements)
- ▶ Training (for end users or administrators)

It is also critical that any documentation produced be reviewed by other stakeholders in the organization to make sure that it meets their needs as well, and to simply get input from other sources. For technical procedures, the document also must be tested and "walked through." With a review process of this sort, the document will be more useful and more accurate. For example, a server build document that has gone through this process (that is, reviewed by the IT manager and security administrator) is more likely to be complete and useful in case the server in question needs to be rebuilt in an emergency.

Documentation that is not historical and that is intended to be used for supporting the network environment or to educate on company policies should be reviewed periodically to make sure that it is still accurate and reflects the current corporate policies and processes.

The discipline of creating effective documentation that satisfies the requirements of the appropriate support personnel as well as management is also an asset to the company and can have dramatic effects. The material in this chapter gives a sense of the range of different ISA-related documents that can have value to an organization and should help in the process of deciding which ones are critical in the organization.

Documenting the ISA Server 2006 Design

The process of designing an ISA Server environment can include multiple design decisions, various decision rationales, and specific implementation settings. It is often difficult, after the design is complete, to retain the knowledge of why particular decisions were made during the design process. Subsequently, one of the first and most important sets of documentation for an ISA environment relates to the design of the environment itself.

This type of documentation can take many forms, but typically involves a formal design document, a server as-built document, and specific information on configured rules and settings, which can be ascertained through the creation of a custom script. Examples of this type of script, which can be extremely valuable in the documentation of ISA settings, is provided in this section of the chapter.

For more information on designing an ISA Server environment, refer to Chapter 4, "Designing an ISA Server 2006 Environment."

Documenting the ISA Design Process

The first step in the implementation of an ISA Server 2006 environment is the development and approval of a design. Documenting this design contributes to the success of the project. The design document records the decisions made during the design process and provides a reference for testing, implementation, and support. The key components to a design document include the following:

- ▶ The goals and objectives of the project
- ▶ The background or what led up to the design
- ▶ The approach that will be used to implement the solution
- ▶ The details of the end state of the project

Goals and objectives can be surprisingly hard to pin down. They need to be detailed and concrete enough to define the results that you want while staying at a high level. For instance, "reduce down time" is too vague to be considered a functional goal, whereas "implement Network Load Balancing with ISA Server 2006 Enterprise Edition to reduce downtime to less than one minute in the case of single server failure" is much more specific.

Including the background of meetings and brainstorming sessions that led up to the decisions for the end state of the project provides the groundwork for the detailed designs provided later in the document. For example, a decision may have been made "because the CEO wants it that way," which affects the post-migration environment. Other decisions may have come about after many hours of debates over the particulars and required technical research to come up with the "right" answer. Recording this level of information can be extremely useful in the future if performance issues are encountered or additional changes to the network are being considered.

The description of the end state to be implemented can be very high level or can drill down to more specific configurations of each server, depending on the document's audience. However, it is recommended that the design document not include step-by-step procedures or other details of how the process is to be accomplished. This level of detail is better handled, in most cases, in dedicated configuration or training documents, as discussed later in this chapter.

Formalizing ISA Server Configuration with As-Built Documentation

The configuration document, often referred to as an *as-built*, details a snapshot configuration of the ISA Server 2006 system as it is built. This document contains essential information required to rebuild a server.

One way to create an as-built document is to export settings on a server using tools such as the script illustrated in the next section of this chapter and with built-in Windows utilities such as WinMSD. WinMSD is a simple export utility that is included in the base Windows operating system, and exports server-specific settings to a text file. This data can then be imported into formal documentation easily.

To export the configuration of an ISA server using WinMSD, perform the following steps:

1. Log in to the ISA server as a local administrator.
2. Go to Start, Run, and type **winmsd** and click Run.
3. From the System Information dialog box, shown in Figure 20.1, go to File, Export.

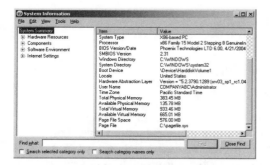

FIGURE 20.1   Using WinMSD to export Windows settings for ISA documentation.

4. Enter a name and a location for the exported text file and click Save.

After the specific settings on an ISA server have been acquired, they can be formalized into as-built documentation. The following is an example of an ISA Server 2006 as-built document template:

```
Introduction
The purpose of this ISA Server 2006 as-built document is to assist an
experienced network administrator or engineer in restoring the server in the
event of a hardware failure. This document contains screen shots and
configuration settings for the server at the time it was built. If settings
are not implicitly defined in this document, they are assumed to be set to
defaults. It is not intended to be a comprehensive disaster recovery plan with
step-by-step procedures for rebuilding the server. For this document
to remain useful as a recovery aid, it must be updated as configuration
settings change.

System Configuration
    Hardware Summary
    Disk Configuration
        Physical Disk Configuration
        Logical Disk Configuration
    System Summary
    Device Manager
    RAID Configuration
    TCP/IP Configuration
ISA Configuration
```

```
Networks        Network Rules
Firewall Policy Rules
VPN Configuration
Antivirus Configuration
```
Add-Ons

Documenting Specific ISA Configuration with Custom Scripting

The ISA Server Console gives easy view access to firewall policy rules, network rules, VPN configuration, and other ISA settings. Although individual elements and entire configurations can be exported for backup or migration purposes, there is no built-in way to export these settings to simple text format for documentation purposes.

Fortunately, the ISA Server development team included a relatively straightforward scripting mechanism called the FPC object that allows for the export of ISA settings to text, CSV, or other formats. This enables administrators with scripting knowledge to generate documentation from an ISA server easily, without having to decipher the XML export files. For more information about the FPC object, reference the following Microsoft website:

http://msdn2.microsoft.com/en-us/library/Aa489786.aspx

The following custom script gives an example of the type of capabilities that the FPC object can give an administrator who is tasked with the documentation of ISA rules. It exports the ISA firewall policy rules on the local server on which it is run. All the rules information is exported to a CSV file.

> **NOTE**
>
> The isaconfig.wsf script, along with others referenced in this book, can be downloaded from the Sams Publishing website by searching for this book title, and then clicking on the link entitled Downloads.

This particular script can be run by executing the following command from the directory where the script is located, as illustrated in Figure 20.2:

```
Cscript isaconfig.wsf /path:C:\Documentation
```

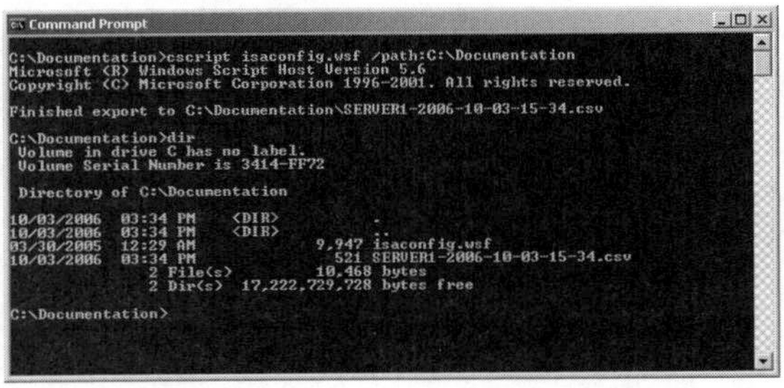

FIGURE 20.2   Running the ISA Configuration Backup script.

20

Listing 20.1 shows the code for the custom documentation script.

LISTING 20.1   Examining the isaconfig.wsf Documentation Script

```
<?xml version="1.0" ?>
<package>
 <job id="isaconfig">
  <runtime>
    <description>
***************************************************************
ISA Configuration Report Job
***************************************************************
    </description>
      <named name="path" helpstring="The UNC or file path you want to export the
      configuration report to."type="string" required="1" />
      <named name="silent" helpstring="Runs script in silent mode." type="simple"
      required="0" />
    <example>
Example:
cscript isaconfig.wsf /path:"\\remoteserver\sharename"
cscript isaconfig.wsf /path:"c:\isainfo"
    </example>
  </runtime>
  <form>

  </form>
  <script language="VBScript">
<![CDATA[
'====================================================================
' Comments about the script
'====================================================================
' This script uses the FPC object to produce a report of the policies in an
' ISA configuration.  As currently written, this script can be run only on the
' local ISA server that you are trying to export the configuration from.
In conjunction with the FPCArray object the
' script can be modified to produce a script that would allow for a centralized
' report of all ISA servers in an organization.
'
' It is also important to note that this script was developed in an effort to
' try to give a visual representation of the policy configuration that is
' present on an ISA server.  Not all the elements that are in a policy are
' represented in the report.  The report is therefore not a complete
' configuration and should be used only to document the current policies that
' are in place.
'
```

```
' To expand upon the script and for more information about the FPC object
' please see the following URL:
'
' http://msdn.microsoft.com/library/default.asp?url=/library/en-
  us/isasdk/isa/fpc_object.asp
'
' Please note that in all cases usage of the FPC object is limited to a
' server that has ISA 2004/2006 or greater installed on it.
'
'====================================================================
' Check args
'====================================================================
If WScript.Arguments.Named.Exists("path") = FALSE Then
  WScript.Arguments.ShowUsage()
  WScript.Quit
End If

Const ForWriting = 2
Dim FSO, WSHNetwork
Dim objLogFile
Dim strPath
Dim strFileName
Dim dtmThisMinute, dtmThisHour
Dim dtmThisDay, dtmThisMonth, dtmThisYear

Set WSHNetwork = CreateObject("WScript.Network")

strPath = WScript.Arguments.Named("path")
Set FSO = CreateObject("Scripting.FileSystemObject")

dtmThisMinute = PadDigits(Minute(Now), 2)
dtmThisHour = PadDigits(Hour(Now), 2)
dtmThisDay = PadDigits(Day(Now), 2)
dtmThisMonth = PadDigits(Month(Now), 2)
dtmThisYear = Year(Now)

strFileName = WSHNetwork.ComputerName & "-" & dtmThisYear & "-" & dtmThisMonth
& "-" &_
        dtmThisDay & "-" & dtmThisHour & "-" & dtmThisMinute & ".csv"

Set objLogFile = FSO.OpenTextFile(strPath & "\" & strFileName, ForWriting, true)

Dim objRoot    ' The FPCLib.FPC root object
Dim isaArray   ' An FPCArray object
```

```
Set objRoot = CreateObject("FPC.Root")
Set isaArray = objRoot.GetContainingArray()

'--------------------
' Write Headers
'--------------------
objLogFile.Write("Order")
objLogFile.Write(",")
objLogFile.Write("Name")
objLogFile.Write(",")
objLogFile.Write("Action")
objLogFile.Write(",")
objLogFile.Write("Type")
objLogFile.Write(",")
objLogFile.Write("Protocols")
objLogFile.Write(",")
objLogFile.Write("From/Listener")
objLogFile.Write(",")
objLogFile.Write("To")
objLogFile.Write(",")
objLogFile.Write("Condition")
objLogFile.WriteLine()

For Each Policy in isaArray.ArrayPolicy.PolicyRules
  objLogFile.Write(Policy.Order)
  objLogFile.Write(",")
  objLogFile.Write(Policy.Name)
  objLogFile.Write(",")

  strPolicyAction = Policy.Action

  If strPolicyAction = 0 Then
    objLogFile.Write("Allow")
  Else
    objLogFile.Write("Deny")
  End If

  objLogFile.Write(",")

  strPolicyType = Policy.Type

  '--------------------
  ' Policy Type Cases
  '--------------------
  ' There are three basic ISA Policy Types (Access Rule, Server Publishing Rule,
  ' Web Publishing Rule)
```

```
Select Case strPolicyType
  Case "0"
    objLogFile.Write("Access Rule")
    objLogFile.Write(",")

    '- - - - - - - - - - - - - - - - - -
    ' Get Protocol Information
    '- - - - - - - - - - - - - - - - - -
    j = 1

    strProSelctMethod = Policy.AccessProperties.ProtocolSelectionMethod

    If strProSelctMethod = 0 Then
      objLogFile.Write("All Outbound Taffic")
    ElseIf strProSelctMethod = 2 Then
      objLogFile.Write("All Except:")
    End If

    For Each Item in Policy.AccessProperties.SpecifiedProtocols
      objLogFile.Write(Item)

      If j <> Policy.AccessProperties.SpecifiedProtocols.Count Then
        objLogFile.Write("; ")
      End IF

      j = j + 1
    Next

    objLogFile.Write(",")

    '- - - - - - - - - - - - - - - - - -
    ' Get Source Network Information
    '- - - - - - - - - - - - - - - - - -
    GetNet(Policy.SourceSelectionIPs)

    '- - - - - - - - - - - - - - - - - -
    ' Get Destion Network Information
    '- - - - - - - - - - - - - - - - - -
    GetNet(Policy.AccessProperties.DestinationSelectionIPs)
    '- - - - - - - - - - - - - - - - - -
    ' Get Conditions
    '- - - - - - - - - - - - - - - - - -
    GetConditions(Policy.AccessProperties.UserSets)
```

20

```
Case "1"
  objLogFile.Write("Server Publishing Rule")
  objLogFile.Write(",")

  '.....................
  ' Get Published Protocol
  '.....................
  objLogFile.Write(Policy.ServerPublishingProperties.PublishedProtocol)
  objLogFile.Write(",")

  '.....................
  ' Get Source Network Information
  '.....................
  GetNet(Policy.SourceSelectionIPs)

  '.....................
  ' Get Published Server
  '.....................
  objLogFile.Write(Policy.ServerPublishingProperties.PublishedServerIP)

Case "2"
  objLogFile.Write("Web Publishing Rule")
  objLogFile.Write(",")

  '.....................
  ' Get Web Server Type
  '.....................
  strWebPubType = Policy.WebPublishingProperties.PublishedServerType

  If strWebPubType = 0 Then
    objLogFile.Write("HTTP")
  ElseIf strWebPubType = 1 Then
    objLogFile.Write("HTTPS")
  ElseIf strWebPubType = 2 Then
    objLogFile.Write("HTTP & HTTPS")
  ElseIf strWebPubType = 3 Then
    objLogFile.Write("FTP")
  End If

  objLogFile.Write(",")

  '.....................
  ' Get Web Listener
  '.....................
  objLogFile.Write(Policy.WebPublishingProperties.WebListenerUsed)
  objLogFile.Write(",")
```

```
        '- - - - - - - - - - - - - - - - - - -
        ' Get Published Web Site Name
        '- - - - - - - - - - - - - - - - - - -
        objLogFile.Write(Policy.WebPublishingProperties.WebSite)
        objLogFile.Write(",")


        '- - - - - - - - - - - - - - - - - - -
        ' Get Conditions
        '- - - - - - - - - - - - - - - - - - -
        GetConditions(Policy.WebPublishingProperties.UserSets)

    Case Else
  End Select

objLogFile.WriteLine()

Next

If WScript.Arguments.Named.Exists("silent") = FALSE Then
  WScript.Echo("Finished export to " & strPath & "\" & strFileName)
End If

'====================================================================
' Functions
'====================================================================
'- - - - - - - - - - - - - - - - - - -
' Pad Digits
'- - - - - - - - - - - - - - - - - - -
' This function is used to pad date variables that contain only one digit.
Function PadDigits(n, totalDigits)
  If totalDigits > len(n) then
    PadDigits = String(totalDigits-len(n),"0") & n
  Else
    PadDigits = n
  End If
End Function


'- - - - - - - - - - - - - - - - - - -
' Get Conditions
'- - - - - - - - - - - - - - - - - - -
' This function is used to get the conditions of a rule.
Function GetConditions(ObjectPath)
  Dim objConditions, objConditionsDict
  Set objConditions = ObjectPath
  Set objConditionsDict = CreateObject("Scripting.Dictionary")
```

```
  j = 1

  For Each Item in objConditions
    objConditionsDict.Add j, Item

    j = j + 1
  Next

  j = 1

  For Each Condition in objConditionsDict
    objLogFile.Write(objConditionsDict.item(Condition))

    If j <> objConditionsDict.Count Then
      objLogFile.Write("; ")
    End If

    j = j + 1
  Next

  Set objConditionsDict = Nothing
  Set objConditions = Nothing
End Function

'--------------------
' Get Network Information
'--------------------
' This function is used to get the network information for a rule.
Function GetNet(ObjectPath)
  Dim objNet, objNetDict
  Set objNet = ObjectPath
  Set objNetDict = CreateObject("Scripting.Dictionary")

  j = 1

  For Each Item in objNet.AddressRanges
    objNetDict.Add j, Item

    j = j + 1
  Next

  For Each Item in objNet.Computers
    objNetDict.Add j, Item

    j = j + 1
  Next
```

```
    For Each Item in objNet.ComputerSets
      objNetDict.Add j, Item

      j = j + 1
    Next

    For Each Item in objNet.Networks
       objNetDict.Add j, Item

       j = j + 1
    Next

    For Each Item in objNet.NetworkSets
      objNetDict.Add j, Item

      j = j + 1
    Next

    For Each Item in objNet.Subnets
      objNetDict.Add j, Item

      j = j + 1
    Next

    j = 1

    For Each Net in objNetDict
      objLogFile.Write(objNetDict.item(Net))

      If j <> objNetDict.Count Then
        objLogFile.Write("; ")
      End If

      j = j + 1
    Next

    objLogFile.Write(",")

   Set objNetDict = Nothing
   Set objNet = Nothing
End Function
]]>
  </script>
 </job>
</package>
```

20

> **NOTE**
>
> This script will work for both ISA 2004 and ISA 2006 servers.

Developing Migration Documentation

If migrating from existing security infrastructure, or from previous versions of ISA, it is wise to produce migration documents at the same time or shortly after the design documentation to provide a roadmap of the ISA Server 2006 migration.

> **NOTE**
>
> The results of testing the design in a prototype lab or pilot might alter the actual migration steps and procedures. In this case, the migration plan document should be modified to take these changes into account.

The following is an example of the table of contents from a typical ISA Server 2006 migration plan:

```
ISA Server 2006 Migration Plan
Goals and Objectives
Approach
Roles
Process
     Phase I - Design and Planning
     Phase II - Prototype
     Phase III - Pilot
     Phase IV - Implementation
     Phase V - Support
Migration Process
Summary of Migration Resources
Project Scheduling
ISA Server 2006 Training
Administration and Maintenance
```

Creating Project Plans

A project plan is essential for more complex migrations and can be useful for managing smaller projects—even single-server deployments.

Tools such as Microsoft Project facilitate the creation of project plans and enable the assignment of one or more resources per task and the assignment of durations and links to key predecessors. The project plan can also provide an initial estimate of the number of hours required from each resource and the associated costs if outside resources are to be used. "What if" scenarios are easy to create: Simply add resources to more complex tasks or cut out optional steps to see the effect on the budget.

Note that it's a good idea to revisit the original project plan after everything is completed (the baseline) to see how accurate it was. Many organizations fail to take this step and miss the opportunity of learning from the planning process to better prepare for the next time around.

Developing the Test Plan

Thorough testing is critical in the success of any implementation project. A test plan details the resources required for testing (hardware, software, and lab personnel), the tests or procedures to perform, and the purpose of the test or procedure.

It is important to include representatives of every aspect of the network in the development of the test plan. This ensures that all aspects of the ISA Server 2006 environment or project and its impact are included in the test plan.

Numbering Server Migration Procedures

High-level migration procedures should be decided during a design and planning process and confirmed during a prototype/testing phase. The initial migration document also should focus on the tools that will be used to migrate data, users, and applications, as well as the division of labor for these processes.

A draft of the document can be put together, and when the process is tested again, it can be verified for accuracy. When complete, this information can save a great deal of time.

The procedures covered can include the following:

- Server hardware configuration details
- Service pack (SP) and hotfixes to install on each server
- Services to enable or disable and appropriate settings
- Applications (such as ISA add-ons) to install and their appropriate settings
- Security settings
- Steps required to migrate functionality to the new server(s)
- Steps required to test the new configuration to ensure full functionality
- Steps required to remove old servers or firewalls from production

Establishing Migration Checklists

The migration process can often be a long process, based on the amount of security functionality that must be migrated. It is very helpful to develop both high-level and detailed checklists to guide the migration process. High-level checklists determine the status of the

20

migration at any given point in the process. Detailed checklists ensure that all steps are performed in a consistent manner. This is extremely important if the process is being repeated for multiple sites.

The following is an example of an ISA Server 2006 server build checklist:

```
Task:                            Initials       Notes
Verify BIOS and Firmware Revs
Verify RAID Configuration
Install Windows Server 2003 Standard Edition
Configure Windows Server 2003 Standard Edition
Install Windows Server 2003 Service Pack 1
Install Windows Server 2003 R2 Edition
Install Security Patches
Install System Recovery Console
Install ISA Server 2006 Standard Edition
Install ISA Patches
Install ISA Add-Ons
Configure ISA Networks
Configure ISA Firewall Policy Rules
Install and Configure Backup Agent
Set Up and Configure Smart UPS
Configure MOM/SCOM Agent


Sign off:                        Date:
```

Creating Administration and Maintenance Documentation for ISA

Administration and maintenance documentation can be critical in maintaining a reliable ISA environment. These documents help an administrator of a particular server or set of servers organize and keep track of the different steps that need to be taken to ensure the health of the systems under his or her care. They also facilitate the training of new administrators and reduce the variables and risks involved in these transitions.

Note that ISA Server 2006 systems, as discussed previously, can serve several different functions on the network, such as edge firewalls, VPN servers, content-caching servers, or reverse-proxy servers. The necessary maintenance procedures may be slightly different for each one based on its function and importance in the network.

One key component to administration or maintenance documentation is a timeline detailing when certain procedures should be followed. As Chapter 17, "Maintaining ISA Server 2006," discusses, certain daily, weekly, monthly, and quarterly procedures should be followed. These procedures should be documented, and the documentation should include clearly defined procedures and the frequency with which they should be performed.

Preparing Step-by-Step Procedure Documents

Administration and maintenance documentation contains a significant amount of procedural documentation. These documents can be very helpful for complex processes, or for processes that are not performed on a regular basis. Procedures range from technical processes that outline each step to administrative processes that help clarify roles and responsibilities.

Creating Documented Checklists

Administration and maintenance documentation can be extensive, and checklists can be quick reminders for essential processes and procedures. Develop comprehensive checklists that will help administrators perform their scheduled and unscheduled tasks. A timeline checklist highlighting the daily, weekly, monthly, and quarterly tasks helps keep the ISA environment healthy. In addition, these checklists function as excellent auditing tools.

Outlining Procedural Documents

Procedural documents can be very helpful for complex processes. They can apply to technical processes and outline each step, or to administrative processes to help clarify roles and responsibilities.

Flowcharts from Microsoft Visio or a similar product are often sufficient for the more administrative processes, such as when testing a new ISA patch, approving the addition of a new server to the network, or scheduling network downtime.

Preparing Disaster Recovery Documentation

Disaster recovery policies and procedures are highly recommended for an ISA environment. Every organization should go through the process of contemplating various disaster scenarios. For instance, organizations on the West Coast may be more concerned with earthquakes than those on the East Coast. Each disaster can pose a different threat. Therefore, it's important to determine every possible scenario and begin planning ways to minimize the impact of those disasters.

Equally important is analyzing how downtime resulting from a disaster may affect the company (reputation, time, productivity, expenses, loss in profit or revenue) and determine how much should be invested in remedies to avoid or minimize the effects.

A number of different components comprise disaster recovery documentation. Without this documentation, full recovery is difficult at best. The following is a table of contents for the areas to consider when documenting disaster recovery procedures:

```
Executive Summary or Introduction
Disaster Recovery Scenarios
Disaster Recovery Best Practices
        Planning and Designing for Disaster
Business Continuity and Response
```

20

Outlining Disaster Recovery Planning

The first step of the disaster recovery process is to develop a formal disaster recovery plan. This plan, while time consuming to develop, serves as a guide for the entire organization in the event of an emergency. Disaster scenarios, such as power outages, hard drive failures, and even earthquakes, should be addressed. Although it is impossible to develop a scenario for every potential disaster, it is still helpful to develop a plan to recover for different levels of disaster. It is recommended that organizations encourage open discussions of possible scenarios and the steps required to recover from each one. Include representatives from each department, because each department will have its own priorities in the event of a disaster. The disaster recovery plan should encompass the organization as a whole and focus on determining what it will take to resume normal business function after a disaster.

Documenting for Backup and Recovery

Backup procedures encompass not just backing up data to tape or another medium, but also a variety of other tasks, including advanced system recovery, offsite storage, and retention. These tasks should be carefully documented to accurately represent what backup methodologies are implemented and how they are carried out. Step-by-step procedures, guidelines, policies, and more may be documented.

Periodically, the backup documents should be reviewed and tested, especially after any configuration changes. Otherwise, backup documents can become stale and can only add more work and more problems during recovery attempts.

Recovery documentation complements backup documentation. This documentation should include where the backup data resides and how to recover from various types of failures (such as hard drive failure, system failure, and natural disaster). As with backup documentation, recovery documentation can take the form of step-by-step guides, policies, frequently asked questions (FAQs), and checklists. Moreover, recovery documents should be reviewed and revised if necessary.

ISA backup and recovery provides for unique capabilities, such as import and export to XML files, so particular attention should be placed on the individual needs of ISA in a recovery situation. For more information on ISA's backup and restore capabilities, see Chapter 18, "Backing Up, Restoring, and Recovering an ISA Server 2006 Environment."

Outlining Monitoring and Performance Documentation for ISA

Monitoring is not typically considered a part of disaster recovery documentation. However, alerting mechanisms can detect and bring attention to issues that may arise. Alerting mechanisms can provide a proactive way to determine whether a disaster may strike. Documenting alerting mechanisms and the actions to take when an alert is received can reduce downtime and administration.

Documenting Change Management Procedures

Changes to the environment may occur all the time in an organization, yet often those changes are either rarely documented or no set procedures are in place for making those changes. IT personnel not responsible for the change may be oblivious to those changes, and other administration or maintenance may be adversely affected.

Documented change management seeks to bring knowledge consistency throughout IT, control when and how changes are made, and minimize disruption from incorrect or unplanned changes. As a result, documentation of change procedures should include the processes to request and approve changes, high-level testing procedures, the actual change procedures, and any rollback procedures in case problems arise.

Change control can be particularly important in an ISA Server environment, where improper configuration of an ISA server can leave a network vulnerable to attack. Implementing either a formal or information change control process is therefore highly recommended.

20

Understanding the Importance of Performance Documentation

Documenting performance-related information is a continuous process because of the ever-changing metrics involved and the evolving nature of business. This type of documentation begins by aligning with the goals, existing policies, and SLAs for the organization. When these areas are clearly defined and detailed, baseline performance values can be established through use of the System Monitor, Microsoft Operations Manager (MOM), or third-party tools (such as PerfMon and BMC Patrol). Performance baselines capture performance-related metrics, such as how much memory is being used, average processor utilization, and more; they also illustrate how the ISA Server 2006 environment is performing under various workloads.

After the baseline performance values are documented and understood, the performance-related information that the monitoring solution is still capturing should be analyzed periodically. More specifically, pattern and trend analysis needs to be examined on a weekly basis, if not on a daily basis. This analysis can uncover current and potential bottlenecks and proactively ensure that the system operates as efficiently and effectively as possible.

Producing Routine Reporting

Although the System Monitor can log performance data and provide reporting when used with other products such as Microsoft Excel, it behooves administrators to use products such as Microsoft Operations Manager (MOM) 2005 for monitoring and reporting functionality. For example, MOM can manage and monitor multiple systems and provide graphical reports with customizable levels of detail.

For more information on using MOM 2005 with ISA Server 2006, see Chapter 19, "Monitoring and Troubleshooting an ISA Server 2006 Environment."

Implementing Management-Level Reporting

Management-level reporting on performance data should be concise and direct but still at a high level. Stakeholders don't require an ample amount of performance data, but it's important to show trends, patterns, and any potential problem areas. This extremely useful information provides a certain level of insight to management so that decisions can be made as to what is required to keep the systems operating in top-notch condition.

For instance, administrators identify and report to management that, if trends on ISA server processor utilization continue at the current rate of a 5% increase per month, additional processors will be required in 10 months or less. Management can then take this report, follow the issue more closely over the next few months, and then determine whether to allocate funds to purchase additional processors. If the decision is made to buy more processors, management has more time to negotiate quantity, processing power, and cost, instead of having to potentially pay higher costs for the processors at short notice.

Detailing Technical Reporting

Technical performance information reporting is much more detailed than management-level reporting. Details are given on many different components and facets of the system. For example, many specific counter values may be given to determine disk subsystem utilization. In addition, trend and pattern analysis should also be included to show historical information and determine how to plan for future requirements.

Writing Training Documentation

Training documentation can entail a myriad of options. For example, an organization can have training documentation for maintenance and administration procedures, installation and configuration of new technologies, common end-user tasks, ways various network components can be used, future technologies, and much more. The documentation should match current training procedures, and it can also help define what training will be offered in the future.

Outlining Technical Training

Administrators are responsible for the upkeep and management of the ISA environment. As a result, they must be technically prepared to address a variety of issues such as maintenance and troubleshooting. Training documentation should address why the technologies are being taught and how the technologies pertain to the network environment, and it should also provide step-by-step hands-on procedures to perform the tasks.

Documenting End-User Training

Training materials and other forms of documentation for end users offer the users a means for learning how to use ISA for VPNs, how to log in to OWA through an ISA forms-based authentication page, and much more. End-user training documentation also serves as a great reference tool after training has been concluded.

Detailing System Usage Policies

To gain control over how the system is to be used, it's important for an organization to implement system usage policies. Policies can be set on end users as well as on the IT personnel. Policies for end users may include specifying which types of access through the ISA firewall are provided, that instant messaging is not allowed on the local machine or the network, and that users must follow specific steps to obtain technical support, for example. On the other hand, IT personnel policies may dictate that routine system maintenance can occur only between 5:00 a.m. and 9:00 a.m. on Saturdays, for example.

Summary

Most, if not all, aspects of an ISA Server 2006 network environment can be documented. However, the type of documentation that may benefit the environment depends on each organization. Overall, documenting the environment is an important aspect of the network and can assist with all aspects of administration, maintenance, support, troubleshooting, testing, and design.

Best Practices

► Make use of the FPC object for scripting the export of ISA configuration for documentation purposes.

► Have documentation reviewed and approved by other stakeholders in the organization to make sure that it meets their needs as well, and to simply get input from another source. For technical procedures, the document also must be tested and walked through.

► Consolidate and centralize documentation for the organization.

► Document the company's policies and procedures for security and maintenance.

► Create well thought-out and professional planning and design documentation to avoid costly mistakes in the implementation or migration process, such as buying too many server licenses or purchasing too many servers.

► Baseline and document the state of an ISA server so that any changes in its performance can be identified at a later date.

► Use tools such as Microsoft Project to facilitate the creation of project plans, enable the assignment of one or more resources per task, and enable the assignment of durations and links to key predecessors.

► Create disaster recovery documentation that includes step-by-step procedures for rebuilding each ISA server to minimize downtime and administration.

► Document daily, weekly, monthly, and quarterly maintenance tasks to ensure the health of the ISA environment.

► Use documentation to facilitate training.

► Document business and technical policies for the organization.

Index

Symbols

A

attachments (HTTP), restricting, 392

attacks. *See* threats

audit trail, logging as, 488

audits, security, 465-466

Authentication Delegations tab options (configuring web publishing rules), 396

authentication methods

forms-based authentication, Exchange mobile services, 353-354

RADIUS environment, integrating ISA Server 2006 with, 24

site-to-site VPN deployment scenario, 279, 285

IPSec Tunnel Mode configuration, 292-294

L2TP configuration, 288-292

PPTP configuration, 286-288

for VPN clients, 233-234

RADIUS, 236-243

VPN protocols, 224

authorization. *See* permissions

auto-discovery

configuring

with DHCP, 302-303

with DNS, 303-304

enabling, 304

of proxy settings, 216-218

autoenrollment of certificates, 258-259

automated group policy installation of firewall clients, 307-308

Automated System Recovery (ASR) sets, updating, 463-464

Automatic Updates client, 453

automatically configuring client proxy settings, 214-215

automating export features with custom scripts, 478-483

B

back firewall template, 72

back-end servers

RPC over HTTP configuration, 363

supporting OMA and ActiveSync on, 349-351, 353

backup and recovery documentation, 534-535

backup and recovery tools, 469-470

components to backup, 470

export and import features, 470

automating with custom scripts, 478-483

exporting ISA settings

individual rule sets, 471-472

server configuration, 472

system policy, 472-473

URLsets, 473-475

importing ISA settings

individual ISA components, 475-476

server configuration, 476-477

URL sets, 477-478

third-party tools, 483-484

backups, 26

validating, 463

verifying, 457-458

bandwidth

constraints with VPNs, 224-225

content download jobs and, 100

baseline performance documentation, 517, 536

management-level reporting, 536

with MOM (Microsoft Operations Manager), 536

technical reporting, 537

E

J–K–L

NLB array network, creating, **173**

nodes (Management Console)

Add-ins, 100

application filters, 101-102

web filters, 102

Cache, 97

cache rules, 99

content download jobs, enabling and configuring, 100

enabling caching, 98

Firewall Policy, 79-80

firewall access rules, 80-81

Firewall Policy toolbox, 84-86

server publishing rules, 82

system policy rules, 82

General, 103

certificate revocation, 107

delegating administration, 103-105

dial-up preferences, configuring, 106

DiffServ settings, 110

firewall chaining, 105

firewall clients, configuring, 105

flood mitigation settings, 108-109

HTTP Compression settings, 111

intrusion detection settings, 109

IP protection, configuring, 110

link translation, 106

RADIUS and LDAP servers, configuring, 109-110

server details, viewing, 108

list of, 67

Monitoring, 86-87

connectivity, verifying, 90-91

dashboard, configuring, 87

logging information, 91

monitoring sessions and services, 88

reports, generating, 88-90

viewing alerts, 87-88

Network, 68

network rules, 73-74

network sets, 71

Network Template Wizard, 74-78

network templates, defining, 72-73

networks versus subnets, 69-71

web chaining, 79

VPN, 91

client access, enabling and configuring, 93-95

remote access, configuring, 95

remote site networks, creating, 96

VPN quarantine, 96-97

NTBackup, 483-484

numbering migration procedures, 531

O

objectives. *See* security goals/objectives

Open System Interconnection (OSI) Reference model, layers in, **136-137**

operating systems

for ISA Server 2006, selecting, 19

patching, 42-44, 453-456

prerequisites for ISA Server 2006, 35

Windows Server 2003 Standard edition, installing, 38-40

OpsMgr (Operations Manager). *See* MOM (Microsoft Operations Manager)

optimization of server hardware, 37-38

P

R

RADIUS (Remote Access Dial-Up Service), 236, 279

    integrating ISA Server 2006 with, 24

    Message Authentication in, 241

    servers, configuring, 109-110

    VPN client authentication, 236-243

RDP access, enabling, 444-446

reassessing security goals/objectives, 466-467

recovery. *See* **backup and recovery tools**

redirecting clients to Exchange virtual directory, 326-328

redundancy with ISA security appliances, 196

Registry, RPC over HTTP configuration, 364

relationships. *See* **network rules**

remote access, configuring, 95. *See also* **RADIUS; VPN**

Remote Access Dial-Up Service. *See* **RADIUS**

Remote Access Policies, creating in IAS, 239-241

Remote Access Quarantine Service (RQS)

    configuring

        protocol definition, 269-270

        rules, 270-271

    installing, 268-269

remote administration, 441

    enabling RDP access, 444-446

    installing ISA Server Management Console, 441-444

Remote Procedure Call traffic. *See* **RPC traffic**

remote site networks, creating, 96

renaming servers in Management Console, 448

reports. *See also* **monitoring**

    customizing, 501

    generating, 88-90, 501-502

    management-level reporting, 536

    scheduling generation of, 502-503

    technical reporting, 537

    types of, 500-501

requesting certificates

    for ISA servers, 253-254

    for VPN clients, 254-255

requirements. *See* **prerequisites**

restores, 26

    from automatic export scripts, 483

    importing ISA settings

        individual ISA components, 475-476

        server configuration, 476-477

        URL sets, 477-478

restricting

    HTTP attachments, 392

    HTTP headers, 392

    HTTP methods, 391-392

    HTTP signatures, 392-393

    RPC traffic, filtering versus, 415

reverse proxy deployment scenario, 20-21, 185

    applying network template, 189-190

    capabilities of, 188

    configuring existing firewalls for, 191-192

    in enterprise environments, 196-197

    preconfigured hardware appliances, 190-191

    web server publishing rules, 188, 193

        for Outlook Web Access, 193-195

        for web services, 195

    within security infrastructure, 186-187

S